SEVEN
Vital Truths
for God's Children

by Michael D. Miesch Jr. PhD OP

outskirtspress
DENVER, COLORADO

THIS BOOK IS DEDICATED
TO MY WIFE
LANETTA ANN MIESCH

AND

TO MY SONS
MICHAEL D. MIESCH III
MARK DAVID MIESCH
AND
PAUL MARTIN MIESCH

My deepest appreciation to my dad and mother, Donovan and Alma Miesch, for their constant love and encouragement, especially when I was struggling through grade school, high school and college with a severe hearing loss and speech impediment.

Indebtedness is expressed to my brother, Dr. Pete Miesch, who started school with me at the age of four, and helped me through grade school, high school and parts of college. To my Aunt Julia Miesch, for my religious training and insisting that I attend two weeks of Bible school every summer even through my sophomore year in college.

Last, but not least, is my deep love and appreciation to my wife, Ann, for her help in the preparation of this manuscript and for her patience for the time I spent on the manuscript.

The author is extremely grateful to Bill Ivie who introduces me to the life in the Spirit and to Ruth Kageler who guided me in the life in the Spirit after my baptism in the Spirit in 1970.

Deep appreciation to my many prayer partners: Barney Bailey, Dr. Dan Morgan, Roger Boos, Al Bastinelli, George Allman, Bill Alexander, Conrad Hopperstead, Jeff Romeo and Michael D. Miesch III for their role in seeking the Lord's discernment and guidance in the preparation and writing of this manuscript.

The author wishes to express his gratitude to Robert Mock, Mark David Miesch and Bill Malloy for proofreading the manuscript, and to Mrs. Katherine Morgan for reading part of the manuscript. The author is deeply indebted to Trudy Smith, Reverend Philip N. Powell O.P. and Nancy Ward for editing the manuscript. The writer is grateful to Michael D. Miesch III, Paul Martin Miesch and Karen Fields for suggestions and help in preparation of this manuscript.

Appreciation is expressed to Jo Ann Glasco for the words of knowledge that it is time to get the book published. The author is very grateful to daughter-in-law, Tracy Lynn Miesch for designing the cover for the books.

Declaration

This is not a book on Catholic doctrines and teachings. This is a book of private revelations received in prayer.

Table of Contents

*Received words from the Lord in middle of night to write papers on Chlordane and DDT. I have not been able to get these papers published. They will be published here.

Preface

After I had finished my manuscript on the book of Revelation "Lifting the Veil of Revelation", I had knowledge that I was supposed to write a chapter on the nature of God. I was puzzled, as this did not seem to fit in with Revelation. I asked a prayer partner to pray with me for discernment and understanding. While in prayer the following words were spoken to me:

> My son, when you begin to write about My Nature, I would have you to pray in the Holy Spirit. Begin at the beginning with what I have given you so far in regard to My Nature. I say to begin at the beginning of the Holy Word. It is in the first few chapters of My Word that you will come to an understanding of My Triune Nature. Seek out what it is about My Holy Spirit that is revealed in the early writings of the book of Genesis, for it is in the beginning I was.

> It is in the writings of the prophets that the presence of My Son is first revealed. Carry this particular part of your work on through the New Testament. Flow with the wind of the Holy Spirit. Allow the flow and movement to be the movement of the Holy Spirit. Allow Him to come upon you to engulf you, to refresh you, and to use you to bring about what My love is.

> I would have the movement of your writings be that of a symphony by starting slowly moving toward a crescendo all the time, allowing the beauty of My Nature to be

revealed. Move slowly, but exactly, for this is an important part of My overall work that you are presenting in your writing. I love you for your diligence. I have many blessings in store for you. For he who reads My Word and believes shall have everlasting life.

After finishing the two chapters on the "Triune Nature of God" and "God's Son, the Man, Jesus and His plan for Salvation," I asked the Lord if He wanted me to write about the Holy Spirit. My prayer partner spoke the following words to me while we were in prayer.

My words at this moment are on their way to you. My thoughts in regard to the prayer of faith you already know. Be direct, descriptive, and scriptural. Brevity is important. Directness of trust is imperative. Begin with the description about the Spirit. Begin with a description of the power of praying in the Spirit. All else will flow as the river of life flows in the Eternal City in Paradise. Ask the saints to pray for you because the resistance of the Adversary is strong. Call on your patron saint to stand with you, and ask for divine guidance. I am pleased with your cooperation and collaboration with My Holy Spirit. Pray as you write and My thoughts will come forth for you.

I sought the Lord's guidance in writing each of the chapters in this book. I was under the impression the Lord wanted these chapters to be a part of the book on Revelation. In a dream, a friend (not one with whom I pray) spoke and said, "Mike, you are to divide your book into two books." This made sense, as the two sections were not related.

Because of the many different subjects discussed in this book, I could not think of a title that would tie all the chapters together. While in prayer with my friend, we received understanding that the book was to be called (number of chapters) Vital Truths for God's Children.

While reflecting on the name of the book, I realized that water baptism had not been discussed. Turning to the Lord in prayer, I received knowledge that I was to write on water baptism.

I realized that I am a layman and have had no theological training. Several people, including a member of the clergy, told me that I was out of my field and did not have enough training or understanding to write on this subject and that these manuscripts should not be published. The only reason I wrote these two books was because I believed I had heard the Lord tell me to do so.

It must be remembered that when Jesus started His Church, He did not go to the educated and learned men of the Law, but chose the uneducated men of Galilee to build His Church.

While in prayer one day, the following words were spoken to me by one of my prayer partners:

I have given you the means by which I can give My people the solutions to their problems. My book is near completion. Keep in mind My attitude about prayer. Vigilance, persistence and self-denial are the necessary ingredients for successful and victorious encounters against the Adversary. My scripture is the embodiment of all truth. Write as I have instructed you in the past, with an open mind, a contrite heart and diligence for the truth. My Word will speak for itself. Concern yourself with only the truth. Trust Me for I am with you always.

Praying before the Blessed Sacrament after Mass the Lord said:

> I want you to show My people My mercy throughout your book that I gave you. When there is a tragedy or calamity, show My mercy to My people, My children. Show how I love them. I will give you the words to write. My words will be understood by children as well. They will be simple and they will be Mine. I want My children to know why I am doing this for them. I do not want them to have fear. I would have them to be joyous and happy that I would do this for them. My words will be full of peace and love.

The Lord said: "This book may cause controversy; controversy is not always bad; controversy can do a lot of good."

What is written is written

I have received many visions and powerful personal messages which I had knowledge that they were to be shared and published. After finishing the writing of the manuscript and being concerned about sharing these very personal visions and messages, I asked the Lord if I should remove these very personal messages. The Lord said:

"What is written is written. Do not make any changes".

While I was praying for those reading my manuscript, the Lord said:

Walk a straight line, Mike. This line exemplifies the Holy Spirit. This Spirit is Who wrote your book. Do not yield to any spirit other than Mine. Your book shall be carried to all nations, so that they may hear. Do not modify or change it in any way. Critics, in whom you have a great deal of respect, will try to change your book. But they were not of the anointing of the Spirit, when your pen was in action. So listen to no one, except those with whom you pray for learning of my truths.

While in prayer, the Lord revealed to me that He wanted me to get the manuscript blessed. I asked the Lord, whom I should get. He said:

Mike, it makes no difference who blesses the book. The person does not carry the blessing. The person only administers the blessing. The blessing is Mine to give. The person is for you to choose. Anyone with the office of presbyter that you choose, I will honor.

I was having trouble deciding between two priests. Finally, the Lord told me to use both of them. I asked the Lord why two priests?

Two priests are used in the blessing of this book, for it is through them that I send My glory and My honor, glory and honor that many angels can use to minister the fruits of your labor. When one prays, a thousand angels are put to flight. Prayer, like sacred blessings, is the extension of man's realm into the presence of God. When one asks Me to come into his presence, I come. The petition must be made, however, for the will of man cannot be made united with the will of God unless the prayer or blessing has been committed. It is a form of respect and love for Me, which I will in no way reject. My army is fortified by prayers and communal blessings that men on earth supply Me in their devotion to Me. Love others as I have loved you, by expressing to them what I have given you and the road to joy and happiness will be simple and straight forward.

The book has doubled in size since it was original blessed by Reverend Daniel Clayton and Reverend Don Fisher. I asked Reverend Andrew Kolzow O.P. to give the book another blessing.

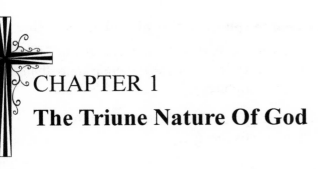

CHAPTER 1

The Triune Nature Of God

Three persons in one God

Triune means three in one. The triune nature of God means there is one God but three different individual persons in one Godhead. The three persons are the Father, the Son and the Holy Spirit.

How do we know there is only one God?

The following scriptures teach that there is only one God.

Isaiah 45:5: I am the Lord, and there is no other; beside Me there is no God....(1).

Isaiah 46:9:...I am God, and there is no one like Me (1).

Isaiah 44:6: This is what the Lord says - Israel's King and Redeemer, the Lord Almighty: I am the first and I am the last; apart from me there is no God (2).

Deuteronomy 32:39-40: See now that I, I am He, and there is no god beside Me; It is I who put to death and give life. I have wounded, and it is I who heal; and there is no one who can deliver from My hand. Indeed, I lift up My hand to heaven, and say, as I live forever. (1)

These scriptures speak of only one God.

What evidences are there of the plural nature of God or the Trinity?

In Genesis when God created everything, the Hebrew word Elohim was used for God. Elohim is plural, indicating that there is more than one person in God. The following scriptures teach that God is plural.

> Genesis 1:26: Then God said, "Let Us make man in Our image, according to Our likeness;…(3).

> Genesis 3:22: Then the Lord God said, "Behold, the man has become like one of Us knowing good and evil.…(1).

"Us" and "Our", being plural, show that there is more than one person in God. "One of Us" shows a plural nature in God. (4)

Three persons of God

Isaiah speaks of three persons being eternal in nature.

> Isaiah 48:16:…From the first I have not spoken in secret; from the time it took place, I was there. And now the Lord God has sent Me and His Spirit (1).

"From the first" and "from the time it took place", "I" was spoken of as being there. This shows that the person "I" is God. Three different persons, each one God, are mentioned in the same verse.

1. The Lord God - the Father
2. I or Me - the Son of God
3. His Spirit - the Holy Spirit

The three persons of God are seen when Jesus, the Son of God, was baptized.

> Matthew 3:16-17: And after being baptized, Jesus went up immediately from the water; and behold, the heavens were opened, and he saw the Spirit of God descending as a dove and coming upon Him, and behold, a voice out of

the heavens saying, "This is My beloved Son, in whom I am well-pleased". (1)

This scripture shows the presence of the Father, the Son and the Holy Spirit all at the same time. All three are separate Persons. Jesus is seen as the Son of God. The Holy Spirit is seen in a bodily form as a dove. God the Father speaks from heaven saying, "Thou art my beloved Son."

The Lord appeared as three men to Abraham.

> Genesis 18:1-3: Now the Lord appeared to him by the oaks of Mamre, while he was sitting at the tent door in the heat of the day. And when he lifted up his eyes and looked, behold, three men were standing opposite him; and when he saw them, he ran from the tent door to meet them, and bowed himself to the earth, and said, "My lord, if now I have found favor in your sight, please do not pass your servant by." (1)

The scripture says the Lord appeared to Abraham. When Abraham looked up, he saw three men. He ran to them, fell down at their feet and said, "My Lord." The following scripture shows that if the three men were angels, they would not have permitted Abraham to bow down to them.

> Revelation 22:8-9: And I, John, am the one who heard and saw these things. And when I heard and saw, I fell down to worship at the feet of the angel who showed me these things. And he said to me, "Do not do that;…worship God." (1)

When the three men were leaving going toward Sodom and Gomorrah, Abraham walked with them. The scripture shows the Lord asking a question.

> Genesis 18:17, 20-22: And the Lord said, "Shall I hide from Abraham what I am about to do."…And the Lord said, "The outcry of Sodom and Gomorrah is indeed

great, and their sin is exceedingly grave. I will go down now, and see if they have done entirely according to its outcry, which has come to Me; and if not, I will know." Then the men (two of them) turned away from there and went toward Sodom, while Abraham was still standing before the Lord. (1)

Though there were three men, the scripture says it was the Lord Who was talking to Abraham. The Lord told Abraham that He was going to Sodom and Gomorrah at that moment to see if the outcry is true. The two men were the ones Who left immediately to go to Sodom while the Lord remained with Abraham. This shows that the two men walking toward Sodom and Gomorrah were the Lord. Abraham pleaded with the Lord not to destroy Sodom and Gomorrah as his nephew, Lot and family lived in Sodom.

When the two men came into Sodom, Lot bowed down to them. If these two men were angels, they would not have allowed Lot to bow down to them (Revelation 22:8-9).

Two Lords

After these men led Lot and his family out of Sodom, the scripture says the Lord on earth called down fire from the Lord in heaven.

> Genesis 19:24: Then the Lord rained on Sodom and Gomorrah brimstone and fire from the Lord out of heaven (1).

Two Lords are mentioned in the same scripture. This confirms that the men that appeared to Abraham and Lot were both Lord. Two Lords are also mentioned in other scriptures (Psalm 110:1 and Matthew 22:44).

> Psalm 110:1: The Lord says to my Lord: "Sit at My right hand, until I make thine enemies a footstool for Thy feet" (1).

There are three persons in the Trinity, each one is called Lord and each one is called God, yet there is only one Lord, God.

Let us review the facts.

1. The scripture says the Lord appeared to Abraham. In reality, three men appeared to Abraham.
2. Abraham bowed down to the three men and called them "my Lord."
3. If these men were angels, they would not have permitted Abraham to bow down to them. (Revelation 22:8-9).
4. The Lord told Abraham that He was going to Sodom at that moment to check things out. In reality, two men went to Sodom, while the Lord remained behind with Abraham. This shows that the two men that went to Sodom were also the Lord.
5. Abraham pleaded with the Lord not to destroy Sodom and Gomorrah.
6. Lot bowed down to the two men. If the two men were angels they would not have permitted Lot to do this (Revelation 22:8-9).
7. The scripture shows that the Lord on earth called fire down from the Lord in heaven. The Lord on earth had to be the two men Who went to Sodom.

Since the three men standing before Abraham were the Lord (plural) then, they had to be the Father, the Son and the Holy Spirit.

God the Father is called God and is seen as a different Person from the Son.

> I Corinthians 1:3,9: Grace to you and peace from God our Father and the Lord Jesus Christ....God is faithful, through whom you were called into fellowship with His Son, Jesus Christ our Lord (1).

This scripture speaks of the Father as God and Jesus as His Son, our Lord. This shows that the Father and the Son are two different Persons.

God the Father called the Son God.

> Hebrew 1:1-2, 8-9: God, after He spoke long ago to the

fathers in the prophets…, in the last days has spoken to us in His Son, whom He appointed heir of all things, through whom also He made the world.…But of the Son He says, "Thy throne, O God, is forever and ever,… therefore God, Thy God hath anointed Thee with the oil of gladness.…" (1)

God the Father called his Son "God," through whom He created the world. Since the Son was the One who created the world, He would have to be God. This scripture shows that both the Father and the Son are called God.

In Titus, Jesus is spoken of as God and Savior.

Titus 2:13: looking for the blessed hope and appearing of the glory of our great God and Savior, Christ Jesus; (1)

The Spirit of God is a separate, distinct person from the Father and the Son.

At the baptism of Jesus, the Holy Spirit or the Spirit of God was seen in a bodily form as a dove in the presence of the Father and the Son (Matthew 3:16-17, Luke 3:21-22). The Holy Spirit is spoken of as a Person, a helper and "He who abides in you".

John 14:16-17, 26: And I will ask the Father, and He will give you another Helper that He may be with you forever; that is the Spirit of truth, whom the world cannot receive, because it does not behold Him or know Him but you know Him because He abides with you, and will be in you.…But the Helper, the Holy Spirit, whom the Father will send in My name, He will teach you all things, and bring to your remembrance all that I said to you. (1)

John 15:26: When the Helper comes, whom I will send to you from the Father, that is the Spirit of truth, who proceeds from the Father, He will bear witness of Me, (1).

Romans 8:9, 16: However you are not in the flesh but in the Spirit, if indeed the Spirit of God dwells in you....The Spirit Himself bears witness with our spirit that we are children of God (1).

The above scriptures show that the Holy Spirit is a separate, distinct Person from the Father and the Son and is referred to as He, Himself, and the Helper who abides in us. Jesus sends the Helper, the Holy Spirit from the Father.

The Holy Spirit is God

When Jesus was baptized in Matthew 3:16-17, the Holy Spirit was described as the Spirit of God, seen in a bodily form as a dove. This shows that the Holy Spirit is a different person from the Father and the Son.

Jesus said that a sin against Him will be forgiven, but a sin against the Holy Spirit will not be forgiven in this world or in the world to come. A sin against the Holy Spirit is the unpardonable sin. If the sin is unpardonable, the Holy Spirit has to be God.

Matthew 12:31-32: Therefore I say to you, any sin and blasphemy shall be forgiven men, but blasphemy against the Spirit shall not be forgiven. And whoever shall speak a word against the Son of Man, it shall be forgiven him; but whoever shall speak against the Holy Spirit, it shall not be forgiven him, either in this age, or in the age to come. (1)

When Ananias lied to the Holy Spirit, Peter said he lied to God

The following scripture shows that Ananias committed a sin against the Holy Spirit by lying.

Acts 5:3-4: But Peter said, "Ananias, why has Satan filled your heart to lie to the Holy Spirit, and to keep back some of the price of the land?...You have not lied to men, but to God" (1).

Peter said that when Ananias lied to the Holy Spirit, he lied not unto men but to God. This scripture shows that the Holy Spirit is God.

How can there be one God and three persons in God?

The triune nature of God is a mystery we do not understand. Reverend Monsignor Francis Miesch of the Diocese of Dallas once said the best explanation of the triune nature of God he has ever heard of was the example of water. Water is chemically known as H2O. Water exists in three different states: ice (solid), liquid and gas (steam or vapor). All three states can exist at the same time. Yet, all three states are one substance, H2O, water. This is just an analogy to help us understand the triune nature of God.

The scriptures teach that there is one God but three different, distinct persons in God. This is the nature of water: Water is one substance but exists in three different states.

I heard a priest give two examples of the Trinity using the family and the finger. There is the father, mother and child, who are three separate individual but yet they are one family. There are three bones in the middle finger. Each bone is different but there is one finger.

The Father and the Son are spoken of as being one.

The scriptures teach that the Father and the Son are one. The Father and the Son will dwell in His people and become one with them.

John 10:30: I and the Father are one (1).

John 17:11:...Holy Father, keep them in Thy name, the name which Thou hast given Me, that they may be one, even as We are (1).

John 17:20-23,26: I do not ask in behalf of these alone, but for those also who believe in Me through their word; that they may all be one; even as Thou, Father, art in Me, and I in Thee, that they also may be in Us....And the glory which Thou hast given Me I have given to them; that they may be one, just as We are one; I in them, and Thou in Me, that they may be perfected in unity,…that the love wherewith Thou didst love Me may be in them, and I in them. (1)

The Father dwells in the Son. The Son dwells in His people. Through this union, all become one.

When a man and a woman get married they become one flesh.

Mark 10:7-8: For this cause a man shall leave his father and mother, and the two shall become one flesh; consequently they are no longer two but one flesh (1).

This scripture explains that when a man and a woman get married, they are joined together by God to become one flesh. The scripture teaches that a man and a woman are no longer two but one. Likewise, when a man has sexual relations with a harlot they become one body.

I Corinthians 6:16: Or do you not know that the one who joins himself to a harlot is one body with her? For He says, "The two will become one flesh" (1).

Whereas, he who joins himself to the Lord becomes one with the Lord.

I Corinthians 6:17: But the one who joins himself to the Lord is one spirit with Him (1).

How can the Father dwell in the Son or the Son in the Father and together be one? How can the Father, the Son and the Holy Spirit dwell in us, and we become one with them? How can a man and a woman when they get married become one flesh not two? How can a man, when he has relations with a harlot, become one body with the harlot? How can there be three persons in one God? How can one be one with another or become one with another? These are all mysteries that we do not understand. There is definitely a spiritual and a physical bond or union in each case which makes each one, one with the other.

The Father, the Son and the Holy Spirit worked together in creating the world.

> Genesis 1:26: Then God said, "Let Us make man in Our image, according to Our likeness;..." (1).

The three persons of the one Godhead all worked together in union with one another to bring forth creation. The Father is looked to as the head. The Son is the Word that spoke creation into existence. The Holy Spirit is the Power who acted with the spoken Word, bringing creation into existence.

The world was created through the Son.

> John 1:1-3, 10, 14: In the beginning was the Word, and the Word was with God, and the Word was God. He was in the beginning with God. All things came into being through Him; and apart from Him nothing came into being....He was in the world, and the world was made through Him, and the world did not know Him....And the Word became flesh and dwelt among us,...(1)

> Colossians 1:3, 13, 15-17: We give thanks to God, the Father of our Lord Jesus Christ,...For He delivered us from the domain of darkness, and transferred us to the kingdom of His beloved Son,...And He is the image of the invisible God, the firstborn of all creation. For in Him all things were created, both in the heavens and on earth, visible and invisible, whether thrones or dominions or rulers or authorities - all things have been created through Him and for Him. And He is before all things, and in Him all things hold together. (1)

These scriptures teach that the world was created through the Son, the eternal Word of God, who became flesh in the man - Jesus Christ.

The Son of God spoke the Word, which brought everything in heaven, on earth and in the world into existence.

Vision of a cloud that was shaped like a fully open rose with many petals. I was looking directly into the center of the rose:

> As you saw the vision looking into the center of the rose, Jesus said, "I am the center of the universe. All things are created through Me, for I am the center of life. All life proceeds from Me." He opens Himself to you just as a petal of the rose opens and releases the sweet smelling fragrance of new life.

The Spirit of God was the force through which everything was created.

In the following scripture, the Lord was telling Zerubbabel to have courage, for it was not by human might or human power but by the power of His Spirit.

> Zechariah 4:6:...This is the word of the Lord to Zerubbabel saying, "Not by might nor by power, but by My Spirit," says the Lord of hosts (1).

In Genesis, it was the Spirit of God that moved over the surface of the waters, bringing forth the creations that were spoken into existence.

> Genesis 1:1-3: In the beginning God created the heavens and the earth. And the earth was formless and void, and darkness was over the surface of the deep; and the Spirit of God was moving over the surface of the waters. Then God said, "Let there be light; and there was light. (1)

Job, Psalms and Ezekiel speak of man being created by the Spirit of God. The Spirit of God is Life, Itself and the Giver of life.

> Job 33:4: The Spirit of God has made me, and the breath of the Almighty gives me life (1).

Psalm 104:29-30:…Thou dost take away their spirit, they expire, and return to their dust. Thou dost send forth Thy Spirit, they are created; and Thou dost renew the face of the ground (1).

Ezekiel 37:9-10:…Thus says the Lord God: From the four winds come, O spirit, breathe into these slain that they may come to life.…and the spirit came into them; they came alive and stood upright, a vast army. (3)

In Genesis, when God said, "Let us make man in Our image, according to Our likeness," the scripture shows the plural nature of God creating man. The scriptures teach that all creation took place through the Son. Yet, the actual creation was shown to be created by the Spirit of God. The Father, the Son and the Holy Spirit were all involved in the creation. The Son was the Word that spoke creation into existence. The Spirit of God is the force that acted with the spoken word to bring forth creation.

The Father, the Son and the Holy Spirit are three persons of one God and all are equal in statue.

When Jesus gave the command to His disciples to baptize in the name of the Father, the Son and the Holy Spirit, He indicated that each of the three persons was God, and they were all equal in stature.

Matthew 28:19: Go therefore and make disciples of all the nations, baptizing them in the name of the Father and the Son and the Holy Spirit, (1).

The scriptures teach that the Father, the Son and the Spirit are all three different persons; each one is God, each one working together in one union as one God. This is the triune nature of God.

CHAPTER 2

Sin, The Fall Of Man, And God's Love

In the beginning was God. God created the angels with a free will and put them before the throne without testing them. Satan, known as Lucifer was the most beautiful of the angels. Lucifer was the prince of the angels being second in command, next to the Lord. The scripture says that pride entered Lucifer's heart, and he decided to exalt himself above the throne of God.

> Isaiah 14:12-14: How you have fallen from heaven, O morning star, son of dawn! You have been cast down to the earth,...You said in your heart, I will ascend to heaven; I will raise my throne above the stars of God; I will sit enthroned on the mount of assembly, on the utmost heights of the sacred mountain. I will ascend above the top of the clouds; I will make myself like the Most High. (2)

Lucifer would have never attempted to overthrow the Lord unless he thought he could succeed. He thought he could succeed by getting most of the angels on his side. The scripture tells us that when the final count was made, only one-third of the angels chose to go with Satan (Revelation 12:4, 9). Satan and his angels were cast out of heaven.

After Satan's rebellion, God apparently decided to never again create a spirit being with a free will and allow him to come into the kingdom without first testing him. Under this plan, God made man. God could see man and knew man's every thought, word and deed, but man could not see God. God's Spirit dwelt in man. He revealed to man that he could do anything except eat of the forbidden fruit.

13

When man sinned, this offended God very much. However, God, in His mercy, said He would give man another chance. In order to redeem man from his sins, He would send His only Son into the world to be offered as a sacrifice. God loved man so much that He freely gave His Son to save man.

> John 3:16-17: For God so loved the world, that He gave His only begotten Son, that whoever believes in Him should not perish, but have eternal life. For God did not send the Son into the world to judge the world; but that the world should be saved through Him. (1)

Messiah came into the world as a babe.

The scriptures foretold that the Messiah would come into the world as a babe and that He would be born of a virgin.

> Isaiah 7:14: Therefore the Lord Himself shall give you a sign. Behold, the young woman who is unmarried and a virgin shall conceive and bear a son, and shall call his name Immanuel - God with us. (5)

> Isaiah 9:6: For to us a child is born, to us a son is given; and the government shall be upon His shoulder, and His name shall be called Wonderful Counselor, Mighty God, Everlasting Father, Prince of Peace. (5)

These prophecies were fulfilled in the Gospels when the angel told Mary she was to be the mother of God's Son.

> Luke 1:26-27,30-35: Now in the sixth month the angel Gabriel was sent from God to a city in Galilee, called Nazareth, to a virgin engaged to a man whose name was Joseph, of the descendants of David; and the virgin's name was Mary....And the angel said to her, "Do not be afraid, Mary; for you have found favor with God. And behold, you will conceive in your womb, and bear a son,

and you shall name Him Jesus. He will be great and will be called the Son of the Most High; and the Lord God will give Him the throne of His father David; and He will reign over the house of Jacob forever; and His kingdom will have no end. And Mary said to the angel, "How can this be, since I am a virgin?" And the angel answered and said to her, "The Holy Spirit will come upon you, and the power of the Most High will overshadow you; and for that reason the holy offspring shall be called the Son of God." (1)

God became the man – Jesus.

While Mary was a young virgin, before her marriage, she was chosen to be the mother of God's Son. The three persons of God, the Father, the Son, and the Holy Spirit were all involved in the conception of the child Jesus. When the power of the Most High, the Father, overshadowed Mary and the Holy Spirit came upon her, she conceived a child in her womb. At the moment of conception, the Son, the second person of the Trinity became the child, a human being. This is the incarnation of God into a human body with a human soul.

> John 1:1-2,14: In the beginning was the Word, and the Word was with God, and the Word was God. He was in the beginning with God....And the Word became flesh, and dwelt among us,...(1).

This child is the Son of God because the Second Person of God was incarnated into a human body. This child is the Son of Man because He was born of woman. This child is wholly and truly God, and wholly and truly man. "Jesus" is the name the angel Gabriel told Mary to call her Son. Jesus means savior. Jesus is God who came into the world as a man to save men from their sins.

Jesus, the Messiah, emptied Himself of His nature as God to be like man.

The Son of God emptied Himself of His divine nature as God of knowing everything and came into the world as a babe with a human body and a human soul (mind). Jesus was truly God, but the divine nature of God of knowing everything was not manifested. He was like man in every respect except sin.

> Philippians 2:5-8:...Christ Jesus, who, although He existed in the form of God, did not regard equality with God a thing to be grasped, but emptied Himself, taking the form of a bond-servant, and being made in the likeness of men. And being found in appearance as a man, He humbled Himself by becoming obedient to the point of death, even death on a cross. (1)

The Messiah as a child had to learn right from wrong.

This child, the Messiah, will feed on milk and honey before He learns to choose between right and wrong. If the nature of God of knowing everything was manifested in Jesus, He would not have to learn right from wrong. Jesus as God cannot learn right from wrong. Only Jesus as man can learn right from wrong.

> Isaiah 7:15-16: He shall be living on curds and honey by the time he learns to reject the bad and choose the good. For before the child learns to reject the bad and choose the good,...(3).

Jesus was like any other Hebrew child. He had to learn to crawl before He could learn to walk. A baby has to grow before it reaches a point where He knows the difference between right and wrong. Jesus had to study the scripture to learn about Himself and His Father in heaven.

Jesus grew in wisdom and knowledge.

As Jesus grew, He increased in wisdom, knowledge and stature.

> Luke 2:40: And the Child continued to grow and become strong, increasing in wisdom, and the grace of God was

upon Him (1).

Luke 2:52: And Jesus kept increasing in wisdom and stature, and in favor with God and men (1).

If Jesus had not emptied Himself of His Divine Nature as God of knowing everything and become like man in every respect except sin, there would be no way for Jesus to grow in wisdom and knowledge. If the Divine Nature of God had been manifested in Jesus, He would have known everything. Only Jesus as Man can grow in wisdom and knowledge.

Jesus asked who had touched Him?

In Mark 5:25-34, a woman with hemorrhage touched Jesus' garment and was healed. Jesus turned around and asked "Who touched my clothes?" as He felt healing power leaving Him. Jesus aware at once that power had gone out from him, turned around in the crowd and asked, "Who has touched my clothes?"...The woman realizing what had happened to her, approached in fear and trembling. She fell down before Jesus and told him the whole truth.

Jesus felt healing power leaving His Body but He did not know who touch Him. He had to ask who had touched Him.

Jesus did not know everything.

The apostles asked Jesus when He was coming back for the second time and when the end of the age would come? (Matthew 24:3, Acts 1:7).

Matthew 24:36: But of that day and hour no one knows, not even the angels of heaven, nor the Son, but the Father alone (1).

Mark 13:31-32: Heaven and earth will pass away, but My words will not pass away. But of that day or hour no one knows, not even the angels in heaven, nor the Son, but the Father alone (1).

Jesus did not know the time the Father had fixed for His Second Coming or the end of the age. Jesus, as man, did not know everything.

Pope Benedict XVI wrote that the two Apostles, Andrew and Philip had served as interpreters and mediators of a small group of Greeks with Jesus. Jesus did not know the Greek language. (6)

The Holy Spirit descended on Jesus when He was baptized by John the Baptist.

> Luke 3:21-22 Now it came about when all the people were baptized, that Jesus also was baptized, and while He was praying, heaven was opened, and the Holy Spirit descended upon Him in bodily form like a dove, and a voice came out of heaven, "Thou art My beloved Son, in Thee I am well-pleased. (1)

> Isaiah 61:1: The Spirit of the Lord God is upon me, because the Lord has anointed me to bring good news to the afflicted; He has sent me to bind up the brokenhearted, to proclaim liberty to captives and freedom to prisoners. (1)

Jesus was led by the Spirit of God

After His baptism, the scriptures say that Jesus was led and guided by the Spirit from that point on. Jesus had all the gifts of the Spirit guiding Him. Jesus was setting an example for us to be led and guided by the Spirit.

Jesus did not come to do His will but the Father's will.

> John 6:38: For I have come down from heaven, not to do My own will, but the will of Him who sent Me (1).

Peter in speaking to Cornelius told how God had anointed Jesus with the Holy Spirit and with power.

> Acts10:38: how God anointed Jesus of Nazareth with the Holy Spirit and power. He went about doing good and

healing all those oppressed by the devil for God was with him (3A).

Jesus was anointed and guided by the Holy Spirit. Jesus was sensitive to His Father's voice and the guidance of the Holy Spirit. He did what His Father wanted Him to do. Jesus wants all of us to be sensitive to the anointing, prompting, and guidance of Holy Spirit just as He was. If the nature of God was manifested in Jesus, He would know everything. There would be no need of the Holy Spirit to lead and guide Him. In the days of the Apostles, great emphasis was put on being baptized in the Holy Spirit. We do not have this emphasis today. Most of us are not sensitive to the anointing, prompting, and guidance of the Spirit. To be sensitive to the anointing, prompting, and guidance of the Spirit requires that we spend time in prayer. Jesus spent considerable amount of time in prayer.

I had a vision of Jesus kneeling by a large rock:

God the Father said, "When My Son, Jesus, walked the face of the earth, He prayed without ceasing."

> Luke 6:12:...He went off to the mountain to pray, and He spent the whole night in prayer to God (1).

Mark tells of Jesus getting up long before daybreak to go out alone to pray.

> Mark 1:35: Very early in the morning, while it was still dark, Jesus got up, left the house and went off to a solitary place, where he prayed (2).

Jesus was led by the Spirit into the wilderness of Judea where He fasted and prayed for forty days and nights. Jesus was a man of prayer. He was tempted in every respect by Satan to sin (Luke 4:1-18).

> Luke 4:1-2: And Jesus, full of the Holy Spirit, returned from the Jordan and was led about by the Spirit in the wilderness for forty days, while tempted by the devil. He

ate nothing during those days; (1).

After three years of public ministry, the time had come for Jesus to be offered up as a sacrificial lamb for the sins of men. Jesus was betrayed by one of His own men for thirty pieces of silver. After the Last Supper (Passover meal), Jesus went to the garden to pray. As Jesus prayed in the garden, sweat of blood dripped off of His head and face (Luke 22:44). The burden of His coming torture, sacrifice and death was more than He could bear.

It is reported that people going through a severe crisis, such as a person facing death, will sometimes sweat perspiration of blood. This is caused by the rupture of the fine capillaries around the sweat glands (Hematidrosis). (7)

Jesus prayed to His Father and said.

> Matthew 26:39: "My Father, if it is possible, let this cup pass from Me, yet not as I will, but as Thou wilt" (1).

> Matthew 26:42: He went away again a second time and prayed, saying, "My Father, If this cannot pass away unless I drink it, Thy will be done" (1).

Jesus was a human being in every respect in suffering: agonizing in the garden, sweating perspiration of blood over His coming scourging, crowning of thorns, crucifixion and death. Jesus prayed, asking His Father to let this cup pass from Him, but that not His will but His Father's will be done. Jesus knew the will of His Father. This is the reason Jesus prayed with the word "if" - "If it is possible." He knew He had to go through with it.

The High Priest and the Jews hated Jesus. They were looking for an opportunity to arrest, condemn, and kill Jesus. Jesus was betrayed by Judas, arrested and tried by the Sanhedrin Court. Jesus was indicted because He admitted that He was the Son of God. Caiaphas, the High Priest, called this blasphemy. The Jews began to slap Him, spit on His face and beat Him. Since the Jews did not have the right to condemn a man to death, they brought Jesus to Pilate. Pilate gave in to the wishes of the Jews and ordered Jesus scourged and condemned to death by crucifixion.

Scourging

Scourging was a punishment in the Old Testament that was inflicted upon an individual by the use of a horsewhip. Deuteronomy 25:1-3 limited the number of blows in a legal punishment to forty.

During the time of Christ, the Romans used whips made with leather cut into strips. The tips of the strips were spiked with metal or bone fragments. *McKenzie's Dictionary of the Bible* reported that the scourging done by the Romans on slaves was horrible and often fatal. (8)

The Shroud of Turin, the garment in which Jesus' body was wrapped after His crucifixion, gives some insight into the cruelty, severity and inhumanity of the scourging and crucifixion. This garment was featured in the June 1980 "National Geographic." The Shroud of Turin was put on public display in 1978. It was thoroughly investigated by scientists using photographs, x-rays, and ultraviolet fluorescent photographs, along with microscopic and chemical analyses. They were convinced that the Shroud of Turin is not a painting or a hoax. They believed that the Shroud of Turin had truly been used as a burial cloth for a victim that had suffered a severe, savage scourging and crucifixion. The ultraviolet fluorescence photographs in the "National Geographic" show over 546 scourge marks. The victim of this shroud was scourged with different types of whips, including a special three-lash whip spiked on the tips with metal barbs. These metal barbs cut into the victim, tearing out pieces of flesh with each blow. The outline of the markings on the shroud was shown to be anatomically correct for a bearded man five feet and eleven inches tall. The shroud shows crucifixion nail wounds on wrists and feet and a spear type wound on the left side. The five wounds on the victim in the shroud correspond to the Biblical account of the crucifixion of Jesus. (9)

A sudarium in Oviedo, Spain is believed to be the linen cloth that covered Christ's face and head that is mentioned in the Gospel of John before He was buried in a shroud. While the shroud has an unknown history, the sudarium has been revered and preserved as a relic from the days of the crucifixion. A presbyter named Philip carried this cloth while he and other Christians were fleeing Palestine in 616 A.D. ahead of the Persian invasion. They traveled through Alexandria, Egypt, and on to Cartegena, Spain. The oak chest containing the sudarium was given to Leandro, the bishop of Seville. This cloth has been in Spain since 631 A.D.

The sudarium was placed on Christ's head while waiting for permission from Pontius Pilate to remove the body from the cross for burial. Studies show the stains indicate that the body was in a vertical position with the head at an angle. There are stains from deep puncture wounds on portions of the cloth covering the back of the head, which are consistent with the puncture marks found on the Shroud of Turin. These puncture marks are consistent with the crown of thorns. The sudarium is impregnated with blood and lymph stains that match the blood type on the Shroud of Turin.

Dr. Alan Whanger of Duke University used a polarized image overlay to compare the correlations between the Shroud of Turin and Sudarium of Oviedo. He found an astounding 70 points of correlation on the front and 50 on the back. Mark Guscin, author of "The Oviedo Cloth," said, "The only reasonable conclusion is that the Sudarium of Oviedo covered the same head as that found on the Shroud of Turin."

Studies done by Max Frie of Switzerland show specific pollens from Palestine are found on both relics. The sudarium has additional pollens from Egypt and Spain that are not found on the shroud, consistent with its history of travel. The shroud has pollens from Turkey that are not on the sudarium suggesting it took a different journey after leaving Jerusalem.

In a study in 1978, a sample of dirt was taken from the foot area of the shroud, which was found to contain travertine argonite crystals, a relatively rare form of calcite, found near the Damascus gate in Jerusalem where the tomb of Christ is purported to be (10).

A note should also be made that the shroud was made from cotton grown in the Middle East. The cloth was of a type of a weave known and used in the Middle East at the time of Christ (9).

The Sudarium of Oviedo, with a known history, has been revered and preserved as a relic of the crucified Christ. Studies show the sudarium and shroud covered the face of the same person. The pollens and calcite dirt on the shroud strongly indicate that the shroud originated in Jerusalem. The comparative studies between Sudarium of Oviedo and the Shroud of Turin strongly question the validity of the carbon 14 dating that was done on the shroud in 1978. Later studies showed that carbon 14 dating was done on newer cloth that was used to repair the damaged area of the shroud that was scorched in a fire. Scientists say the relic authenticates the Shroud of Turin as the actual burial cloth of Christ. (10)

Since the image on the sudarium matches the image on the shroud perfectly, and the sudarium has been revered as a relic of our Lord since the days of the Crucifixion, then the shroud should be revered as the burial cloth of Christ.

When someone has been wrapped up in a shroud, the cloth is not retrieved as the body begins to decompose and stink and the cloth becomes soiled and rotten. The question is if the shroud is really and truly a burial cloth, as scientists believe it to be, why was it retrieved and kept? The only logical reason for the shroud and sudarium to be retrieved would be that this was truly the burial cloth of Christ and that He was truly raised from the dead three days after His death.

The scourging of Jesus

The five wounds, the 546 scourging marks on the Shroud of Turin and the deep puncture marks by the crown of thorns on both cloths show the painful, cruel, horrible, savage-like, mutilation and crucifixion our Lord endured. (9)

Crown of thorns

The Roman soldiers weaved a crown of thorns, which was pressed and imbedded upon His head. Jesus was mocked as the King of the Jews.

Soldiers used the flats of their swords to force the crown on His head (11). Jesus, in a prophetic message to Louise Tomkiel, said He was crowned with three- to four-inch long thorns, of which many thorns penetrated His skull and came out of His forehead near His eyes (12). Three of the thorn wounds were reported to be mortal (13).

Jesus was forced to carry His cross.

Jesus severely weakened from the painful scourging and loss of blood, was forced to carry His cross to Calvary. Jesus, according to tradition, fell down three times with the heavy cross on His shoulder before the soldiers made Simon the Cyrenian help Him carry the cross.

The crucifixion

Jesus was stripped of His clothing and completely humiliated before the people. He was nailed by His wrists and ankles to the cross. His arms were pulled out of their sockets and stretched to fit over the nail holes prepared on the cross where His hands were nailed. His feet were pulled and positioned to fit into a man-made inhuman position and nailed to the cross. (13)

Jesus was on the cross for six hours.

Jesus hung on the cross for six hours, i.e. from the third hour in the morning to the ninth hour in the afternoon.

> Mark 15:25-26,33: And it was the third hour when they crucified Him. And the inscription of the charge against Him read, "THE KING OF THE JEWS."....And when the sixth hour had come, darkness fell over the whole land until the ninth hour. (1)

At the ninth hour, Jesus cried up to His Father in a loud voice, saying "My God, my God, why has Thou forsaken Me?" The pain was more than He could bear. Then Jesus cried out once more and died (Mark 15:34, 37).

When Joseph of Arimathea asked Pilate for the body of Jesus, Pilate could not believe that Jesus was dead. Pilate summoned the Roman centurion to determine if Jesus was dead. Ordinarily, one will hang on a cross for several days before dying by crucifixion. To speed up death by crucifixion, a blow is given to each knee or leg to break the bone so the victim cannot stand or push up to get a breath of air. The weight of the body pulling on both arms makes it difficult to breathe. The victim pushes up on his legs in order to breathe. When the legs are broken, suffocation and death comes quickly.

They did not break a bone in Christ's legs, as He was already dead. The soldier struck a spear into His side and heart. This fulfilled the prophecy spoken in Psalm 34:20 where it says not a bone was broken. The two criminals on both sides of the Lord had their legs broken.

> John 19:32-34, 36-37: The soldiers therefore came, and broke the legs of the first man, and of the other man who was crucified with Him; but coming to Jesus, when they saw that He was already dead, they did not break His legs; but one of the soldiers pierced His side with a spear, and immediately there came out blood and water....For these things came to pass, that the scripture might be fulfilled, "Not a bone of Him shall be broken."...They shall look on Him whom they pierced. (1)

Why did Jesus die after only six hours on the cross?

A person nailed to a cross will live several days before dying. For this reason the bones in both legs of the criminals are broken to speed up their death by suffocation. Yet no bones in Christ's body were broken for He was already dead. Why was Christ dead after only six hours on the cross? The fact Christ died in six hours indicates that Christ was severely beaten and mutilated by the scourging. He had to have lost a tremendous amount of blood. This is supported by the scripture in Psalms, which refers to His tongue cleaving to His jaws.

> Psalm 22:15: My strength is dried up like a potsherd, and my tongue cleaves to my jaws; (1).

When a person loses a lot of blood, the mouth will become very dry because there is no fluid to moisten the mouth. Christ's death during the crucifixion was hastened by the severe scourging and loss of blood. As the *McKenzie's Dictionary of the Bible* points out, scourging done by the Roman soldiers on their slaves was often fatal. This was the case with Jesus.

The suffering of Jesus according to Benedetta Da. S.S., and Pope Leo XIII, in Rome, April 5, 1890.

> Be it known that the number of armed soldiers were 150; those that trailed me while I was bound were 23. The executioners of justice were 83; the blows received on my head were 150; those on my stomach, 108; kicks on my shoulders, 80. I was led bound with cords by the hair 24 times; spits in the face were 180. I was beaten on the body 6666 times; beaten on the head, 110 times. I was roughly pushed and at 12 o'clock was lifted up by the hair; pricked with thorns and pulled by the beard 23 times; received 20 wounds on the head; thorns of marine junks, 72; pricks of thorn in the head, 110; mortal thorns in the forehead, 3. I was afterwards flogged and dressed as a mocked king; wounds in the body, 1000. The soldiers, who led me to the Calvary, were 608; those who watched me were 3, and those who mocked me were 1008; the drops of blood, which I lost, were 28,430. (13)

I was of the opinion that Jesus was nailed to the cross at 9 in the morning as reported in the gospel of Mark. I was reluctant to print the above information, which stated that Jesus was lifted by the hair at 12 o'clock. I asked my prayer partner to pray with me for an understanding. If Jesus was nailed to the cross at 9 in the morning, how could He be lifted by the hair at noon? This is what the Lord said:

> Jesus was indeed lifted by the hair at noon by the soldiers to see if He was still alive.

We received understanding that the cross was not high off the ground, and the soldiers were able to reach up to lift Jesus by the hair to see if He was still alive.

Is there a conflict between the gospels of John and Mark?

There appears to be a conflict between the gospel of John and the gospel of Mark. The gospel of John stated that Jesus was condemned to death by Pilate at the noon hour while the gospels of Matthew and Luke support the gospel of Mark in that Jesus was on the cross long before the noon hour when darkness came over the land.

> John 19:13-14: When Pilate heard these words he brought Jesus out and seated him on the judge's bench in the place called Stone Pavement, in Hebrew, Gabbatha. It was preparation day for the Passover, and it was about noon. (3A)

A friend, Wayne McGowen, did some research to understand the conflict between the Gospel of John and the other three gospels. He found that John had used the Roman time, which starts at midnight, while Mark, Matthew and Luke used the Hebrew time, which begins at sunrise or sunset. The original translation of John 19:13-14 reported Jesus was condemned to death at the sixth hour, which using Hebrew time was translated the noon hour indicating Jesus was on the cross for only three hours.

Mark reported that as soon as morning came, which is sunrise, not noon that Jesus was taken to Pontius Pilate. Jesus was actually condemned to death about six in the morning not noon.

> Mark 15:1: As soon as morning came, the chief priests with elders and scribes, that is the whole Sanhedrin, held council. They bound Jesus, led him away, and handed him over to Pilate (3A).

The sixth hour Roman time would be sunrise Hebrew time. Jesus was nailed to the cross at third hour of the day Hebrew time. This shows that there is no conflict between the Gospel of John and the other gospels.

Jesus was on the cross six hours, not three hours as most believe.

Jesus was crowned with thorns three times.

The Lord Jesus Christ told Luisa Piccarretta that crown of thorns was driven into His head three times. The crown of thorns was placed on his head at the time He was scourged while He was stripped of His garment. The crown of thorns was taken off so they could put His garment back on. The crown of thorns was driven back on His head for the second time. At the crucifixion, the crown of thorns was taken off so Jesus could be stripped of His garment. The crown of thorns was driven back onto His head for the third time.

> Jesus said: "My daughter, not only was the crowning with thorns triple, but almost all the pains I suffered in my Passion were triple. Triple were the three hours of agony in the garden; triple was the scourging, as they scourged Me with three different types of lashes; three times did they strip Me, and as many as three times was I condemned to death: at nighttime, early in the morning, and in broad daylight. Triple were my falls under the Cross; triple the nails; three times did my Heart pour out blood: in the garden by Itself; in the act of the crucifixion from Its very center, when I was stretched well on the Cross - so much so that my body was all dislocated and my Heart was smashed inside and poured out blood; and after my death, when my side was opened with a lance. (14)

Jesus described His scourging, crucifixion and death.

Jesus revealed the information below to Maria as a gift in return for the huge act of suffering she had offered to Him. There is every reason to believe that the revelation below is true. A person nailed to a cross will live for days before death occurs. One does not die after a few hours on the cross unless there was a tremendous scourging and loss of blood. The scourging described below was so severe that it would be only a matter of hours for death to occur. The men who scourged Jesus were furious and beat Him severely because He would not cry out for mercy. They wanted Jesus to beg for mercy. The Scripture says Jesus was silent and did not open His mouth. Jesus had no intention of crying out for mercy to those who scourged Him. Jesus did not cry out until the very end when He cried out to God His Father: My God, My God, why have you forsaken me?

> Isaiah 53: He was oppressed and afflicted, yet he did not open his mouth; he was led like a lamb to the slaughter, and as a sheep before her shearers is silent, so he did not open his mouth. (2)

It was reported that it took hours for Jesus to carry His cross to Calvary. He was kicked, hit and beaten all the way to Calvary. Jesus was condemned to death by Pontius Pilate at sunrise (6 am). He could hardly stand before Pilate. If Jesus had not been severely beaten, tortured and scourged, He would not have died on the cross. He would have had his leg broken like the thieves.

> John 19:36:…Scripture might be fulfilled, "Not a bone of Him shall be broken." (1)

He fell, fainted and passed out a number of times. It was not the nailing to the cross that killed Jesus; it was the severe scourging and loss of blood that was fatal.

I had a very close, colorful vision of the Lord Jesus Christ from the waist up with a crown of thorns on His head. His body was very, very bloody.

> Jesus said He will be sending this vision to me many times in my life time as He wants me to truly realize the suffering He experience on the cross.

29

Jesus revealed His suffering to Maria

My dearly beloved daughter My time for more suffering will come about as My Passion on the cross will be commemorated. No man understands the extent of My suffering during My crucifixion or the way in which I was scourged. My scourging was the worst. I was beaten savagely by ten men and every inch of My body was slashed. The flesh on My back was torn and My shoulder blades were visible. I could barely stand and one eye was bruised and crushed. I could only see through My left eye. By the time they took Me before Pontius Pilate and placed the crown of thorns on My head I could barely stand up. They then stripped Me bare before placing a short red garment over My head and then placed a palm branch in my right hand. Each thorn was like a needle so sharp was it. One of these thorns also pierced My right eye which left Me barely able to see. I lost so much blood that I vomited and was so dizzy that when I began My ascent to Calvary I could not hold the cross. I fell so many times that it took hours before I reached the top of the hill. I was scourged and whipped each step of the way. My body was bloody all over and covered with a thick sweat produced by a scorching sun. I fainted a few times. Much as this was painful and agonising the most frightening of all was the hatred shown to Me, not just by the adults along the way, but by young children who kicked Me because they were following their parents' example. The screams that poured out from their mouths and the hatred was nothing compared to the fear they had of Me. Because, behind it all, they were still not sure whether or not I was, in fact, the Messiah they were awaiting for so long. It was easier, therefore, to hate Me, denounce Me rather than accept Me for that would have meant that they would have had to change their ways. My most agonising moment was when I lay on the ground on My side, having being kicked in the back again, and saw My beloved Mother looking at Me. She was heart broken and had to be held up by two of My disciples. I could only see her through the one remaining eye and I could not bear to watch her torment. The jeers, screams and roars from the crowds of hundreds could be felt from the ground I lay on and it took six hundred soldiers to organise and supervise the crucifixion of Myself and six others. I was the main focus of their attention and the others did not suffer like I did. When My wrists, at the base of My thumbs, were nailed to the cross I could no longer feel. My body was so battered and bruised that I have gone into shock. My shoulders were dislocated and My arms were torn out of their sockets. The worst physical damage was inflicted on My body before I was nailed to the cross. I let out no scream. No protest. Only a whisper. This infuriated My executioners who wanted a reaction to satisfy their lusts. I never engaged with them for to do so would have meant that I would have had to engage with Satan and his demons who infested their souls. This is why their viciousness towards Me was so intense. I was hanging on the cross for five hours. The sun was scorching without clouds to help reduce the burning of My skin. As soon as I took My last breath My Father sent forth black clouds as well as thunder and lightning. The storm that took place was of such a frightening magnitude and so sudden that My spectators were left in no doubt at that stage that I was, indeed, the Saviour that had been sent by God the Father. I reveal this to you My daughter as a gift to you in return for the huge act of suffering you have offered Me. Tell My children that I do not regret My Passion on the Cross. What I do regret is that My sacrifice has been forgotten and that so many deny that My crucifixion took place. Many have no idea as to what I had to suffer as many of My apostles did not witness My climb to Calvary. What hurts Me today is that so many deny Me still. My appeal to you, My followers, is do not allow My Crucifixion to go to waste. I died for ALL sins including those committed today. I want and I need to save even those who deny Me even today. Your Beloved Saviour, Jesus Christ. (15)

God's love for man

The Lord freely gave us His Son to be offered up as a sacrificial lamb for the sins of men. Jesus, who was God, willingly emptied Himself of His Divine Nature as God and took on the nature of man. Jesus knew beforehand the intensity and pain of the scourging, crowning of thorns, the carrying of His cross, crucifixion and death. During His agony in the garden, Jesus sweated blood over the pain, suffering and death that He knew was coming. Jesus pleaded with His Father saying, "If it is at all possible, let this cup pass from Me. But not My will, but Thy will be done." While on the cross just before He died, Jesus cried out to His Father and said, "My God, My God, why has Thou forsaken Me?" The pain, loss of blood, difficulty breathing and suffering on the cross were more than He could bear. He felt He had been forsaken and abandoned. God, the Father, had to back off at this moment to allow sin to do its work. The Son is one with the Father and the Father is one with the Son. The Son did nothing except what the Father willed. The Father was the head while the Son was the body. Only in allowing the body to die was there a possibility of new life. When the Father pulled back to allow Satan to work, the Son was without the presence, comfort and direction of the Father, His head. Thus He cried out, "My God, My God, why have Thou forsaken Me?"

Jesus knew beforehand the price He had to pay. He fully accepted this responsibility to set man free. What greater love can one give than to knowingly and willingly accept the horrible scourging, crucifixion and giving of His life so that men may live? Jesus has done His part. He paid the price for the salvation of men with His life. Salvation is a free gift from God. Nevertheless, man has to do his part. Man has to accept this gift of salvation. God has extended His hand down to help man. Man has to reach up and take a hold of God's hand and complete this act.

Salvation involves three things: belief in and accepting the Lord Jesus Christ as God and Savior, repenting for our sins and water baptism. We will discuss water baptism first.

Water Baptism

Water baptism is one of the commandments of Christ.

> Matthew 28:19-20: Go therefore and make disciples of all nations, baptizing them in the name of the Father and the Son and the Holy Spirit, teaching them to observe all that I commanded you;...(1).

Jesus said one must believe and be baptized to be saved.

Water baptism is one of the commandments of Christ for salvation.

> Mark 16:15-16: He said to them, "Go into all the world and preach the good news to all creation. Whoever believes and is baptized will be saved, but whoever does not believe will be condemned (2).

Jesus did not say whoever believes would be saved. He said, "Whoever believes and is baptized will be saved."

Peter spoke of water baptism saving us.

> 1 Peter 3:20-21:...In it only a few people, eight in all, were saved through water, and this water symbolizes baptism that now saves you also -...(2).

Water Baptism takes away sins

Ezekiel foretold the day when water would be sprinkled on the people to clean them of their defilement.

Ezekiel 36:25-26: I will sprinkle clean water on you, and you will be clean; I will cleanse you from all your impurities and from all your idols. I will give you a new heart and put a new spirit in you; I will remove from you your heart of stone and give you a heart of flesh. (2)

Paul spoke of water baptism washing away his sins. Ananias said to Paul,

Acts 22:16: "And now why do you delay? Arise, and be baptized and wash away your sins, calling on His name" (1).

Another translation says,

And now, why delay? Go and be baptized, and be cleansed from your sins, calling on the name of the Lord (16).

In Acts, Peter spoke of water baptism taking away our sins.

Acts 2:38:...Repent, and let each of you be baptized in the name of Jesus Christ for the forgiveness of your sins;...(1).

Other translations say:

Turn away from your sins, each one of you, and be baptized in the name of Jesus Christ, so that your sins will be forgiven;...(17).

You must repent,...and every one of you must be baptized in the name of Jesus Christ for the forgiveness of your sins;"...(18).

Repent - change your views, and purpose to accept the will of God in your inner selves instead of rejecting it - and be baptized every one of you in the name of Jesus Christ for the forgiveness of and release from your sins;" (5).

Repent, Peter said to them, and be baptized every one of you, in the name of Jesus Christ, to have your sins forgiven;...(19).

Can any man forbid the water that these Gentiles should not be baptized?

Peter was told by the Spirit to go and tell the Gentiles about the Lord. As Peter was preaching the gospel, the Holy Spirit came upon the Gentiles. Then Peter said,

> Acts 10:47: "Can anyone keep these people from being baptized with water? They have received the Holy Spirit just as we have." So he ordered that they be baptized in the name of Jesus Christ (2).

Peter commanding that the gentiles be baptized immediately shows that he considered baptism to be of utmost importance. This scripture also shows that the baptism of water and the baptism of the Holy Spirit are two separate events.

Baptism of water and the baptism of the Holy Spirit are two separate events

> Acts 8:5,12,14-17: Philip went to the city of Samaria and preached the Messiah to the people there....But when they believed Philip's message about the Good News of the Kingdom of God and the name of Jesus Christ, they were baptized, both men and women....The apostles in Jerusalem heard that the people of Samaria had received the word of God; so they sent Peter and John to them. When they arrived, they prayed for the believers that they might receive the Holy Spirit. For the Holy Spirit had not come down on any of them; they had only been baptized

35

in the name of the Lord Jesus. Then Peter and John placed their hands on them, and they received the Holy Spirit. (17)

The people of Samaria were baptized with water. Later, at another time, Peter and John came to Samaria to pray with these people for the baptism of the Holy Spirit. This scripture shows that the baptism of water and the baptism of the Holy Spirit are two separate acts and events.

The water baptism of John the Baptist cannot be substituted for the water baptism of Jesus.

Apollos, an eloquent man, well versed in scripture, was teaching that Jesus was the Messiah. He had converted some of the people and baptized them in the baptism of John.

> Acts 18:24-25,27-28: Meanwhile, a Jew named Apollos,...a learned man, with thorough knowledge of the scriptures. He had been instructed in the way of the Lord, and he spoke with great fervor and taught about Jesus accurately, though he knew only the baptism of John....he was a great help to those who by grace had believed. For he vigorously refuted the Jews in public debate, proving from the Scriptures that Jesus was the Christ. (2)

Paul later came upon these disciples of Apollos and asked them under whose baptism they were baptized.

> Acts 19:1-5: While Apollos was at Corinth, Paul took the road...and arrived at Ephesus. There he found some disciples and asked them, "Did you receive the Holy Spirit when you believed?" They answered, "No, we have not even heard that there is a Holy Spirit." So Paul asked, "Then what baptism did you receive?" "John's baptism," they replied. Paul said, "John's baptism was a baptism of repentance. He told the people to believe in the one coming after him, that is, in Jesus." On hearing this, they were baptized into the name of the Lord Jesus. (2)

Paul immediately told the disciples of Apollos that there was a difference between the baptism of John and the baptism of Jesus. Though these disciples had been baptized in the water of John's baptism, Paul told them that it was essential to be baptized in the baptism of Jesus. The baptism of John was a baptism of repentance, which did not wash away sins or save anyone. Jesus' baptism is a baptism of water in the name of the Father, and the Son and the Holy Spirit, which washes away sins, enabling a person to be born again with a new heart and a new spirit to enter into the kingdom of God.

You must be born of the water and the Spirit to enter into the Kingdom of God.

A Baptist friend, who is one of my prayer partners, heard a prominent minister give a teaching on John 3 wherein Jesus told Nicodemus that one must be born again of the water and the Spirit to enter into the kingdom of God.

> John 3:3-7: Jesus answered and said to him, "Truly, Truly, I say to you, unless one is born again, he cannot see the kingdom of God." Nicodemus said to Him, "How can a man be born when he is old? He cannot enter a second time into his mother's womb and be born, can he?" Jesus answered, "Truly, truly, I say to you, unless one is born of water and the Spirit, he cannot enter into the kingdom of God. That which is born of the flesh is flesh; and that which is born of the Spirit is spirit. Do not marvel that I said to you, "You must be born again." (1)

The minister had convinced my friend that the water to which Jesus was referring in John 3 was the water of childbirth. My friend and I got into a discussion on water baptism. It did not matter what scriptures I quoted, I was not able to convince him that water baptism was one of the commandments for salvation. I told my friend that if he wanted to believe that water baptism was not a commandment from the Lord for salvation that was his privilege. I was not going to allow a disagreement to come between us as friends.

Two weeks later, he came to me saying that the Lord had spoken to him about water baptism. He said that if people are preaching water baptism when it is not necessary, we need to set them straight. When I had read the following words of knowledge the Lord had given my friend, I told him that these words do not support his view but support water baptism. These words show that the water in John 3 is not childbirth's water, but is water in which one is baptized.

> Water is a medium for the existence of physical life on earth. It is present in every living thing. Without it, we would surely die. This chemical formula is only a foundation for life on earth.

> What I said in John 3 pertains to the reverence one must give when he received Me as his personal Savior and comes to the current spiritual rebirth. I use water as a symbolic figure for the existence of man. In this world, water is man's only foundation of existence and represents his coming into God's spiritual world.

> Silver is given in exchange for material possession because it holds value. In the same manner, water is given in exchange for the Spirit because it holds value pertaining to the existence of life on earth. It is spiritual reverence in redeeming value for man to have eternal life. I told the Pharisees that the Sabbath is made for man, not man for the Sabbath.

> Without Me, water baptism has no power whatsoever. With Me, water baptism is the fruit of man's devotion to life as a witness and remembrance to Me. Water by itself has no power except to sustain a man's life, but with Me, it symbolizes that he has brought his physical presence into eternal life through his faith in Me.

While in prayer, my friend wrote down these words as they came to him. He was so convinced that the water Jesus spoke of in John 3 was childbirth water and that water baptism was not a commandment for salvation. When I had read the following words of knowledge the Lord had given my friend, I told him that these words do not support his view but support water baptism.

This revelation shows that the water of which Jesus was speaking in John 3 is baptismal water, not childbirth water. Just as silver holds value in exchange for food, clothing and the things we need or want, water also holds value for life since without it we cannot live. Water in baptism, like silver, has a spiritual redeeming value for man, which is given in exchange for eternal life.

When Jesus uses the words, "Truly, truly, I say to you," in the scripture, He is emphasizing that what He is about to say is of utmost importance. Jesus uses these words in speaking to Nicodemus, when He said, "Truly, truly, I say to you, unless one is born again, he cannot see the kingdom of God."

Nicodemus asked Jesus how he could enter his mother's womb to be born again. Jesus, putting heavy emphasis on what He was about to say, replied, "Truly, truly, I say to you, unless one is born of water and the Spirit, he cannot enter into the kingdom of God....Do not marvel that I say to you, you must be born again." Jesus put emphasis on being born again. How can one be born a second time? How can one be born again except through water baptism?

The water about which Jesus was talking in John 3 is the baptismal water that Ezekiel, Paul and Peter spoke of as cleansing us of our defilement and sins. This is the baptismal water of which Peter spoke when he asked if any man could forbid the water that the Gentiles should not be baptized. This is the baptismal water of which Peter spoke of in 1 Peter 3:20-21 that saves us. This is the baptismal water that Jesus spoke of in Mark 16:15-16 when He said you must believe and be baptized to be saved. This is the baptismal water that Jesus was referring to in John 3:3-7 when He said, "You must be born of water and the Spirit to enter into the kingdom of God. The water in John 3 is not childbirth water, for childbirth water has no power to remove sin and save us.

39

When Jesus said, "Truly, truly, I say to you, you must be born again," it is through water baptism that one is born again. It is my opinion that most adults when baptized with water feel an anointing from the Lord at that moment. They know something has happened. They know that they are different. They know that they have a new heart and a new spirit. They have a spirit of peace. They know they have been born again.

This water of which Jesus spoke in John 3 is baptismal water that enables one to enter into the kingdom of God. The scriptures show that Jesus, Peter and Paul placed utmost significance on the importance of being baptized with water.

Go and baptize in the name of the Father and the Son the Holy Spirit.

A close friend had a neighbor that was teaching water baptism in Jesus' name only. There are a number of scriptures, which speak of water baptism in Jesus' name. Our friend was confused, as she had been baptized in the name of the Father and the Son and the Holy Spirit. While she was in prayer, the following words were spoken to her: "Do as My Son says." In Matthew, Jesus said,

> Matthew 28:19-20: Go therefore and make disciples of all the nations, baptizing them in the name of the Father and the Son and the Holy Spirit, teaching them to observe all that I commanded you: (1).

There is only one baptism.

> Ephesians 4:4-6: There is one body and one Spirit - just as you were called to one hope when you were called - one Lord, one faith, one baptism; one God and Father of all, who is over all and through all and in all. (2)

One can be baptized only one time. The scripture does not speak of a second water baptism.

How should one be baptized?

Jesus did not give any teaching on the manner one should be baptized, except for baptizing in the name of the Father, and the Son and the Holy Spirit. Most Bible translations of Ezekiel 36:25 speak of water being sprinkled on the people to clean them of their defilement. Several translations speak of water being poured upon the people to clean them of their defilement.

> Ezechiel 36:25-26: And I will pour upon you clean water and you shall be cleansed from all your filthiness and I will cleanse you from all your idols. And I will give you a new heart, and put a new spirit within you; and I will take away the stony heart out of your flesh, and will give you a heart of flesh. (20)

Another translation says,

> I will sprinkle clean water upon you to cleanse you from all your impurities, and from all your idols I will cleanse you. I will give you a new heart and place a new spirit within you, taking from your bodies your stony hearts and giving you natural hearts. (20A)

> And then I will pour cleansing streams over you, to purge you from every stain you bear, purge you from the taint of your idolatry. I will give you a new heart, and breathe a new spirit into you; I will take away from your breasts those hearts that are hard as stone, and give you human hearts instead. (19)

Some think the above scripture does not pertain to water baptism. This scripture speaks of water being sprinkled or poured on the people to cleanse them of their sins and giving them a new heart and a new spirit. This is exactly what happens when one is baptized with the water baptism of Jesus.

Most movies depicting the baptism of Jesus show Him to be standing in the water with John the Baptist using a gourd to pour water upon His head. Others speak of immersion in water. They believe that Christ or the Ethiopian eunuch was immersed in water because the scriptures speak of them going down into the water and coming up out of the water. Philip also went down into the water and came up out of the water with the eunuch.

> Acts 8:38-39: "... and they both went down into the water, Philip as well as the eunuch; and he baptized him. And when they came up out of the water, . ." (1).

Since Philip went down into the water and was not immersed or baptized, the term "going down into the water and coming up out of the water" cannot be interpreted to mean or to prove that a person was baptized by immersion. If John the Baptist had poured water on Jesus' head with a gourd, Jesus would also have to walk up to the shore to come out of the water. It cannot be proven by scriptures whether Jesus or the eunuch was baptized by immersion.

Paul and Silas baptized the jailer and his family at midnight.

> Acts 16:25-34: But about midnight Paul and Silas were praying and singing hymns of praise to God, and the prisoners were listening to them; and suddenly there came a great earthquake, so that the foundations of the prison house were shaken; and immediately all the doors were opened, and everyone's chains were unfastened. And when the jailer had been roused out of sleep and had seen the prison doors opened, he drew his sword and was about to kill himself, supposing that the prisoners had escaped. But Paul cried out with a loud voice, saying, "Do yourself no harm, for we are all here!" And he called for lights and rushed in and, trembling with fear, he fell down before Paul and Silas, and after he brought them out, he said, "Sirs, what must I do to be saved?" And they said, "Believe in the Lord Jesus, and you shall be saved, you and your household." And they spoke the word of the

Lord to him together with all who were in his house. And
he took them that very hour of the night and washed their
wounds, and immediately he was baptized, he and all his
household. And he brought them into his house and set
food before them, and rejoiced greatly, having believed
in God with his whole household. (1)

It is doubtful that Paul and Silas took the jailer and his family to a
river or a pool to baptize them by immersion for several reasons:

1. It was the midnight hour and a light was needed to see.
2. Everyone was shaken as they just had an earthquake.
3. Paul and Silas had been beaten and were wounded.
4. The jailer was concerned about the prisoners trying to escape and
   would not want to leave the prisoners unattended.
5. When the jailer woke up, he could see that the jail doors were
   opened. This shows that the jailer's house was part of the jail or
   right next to the jail. There is no indication that they left the jail
   area; for the jailer and his family were baptized immediately after
   he washed Paul's and Silas' wounds.

For these reasons, it is most likely that the jailer and his family were
baptized in the manner spoken of in Ezekiel 36:25. It is interesting that
Paul felt that the jailer and his family should be baptized immediately
even though it was the midnight hour.

Bapto is a Greek word meaning to whelm i.e. to cover wholly with
a fluid. However, according to "Strong's Concordance," *bapto* in the
New Testament time also meant to moisten a part of one's body. Though
baptizo and *baptismo* are Greek words meaning baptize and baptism,
they also mean wash and washing. Paul, Peter and Ezekiel, all spoke
of baptism as washing away of one's sins and cleaning a person of his
defilement.

Since baptism is a commandment for one's salvation, certainly the
Lord did not intend to limit the condition by which a person is baptized.
This would certainly be the case if a person can be baptized only by

immersion. A person in the frozen north would have difficulty being immersed because of the scarcity of water. A terminally ill person would not be able to be immersed because of illness. Because of the severe drought and famine in Ethiopia and Sudan, people are dying due to the lack of food and water. Being baptized by immersion would put restrictions on certain people wishing to be baptized while sprinkling or pouring some water on their forehead would not.

Sprinkling or pouring of water or being immersed in water are all acceptable for water baptism, as baptism is not the washing of dirt off the body, but is the answering of a good conscience toward God.

> 1 Peter 3:21: And corresponding to that, baptism now saves you - not the removal of dirt from the flesh but an appeal to God for a good conscience through the resurrection of Jesus Christ (1).

The Living Bible says:

> In baptism we show that we have been saved from death and doom by the resurrection of Christ: not because our bodies are washed clean by the water, but because in being baptized we are turning to God and asking him to cleanse our hearts from sin. (16)

As Jesus began to wash His disciples' feet, He came to Peter. Peter told the Lord that He was not going to wash his feet. The Lord told Peter that unless He washed his feet, he could not have any part of Him. Peter replied, Lord, wash not only my feet but also my hands and my head as well.

> John 13:10-11: Jesus answered, "A person who has had a bath needs only to wash his feet; his whole body is clean. And you are clean, though not every one of you." For he knew who was going to betray him, and that was why he said not every one was clean. (2)

Though the washing of one's feet has nothing to do with water baptism, Jesus showed Peter that it wasn't the washing of his whole body that made him clean. Likewise, in baptism, it isn't the washing of one's whole body that cleanses him of his defilement, but it is an act of obedience toward God that enables one to be born again into the kingdom of God.

Water baptism is symbolic of dying, being buried and resurrected with Christ.

In Romans 6:1-11, Paul speaks of water baptism as being united with Christ in His death, burial and resurrection.

Death – one must repent and die to sin before being baptized (circumcision of the heart).

Burial - being baptized with water to remove the heart of stone, to wash away sins and to bury or cast away the old nature of sin.

Resurrection - receiving a new heart and a new spirit.

Romans 6 is a confirmation to the words spoken in Ezekiel 36:25 where the Lord said He would sprinkle or pour clean water on His people to clean them of their sins and put a new heart and a new spirit in them.

Why infant baptism? Water baptism reconciles a man with God.

When Adam and Eve sinned, man was cut off from God. As a consequence of that sin, all men are born defiled, inheriting a spirit of sin, which results in sickness, disease, and death. The following scriptures show that man is tainted with sin at the moment of conception and going astray at the moment of birth.

1. Job 14:4: Who can make him clean that is conceived of unclean seed? Is it not thou who only art? (20A).

Other translations say:

How can you demand purity in one born impure? (16).

Who can cleanse what is born of tainted stock, save Thou

45

alone, who alone hast being? (19).

Nothing clean can ever come from anything as unclean as man (19).

2. Psalm 50:7 (51:5): For indeed, I was born in sin; guilt was with me already when my mother conceived me (19).

    Other translations say:

    Psalm 51:5: You know I was born guilty, a sinner from the moment of conception (18).

    But I was born a sinner from the moment my mother conceived me (16).

3. Psalm 58:3: These men are born sinners, lying from their earliest words (16).

    Other translations say:

    Even from birth the wicked go astray; from the womb they are wayward and speak lies (2).

    Psalm 57:4 (58:3): Sinners that left the womb only to go a-straying; renegades and liars their mothers bore them! (19).

A person is a single cell at the moment of conception. The Psalms show that man was in sin at the moment he was conceived, while he was a single cell.

Before the crucifixion, death and resurrection of our Lord Jesus Christ, no man could enter into the kingdom of heaven, not even innocent babes that died without actual sin.

Romans 5:12: When Adam sinned, sin entered the entire human race. His sin spread death throughout all the world, so everything began to grow old and die, for all sinned (16).

Romans 5:18: So then, as the one sin condemned all men, in the same way the one righteous act sets all men free and gives them life (17).

When Adam sinned, the door to the kingdom of heaven was closed. Sin had entered the entire human race. All men including women, children and infants were condemned and could not enter into the kingdom of heaven.

God sent His Son into the world so that all men could be saved.

John 3:16-17: For God so loved the world, that He gave His only begotten Son, that whoever believes in Him should not perish, but have eternal life. For God did not send the Son into the world to judge the world; but that the world would be saved through Him. (1)

No one, including infants, could be saved before the coming of our Lord Jesus Christ. Jesus said He is the door to the kingdom of heaven.

John 10:9: I am the door. Whoever comes in by me will be saved;…(17).

Jesus opened the door with His crucifixion, death and resurrection. Before Jesus opened the door, no one, not even infants, could enter into the Kingdom of Heaven. Abraham and all the prophets and saints of the Old Testament were in Hades waiting for the Lord to open the door. Adam's sin affected all people, including infants.

Why were innocent babes that knew no sin unable to enter the kingdom of heaven? This reasoning and understanding shows that all men regardless of their innocence are under the curse of the first sin of Adam and Eve. It was through the crucifixion, death and resurrection of Jesus Christ that man was able to be reconciled with God. It is through the cleansing of water baptism that the curse of the sin of Adam and Eve is washed away, enabling man to be reconciled with God.

Though water baptism takes away man's sin, it is used only one time. Its main purpose is to remove the inherited curse of a spiritual death due to the sin of Adam and Eve so that man can be reconciled with God.

The innocent infants of today are no different than the infants of the Old Testament. Just as the infants of the Old Testament needed to be reconciled with God so do the infants today need to be reconciled with God. Though young children have not reached the age of reasoning and have no actual sin, they need to be baptized for reconciliation with God. Each child is reconciled with God by having the inherited curse of the sin of Adam and Eve washed away and having the seal of the living Triune God placed on him. The child that is bathed in God's baptismal grace is spiritually protected until such time that the child is old enough to make a profession of faith on his own.

Water is a symbol of life. Without it nothing can live. It is only appropriate that the Lord chose water as a means to reconcile man to Himself. Jesus said, "Unless a man is born again of water and the Spirit, he cannot enter the kingdom of heaven" (John 3:5).

Hold firm to the tradition you have been taught by word of mouth.

Jesus never instructed the apostles to write about the things He said or did. Everything Jesus said or did was not written down or recorded.

> John 20:30-31: Jesus did many other mighty works in his disciples' presence which are not written down in this book. These have been written that you may believe that Jesus is the Messiah, the Son of God, and that through this faith you may have life in his name. (17)

> John 21:25: Now there are many other things that Jesus did. If they were all written down one by one, I suppose that the whole world could not hold the books that would be written (17).

Most of the apostles did not write anything but taught by the word of mouth. Paul told the Corinthians and the Thessalonians to stand firm and hold to the traditions taught by the word of mouth.

> 1 Corinthians 11:2: Now I praise you because you

remember me in everything, and hold firmly to the traditions, just as I delivered them to you (1).

2 Thessalonians 2:15: So then, brethren, stand firm and hold to the traditions which you were taught, whether by word of mouth or by letter from us (1).

Infant baptism – a tradition since the time of the Apostles.

Saint Irenaeus (140 - 205 A.D.), the Bishop of Lyons, who was born shortly after the death of Apostle John, is called John's grandson in the faith. Saint Irenaeus was carefully instructed by the martyr, Saint Polycarp, the Bishop of Smyrna, who was an immediate disciple of John, the Apostle (21). Saint Irenaeus wrote:

> He came to save all who through him are born again unto God: infants, children, boys, youths and elders (22).

Saint Irenaeus would certainly know from St. Polycarp if infant baptism was practiced during the time of the apostles.

Origen (185-255) wrote that the power of baptism to forgive sins applies not only to adults but even to small children. Small children are baptized to remove the taint that we have at the moment of birth. (*In Lt. hom. XIV*).

The scripture says:

> Jobs 14:4: No one is free from taint, not even he whose life upon earth lasts but a day.

Origen said the reason children are in sin is because the child is conceived in a sinful body, in a mortal and lowly body. He wrote that infant baptism, which blots out this taint, is an "ecclesiastical practice" going back to the apostles (*Comm. in epist. ad Rom. V:9*) (23).

Origen at the end of his life wrote:

> The church received from the apostles the tradition of

giving baptism even to little children, (Comm. in epist. as Rom. 5:9; cf. In levit. Hom. 8:3).

This testimony carries weight. Origen knew that the baptism of little children was an Apostolic tradition as he had traveled widely spending a lot of time in Egypt and Palestine, and had visited Rome, Arabia (two or three times), Greece and possibly Asia Minor. (24)

Saint Cyprian and the bishops of the Third Council of Carthage in 235 A.D. were the leaders of the Church at that time. This council occurred 150 years after the death of Apostle John and 140 years before certain writings were determined to be inspired and compiled into a book called the New Testament. These leaders publicly stated that children should be baptized as soon as possible after birth. (25)

Tombstones' inscriptions show that young children were baptized.

Joachim Jeremias in his book, "Infant Baptism in the first Four Centuries", has some drawings of tombstones, plus a number of inscriptions of tombstones of children from the second, third and fourth centuries. These children range in age from eight months to nine years. The inscriptions on these tombstones show the children's age at death, that they were baptized and in some cases their age when baptized. One inscription stated that a twelve-year-old boy was baptized on his deathbed. (22)

Apostle John spoke of the children's sins being forgiven in Jesus' name.

1 John 2:12-13: I write to you, dear children, because your sins have been forgiven on account of his name. I write to you, fathers, because you have known him who is from the beginning. I write to you young men, because you have overcome the evil one. (2)

Another translation says:

I am writing to you little children, because your sins are

forgiven you for His name's sake (1).

The fact that John spoke to the little children along with the fathers and young men, shows that he was definitely speaking of little children when he talked about their sins being forgiven. This scripture is a strong indication that these children had been baptized, as it is through water baptism in Jesus' name (i.e. in the name of the Father, of the Son and of the Holy Spirit) that sins are washed away and forgiven.

Children are sometimes spoken of as being innocent and without sin. If this is the case, to what kind of sins was the Apostle John referring of which these children were forgiven?

After Jesus' ascension into heaven, the apostles went to all nations preaching the gospel. The teachings and traditions of the early church were taught primarily by word of mouth. Infant baptism was a tradition at the time of Irenaeus and Origen, who were only one or two generations removed from the time of the apostles. They would certainly know from their predecessors if infant baptism was practiced during the time of the apostles.

The bishops from the different nations at the Third Council of Carthage all reaffirm infant baptism. If infant baptism was widely practiced as Saint Irenaeus, Origen, Saint Cyprian and the bishops of the Third Council of Carthage indicated, then it was certainly going on at the time Apostle John was alive. Apostle John did not make any known attempt to discourage infant baptism. A scripture by John in 1 John 2:12 supports the fact that infant baptism was practiced by the apostles.

These references show that infant baptism was definitely taught and practiced by the leaders of the early church.

Each writer of the books of the New Testament gave a teaching or shared something that was not revealed or shared by other writers of the New Testament. If it were not for Paul being in jail, writing letters, (the epistles of Paul), we would not have the teachings and understanding we have today.

Though infant baptism was not directly mentioned in the writings that were compiled to form the New Testament, it was indirectly indicated by Apostle John, and it was definitely shown by the writings of Saints Irenaeus, Origen and Saint Cyprian to be a tradition that was widely taught and practiced by the early leaders of the church.

Infant baptism was practiced for 1500 to 1600 years before it was ever questioned. There are many denominations that still practice infant baptism. These include the Roman Catholic, the Greek Orthodox, the Episcopalian or Anglican, the Lutheran, the Methodist and Presbyterian. (26)

Everyone, including infants, should be baptized. For it is through water baptism that man is reconciled with God, washing away the inherited curse of the sin of Adam and Eve and having the seal of God, the Father, the Son and the Holy Spirit placed on him, releasing him from the grip of a spiritual death.

What about the good thief on the cross who was not baptized?

The good thief on the cross was like the Old Testament saints that died under the old covenant. Water baptism was a commandment under the new covenant after Jesus' death and resurrection.

The scripture in 1 Peter 3:19 and 1 Peter 4:6: tells us that Jesus, after His death on the cross, descended into Hades to preach to the good people that had died and were unable to enter into the kingdom of heaven before Jesus' crucifixion, death and resurrection. Why did Jesus preach to the spirits in prison? Did Jesus tell those in prison that they had to repent for their sins and believe that He was the Son of God to be saved? The scriptures teach that man is conceived impure and in sin. This is obvious, as infants who knew no actual sin were not able to enter into the kingdom of heaven before Jesus' crucifixion, death and resurrection. Did Jesus do as Peter did on the day of Pentecost and tell the spirits in prison that they needed to be baptized in the name of the Father, the Son and the Holy Spirit to wash away their sins, to be sealed and reconciled with God? What type of a response was Jesus expecting from these people to whom He was preaching?

Those that have questions about water and the desire for water in the spiritual world need to read about Lazarus and the rich man in Hades.

Luke 16:23-24: And in Hades he lifted up his eyes, being in torment, and saw Abraham far away, and Lazarus in his bosom. And he cried out and said, "Father Abraham, have mercy on me, and send Lazarus, that he may dip the tip of his finger in water and cool off my tongue; for I am in agony in this flame." (1)

Though Abraham and Lazarus were also in Hades, they were separated from the rich man by a large gulf. There was no way Lazarus could cross over to where the rich man was. Though the rich man had died and was in Hades as a spirit, he was asking for water.

Water is the symbol and source of life. In John 4, Jesus said He was the source of the living water whereby one will never thirst again. While Abraham and Lazarus had water, the rich man did not.

We have no way of knowing what Jesus preached to the spirits in prison or what He asked of them. It is interesting that Peter spoke of water baptism saving us immediately after he spoke of Jesus preaching to the spirits in prison.

When Adam and Eve were in the Garden of Eden, they were told not to eat of the fruit of the tree of knowledge of good and evil (the tree of death). There was a tree in the garden called "the tree of life" of which they could eat the fruits. When Adam and Eve had eaten the fruit of the tree of death, the Lord stationed cherubs with flaming swords to guard the tree of life to prevent Adam and Eve from partaking of the fruits of this tree in their sinful state. Yet, in Revelation 2:7, the Lord said He would grant to those that overcome the right to eat from the tree of life. Why do those that have died and have been resurrected to a new life, need to partake of the fruit of the tree of life, the same tree of which Adam and Eve had an opportunity to partake when they were on earth?

Just as we will be given the right to partake of the fruits of the tree of life after we have been raised from the dead, it is also possible that when Jesus preached the good news to the spirits that lived and died before His coming, that He asked them to respond to His preaching by being baptized with water. This response would wash away the stain of the sin of Adam and Eve, reconciling them to God, sealing them with everlasting life in the name of the Father, of the Son and of the Holy Spirit.

The spirits in prison were obviously good people that had lived and died before the coming of our Lord Jesus Christ. These people were unable to enter into the kingdom of heaven before the crucifixion, death and resurrection of Jesus Christ. Jesus preached to these people because they needed to be reconciled with God.

> 1 Peter 3:18-21: For Christ died for sins once for all, the righteous for the unrighteous, to bring you to God. He was put to death in the body but made alive by the Spirit, through whom also he went and preached to the spirits in prison who disobeyed long ago when God waited patiently in the days of Noah while the ark was being built. In it only a few people, eight in all, were saved through water, and this water symbolized baptism that now saves you also…(2)

> 1 Peter 4:6: For this is the reason the gospel was preached even to those who are now dead, so that they might be judged according to men in regard to the body, but live according to God in regard to the spirit. (2)

What about those people who believe in Jesus but were never baptized?

I am not naive enough to say that people who believe in Jesus Christ but were not baptized will go to hell. I know that our God is an all-merciful God. Those who believe and were not baptized will fall on His mercy for Jesus said in Mark 16:15-16 that one must believe and be baptized to be saved.

Water baptism, through Jesus Christ, has redeeming power, enabling one to be born again, to be saved, washing away his sins, making him a new creation with a new heart and a new spirit, opening the door for him to enter into the kingdom of God.

Comment – The Lord has given me a gift of praying for people in purgatory (Chapter 9). The Lord allowed people who had not been baptized to be baptized.

Salvation

Salvation is a free gift from God and cannot be earned.

> Ephesians 2:8-9: For by grace you have been saved through faith: and that not of yourselves, it is a gift of God; not as a result of works, that no one should boast (1).

Nevertheless, there are certain conditions that must be met to receive this free gift.

What must one do to be saved?

On the day of Pentecost, after the outpouring of the Holy Spirit, approximately three thousand Jews gathered around the apostles to see what all the commotion was about. Peter stood up and preached the gospel, which is the good news of Jesus Christ.

> Romans 1:16: For I am not ashamed of the gospel, for it is the power of God for salvation to every one who believes,…(1).

The three thousand Jews were touched and pierced to their hearts by the words Peter spoke. They turned to Peter and to the rest of the apostles and said, "Brethren, what must we do?" Peter replied,

> Acts 2:38-39:…Repent, and let each of you be baptized in the name of Jesus Christ for the forgiveness of your sins; and you shall receive the gift of the Holy Spirit. For the promise is for you and your children, and for all who are far off, as many as the Lord our God shall call to Himself. (1)

Salvation involves belief in the Lord Jesus Christ, repenting for one's sins and water baptism.

One must believe that Jesus Christ is the Son of God.

> John 3:17-18: For God did not send his Son into the world to condemn the world, but to save the world through him. Whoever believes in him is not condemned, but whoever does not believe stands condemned already because he has not believed in the name of God's one and only Son. (2)

Jesus said He was the way, the truth and the life (John 14:6).

Jesus is the One who saves

> Acts 4:12: Salvation is found in no one else, for there is no other name under heaven given to men by which we must be saved (2).

Jesus said,

> John 11:25-26:...I am the resurrection and the life; he who believes in Me shall live even if he dies, and every-one who lives and believes in Me shall never die....(1).

In John 10:9, Jesus said, "I am the door; if anyone enters through Me, he shall be saved,..." No one can enter the kingdom of heaven except through Jesus Christ (John 10:1).

All have sinned

> Romans 3:23: for all have sinned and fall short of the glory of God, (1).

> I John 1:8-9: If we claim to be without sin, we deceive ourselves and the truth is not in us. If we confess our sins, he is faithful and just and will forgive us our sins and purify us from all unrighteousness (2).

Now is the time for salvation.

> 2 Corinthians 6:2:...behold, now is the acceptable time, behold, now is the day of salvation, (1).

> John 1:12: But as many as received Him, to them He gave the right to become children of God, even to those who believe in His name (1).

Accepting Jesus Christ as your Lord and Savior.

If one wants to accept Jesus Christ as his Lord and Savior, one can say the following prayer:

> Heavenly Father have mercy on me, a sinner. I confess with my mouth and acknowledge that Jesus Christ is the Son of God. I believe that He was scourged, crucified and died for my sins, and on the third day was raised from the dead. Father, through your Son, Jesus, I ask that you forgive me of all my sins (name them). I commit myself to turn away from all sins, occasions that may lead to sin or anything that will offend you, my Lord. By faith, I (name), now accept You, Jesus Christ, as my Lord and Savior. Please fill me with the power of your Spirit to enable me to live a strong Christian life.

New Life

If we confess our sins, the Lord is faithful and just to forgive us our sins and cleanse us from all unrighteousness. Scripture says the eye has not seen, the ear has not heard nor has it entered into the heart of man all that God has prepared for those who enter into His kingdom (I Corinthians 2:9).

Words received in prayer

While my friend and I were in prayer, the following words came to us:

Our Lord Jesus came into the world as a human, born of the flesh, but with a spirit as supreme as God Almighty, for He was God. In order to impart to this world the power necessary to overcome evil and darkness, Christ was presented on a level much lower than the Holy Angels in order to go into battle.

The world was His battlefield, so that the armor of God could be made manifest. Jesus Christ shed His blood for man. This sacrificial blood bridged the gap between man's sinful nature and God's most perfect existence. Jesus' blood was His very life and whoever believes that Jesus is the Son of God and was resurrected and glorified after three days, will receive this blood of life for all eternity.

Believing this is essential, for this kind of faith in Christ, His Deity and His resurrection makes man acceptable to God for reconciliation. God accepts sincere faith as Holy Reverence to His name and is the only real action we can take to appease God. So, in terms of accepting Christ as the Son of God, our Savior and Redeemer, we must utilize this vehicle of faith to unite us with the blood of Christ.

In seeking the Lord for an understanding in regard to the armor of God, the following analogy was given to us:

Spiritual battles are dealt with much in the same way as physical battles. A nation can fight and successfully win a war only if it knows where the enemy hides. Without knowledge of the occupation of the enemy, the battle is fruitless. This does not imply the manner in which the nation fights; it only identifies where the battle is fought.

Christ's battle was fought here on this earth. The enemy was Satan and his legions of angels that powered the forces of darkness. In order for Christ to impart the armor of God, He had to come to this earth and fight the battle in a human form.

Ephesians 6 speaks of salvation, righteousness, truth, peace, faith, the word of God and praying at all times in the Spirit as the Armor of God. These are essential to fight and overcome the powers of darkness, for our battle is not against flesh and blood but against the unseen powers and rulers of darkness.

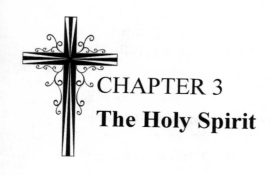

CHAPTER 3
The Holy Spirit

The Holy Spirit is God. He is also the Third Person of the Blessed Trinity. The Holy Spirit is the Comforter Who dwells within us and brings forth new life to make us strong Christians and soldiers for Jesus Christ.

In the Old Testament only the prophets and certain individuals, such as King David, had the Holy Spirit. David pleaded with the Lord not to take the Holy Spirit from him.

> Psalm 51:11-12: Do not cast me away from Thy presence, and do not take Thy Holy Spirit from me. Restore to me the joy of Thy salvation, and sustain me with a willing spirit (1).

David wanted the presence, the pleasure, the comfort and the anointing of the Spirit of God dwelling within him.

The Lord promises to pour His Spirit out on all the people.

> Joel 2:28-29:…I will pour out My Spirit on all mankind; and your sons and daughters will prophesy, your old men will dream dreams, your young men will see visions. And even on the male and female servants I will pour out My Spirit in those days. (1)

> Ezekiel 36:27: And I will put My Spirit within you and cause you to walk in My statutes, and you will be careful to observe My ordinances (1).

The Holy Spirit was compared to the new life that springs forth when water is poured on thirsty land.

In Isaiah, the Lord compared the pouring out of His Spirit on the people to the new vegetation that comes forth when water is poured out on dry, parched land.

> Isaiah 44:2-4: Thus says the Lord who made you and formed you from the womb, who will help you. Do not fear, O Jacob My servant,...For I will pour out water on the thirsty land and streams on the dry ground; I will pour out My Spirit on your offspring and My blessing on your descendants; and they will spring up among the grass like poplars by streams of water. (1)

Persons filled with the Spirit will be like poplar trees growing by a stream; they are in constant contact with the living water that gives and brings forth new life. Just as water brings forth new vegetation and new life on thirsty soil, the Holy Spirit also brings forth new life within a person.

Pouring water on the ground during the Feast of the Tabernacles was symbolic of the outpouring of the Holy Spirit which was yet to come.

During the Feast of the Tabernacles, water was taken from the spring of Gihon and poured out on the ground at the foot of the altar. This water was poured out in a symbolic anticipation of the outpouring of the Holy Spirit, which was yet to come, as only the prophets and certain individuals had the Holy Spirit during the Old Testament time (27).

John the Baptist foretold that Jesus was the one who would baptize with the Holy Spirit and with Fire.

John the Baptist said,

> Matthew 3:11: As for me, I baptize you in water for re-pentance, but He who is coming after me is mightier than

I,…He Himself will baptize you with the Holy Spirit and fire (1).

Jesus spoke of the outpouring of the Holy Spirit during the great Feast of the Tabernacles.

John 7:37-39: On the last and greatest day of the feast, Jesus stood up and exclaimed, "Let anyone who thirsts come to me and drink. Whoever believes in me, as the scripture says, "Rivers of living water will flow from within him." He said this in reference to the Spirit that those who came to believe in him were to receive. There was, of course, no Spirit yet, because Jesus had not yet been glorified. (3A)

The Feast of the Tabernacles was one of the three great yearly feasts in which all males were obligated to present themselves before the Lord. This feast was celebrated after the harvest (28). During this feast, at the moment the vessels of water were being poured out on the ground in anticipation of the outpouring of the Holy Spirit that was to come, Jesus stood up and began to speak, saying "If any man is thirsty, let him come to Me and drink. He who believes in Me, from his innermost being shall flow rivers of living water." Jesus spoke of the living water as being the Holy Spirit that was to be poured out after He had been glorified (27).

Vision - though it was not raining, there was clear water everywhere. I could see lawns with tips of grass just sticking out of the water. Water was flowing down the street from the top of the hill. The Lord said:

Have I not said with streams of living water I will pour out on mankind? This living water will wash away sins. It will fill the thirst of the world if they will drink of it. This water is also the water of baptism that cleans us from sin.

Disciples were not to leave Jerusalem until they had received Holy Spirit.

In the Acts of the Apostles, just before He ascended into heaven, Jesus spoke to His disciples and followers and told them not to leave Jerusalem until they had been baptized with the Holy Spirit.

> Acts 1:4-5,8:...He commanded them not to leave Jerusalem, but to wait for what the Father had promised,...for John baptized with water, but you shall be baptized with the Holy Spirit not many days from now....you shall receive power when the Holy Spirit has come upon you;...(1)

The Holy Spirit came upon a group of 120 people on the day of Pentecost, ten days after Jesus ascended into heaven (Acts 1:15). This was the moment which the people in the Old Testament had been looking forward to. This was the first time the Holy Spirit had been poured out on a community of people.

> Acts 2:1-4: And when the day of Pentecost had come, they were all together in one place. And suddenly there came from heaven a noise like a violent, rushing wind, and it filled the whole house where they were sitting. And there appeared to them tongues as of fire distributing themselves, and they rested on each one of them. And they were all filled with the Holy Spirit and began to speak with other tongues, as the Spirit was giving them utterance. (1)

Just prior to the outpouring of the Holy Spirit, the disciples and followers of Jesus went into hiding, because they were afraid of the Jews. On the day of Pentecost, when the Holy Spirit was poured out on them, they were no longer afraid and became bold. A mighty wind stirred the city. They began to speak in tongues, praising God, raising all kinds of commotion. At this time, there were Jews from many nations of the world living in Jerusalem. Many of the Jews came to see what the commotion was about. These Jews heard the Galileans praising God in the languages of their own countries.

> Acts 2:5-13: Now there were Jews living in Jerusalem, devout men, from every nation under heaven. And when this sound occurred, the multitude came together, and were bewildered, because they were each one hearing them speak in his own language. And they were amazed and marveled, saying, "Why, are not all these who are speaking Galileans? And how is it that we each hear them in our own language to which we were born? Parthians and Medes and Elamites, and residents of Mesopotamia, Judea and Cappadocia, Pontus and Asia, Phrygia and Pamphylia, Egypt and the districts of Libya around Cyrene, and visitors from Rome, both Jews and proselytes, Cretans and Arabs - we hear them in our own tongues speaking of the mighty deeds of God." And they continued in amazement and great perplexity, saying to one another, "What does this mean?" But others were mocking and saying, "They are full of sweet wine." (1)

The Apostle Peter spoke:

> The Jews from all nations were amazed. Peter began to preach.

> Acts 2:15-21: These people are not drunk, as you suppose, for it is only nine o'clock in the morning. No, this was what was spoken through the prophet Joel: 'It will come to past in the last days,' God says, that I will pour out a portion of my spirit upon all flesh. Your sons and daughter shall prophesy, your young men shall see visions, your old men shall dream dreams. Indeed, upon my servants and my handmaids I will pour out a portion of my spirit in those days, and they shall prophesy. I will work wonders in heaven above and signs on earth below: blood, fire, and a cloud of smoke. The sun shall be turned

to darkness and the moon to blood, before the coming of the great and splendid day of the Lord, and it shall be that everyone shall be saved who calls on the name of the Lord. (3A)

Peter witnessed about Jesus who was crucified. The Jews were pierced to their hearts and asked Peter and the disciples what they must do. Peter said:

> Acts 2:38-39: Repent and be baptized, every one of you, in the name of Jesus Christ so that your sins may be forgiven. And you will receive the gift of the Holy Spirit. The promise is for you and your children and for all who are far off – for all whom the Lord our God will call. (2)

The promise of the Holy Spirit was not only to the Jews and their children but to those far off, who include you and me.

Father gives the Holy Spirit.

> Luke 11:11-13: What father among you would hand his son a snake when he asks for a fish? Or hand him a scorpion when he asks for an egg? If you then who are wicked, know how to give good gifts to your children, how much more will the Father in heaven give the Holy Spirit to those who ask him? (3A)

Jesus baptizes with the Holy Spirit

John the Baptist said he baptized with water for repentance but Jesus coming after him will baptize with the Holy Spirit and with fire (Matthew 3:11, Luke 3:16). Jesus told his disciples to wait in Jerusalem until they have been clothed with power from on high.

> Acts 1:8: but you shall receive power when the Holy Spirit has come upon you; and you shall be My witness both in Jerusalem, and in all Judea and Samaria, and even to the remotest part of the earth (1).

Philip preached to the people in Samaria.

> Acts 8:5-8, 14-17: And Philip went down to the city of
> Samaria and began proclaiming Christ to them. And the
> multitudes with one accord were giving attention to what
> was said by Philip, as they heard and saw the signs which
> he was performing. For in the case of many who had un-
> clean spirits, they were coming out of them shouting with
> a loud voice; and many who had been paralyzed and lame
> were healed. And there was much rejoicing in that city....
> Now when the apostles in Jerusalem heard that Samaria
> had received the word of God, they sent them Peter and
> John, who came down and prayed for them, that they might
> receive the Holy Spirit. For it had not yet fallen upon any
> of them; they had simply been baptized in the name of the
> Lord Jesus. Then they began laying their hands on them,
> and they were receiving the Holy Spirit. (1)

Philip had preached to the people with signs and wonders and people
were healed. The people had readily accepted Jesus and were baptized
with water but had not received the Holy Spirit. When Peter and John
heard that the people had not received the Holy Spirit, they immediately
went to Samaria and prayed with the people that they might receive the
Holy Spirit.

In Acts 10, Peter was invited to preach to Cornelius, a gentile, a
centurion, a righteous and God-fearing man. While Peter was preaching,
the Holy Spirit fell upon Cornelius and all who were listening. Peter
asked, "Can anyone forbid the water that they who have received Holy
Spirit just as we have from being baptized?"

In Acts 19:1-6, Paul met some disciples of John the Baptist who
were preaching Jesus. Paul did not see any gifts of the Holy Spirit being
manifested. He asked if they had received the Baptism of the Holy
Spirit since they believed. They had never heard of the Holy Spirit. Paul
then asked with whose baptism they were baptized. They said, "The
baptism of John the Baptist." Paul explained that John's baptism was for
repentance; they must be baptized in the name of Jesus. After they were

baptized, Paul laid hands on them and they received the Holy Spirit and began speaking in tongues and prophesying.

Peter, John, and Paul knew it was essential that these people receive the baptism of the Holy Spirit with the gifts of the Spirit. It is also important for us to be baptized with the Holy Spirit and to receive the gifts of the Spirit. The Lord wants all of His people to be filled with the Holy Spirit just as Philip, the apostles and Cornelius.

We receive the Holy Spirit when we are baptized with water. The difference in water baptism and the baptism of the Holy Spirit is the power we received. Water baptism is like a pilot light in contrast to a blazing furnace such as the apostles received on the day of Pentecost. The Lord promised in the Old Testament to pour out His Spirit on all mankind. The Lord wants all of us to be clothed in the power of the Most High. The Holy Spirit enables us to be strong Christians and soldiers for Jesus Christ. We should desire and seek the baptism of the Holy Spirit and the gifts of the Spirit with the power of God operating in our lives. To receive the baptism of the Holy Spirit, we have to repent, turn away from sin, and strongly desire and seek the Holy Spirit with all that is within us.

Some people are concerned that if they allow the Spirit to operate within them, that they will have no control over what they do. This is not true. A person has complete control over his body. The Spirit of God within a person does not control a person. It is just like committing a sin. The Lord has given us a free will. We can do what we want to do. If we want to commit a sin, God does not stop us. The Spirit does not force us to do anything against our will. There are times when some people get excited and emotional; however, they are doing this in the flesh. God's Spirit is gentle, comforting and loving. This is the reason King David pleaded with the Lord not to take away the presence and comfort of His Most Holy Spirit.

Paul tells us to earnestly desire and seek after the greater gifts of the Spirit.

There are many gifts of the Holy Spirit.

I Corinthians 12:4-11: Now there are distinctive varieties and distributions of endowments (extraordinary powers distinguishing certain Christians, due to power of divine grace operating in their souls by the Holy Spirit) and they vary, but the (Holy) Spirit remains the same. And there are distinctive varieties of service and ministration, but it is the same Lord (Who is served). And there are distinctive varieties of operation - of working to accomplish things - but it is the same God Who inspires and energizes them all in all. But to each one is given the manifestation of the (Holy) Spirit - that is, the evidence, the spiritual illumination of the Spirit - for good and profit. To one is given in and through the (Holy) Spirit (the power to speak) a message of wisdom, and to another (the power to express) a word of knowledge and understanding according to the same (Holy) Spirit; To another (wonder-working) faith by the same (Holy) Spirit, to another the extraordinary powers of healing by the one Spirit; To another the working of miracles, to another prophetic insight - that is, the gift of interpreting the divine will and purpose; to another the ability to discern and distinguish between (the utterance of true) spirits (and false ones), to another various kinds of (unknown) tongues, to another the ability to interpret (such) tongues. All these (achievements and abilities) are inspired and brought to pass by one and the same (Holy) Spirit, Who apportions to each person individually (exactly) as He chooses. (5)

The nine gifts of the Holy Spirit.

1 Corinthians 12:3-11 speaks of nine gifts of the Holy Spirit.

1. Gift of wisdom
2. Gift of knowledge
3. Gift of faith
4. Gift of healing

5. Gift of miracle
6. Gift of prophecy
7. Gift of discernment of spirit
8. Gift of tongues
9. Gift of interpreting tongues

Gift of wisdom

There is human wisdom. There is divine wisdom, which comes from the Holy Spirit to people in certain circumstances. Divine wisdom is imparted by the Holy Spirit, giving a person an understanding in what to say, to do or how to respond in a certain moment and time. An example is given in Matthew.

> Matthew 10:18-20: and you will be led before governors and kings for my sake as a witness before them and pagans. When they hand you over, do not worry about how you are to speak or what you are to say. For it will not be you who speak but the Spirit of your Father speaking through you. (3A)

If anyone lacks wisdom, let him ask of the Lord

> James 1:5-8: If any of you lacks wisdom, he should ask God, who gives generously to all without finding fault, and it will be given to him. But when he asks, he must believe and not doubt, because he who doubts is like a wave of the sea, blown and tossed by the wind. That man should not think he will receive anything from the Lord; he is a double-minded man, unstable in all he does. (2)

We need to ask the Lord for wisdom, understanding, and guidance in ministering to and praying for people.

Gift of knowledge or words of knowledge

This is a very important gift. Supernatural knowledge is knowledge revealed to an individual which he has no natural way of knowing. This gift is widely used in the healing ministry, in discernment of spirits and in prayer meetings. Knowledge can be imparted by visions, dreams, words or understanding received or by prophecy. The Lord will often reveal sins that need to be repented before a healing can take place.

An example of supernatural knowledge is found in 1 Corinthians. The scripture speaks of the secrets of a man's heart being revealed by those in prayer.

> 1 Corinthians 14:25: the secrets of his heart are disclosed; and so he will fall on his face and worship God, declaring God is certainly among you (1).

The Spirit speaks to us by thoughts. The Spirit gives us knowledge and understanding.

The Spirit speaks to us through thoughts that pass through our mind. I was seeking the Lord for understanding on how to prove that the invasion of Israel by the nations of the north in Ezekiel 38 and 39, and the battle of Armageddon in Revelation 16:16-21 is one and the same event. A comparison of the scriptures in Chapter 4 in my book *Lifting the Veil of Revelation* (29) shows that the identical events that take place in Ezekiel also occur at the battle of Armageddon. One of the events shows the mountains of Israel being leveled by a severe earthquake. I said, "Lord, I see the comparison. How can I show that the invasion of Israel by the nations of the north in Ezekiel and the battle of Armageddon in Revelation is one and the same event?" I prayed about this for three days. I was up early one Sunday morning for my personal prayer time. While I pacing the floor praising the Lord, a very heavy thought came to me. The thought was so strong that I knew it was not my thought. The thought was:

> "If the invasion of the nations of the north is a separate event from the battle of Armageddon, and the mountains of Israel are leveled when the nations of the north invade Israel, where are the mountains to be leveled a second time at the battle of Armageddon?"

The mountains of Israel can be leveled only one time. If they have already been leveled, there will be no mountains to be leveled at the battle of Armageddon. Yet, the scriptures say the mountains are leveled at the battle of Armageddon. This reasoning shows that the invasion of Israel by the nations of the north and the battle of Armageddon are both one and the same event.

The Lord can speak to us with thoughts that pass through our mind, which we recognize as not being our thoughts. The revelation of proving that the invasion of Israel by the nations of the north and the battle of Armageddon are both one and the same event is an example of how the Spirit teaches and gives us knowledge and understanding.

Gift of faith and gift of healing are discussed in Chapter 4. There is a measure of faith which everyone has. There is supernatural faith which the Lord gives. There many examples of supernatural faith in both the Old Testament and the New Testament. Jesus cursed a fig tree because it had no fruit. Peter remembered the Lord cursing the fig tree and said to Jesus:

> Mark 11:21-24: Rabbi, look! The fig tree you cursed has withered!" "Have faith in God," Jesus answered, "I tell you the truth, if anyone says to this mountain, 'Go, throw yourself into the sea', and does not doubt in his heart but believes that what he says will happen, it will be done for him. Therefore I tell you, whatever you ask for in prayer, believe that you have received it, and it will be yours," (2)

Those involved with extraordinary healings are working with supernatural faith.

In 1980, Barry McGill and I took a group of Boy Scouts on a canoe trip into a wilderness canoe area in Canada. While in the middle of a large lake, rain clouds moved in. Our guide told us we had to go to an island in the middle of very large lake. Barry and I told the guide we did not need to get off the lake as we would pray that it would not rain on us. The guide made us get off the lake. The guide was completely amazed to see heavy rain falling on the lake in a complete circle around and away

71

from the island but not on us.

Gift of miracle is where unusual phenomena occurs such as raising the dead, the multiplication of food, etc. Father Rich Thomas and his prayer group in El Paso, Texas took some food to the garbage dump in Juarez, Mexico on Christmas day to feed the poor people living there. There were more people than they had food. The Lord miraculously multiplied the food and there was food left over.

While attending a Full Gospel Business Men convention in Dallas in 1970, a minister prayed for a lady wearing a shoe with a three inch lift. I was sitting on the front row. As she sat in a chair the minister held her legs side by side. As he prayed the short leg grew three inches right before my eyes. She had to take her shoes off to stand or walk evenly.

The raising of the dead by the apostles Peter and Paul was a miracle. (Acts 9:36-42, Acts 20:7-12) Father Rich Thomas, a Jesuit priest in El Paso, Texas was reported to have raised a number people from the dead.

An amazing miracle deals with eight Jesuit priests that survived the atomic bomb in Hiroshima, Japan on August 1945 while everyone within one mile radius was killed. The priests lived eight blocks from the center of the blast. The priests did not suffer from radiation and lived long lives (30).

Gift of prophecy is a very important gift. It is mostly used to exhort and edify the people. It is occasionally used to foretell things that are to come. The Book of Revelation is full of prophetic events that are yet to come.

> 1 Corinthians 14:3: But one who prophesies speaks to men for edification and exhortation and consolation (1).

Gift of discernment of spirits

This gift is for detecting evil spirits. There are both good and evil spirits. The apostle Peter had the gift of discernment when he asked Ananias, why he had lied to the Holy Spirit about the donation of his money. Ananias and his wife sold their property and claimed that they had given all the money to the community.

Acts 5:3-5: But Peter said, "Ananias, why has Satan filled your heart to lie to the Holy Spirit, and to keep back some of the price of the land? While it remained unsold, did it not remain your own? And after it was sold, was it not under your control? Why is it that you have conceived this deed in your heart? You have not lied to men but to God." And as he heard these words, Ananias fell down and breathed his last; and great fear came upon all who heard of it. (1)

Paul had the gift of discerning the presence of evil spirits. Paul cast an evil spirit out of a girl who brought her master much money.

Acts 16:16-18: And it happened that as we were going to the place of prayer, a certain slave girl having a spirit of divination met us, who was bringing her master much profit by fortunetelling. Following after Paul and us, she kept crying out, saying, "These men are bond-servants of the Most High God, who are proclaiming to you the way of salvation." And she continued doing this for many days. But Paul was greatly annoyed, and turned to her and said to the spirit, "I command you in the name of Jesus Christ to come out of her!" And it came out that very moment. (1)

This gift is used to discern whether a message, vision or dream is from the Lord. The Lord provided me with prayer partners to help discern whether the messages, visions or dreams I received were from the Lord.

Gift of tongues is discussed in Chapter 5. The Lord told me to begin with a description of the power of praying in the Spirit. Praying in the Spirit is the same as praying in tongues. Praying in tongues is a very powerful way to pray as the Holy Spirit intercedes for the saints according to the will of God when we do not know how to pray. This gift is mostly used for our personal private prayer time.

Romans 8:26-27:...the Spirit also helps our weakness; for we do not know how to pray as we should, but the

73

Spirit Himself intercedes for us with groanings too deep for words; and He who searches the hearts knows what the mind of the Spirit is, because He intercedes for the saints according to the will of God. (1)

Gift of interpreting tongues and the gift of prophecy are closely related. When someone speaks in tongues at a prayer meeting, there is a need to interpret the message so people will know what was spoken. Those with the gift of prophecy are usually able to interpret the message when someone speaks out in tongues. If there is no one with the gift to interpret the language spoken in tongues they should be quiet. Paul said one who prophesies is greater than one who speaks in tongues unless he interprets, so that the church may be built up (Acts 14:5). At a prayer session Paul said he would rather one speaks five intelligible words that people understand than speak in tongues. Yet, he wished that everyone prayed in tongues. He thanked the Lord that he prayed in tongues more than anyone.

The gifts of the Holy Spirit are wisdom, knowledge, faith, healing, working of miracles, prophecy, discerning and distinguishing between spirits, speaking in tongues and the interpretation of tongues. Paul said we should earnestly desire and seek these greater gifts of the Holy Spirit.

I Corinthians 12:29: Are all apostles? Are all prophets? Are all teachers? Do all work miracles or have the gift of healing? Do all speak in tongues, all have the gift of interpretation of tongues? Set your heart on the greater gifts. (31)

The gifts and manifestation of the Holy Spirit are available to us. We should desire and seek these gifts with the comfort and presence of the Holy Spirit dwelling within us.

Jesus said the Holy Spirit would dwell within us and we would know him but the world would not know him. Jesus said the world would not see Him, but we would see Him as He would not leave us as orphans.

Why did Jesus say that His people would continue to know and see Him after He ascended into heaven?

> John 14:15-20: If you love me, you will obey what I command. And I will ask the Father, and he will give you another Counselor to be with you forever – the Spirit of truth. The world cannot accept him, because it neither sees him nor knows him. But you know him, for he lives with you and will be in you. I will not leave you as orphans; I will come to you. Before long, the world will not see me anymore, but you will see me. Because I live, you also will live. On that day you will realize that I am in my Father, and you are in me and I am in you. (2)

In Acts 2:17-21, Peter spoke the words of Joel the prophet that it will come to pass in the last days that God will pour out a portion of His Spirit upon all flesh.

1. Your sons and daughters shall prophesy, i.e. they will speak the words they are receiving from the Lord.
2. Young men shall see visions, while old men will dream dreams. In these visions and dreams, they will see Jesus, the Blessed Mother, God the Father, the Holy Spirit, angels, and saints.
3. Jesus is present, dwelling, and comforting His people, through visions, dreams and the operation of the gifts of the Holy Spirit.

Walk by the Spirit

> Galatians 5:16, 22, 23: ... walk by the Spirit, and you will not carry out the desire of the flesh....But the fruit of the Spirit is love, joy, peace, patience, kindness, goodness, faithfulness, gentleness, self-control; (1)

For a close walk and relationship with the Lord, it is essential to turn from sin, to spend time in intense prayer, and to fast. Many saints have experienced a close encounter and a relationship with Jesus, the

Blessed Mother, God the Father, the Holy Spirit and the angels. I sought the baptism of the Holy Spirit for five months before I experienced it on the third week of September 1970. The Lord wants all of us to be filled with the baptism of the Holy Spirit.

The best way for a close relationship with the Lord is through the baptism of the Holy Spirit with the gifts of the Holy Spirit operating in our lives.

There are many rewards, honors and levels in the kingdom of heaven. These rewards and honors have to be earned in this life. As shown in my book *Lifting the Veil of Revelation*, the bride of Christ is the prize of the high calling that Paul ran a race with all of his might to win. Many will only make it within the door of the kingdom of heaven with no reward other than making it to heaven. To be a part of the bride of Christ with privilege of following Him wherever He goes, one must run the race that Paul ran (29).

> 1 Corinthians 3:11-15: For no man can lay a foundation other than the one which is laid, which is Jesus Christ. Now if any man builds upon the foundation with gold, silver, precious stones, wood, hay straw,each man's work will become evident; for the day will show it, because it is to be revealed with fire; and the fire itself will test the quality of each man's work. If any man's work which he has built upon remains, he shall receive a reward. If any man's work is burned up, he shall suffer loss; but he himself shall be saved, yet so as through fire. (1)

After Jesus baptism by John the Baptist in the Jordan River, the scriptures say that He was led and guided by the Holy Spirit from that point on. Jesus had all the gifts of the Holy Spirit guiding Him. Jesus wants all of us to seek the gifts of the Holy Spirit and to be sensitive to the anointing, prompting, and guidance of Holy Spirit just as He was.

Cardinal Timothy Manning's Prayer: To activate the Seven Gifts of the Holy Spirit, by inviting the Holy Spirit to work in you and through you by Knowledge, Understanding, Wisdom, Counsel, Piety, Fear of the

76

Lord, and Fortitude:

Holy Spirit of God, take me as your disciple; guide me; instruct me; illuminate me. Bind my hands so that they may do no evil; cover my eyes that they may see evil no more; sanctify my heart so that evil may not dwell within it. Be my guide; be my God! Wherever you lead me, in your strength, I shall go; whatever you forbid me, I shall renounce; whatever you command me, in your strength, I shall do. Lead me, then, into the fullness of your truth. Amen. (32)

The Blessed Mother speaks about receiving the gifts of the Holy Spirit.

My children in the world today do not know how to receive the gifts of the Holy Spirit. Preparation is necessary to become ready and worthily to receive the gifts of the Holy Spirit. It is a very tough journey. She told the person receiving this message that it took a full year to prepare her and it was no easy feat. She said, "Do you remember how hard you found it to surrender your will to prove your humility?"

The Blessed Mother spent ten days in the Upper Room helping the Apostles to be open and ready to receive the Holy Spirit. She had to help them prepare their souls. The Apostles had to surrender their full will, and understand the depth of humility necessary before they were spiritually ready to receive the Holy Spirit. They thought they had learned everything from Jesus. The Blessed Mother said this was pride. When you have pride, you cannot receive the gifts of the Holy Spirit. To receive the gifts of the Holy Spirit, you must become little before my Son, like a small child. Those who receive the gifts of the Holy Spirit are submissive to the wishes of my Son, Jesus. They are not boastful, aggressive, critical, nor mock others, or preach hatred. As the Blessed Mother was preparing the disciples to receive the Holy Spirit many arguments or discussions took place before they accepted what was expected of them. Only when they understood the depth of humility necessary, were they prepared to receive the Holy Spirit.

It takes a person a long time to be given the gift as one must surrender their will to prove their humility. Once you received the gift of the Holy

Spirit you can not take it for granted. One must continue to pray, remain humble of heart and seek redemption every day as the gift can be taken away.

The Blessed Mother wants us to call on her for help in receiving the gift of the Holy Spirit.

Crusade Prayer for Gift of Discernment.

O Mother of God helps me to prepare my soul for the gift of the Holy Spirit. Take me as a child, by hand, and lead me on the road towards the gift of discernment through the power of the Holy Spirit. Open my heart and teach me to surrender in body, mind and soul. Rid me of the sin of pride and pray that I will be forgiven for all past sins so that my soul is purified and that I am made whole so that I can receive the gift of the Holy Spirit. I thank you Mother of Salvation for your intercession and I await with love in my heart for this gift for which I yearn with joy. Amen. (33)

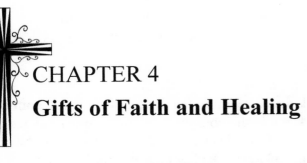

CHAPTER 4

Gifts of Faith and Healing

Wisdom is one of the gifts of the Holy Spirit. The scripture says if any man lacks wisdom, let him ask of the Lord who gives liberally to all men.

> James 1:5-8: If any of you lacks wisdom, he should ask God, who gives generously to all without finding fault, and it will be given to him. But when he asks, he must believe and not doubt, because he who doubts is like a wave of the sea, blown and tossed by the wind. That man should not think he will receive anything from the Lord; he is a double-minded man, unstable in all he does. (2)

The Lord will give wisdom to anyone who asks in faith and does not doubt. Anyone includes you and me.

Daniel asked for wisdom and understanding.

Daniel was a servant under Nebuchadnezzar in the Kingdom of Babylon. Daniel knew from the book of Jeremiah the prophet, that there were to be seventy years of Babylonian Captivity (Daniel 9:2). Daniel knew that the Lord was going to send His Son into the world as the Messiah, and He would sit on the throne of David as the King of Israel.

> Isaiah 9:6-7: For a child will be born to us, a son will be given to us; and the government will rest on His shoulders; and His name will be called Wonderful Counselor, Mighty God, Eternal Father, Prince of Peace. There will be no end to the increase of His government or of peace, on the throne of David and over His kingdom, to establish

it and to uphold it with justice and righteousness from then on and forevermore. The zeal of the Lord of hosts will accomplish this. (1)

Daniel knew from the dream of Nebuchadnezzar that there were to be four more world kingdoms before the coming of the kingdom of stone. The kingdom of stone is the coming kingdom of our Lord Jesus Christ and the kingdom of Israel (Daniel 2). The kingdom of Babylon had passed, the kingdom of Persia had come, and the seventy years of captivity were almost over. It was time to go home, and three more kingdoms were yet to come. Daniel was puzzled as he thought all the world kingdoms would be fulfilled before the seventy years of captivity were over. Daniel turned to the Lord with prayer and fasting, asking for wisdom and understanding. The Archangel Gabriel, appeared to Daniel.

> Daniel 9:21-22: while I was speaking in prayer, the man Gabriel, whom I had seen in the vision at the first, came to me in swift flight.... He came and he said to me, "O Daniel, I have now come out to give you wisdom and understanding." (31)

Spiritual warfare – The Lord uses angels as messengers to answer our prayers.

On another occasion, Daniel asked the Lord for wisdom and understanding concerning the world kingdoms that were to come. Daniel fasted and prayed for twenty-one days before the angel of the Lord appeared to him. This event gives us a tremendous insight into the spiritual warfare involved in asking for wisdom. The angel spoke to Daniel and said:

> Daniel 10:11-14: "... O Daniel, man of high esteem, un-derstand the words that I am about to tell you and stand upright, for I have now been sent to you...." "Do not be afraid, Daniel, for from the first day that you set your heart on understanding this and on humbling yourself be-fore your God, your words were heard, and I have come

in response to your words. But the prince of the kingdom of Persia was withstanding me for twenty-one days; then behold, Michael, one of the chief princes, came to help me for I had been left there with the king of Persia. Now I have come to give you an understanding of what will happen to your people in the latter days, for the vision pertains to the days yet future. "(1)

The Lord heard Daniel's prayer the very first day. The Lord answered Daniel's prayer the very first day by sending an angel to give Daniel wisdom and understanding. The Prince of Persia and his angels prevented the angel of the Lord from reaching Daniel. The angel called for Michael the Archangel and his army. They fought for twenty-one days before the angel of the Lord was able to get through to Daniel. Daniel kept the faith with prayers and fasting until the angel of the Lord got through. In this case, it took twenty-one days. If Daniel had kept the faith with praying and fasting for only twenty days, the angel of the Lord would not have been able to get through. Daniel's faith with praying and fasting provided ammunition for Michael and his angels to fight against the Prince of Persia and his angels. The angels of the Lord can fight against the powers of darkness only as long as we provide ammunition with our faith, prayers and fasting.

In Mark, the disciples were asking Jesus why they could not cast a spirit out of a small boy. Jesus said:

Mark 9:29: And He replied to them, "This kind cannot be driven out by anything but prayer and fasting" (5).

When we ask the Lord for something, there is usually a spiritual battle with the powers of darkness trying to hinder our prayers from being answered.

The Lord said if any man lacks wisdom, let him ask of the Lord who gives liberally to all men, but let him ask in faith without wavering. Daniel asked for wisdom and understanding but had to fight the fight of faith with prayers and fasting for twenty-one days. Most of us waver and quit praying if our prayers are not answered immediately. We have to persist in faith without wavering so the angel of the Lord can get through to answer our prayers.

What is Faith?

> Hebrew 11:1: Now faith is being sure of what we hope for and certain of what we do not see (2).

St. Augustine said:

> Faith is to believe what we do not see. The reward of faith is to see what we believe (34).

Faith is the evidence of the things we pray for but do not see. It is belief that the Lord has answered our prayer the minute we begin to pray. The world says we will believe it when we see it.

Faith believes right now, the moment we begin to pray that our prayers have been answered even though we do not have any evidence. God answered Daniel's prayers the very first day by immediately sending an angel to Daniel. The angel was not able to get through to Daniel until twenty-one days later.

Suppose you call me and say you need one hundred dollars. If I write you a check for one hundred dollars and put it in the mail right away, your request has been answered. I have given you one hundred dollars. However, it may be a day or a few days before you receive your check or the check could get lost in the mail. Regardless, whether you receive the check or not, I have answered your request. The check has been written and put in the mail. The angels of the Lord are messengers the Lord uses to answer our prayers just as the mailman is used to deliver the mail. Just as proper precautions are necessary to ensure the safe delivery of mail, proper precautions are essential to help the angel of the Lord to get through the powers of darkness to answer our prayer.

When you pray, believe that you have received, and then you shall have it.

The Lord spoke to His disciples and said,

Mark 11:22-24: "Have faith in God," Jesus answered, "I tell you the truth, if anyone says to this mountain, 'Go, throw yourself into the sea', and does not doubt in his heart but believes that what he says will happen, it will be done for him. Therefore I tell you, whatever you ask for in prayer, believe that you have received it, and it will be yours," (2)

When you pray and ask the Lord for something, it is essential to believe that the Lord has heard and answered your prayer the moment you began to pray. Faith is a commitment to believe and to hold on to that belief that the Lord has heard and answered your prayers. The Lord heard Daniel's prayer and immediately sent an angel to answer his prayer. Though Daniel's prayer was answered immediately by the Lord, the angel was delayed for twenty-one days by the Prince of Persia.

How fast can an angel answer a prayer request?

Daniel 9:21: while I was speaking in prayer, the man Gabriel, whom I had seen in the vision at the first, came to me in swift flight...(31).

Notice that the angel appeared to Daniel after a swift flight, before Daniel was through praying. In this case, the Prince of Persia either did not try to stop the angel or could not stop the angel from reaching Daniel. Daniel's prayer was answered before he was through speaking.

Fight the fight of faith. Ask the Lord one time then remind him daily by thanking him.

1 Timothy 6:12: Fight the good fight of faith (1);

When we pray, we should ask the Lord one time and then remind the Lord daily by thanking him for answering our prayers. If we ask the Lord a second time, it is like saying the Lord did not answer our prayer the first time. We need to persist in prayer with thanksgiving and praise until the angel gets through and our prayers are answered. Pleading

83

with the Lord to answer our prayer does not work. The Lord has already answered our prayer the moment we began to pray. Pleading does not provide ammunition for the angels to fight the powers of darkness. It is essential that we study the scriptures so that we will know the truth, and the truth will set us free.

The scripture says if any man lacks wisdom let him ask of the Lord who gives liberally to all men, but let him ask in faith without wavering. Daniel was a man who asked for wisdom, but he had to fight the fight of faith with prayer and fasting for twenty-one days before his prayers were answered. If a man doubts, he is like the waves of the sea, tossed to and fro with the wind, he shall not expect to receive anything from the Lord (James 1:5-6).

The Lord blessed Daniel with a gift of wisdom and understanding. Because of Daniel's wisdom, Nebuchadnezzar made Daniel, who was a slave and a servant from Judah, a ruler over the whole province of Babylon. Wisdom is one of the gifts of the Holy Spirit.

Why some people's prayers are answered while others are not.

Almost a year after I had written this chapter on "Faith and the gift of healing," the Lord woke me up from a deep sleep at 2 a.m. to pray. Later in the day while praying with a friend, it was revealed that the Lord wanted me to tell why Jesus could not perform miracles with certain afflicted people. The word of knowledge received in prayer gives a profound insight, in a nutshell, why some people's prayers are answered, and while others are not.

> When Christ went to a certain town, He was unable to heal certain afflicted people because of their unbelief. Today, there stands no one even measurable to the stature of Jesus Christ, so there can be no real substitute for lack of faith. With faith, everything is possible. Without faith, nothing is possible not even to those that are in the body of Christ.

Though Jesus had faith, He was unable to heal certain afflicted people because of their unbelief. Without faith, nothing is possible, not even to those that are in the body of Christ. When we pray, it is essential to believe that our prayers have been answered the moment we begin to pray and to fight the fight of faith rejecting all thoughts of doubt.

Jesus had to pray two times for the blind man to be healed.

> Mark 8:22-25: And they came to Bethsaida. And they brought a blind man to Him, entreated Him to touch him. And taking the blind man by hand, He brought him out of the village; and after spitting on his eyes, and laying His hands upon him, He asked him, "Do you see anything?" And he looked up and said, "I see men, for I am seeing them like trees, walking about." Then again He laid His hands upon his eyes; and he looked intently and was re-stored, and began to see everything clearly. (1)

The first time Jesus prayed, the blind man did not have enough faith to be healed. After recovering some sight, he had the faith to be completely healed the second time Jesus prayed. It is essential that we believe.

Words received in prayer:

Faith is the key to divine healing and all of God's power.

Vision of one and half year old child with a big grin on his face:

The Lord said, "Come to me, like this child with simple child-like faith."

My first experience in praying with faith

Bill Ivie, a friend at work, was always witnessing to people about the Lord. I told him that my wife's parents were Pentecostal, but I did not dare tell him I was Catholic. One day, my boss said to Bill, "How do you like my friend, Mike, a good Roman Catholic?" I said, "Oh boy, he is going to work me over." Bill quoted scriptures to me coming and going about the Holy Spirit, speaking in tongues, etc. In February 1970, my mother had been sick with the flu and pneumonia and was bedridden for about three months. When I talked to her on the phone on Thursday night, her voice was very weak. On Friday, I spoke to my friend, Bill and said, "I would appreciate it if you would pray for my mother." He looked me in the eyes and said, "Expect a miracle." Saturday, I went to my hometown to visit my parents. A miracle had truly taken place. My mother was up walking around.

A few months later, on a Thursday, Bill asked me if I wanted to go with him to the hospital to pray for a little five-year-old boy. This little boy had two malignant tumors behind both eyeballs. He had been in a coma for a week. The doctors refused to operate, because they said there was no hope. I told Bill, I would go to the hospital, but I did not know anything about praying for people. Bill said, "Mike, we are going to do just what the scripture tell us to do." When we walked into the room, the little boy's father, Mr. Boydstun, said if this is the Lord's will, we would accept it. Bill said, "It is not the Lord's will that any should perish. It is His will that we prosper and be in health even as our souls prosper." All three of us prayed for the little boy. The next day, the little boy woke up and sat on the side of the bed. On Saturday, the little boy played all over his room. The doctors said, "OK, we will do surgery on Monday morning." The surgery was supposed to be over at 9 a.m. Bill and I went to the hospital at 11 a.m., just as the doctors were coming out of surgery. Their faces were as white as a sheet of paper. The two tumors had completely disappeared. The doctors said the little boy would be blind as the optic nerves were no longer there. Yet, the little boy had 20/20 vision. This experience had a tremendous impact on me. (I happened to be on the fourth day fast, water only for another intention when we prayed for the little boy)

> 3 John 2: Beloved, I pray that in all respects you may prosper and be in good health, just as your soul prospers (1).

Prophetic message of faith on the day of our wedding.

My wife's parents were adamantly opposed to Ann marrying a Catholic in a Catholic Church. A lady friend of theirs went on a week long fast for discernment about their daughter marrying a Catholic boy.

On the day of the wedding she told my wife's parents that she received understanding that the Lord was in me and that I would come around to their way of thinking, and I would have a faith that they had never known. (Note that this was four years before the beginning of the Catholic Charismatic Renewal in 1967.) My father-in-law did not come to the wedding. My mother-in-law came and gave the message to her daughter. Ann said, "Mom that will never happen." Ann had never accepted the Pentecostal faith and was going to a Baptist church at the time I was dating her. In May 1970, my cousin, Father Francis Miesch was at our house for dinner. I said, "Father, the Lord is sure with those Pentecostal people." He said, "Yes, that is right." I said, "Would it be wrong if I left the Catholic Church and join the Pentecostal Church?" (I certainly had no intention of doing this.) Father Miesch and my wife almost fell off the barstool. Father explained that he had gone to Ann Arbor, Michigan the week before with Bobbie Cavnar and suggested that I get in touch with Bobbie. I attended my first Catholic Pentecostal prayer meeting at Ursuline Academy in Dallas. My wife, Ann, was not happy at all. She told a girl friend that if I accepted the Pentecostal faith, perhaps there is a Holy Spirit. Ann threatened to leave me. For the next nine months we just tolerated each other. In March 1971, I had invited one of Ann's friends to go with me to the prayer meeting at Bishop Lynch High School. I asked Ann if she wanted to go to the prayer meeting. She said she would think about it. About an hour before the prayer meeting, Ann's parents came by on their way home from Florida. Ann said, "I am not going." I said, "Oh yes you are; your parents will go with us." Ann watched her dad, who believed the Catholic Church was the Whore of Babylon, lifting his hands, praising God in a Catholic Pentecostal prayer meeting. Ann knew that this could not happen, except by the power of the Holy Spirit. Afterward, she asked about the prophecy that was spoken of on the day of our wedding in February 1963. This was the first time I had heard about this prophecy.

Ann's mother had a dream in which Ann (now my wife) walked out of her grandmother's house with a coat thrown over one shoulder and her arm in one sleeve. Ann was carrying luggage and walked right passed her mother while her mother was talking to two people in a car. Ann walked off into the distance without saying anything to her mother. Lord gave the following message as the interpretation to the dream.

> I am no longer a part of this family. I am going to be a part of another family that I do not know. Although I will marry this man that God has chosen, I am not marrying the others of his family. I am distressed now but know I will be happy with whom God has chosen. Likewise, it is the same for my children. God has chosen this match (Our son, Mike and his wife, Jean Marie). My Father has them in the palm of his hand. Michael is overcome by what he does not know and innocence. My daughter should not be afraid of the world but take charge as we taught you. Overcome evil with good. Spend time before my mother. Pray the rosary together. Set aside any fear or misgivings.

Tumor

The first of June 1977, my 12 year old son Michael walked up to me with his shirt off and said "Dad, what is this?" There was a large hard tumor on his left breast. The thoughts that went through my mind was when I was a freshman in high school, a boy walked up and pinched and twisted my left breast. This action bruised my breast, and a tumor started growing. By the time I was a senior, it had grown to the size of a hen egg, two-third inside the rib cavity and one-third outside the rib cavity. It was difficult for me to take a deep breath, and it was putting pressure on my heart. I turned to my son and said, "Well, we will have to go to the doctor and get it cut out." My wife, Ann spoke up and said, "Why don't we pray about it?" I said, "Fine". However, I knew anytime you pray for something like this, you have to pray with faith. I told Michael that I wanted him to help his mother and dad pray with faith. I told him that we were going to ask the Father in Jesus' name one time, and we would remind the Father by thanking him daily. I told my son that thoughts would come like, "How can you say you don't have a tumor? Can't you see it? Can't you feel it?" I said, "You will have to come back and say; I am not lying for the scriptures say when you pray, believe that you have received and then you shall have it." In less than a month's time, the tumor completely disappeared.

Faith and doubt

Faith and doubt is like temptation and sin. A man can have thoughts to lust after a woman. If a man rejects these thoughts, he has not committed a sin. If a man cultivates these thoughts, then he commits a sin.

When we pray with faith for something, we have to fight the fight of faith. Thoughts of doubt will come. As long as we reject these thoughts of doubt, we are still standing firm. If we cultivate these thoughts of doubts, then we have wavered. The first chapter of James 1:5-8 says, "A man who doubts is like the waves of the sea, tossed to and fro with the wind. A double-minded man is unstable in all of his ways. Let not that man think he shall receive anything of the Lord."

Thoughts of doubt will usually come creeping in early in the morning before I am awake. This is all right, as long as I reject those thoughts of doubt the minute I realize what is happening. When these thoughts of doubt try to come in, I just simply say to the devil: "You are a liar and a thief and the truth is not in you."

The key to fighting the fight of faith is a positive confession.

> Proverbs 18:21: Death and life are in the power of the tongue; those who make it a friend shall eat its fruit (3A).

When you are praying for something, be optimistic. Talk as though you have already received it. If you make a negative confession, the Lord will not answer your prayers.

A person must have faith to be healed.

I asked the Lord if I could fast and pray and get the victory for someone who had cancer. These are the words I received:

> No healing can take place unless the person the healing is meant for has the faith to receive it. This is the way it has been from the beginning.

There are some exceptions. The Lord will sometimes allow you to fast and pray for a member of the family. My father-in-law was having some heart problems. He said he could not even take a shower without taking nitroglycerin. He had an appointment in a week to see a doctor about running a balloon up his arteries to open up his circulation. I asked someone to pray with me for discernment on whether I could fast and get the victory. The answer was, "Yes, seven days." I called my father-in-law and told him I could get the victory, but I was not going to start fasting until the following week because I did not want to be fasting on my birthday, the coming Friday. I started fasting on Sunday. My father-in-law went to the doctor on Monday. He called me Monday night and said the doctor could not find anything wrong with him. I turned to the Lord and said, "Do you want me to continue the fasting?" He said, "Yes, to seal the victory." I went seven days with nothing but water. My fast was over on Saturday. I called my father-in-law on Sunday to see how he was doing. He said he had been working up a storm. He had cleaned up his yard and hauled off two truckloads of tree limbs and trash without any problem.

Three years later, he came down with cancer. He had a grapefruit size tumor in his lung. Even though I did not receive knowledge that I could get the victory, I went on a ten day fast, drinking only water. The following words were spoken to me after the fast:

> My son, my son, you will be rewarded for your fasting, prayers, and abundant faith. Stand firm in your desire and faith for the healing that will take place. Inform Ann that during the midst of dark waters, when life seems to vanish before our eyes, I still have the authority and power to heal and to bring forth human life with strength that only I can deliver. Know this and believe, for it is I that will receive glory with this healing. Physicians may shun life as one that is lost, but you must know they report what is happening physically. I am the Author of life and the spirit within. Ann, you must believe and stand firm with your husband for his days are not lost as I am the Lord

and Savior that will stand in the gap for any person that believes. I will call forth the spirit of healing, and this will come to pass through your faith.

At the time this prophecy was given to me, I did not realize the Lord was saying that my wife Ann had to stand in the gap with me for this healing to come to pass. My wife is a woman of great faith but for some reason she did not even attempt to fight this fight of faith. I did not feel it was necessary, as I thought the victory was won. My father-in-law was very alert, comfortable, peaceful and talking up to a couple hours of his death. I was shocked, as he did not look like a man close to death. I included the above prophecy to show that the Lord will sometime allow an immediate member of the family to stand in the gap and intercede for a healing, when the person being prayed for does not have the faith to receive it.

In the early 1970s a childhood friend came down with cancer. I went on 12 days water-only fast asking the Lord to heal him. Finally, I said, "Lord, speak to him and tell him he is healed." The Lord did speak to him. He told his wife he was healed. He was not going to die. Yet, he died a day or two later. He did not have the faith or know how to fight the fight of faith to be healed.

Diabetes

Dr. Ernest Laake, a close family friend, came down with diabetes at the age of 89. He had both big toes amputated and then one leg just below the knee by the age of 93. He got a prosthesis and learned to walk again. When he was 98, he fell and hurt his good leg and had to be put in a rest home. The nurses tore the skin on both shoulders while they were trying to help him. One shoulder had exposed flesh 6 to 8 inches in circumference, while the wound on other shoulder was 4 to 5 inches. He always wanted me to turn him, as he had no peace in his body. I could only turn him on his left shoulder, as his right shoulder was too bad to lie on. The last of May, my wife went with me to see him. She left in tears, as she did not think he would make it through the night. I called a friend in Mississippi to pray with me for discernment. I commanded the spirit of diabetes to identify itself. My friend received knowledge that Dr. Laake had been mistreated by a friend. I quoted I John 5:16, which says, "If you see a brother commit a sin which is not unto death, you shall pray, and it shall be forgiven him." I repented for any sins he may have committed in response to this mistreatment. Then I commanded the spirit of diabetes to leave and to never come back. The next week was as different as day and night. Never again did Dr. Laake ask me to turn him. Gradually, the sores on his shoulders healed completely. In October, five months later, I asked Dr. Laake if he was still taking insulin for his diabetes. He said, "Oh no!" He did not know what happened, the diabetes just went away. Dr. Laake died in December at the age of 99. I had several visions of Dr. Laake after death thanking me for the prayer I said for him while he was alive.

I asked the Lord if I had put too many testimonies in this book. His reply was "You can never put too many testimonies in a book." I took this to mean that the Lord wanted me to include a number of my experiences in praying, fighting and winning the fight of faith.

Wood chips

In 1972, Texas Power and Light had men cutting limbs off of trees around power lines. I asked them if they would dump the wood chips from the limbs on my property. Wood chips make good compost for the garden. We have approximately one and three-tenth acres of land. Part of the property is low land, and I wanted to fill this area with wood chips. After receiving a couple loads of wood chips, the wood chips man came in right after a heavy rain. He got stuck and had to get a wrecker to pull him out. After this incidence, he did not come back. I talked to him three different times. He said he would come back, but never did. I knew if I wanted those wood chips, I would have to take it to the Lord in prayer.

> Mark 11:24: Therefore I tell you, whatever you ask for in prayer, believe that you have received it, and it will be yours (2).

In December of that year, I asked the Lord one time to deliver the wood chips to us. Afterward, I reminded the Lord daily by thanking Him for the wood chips. Every time we said the blessings for the meal, I would thank the Lord for the wood chips. It got to the point that every time I thanked the Lord for the wood chips, my sons would turn to their mother and ask, "What wood chips? Where are the wood chips? What is daddy talking about?" Nine months later, in September 1973, I was walking through my yard and I said, "Lord, the year is almost over, and I don't have those wood chips." Then I caught myself and said, "Oh, no, Lord, I thank you for those wood chips." The next day, there was a load of wood chips in my yard. Thereafter the wood chip man brought almost 100 loads of wood chips to fill in the low part of my property. The reason I asked the Lord one time is that if I asked him again, I would be saying that He did not answer my prayer the first time. By thanking the Lord daily, I reminded the Lord of my prayer request with expectant faith.

Heart condition

My mother and her family have had a history of heart problems. In 1950, my mother had a cardiac attack where she was bed ridden for six months. She has since had several cardiac attacks and was always having angina attacks and heart pains. In 1973, she was sent to Baylor Hospital for open-heart surgery. Ann and I went on a fast for a week, asking the Lord to intervene so she would not have to have surgery. The doctors ran all kinds of tests for one week, then debated for the last three days before deciding not to have surgery. I told my mother afterward, any time she senses an attack or pain coming on, to simply lay her hand on her chest and rebuke it in the name of Jesus. For two years afterward, she did not any take heart medicine, but simply took authority over the pain in Jesus' name. My mother was in better condition two years later than she was in 1973. I did not tell my mother to stop taking heart medicine. That was her decision. I want to emphasize that a person should do what their doctor tells them to do. The Lord uses doctors as told in Ecclesiasticus 38.

My heart problem

About 4:30 one morning in October 1975, I came up out of bed like lightning from a dead sleep with tremendous pain in my chest and tightness in my left arm. I took authority over the pain in Jesus' name and confessed with my mouth that I was not accepting any heart condition. I did not say anything to Ann until noon. She was furious and told me I was going to the doctor. I called some friends and told them to pray that the doctor would not find a heart condition. I showed the doctor my left chest, which was black, blue, yellow and green.

The doctor checked me thoroughly with the electrocardiogram and x-rays. He was puzzled and gave me a prescription for pain. He told me to come back in three days. Since the doctor could not find anything wrong, I did not get the medicine. A light pain flared up several times during the next three days. Each time, I would confess that there was nothing wrong. On the third day, I called the doctor and told him I was doing fine and did not need to come in. The moment I hung up the telephone, a tremendous pain hit my chest. The pain lasted for two hours. I kept confessing that I did not have a heart condition until the pain left. I have not had any trouble since.

Hemorrhoids

In 1974, I was given an expense-paid fishing trip to Canada. On Friday, a week before I was to leave, I was in the bathroom. My wife stuck her head in the door and said, "Quit that straining. You are going to come down with hemorrhoids." The next day, I had the most severe case of hemorrhoids. I had hemorrhoids two times before this. The first time, I had surgery. The second time, I did not do anything. The second hemorrhoid turned into a solid knot. I had this knot for eight years.

I went to the prayer meeting on Sunday and prayed about the hemorrhoids but did not tell anyone about it. By Tuesday night, the pain was so intense, I was perspiring all over. The pain went all the way to the bottom of my feet. I asked the prayer community to pray for me. One member of the community had just had surgery for hemorrhoids and mentioned that he could recommend the best doctor in town. I said, "No, thank you." I was determined that these hemorrhoids leave the same way they came, i.e. with the spoken word. I took authority over the knot that had been there for eight years.

In spite of the intense pain and perspiring, I put on a fake smile and went home rejoicing in the Lord that I did not have hemorrhoids. I knew if I had surgery, there would be no way I could go on the fishing trip. When I woke up the next morning, the hemorrhoids were gone, including the solid knot.

Teeth

In 1969 and 1970, I had gold fillings put in eight of my molars. I had a problem of clamping down on my teeth while sleeping. In 1971, a small crack appeared between the filling and the tooth, exposing a nerve. I knew if I had to go to the dentist every year because I clamp down on my teeth, there would soon not be anything left of my teeth after a few visits.

I turned to the Lord and asked him to heal my teeth. I reminded the Lord each day as I went to communion, and as I said the table blessing by thanking him for healing my teeth.

In 1974, I was talking to my mother. She turned to me and asked, "Mike, do you have any cavities?" I answered, "Yes!" She chewed me up one side and down the other. I did not say anything. I just turned to the Lord and told him I could have all the faith in the world, but if He did not take the bad breath and decay away, I would be forced to go to the dentist. The Lord took the bad breath away; however, it would return from time to time. Each time, I would take authority over it, and the bad breath would leave. This attack lasted about three months before I had the victory. Nevertheless, my teeth continued to get worse and worse. I had four cracked teeth, one on each upper and lower side of my mouth. The cracks on the right side were so big that when I put my tongue into the cavity, it felt like the Grand Canyon. I had another tooth that was so badly decayed, the nerve died. When a nerve is dying, it is very sensitive to hot and cold. The pain first hit me one night when I was asleep. I came up out of bed with painful shock waves going through my head. I paced the floor, praising the Lord for 30 minutes before the pain left.

I discovered that if I came against the pain immediately in the name of Jesus, It would stop quickly. The enemy knew I would come against him immediately anytime he hit me with pain. It got to be such a routine thing that the enemy made a slip and hit me with the identical nerve shock throbbing pain on my front tooth instead the very back tooth where the dying tooth was. There was nothing wrong with the front tooth where the pain hit.

During the two months prior to April 1977, I could not chew on the right side. The fillings were loose and were about to come out. Though I had two cavities on my left side, I could still chew on them. The last two months were very painful. Many times, the thoughts would come, "What a fool you have made of yourself. You are going to be embarrassed when you have to go to the dentist!" I would not cultivate these thoughts. I rejected them with everything within me, though it looked like after six years, I was fighting a losing battle. Nevertheless, I knew that the Holy Spirit had witnessed to me many times during the six years to stand firm and fight the fight of faith. One example was taking away the bad breath.

In April 1977, six of us were talking and praying. I turned to my brothers and sisters in the Lord and asked them to pray for my teeth. I made a sweeping motion over my jaw. They laughed at me. They had no idea how serious this was. However, in a split second, the Lord healed four of my teeth. One badly decayed tooth was not healed.

The next morning, a voice said, "Why don't you have the decayed tooth pulled out?" I rejected this as not being from the Lord. During the next few years, cracks would appear in the teeth that were healed. Each time, I would take authority over it and the crack would close up immediately. These cracks would appear sometimes once a month, other times once a week and sometimes, several times a day. On a couple occasions, a tooth would open up for a week before it would close up.

I was praying for a front tooth that was dark due to a dead nerve. When the Lord did not do anything about the front tooth, I started seeking the Lord on whether he wanted me to go to the dentist. I was embarrassed about the back tooth that was decayed below the gum line.

While I was praying, I had a picture of a friend. A voice said, "Do as they do!" I knew what he did. He went to the dentist. However, I continued to seek the Lord because the decayed tooth was one of the teeth from which the Lord took the bad breath away. The Lord gave me Ecclesiasticus 38, which says, "Honor your doctor". He also said, "Wisdom tooth is not wisdom". I did not consider this tooth a wisdom tooth as I had all my wisdom teeth pulled.

I went to the dentist, and he took an x-ray of my whole mouth on one film. He called the decayed tooth a wisdom tooth. I counted all the molars on the x-ray and sure enough, this was an extra tooth. The dentist checked all my teeth and said they were fine except for the chipped place on the front tooth.

Though the Lord healed four of the six teeth I was praying for, the Lord was emphasizing that he wanted us to use dentists and doctors. One of the main reasons, I did what I did was to get the victory over the clamping down and breaking my teeth. With only a few exceptions in the last year, I have not had any problem with clamping down on my teeth in the last thirty years.

The Lord speaks words of encouragement

On February 28, 1983, I was having some problems with some of my teeth including one, which the Lord healed in 1977. These teeth cracked open (fillings and tooth separated) during the weekend of the men's retreat. These teeth closed up briefly for as long as half a day, but for the most part had been open since the men's retreat 22 days earlier. The thought running through my mind was "Do I have to fight the fight of faith all over again for my teeth?" The first fight of faith took six years. In a dream, God the Father embraced me and the thoughts came to me, "No, you don't have to fight the fight of faith all over again." Then I saw a picture of a dark tunnel in which green objects were floating out of the tunnel toward me. My prayer partner spoke the following words to me

> My son, I have given your spirit new life. Your spirit is in union with Mine. Receive the new life that I have for you. I love you for your perseverance and your conviction of

heart. Your prayers are heard and will be answered in My time. Trust your brother, Jesus, to be your guide to Me. Protect yourself with My armor in order that you will come through the valley of darkness into My light. It is the Lord God Yahweh, your Father, Who speaks.

Almost 14 years later, I had a picture or a vision of x-rays showing the top and lower teeth in my mouth. The Lord said,

You are not to have any doubt in your faith. The panoramic view is a witness of your faith to the enemy.

Oak Wilt

In June 1973, I attended a seminar in Irving, Texas where we live in which an Extension Plant Pathologist with Texas A & M University talked about Oak Wilt, a disease that is fatal to oak trees. Once a tree comes down with the disease, there was nothing you can do. The recommendation was to cut the diseased tree down and all other oak trees within fifty feet of the diseased tree. This disease was prevalent in Irving. I came home and told Ann that we were going to have to start praying for the protection of our oak trees. We have some very large oak trees, two of which were 7 1/2 feet and 8 feet in circumference respectively.

On the first of June 1977, a big limb died on one of the big trees. I went up and cut the limb off. The next week, two more limbs died. I said, "Oh, no, Lord, that is Oak Wilt and I do not accept that." More limbs died. Three more trees came down with the disease.

The thought of our home without those large oak trees made me sick to the pit of my stomach. I rejected this feeling with everything within me. I kept confessing that these trees were O.K. How do you look at a limb with dead leaves and say to the limb, you are alive or to a tree with a disease that is fatal and say, "You are O.K.?" I told Ann we had to turn to the Lord and find out what was going on. Have we sinned? Are we out of order? We had prayed faithfully since June 1973 for the Lord to protect our trees. While we were praying, the thoughts came, "Did the blind man sin? No, this is a period of trial and testing! Stand firm." I said,

"Praise the Lord." I did not worry about those trees anymore. I would go out every day and look at those dead limbs and say, "Thank you Jesus, that those limbs are alive." I kept this up all through the summer. In the third week of July, while I was in Kansas City praying, I saw a picture of myself giving a testimony about the healing those trees. When I came home, they looked just as dead-looking as ever. A week later, new buds started popping forth from those dead limbs! The buds put forth new leaves on the first tree that was afflicted. The leaves did not come out on the other trees until the next spring. Even the next spring, the enemy tried to keep the new buds from coming out, while the limbs that were not afflicted with the disease put out new leaves. I took authority over the enemy in Jesus' name. There was a two-week delay in the leaves coming out. I have pictures of the trees when they were dying and afterward when they were healed. In the spring of 1979, two more trees were afflicted in which half of the leaves on the trees wilted and turned brown. These two trees were not among the previous trees that came down with Oak Wilt. Again, I took authority over the enemy, and all my trees are doing fine.

I showed the pictures of the trees to the Extension Plant Pathologist. He said, "Mike, I have never seen a tree that has come down with this disease to ever survive. There is something involved here other than man."

Even though we prayed faithfully for four years, the Lord permitted the enemy to attack our trees. When you have trees that cannot be replaced in 100 years that is not something you want your faith tested on, especially when the disease is fatal.

Lumber

A manufacturing company that made doors and windows, received big crates of glass to make windows and sliding glass doors. When the glass was removed, the crates were thrown away. These crates consisted of lumber 2 inches thick, 10 inches wide and 7 feet long. They let me have a few crates; then they would not let me have any more because it was too much trouble to save the crates. They did not have much room to store them, and it was easier to dump the crates in the trash truck. I tried to get them to save them for me, but every time I went by, they had already been thrown away.

We were planning to build 1200 square foot, two-story addition to our home. We knew that if we were to get this lumber, we would have to take it to the Lord in prayer. My wife and I prayed and fasted for five days, water only. Afterward, the manufacturer not only arranged for me to pick up the crates every day, they provided a truck to haul the crates to my house. The 2 X 10s were ripped into 2 X 4s. The Lord provided all the 2 X4s we needed to build the frame structure for the house.

> James 4:2-3:...Why you don't have what you want is because you don't pray for it; when you do pray and don't get it, it is because you have not prayed properly,...(18).

My dad's heart attack

In June 1977, three weeks before the charismatic conference in Kansas City, my dad had a heart attack. It was so serious that the doctor would not let my dad read the paper or watch TV. My mother told me there was no way they could go to the conference. I said, "Oh, yes, the conference is three weeks away." They kept my dad in the hospital for two weeks. They told him to go home and take it easy. This was one week before we were to leave for the conference early Saturday morning. My dad went to the doctor on Friday afternoon for a check-up. My mother told the doctor that they had planned to go to Kansas City but couldn't go now. The doctor said, "Oh, yes, go ahead. It's all right for him to go to Kansas City. Just take it easy." Always make a positive confession regardless of how hopeless it seems.

Mother's tumor and 28 days fast

In 1983, we went to my parent's house on Wednesday, the day before Thanksgiving. My mother informed me that she had a large tumor on her back next to her spine. When I felt the tumor, it appeared to be two to two and one- half inches in diameter. The doctors were 99% certain that it was malignant. I spoke to Satan and said, "I will turn heaven and hell upside down to get the victory." Starting that night, before I even had a chance to start fasting, I was hit with all kinds of pain and discomfort, some which I had never experienced before. I had a discomfort in which something was stuck in my throat, yet when I drank water, the water would pass on through, but there was no relief. I had severe cramps in my fingers, feet and legs. My chest was bloated with pains. The pains would jump from one area to another. I had never experienced anything like this. This harassment went on all through the night, every night for about 10 days. I ate breakfast Saturday morning and then I started fasting. On the seventh day of the fast, I was at an all-night prayer vigil. About four in the morning, I felt an overwhelming healing type of an anointing. I knew my mother was healed. When the tumor was cut out, it was to the doctor's surprise, benign. I know in my heart that the tumor was malignant before my fast. The Lord told me not to come off the fast, as my mother needed some spiritual healing of some anger and unforgiveness in her heart. This was between Thanksgiving and Christmas. I did not want to be fasting during this time, as there were many parties and a lot of good food to eat. I begged the Lord each day to let me come off of the fast. He always said, "No!" Finally, He said I could come off the fast on the 28th day, which was Christmas Eve. I did not eat any solid food during this fast. I had signed up to donate blood before I started the fast. On the 16th day, I said, "Lord if you do not want me to donate blood, you block it". He didn't block it. Afterwards, I drank some orange juice. When I went to Christmas parties, I would drink a coke. The Lord said He was using my fast to touch the lives of people all over the world. I went home after supper the day before Christmas Eve. The next morning I told my mother I was going to fast that day and would eat Christmas Eve dinner that evening. This was the easiest fast I had ever been on. The Lord protected me. No one, including my mother, could tell that I was on a fast. I was not weak.

Massive Stroke

In 1984, my dad had a massive stroke. There was some paralysis, as he was not able to walk. I started fasting immediately. I asked a friend to pray with me to ask the Lord, how long I needed to fast to get the victory.

My friend received knowledge for five days. He also said the Lord asked him to fast with me. I told him there was no way I could ask him to do it, but if he did, I would greatly appreciate it. After we came off the five-day fast, my dad had another stroke. This time, he could not open one of his eyes. I immediately spoke to Satan and said, "You are a liar, and a thief and the truth is not in you. There is nothing wrong with my dad." Within five days he was on a rapid road to recovery. My mother said that when they went to see the doctor; the doctor walked behind my dad, patting him on the shoulder and said, "You are very lucky. You are not supposed to be alive."

Eye surgery

Around 1985 or 1986, my dad had eye surgery on one eye and was able to see after a few weeks. In early December, he had surgery on the second eye. For almost four months, till the 1st of March, my mother was telling me the operation was not a success, as he could not see. I kept telling her, "Oh, yes, he can see." When they went to the doctor a week later, he had 20 - 20 vision with glasses. Last week, I noticed my 94-year-old Dad reading a handwritten letter without glasses. I cannot read a letter without glasses.

Our dog - Ginger

Ginger was a Golden Retriever. When Ginger was about three years old, one of my sons dropped her over a four-foot fence, severely injuring her left hip. The dog walked with a limp. It was obviously painful for her to attempt to lie down or get up. My son took the dog with him when he went to college, as he and several students were living on a ranch away from the campus. The next year, my son lived on the college campus, so the dog was brought home. It was painful for me to see Ginger suffer. Two or three years after the injury, I laid hands on Ginger and asked the Lord to heal her. The next week I noticed that Ginger was no longer limping. The Lord had healed her. When one of the students that lived with my son on the ranch came by, he could not believe that this dog was Ginger as she did not walk with a limp or struggle to lie down.

Labrador Retriever

My son, Mark has a Labrador Retriever. When the dog was about six-months old, he took the dog with him to visit a friend on a ranch. Mark had trained his dog in obedience and to do a number of tricks. The dog had played long and hard all day and went to sleep under a truck. The dog did not move when the truck started and was run over, breaking a leg and tearing the bone and ligaments from his hip. Though the broken bone healed, the dog was unable to put any weight on his injured leg, and as a consequence walked on three legs. The dog lost a tremendous amount of weight. A year later, surgery was performed hoping to help the dog to walk on the bad leg. Six weeks or so after the surgery, the doctor took x-rays, and found that the bones were deteriorating from bone cancer. The ball that fits into the hip socket was gone. The veterinarian estimated the dog had about six months to live. My son was heart-broken. While in prayer with a prayer partner, I asked the Lord to heal the dog. The dog made a rapid recovery and was able to walk and put weight on his injured leg. The veterinarian called this truly a miracle because he has x-rays that show the bone completely missing.

Molar tooth

In 1997 I had an infection around the root of a molar tooth. After taking some antibiotics, an endodontist wanted to make a four-inch incision and scrape the jawbone. I received an understanding from the Lord that I could get the victory through prayer and fasting. In 1999 I could taste some decay. The dentist said it was coming from the root of this tooth, and he sent me to another endodontist. The endodontist said there was a fracture in the root, and the tooth had to be extracted. When I looked at the x-ray, all I could see was a thin line running up and down the middle of a root. I could not tell that the root was fractured. The tooth became very sensitive and I could not chew on anything that was hard. After seeing the endodontist, I went on a five-day fast with nothing but water, seeking the Lord for an understanding. Did he want me to get my tooth extracted or would he heal my tooth. On the fourth day of the fast, after Mass, I noticed that I could clamp down hard on my tooth, and it did not hurt. Also I could not taste any decay. I said,

"Lord, I accept this healing." I had an inner witness in my spirit that the Lord had healed my tooth. That night as a prayer partner prayed with me, the Lord said, "My son you are healed." When I broke my fast to eat, I had difficulty chewing on the tooth. I spoke to Satan and said, "You are a liar, a thief and the truth is not in you, my tooth is healed." Satan harassed me for the next two days with problems chewing and decay taste in my mouth, which I rejected continuously. Afterward, I did not have any more problems. I went to my dentist three weeks later. To my surprise, the fractured root had broken loose from the tooth and had moved away from the tooth so that there was a large gap between them. The dentist said he had never seen anything like that. Even though half of the root is gone, I could clamp down hard on my tooth and had no trouble chewing on it.

After six months, someone gave me some sticky candy, which pulled the crown off. I said, "Oh no, Lord, do I have to get my tooth extracted?" I received a "No!" I went to my dentist and told him to put the crown back on. Very reluctantly, he glued it back on, knowing that it would not stay on without pins. The crown stayed on for another two months before it came loose. My dentist refused to put the crown on for a second time forcing me to get the tooth extracted. There are three roots in a molar tooth. Unless I could find a dentist that was willing to put pins in the two good roots, the crown would keep coming off. Four different dentists looked at my tooth and said the tooth could not be saved because of the broken root. They also believed the tooth was abscessed. I had already written the testimony above. I said, "Lord do I take this testimony out, since my tooth has been extracted?" He said, "No, the tooth is healed." This is true. I had no decay taste or discomfort with the tooth. For six months, I could bite down hard and chew just as with any other tooth, even though there were only two roots supporting it. Though one root was broken, it was as strong as my other teeth. It is interesting that the dentist who extracted the tooth had a difficult time getting the tooth out because the two remaining roots were strong and would not turn loose from my jawbone. I ended up with a bridge to replace the tooth.

Ankles

In the mid 1980s, I was having problems with my ankles. When I woke up in the morning, I had trouble walking. It felt like the ligaments in my ankle would snap if I tried to walk forward. After taking a few steps, the ligament in my ankles would loosen up. Afterwards, I was all right for the rest of the day. After three months, my ankles were bothering me all day. I asked a friend to pray with me for discernment. I told him I wanted to command the spirit that was attacking my ankles to identify itself. He said, "Oh, Mike, I never prayed this way before." I told him, not to worry if he did not get anything, but if he did get something to let me know. As we began to pray, he said, "Mike, it is a spirit of unbelief." I said, "I do not understand, let's continue to pray." He saw a picture of a loaf of bread. He said, "Mike, do you have any concern about taking care of the need of your family?" I replied, "No, but I do have some concern about my retirement." He said, "That is it. If the Lord takes care of the birds in the air, the fish in the sea and the flowers in the field, how much more does He have concern for us." I repented of my unbelief and my ankles were healed. The spirit tried to attack me two more times. I rebuked it each time. Afterwards, I had no more problems with my ankles.

The Roman Ritual

Early one morning in prayer, a vision of the prayer on exorcism in the Roman Ritual appeared before my eyes. While my prayer partner and I were praying for an understanding, we received the following words:

> The prayers of the Church in the Roman Ritual carry great power. Unfortunately, we are not being taught in our congregations about our powerful heritages.

When one of my sons was small, he was having trouble controlling both of his elimination functions. We received knowledge that there was a spirit involved. We were not having any success in praying for a healing. We were getting desperate. I started reading about exorcism in the Roman Ritual. The introduction to the prayers of exorcism said to pay attention to the prayers or words that cause a reaction, then to repeat them over and over until the person is set free. My son was asleep when I prayed for him. I noticed a reaction in the prayer concerning emotions. I read all the prayers on exorcism for three days with special emphasis on the one concerning emotions. I spent two hours in prayer the first day and one hour the last two days. My son was set free on the third day.

On another occasion, one of my sons had high fever, the fever left immediately after I read the prayers of exorcism.

I started reading the prayers of exorcism for the protection of my mother and dad every day for about six months. During this time, I began including other people. I asked the Lord if my prayers were diluted for my mother and dad when I started including other people. The Lord said:

> Your prayers are not divided or diluted. Its words are more powerful today than 400 years ago. Today, much prayer is needed, and there are too few people to wage war with the enemy. It is the words of the authority of the Church. March on! Do not stop! You are scattering spirits to the point that they are running into each other. I say march on!

Jesus told his disciples not to stop anyone who casts out demons in His name.

> Mark 9:38-40: "Teacher," said John, "we saw a man driving out demons in your name and we told him to stop, because he was not one of us." "Do not stop him," Jesus said. "No one who does a miracle in my name can in the next moment say anything bad about me, for whoever is not against us is for us." (2)

When the Church discourages exorcism, they are doing exactly what Jesus told them not to do.

I had a picture of a priest walking past a man in a wheel chair. In praying for an understanding, a prayer partner received the following words:

106

Part of the authority of a priest is the power to lay hands on the sick, who will recover. Most priests today do not exercise the power given to them nor do they use their authority. God is calling priests to use all of their authority.

James 5:14-16: Is anyone sick? He should call for the elders of the church and they should pray over him and pour a little oil upon him, calling on the Lord to heal him. And their prayer, if offered in faith, will heal him, for the Lord will make him well; and if his sickness was caused by some sin, the Lord will forgive him. Admit your faults to one another and pray for each other so that you may be healed. The earnest prayer of a righteous man has great power and wonderful results. (16)

Mark 16:17-18: And these signs shall follow them that believe; In my name shall they cast out devils; they shall speak with new tongues... they shall lay hands on the sick, and they shall recover (35).

The following words came to my prayer partner while we were in prayer.

Faith is the key to divine healing and all of God's power.

I asked the Lord about the healing of my eyes and ears? He replied:

I have seen your faith. I have read your heart. I know your every thought. I am greatly pleased. Behold, your faith has made you whole. It is not by any man I will do this, but by My sovereign act. Wait for Me with an expectation and joy. In a short time, you will see your heart's desire. Your eyes, your ears, your sister, your friends, your sons, your wife and yourself, I have answered your prayers. Continue to pray with thanksgiving until you see it all come to pass. For I am God. I have decreed it. It will come to pass.

The power to heal is Mine to give when I want to give it. To manifest your healing now is not My plan for you. I love you Mike, be patient. Your healing has been achieved. I will manifest it in My time.

Vision – A large crowd of people and a word was spoken about my ears being healed but nothing happened. Prayer partner received the following words.

People will come from all over the world with advice on how to be healed. Do not pay any attention to them. I have healed you. It will be manifested in My time.

A Mormon friend

I have been praying for a number of people and friends daily by asking the Lord to put a hedge of protection around them and to draw them to His Son, our Lord Jesus Christ. One friend with whom I had worked was a Mormon. He was an analytical chemist. As a youth he spent two years doing missionary work for the Latter Day Saints. I prayed for him daily for over twenty years. One day we ran into each other. I had not seen him in ten years. I told him I had been praying for him every day. He said, "Mike, it must be working because my wife and I are taking instructions to become Catholic." A couple months later, they informed me that they had become Catholic.

I asked the Lord about my parents and why he has not manifested the healing of my ears and speech? He replied:

Be patient, Mike. I have heard your prayers, and I have answered them. You are a special instrument I have raised up. I choose to use you in My way for the greatest good of those who meet you. Your parents are in My hands. I am

108

healing them now through their sufferings. I am with you. Do not fret about delays in seeing My healing on you or on them. Be patient and trust Me, especially when you do not see the results you want. For eternity you will see the results of your prayers. Wait on Me.

Torn rotator cuff and bicep muscle

I had torn my right bicep muscle in 2002 when I had touched the door of a hot wood-burning stove. As I jerked my arm quickly, I tore my bicep muscle. It took six months for the pain to go away. I could always feel the torn muscle in my bicep. In February 2004, I tore a tendon loose from my rotator cuff and injured my bicep muscle for a second time. I could lift my right hand up to my shoulder but I was unable to lift my elbow or arm upward. My rotator cuff was very sore for two months. After a three day fast, I received understanding the Lord wanted me to have surgery on my rotator cuff. Due to complications in taking and retaking a MRI, I did not have surgery until the middle of May. I did not say anything to the doctor about the torn bicep muscle, as it was the least of my worries. After starting my exercise program the bicep muscle started bothering me more and more. For six and one-half months it hurt to carry a cup of coffee in my right hand. It was painful to carry a food tray. I could not lift anything heavy. When I reached around my bicep muscle with my forefinger and thumb, I could almost touch my forefinger with my thumb as there was no bicep ball on my arm. I was greatly concerned as I was not aware that a bicep muscle torn in the middle of the arm can be surgical repaired. I asked my prayer partner to pray with me for understanding. Could I get the victory for my bicep muscle with a long fast on just water? After praying, he received understanding that the Lord wanted me to do a novena. I did a novena to the Sacred Heart of Jesus, which is listed below. This is a very powerful prayer.

Novena of Confidence to the Sacred Heart of Jesus

O Lord, Jesus Christ, to your most Sacred Heart I confide this intention. (Here mention your request) Only look upon me...then do what your heart inspires...Let Your Sacred Heart decide...I count on

It…. I trust in It…. I throw myself on its mercy… Lord Jesus! You will not fail me. Sacred Heart of Jesus, I trust in You! Sacred heart of Jesus, I believe in Your love for me! Sacred Heart of Jesus, Your Kingdom come! O Sacred Heart of Jesus, I have asked for many favors, but I earnestly implore this one. Take it; place it in Your Sacred Heart. <u>When the Eternal Father sees it covered with Your Precious Blood, He will not refuse it. It will be no longer my prayer but Thine, O Jesus</u>. O Sacred Heart of Jesus, I placed my trust in You. Let me never be confounded. Amen. (36)

My arm continued to hurt all through the novena. On the ninth day, I felt strength in my arm with almost no pain. The muscle was large and firm like it was before it was torn. Pain flared up several times the next few days. I fought the fight of faith and kept confessing that my arm was healed. The Lord did heal my muscle. After the 12th day I had no more pain. For six and one-half months prior to this novena, it hurt to carry a cup of coffee. Now I can lift heavy objects with no discomfort. I can no longer feel the torn muscle in my bicep. This has really made a believer out of my wife, Ann, as she has been saying several novenas daily for several months now.

Arthritis in my rotator cuff

In 2004, when the doctor performed surgery on my rotator cuff, he told me I had some arthritis on my rotator cuff. For years, I felt sand-like grains in my rotator cuff when I moved my arms. With my prayer partner, I commanded the spirit of arthritis to identify itself. My prayer partner received understanding that the arthritis was due to unbelief or lack of trust in the Lord. I immediately repented of my unbelief or lack of trust and commanded the spirit of arthritis to leave. I was immediately set free. I no longer have the grain-like irritation in my rotator cuffs.

Vision and dream about high school classmate

I have had pictures of a high school classmate, Pauline Glenn, off and on for over 25 years. I have prayed daily for Pauline for years. In 2004 I heard that she had cancer and had both breasts removed. Pauline told me that in

July 2004 she was given six months to live.

In March of 2005 I had a dream in which I was walking down a long corridor. I passed a room in which a couple, who had kept me in touch with the classmate, was sleeping in bed. I told the couple I was surprised to see them. I asked them about Pauline. Suddenly, Pauline was in bed lying next to the woman and said, "I am here!" I said, "Pauline, I am going to pray for you." The power of God came down so strong that the woman that was in the middle was flipped over on top of her husband. When I prayed with my prayer partner for discernment, he received understanding that Pauline would have peace in her body. In other words she was healed of cancer. This was two months passed the six months she was given. The couple asked me about the significance of them in the dream. I told them that I did not pray about them, but my understanding was that Pauline considered them part of her family, and that they were my contact with her.

In October 2005, while I was praying, I had a picture of Pauline standing before me. She was younger looking, wearing a long, blue, low-cut evening gown. She was shocked, stunned and surprised to see me. I had understanding that she was shocked, stunned and surprised at the effectiveness of my prayers for her. She knew that she had been healed of cancer.

On New Year's Eve 2005, I received a card and letter from Pauline. She said: In 1999 she was diagnosed with breast cancer. In 2002 she had a double mastectomy. In 2004 the cancer had moved into her bones, chest and abdomen. In July 2004 she was told that she had approximately six months to live. In December 2005 a MRI and CT-scan showed no active cancer in her abdomen or pelvis, an ovarian mass had diminished since January 2005, a mass in her lung was gone, and no sign of active cancer in her spine. Pauline was given a blood test that indicates how active cancer is in one system. Normal, indicating no active cancer is 40. At one point her count was 400. Her count now was 42. The doctor told her that there was no trace of cancer in her body. She is completely healed.

The dream and picture was just the Lord letting me know what was going on with Pauline. I saw Pauline at a class reunion in September 2006. She was doing fine, with no trace of cancer in her body. In 2008 the cancer came back. Pauline passed away in 2008 three years after she was healed. It was through my faith that Pauline was healed. I have never had a victory for a healing that I was not severely tested and had to fight the fight of faith to keep the healing.

Neighbor healed of cancer

March 2006 - Hubert and Janie Peek are our next door neighbors. Janie was in the fourth and final stages of cancer. Her left lung had collapsed. She was bedridden and on oxygen. I was aware that her husband had diabetes. I asked my prayer partner to pray with me for discernment. I asked the Lord if I could fast and get the victory for Janie if her husband was not able to fast. My prayer partner received the understanding that I was to fast for three days. I asked Janie if Hubert was able to fast for her. She said, "No!" I told her that I would fast for her. I went three days with only water. After the fast, the Lord said, "You have done your part; the rest is up to me." I continue to lift Janie up every day especially at communion. When I prayed with Janie, she received the gift of tongues. I encourage her to pray in tongues everyday as Roman 8:26 says the Spirit makes intercession for our infirmity when we do not know how to pray.

> Romans 8:26 -27: Likewise the Spirit also helpeth our infirmities: for we know not what we should pray for as we ought: but the Spirit itself maketh intercession for us with groanings which cannot be uttered. And he that searcheth the hearts knoweth what is the mind of the Spirit, because he maketh intercession for the saints according to the will of God. (35)

The Lord revealed to me that no healing can take place unless the person, for which the healing is meant, has the faith to receive it. Hubert and Janie are people of great faith. Janie kept confessing that she was healed regardless how bad she felt. Janie started using vitamins, herbs and health food and continued working with her doctors. In September 2006 Hubert said there was no trace of cancer in her body.

In July 2009 the cancer came back. My wife and I went on a three day fast for Janie. After the fast I had a vision of a large area of green and a small area of purple. The Lord revealed that purple were thoughts of doubts. The Lord said to reject all thoughts of doubts and there would be new life. Fighting doubts when you are in pain and hurting is difficult. Janie passed away the last of September, three years after she was healed.

Oak tree died and yet live.

I need to share another story about my neighbor who is continuously amazed about this tree that was dead and yet lives. Hubert and Janie had just brought and built their home on the property. There is an oak tree on the fence line on the corner edge of both our properties. The tree facing my side was dead with rotten wood and full of woodpecker holes and nests. There were limbs with green leaves on Hubert's side. In the middle of the summer, all the leaves turned brown. The tree appeared to be dead. Hubert said, "I sure hate to lose that tree." Later that day while saying my prayers, I had a picture of that tree with some new growth. I do not recall specifically praying for the tree, nevertheless, I said, "Lord, I accept this new growth". I shared the vision with Hubert. A few weeks later, the tree had a couple new leaves. Six years later, there are many limbs covered with healthy green foliage on Hubert's side while my side of the tree is dead.

Several years ago, three of Hubert's Oak trees came down with Oak Wilt which is a fatal disease. I asked Franciscan Father Bob Hilz to bless Hubert's trees and property and to pray with me and come against Oak Wilt. All the trees have survived.

The Lord is no respecter of person. He looks for any opportunity to show His love, mercy, and grace. He uses everyday circumstances in our lives to do this. All He requires from us is faith. His healings are bountiful to those who will only ask, but they must stand in the gap and fight the fight of faith without wavering or doubting.

Joshua Luke Miesch – a new born son

Our son, Mike III and his wife Jean Marie have not been able to have a family. They tried to adopt a number times including flying to Kazakhstan with no luck. My wife, Ann, had brought a statue of a mother holding a baby prior to their trip to Kazakhstan. She debated about giving this statue to Jean Marie which she did at Christmas. There was silence in the room when she opened this present. Ann said she had bought this statue prior to their trip and decided to give it to her as proof of our faith that they would have a family. Ann and I prayed faithfully everyday. Years later, after 17 years of marriage, Joshua, a healthy baby boy was born on May 20th 2011.

Blessed Mother Interceded for me

January 08, 2012

I had rotor cuff surgery on my right shoulder in 2004. In 2008 I fell backwards and damaged the rotor cuff on my left shoulder. The doctor had great difficulty repairing this rotor cuff. It was six months before I could lift this arm upward above my head. For four years I could not use or lift this left arm sideways to put a letter in a mailbox or to get money from an ATM machine from an open car window. Because of the limited use of my left arm, I had to use my right arm more and more. For a year or so my right shoulder has been tender and sore. It hurt to lift my right arm to comb my hair. As I was lying sideways on my right shoulder on the night of January 7, it felt like one of the tendons snapped. The bicep muscle in my arm seemed to have dropped and was painful. It bothered me all through the night. The thoughts were that I would have to have another rotor cuff surgery.

I got up at 5 am to pray. I said, "Blessed Mother, you've got to help me." Immediately, the Blessed Mother slid her right hand under my left arm and said, "I am the Ark of the Covenant. (The Blessed Mother carried Jesus in her stomach for nine months) Jesus, My Son, is the New Covenant. The New Covenant contains all of my promises, one of which is healing." The pain left immediately. Both arms were healed. I can lift my left arm sideways to the top of my head. Both of my arms are now in

114

excellent shape with no pain or discomfort. There was also healing in my knees, as I am able to walk up and down steps with no discomfort. I have never had a healing for which I did not have to fight the fight of faith before the healing was manifested and afterwards to keep the healing.

Prayer for the Blessed Mother to intercede for me

Remember, O most gracious Virgin Mary, that never was it known that anyone who fled to your protection, implored your help, or sought your intercession was left unaided. Inspired with this confident, I fly unto you, O Virgin of virgins, my mother. To you I come, before you, I stand, sinful and sorrowful. O Mother of the Word Incarnate, despises not my petitions, but in your mercy, hears and answers them.

Prostrate Cancer

Blood work in May 2013 showed PSA readings of 25 and 25.2. A biopsy was positive for prostrate cancer.

When cancer is involved it is usually due to sin. I had what I felt was mild resentment. Nevertheless, resentment is a sin. I went to confession and repented for my resentment. Ann and I went on three day water-only fast two different times for a total of 12 days. Afterward Ann and I both had faith to believe that the cancer was no longer there. I went to my personal physician and asked for another PSA. He asked why? I told him that after the fast we had belief that the cancer was no longer there. If the cancer is no longer there the PSA should drop. He said if there PSA drop, he will start fasting the next day. Read the doctor e-mail below. The PSA drops from 25 to 1.25.

> It looks like you are right. The PSA has come down to 1.25. What an amazing change. Do you want to keep monitoring this? I don't think we should check it again.
>
> Healthcare Associates of Irving

My urologist believed the cancer is still there. For 15 months he has strongly insisted that I be treated for prostrate cancer. After 18 months the PSA reading was 0.9. He is puzzled why the PSA readings have not gone up. He said we will not do anything unless the PSA goes up. I asked him if he was ready to accept a miracle. He said, "No, that he will see me in six months." My personal physician does believe that the cancer is no longer there. After a year and half, the PSA readings have not gone up.

Sin will hinder a prayer from being answered.

There are a number of things that will hinder a prayer from being answered. Some of these sins are unbelief, resentment, bitterness, hatred, unforgiving heart, etc. The scripture says God does not listen to sinners but only those who do His will.

> John 9:31: We know that God does not hear sinners; but if any one is God-fearing, and does His will, He hears him (1).

Sickness and death came into the world with the sins of our first parents, Adam and Eve. However, all sickness is not due to personal sin. The apostles asked Jesus whose sin was responsible for a man being born blind, his or his parents? Jesus said neither the man nor his parents were responsible but that this was for the glory of God. However, the glory of God was manifested when Jesus healed the man.

> John 9:1-3: And as He passed by, He saw a man blind from birth. And His disciples asked Him, saying, "Rabbi, who sinned, this man or his parents, that he should be born blind?" Jesus answered, "It was neither that this man sinned, nor his parents; but it was in order that the works of God might be displayed in him. (1)

Serious sin can lead to serious sickness.

Though not all sickness is due to personal sin, the scriptures do teach that serious sin can lead to serious sickness or death.

1. Not discerning the Body of the Lord

> I Corinthians 11:27-30: Therefore whoever eats the bread

or drinks the cup of the Lord in an unworthy manner, shall be guilty of the body and blood of the Lord. But let a man examine himself, and so let him eat of the bread and drink of the cup. For he who eats and drinks, eats and drinks judgment to himself, if he does not judge the body rightly. For this reason many among you are weak and sick, and a number sleep. (1)

Those who partake of the body and blood of Christ in an unworthy manner may become weak, sick or even die.

2. Destruction of the flesh.

Paul handed a man, who was having sexual relations with his father's wife, over to Satan for the destruction of the flesh so that his spirit may be saved in the day of the Lord.

I Corinthians 5:5: I have decided to deliver such a one to Satan for the destruction of his flesh, that his spirit may be saved in the day of the Lord Jesus (1).

Destruction of the flesh can be a number of things such as cancer, multiple sclerosis, etc. I am not saying that people who have cancer, multiple sclerosis or other serious sickness have committed serious sins. There are many babies with cancer. Babies are not capable of committing sin. I am only saying that cancer and multiple sclerosis are examples of the destruction of the flesh.

3. Body wasting away because of sin.

The Psalms speak of the body wasting away.

Psalm 32:3: When I kept silent about my sin, my body wasted away... (1).

Psalm 31:10: For my life is spent with sorrow, and my

years with sighing; My strength has failed because of my iniquity. And my body has wasted away. (1)

Psalm 38:3: There is no soundness in my flesh because of Thine indignation. There is no health in my bones because of my sin (1).

4. **Envy and anger will shorten one's life, while pride brings on unheard of affliction.**

Sirach 30:24: Envy and anger shorten one's life, worry brings on premature old age (3).

Sirach 10:13: for pride is the reservoir of sin, a source which runs over with vice; because of it God sends unheard-of afflictions and brings men to utter ruin (3).

One who covers his sins shall not prosper.

Proverbs 28:13: He that covereth his sins shall not prosper; but whoso confesseth and forsaketh them shall have mercy (37). (35X)

Proverbs 3:7-8:...Fear the Lord and turn away from evil. It will be healing to your body, and refreshment to your bones (1).

I John 1:9: If we confess our sins, He is faithful and righteous to forgive us our sins and to cleanse us from all unrighteousness (1).

These scriptures teach that serious sins can bring on serious sickness. The scriptures also teach that if we will repent and turn away from sin that the Lord will forgive us of our sins and will bring healing to our body.

James 5:16: Therefore, confess your sins to one another, and pray for one another, so that you may be healed (1).

If a person has any serious sin in his life, he must first deal with the sin before he can expect healing from the Lord. After repenting for our sins, and turning away from them, praying in the spirit is the means to help bring health to our bodies as the Spirit will make intercessions for the saints according to the will of God when we do not know how to pray (Roman 8:26).

Honor the physician. He who has need of a physician should go.

Jesus said it is those who are sick that have need of a physician.

> Luke 5:31: And Jesus answered and said to them, "It is not those who are well who need a physician, but those who are sick (1).

If you are asking for a healing where sickness is involved, seek the Lord and do what he tells you to do. However, remember the Lord created the physicians and said if you have need of a physician, then go.

> Ecclesiasticus 38:1-2: Honour the doctor with the honour that is his due in return for his services; for he too has been created by the Lord. Healing itself comes from the Most High,...(18).

This scripture shows that physicians were created by the Lord to heal the people.

The Lord provides medicines.

> Ecclesiasticus 38:4: The Lord has brought medicines into existence from the earth, and the sensible man will not despise them (18).

The wise man will use the medicine that the Lord provides through the herbs of the earth.

Repent of your sins before you go to the doctor

> Ecclesiasticus 38:9-10: My son, when you are ill, do

119

not be depressed, but pray to the Lord and he will heal you. Renounce your faults, keep your hand unsoiled, and cleanse your heart from all sin (18).

The scripture says to repent of your sins before you go to a doctor. We are to pray to the Lord asking him to heal us though the doctor.

Let the doctor take over for the Lord created him.

Ecclesiasticus 38:12-15: Then let the doctor take over - the Lord created him too - and do not let him leave you, for you need him. Sometimes success is in their hands, since they in turn will beseech the Lord to grant them the grace to relieve and to heal, that life may be saved. (18)

We need to have faith that God will use the doctor to heal us. At the same time we are to pray in the spirit for our infirmities.

Vision of a man in a wheelchair opening his mouth in an expression of protest:

The wheelchair is symbolic of self-pity and excuses. The expression of upset on the face of the man in the wheelchair is symbolic of a complaint against his circumstances. He will complain and feel sorry for himself, but Jesus says, "Get up and walk!" There is no use for fear or self-pity. We are a people of power and truth. What is needed is trust in Jesus. Step out in faith. "Commend our ways to the Lord, and He will do everything for us."

CHAPTER 5

Gift of Tongues

In writing about the Holy Spirit, the Lord said, "Begin with a description of the power of praying in the Spirit." Praying in tongues is the same as praying in the Spirit. When we pray in the spirit, the Spirit intercedes for us according to the will of God when we do not know how to pray. When the Lord wakes me in the middle of the night to pray and I do not know what or how He wants me to pray, I pray in the spirit.

> Romans 8:26-27:...the Spirit also helps our weakness; for we do not know how to pray as we should, but the Spirit Himself intercedes for us with groanings too deep for words; and He who searches the hearts knows what the mind of the Spirit is, because He intercedes for the saints according to the will of God. (1)

The person who prays in tongues does not know what he is saying.

> I Corinthians 14:2, 14-15: For one who speaks in a tongue does not speak to men but to God; for no one understands, but in his spirit he speaks mysteries....For if I pray in a tongue, my spirit prays, but my mind is unfruitful. What is the outcome then? I shall pray with the spirit and I shall pray with the mind also. I shall sing with the spirit and I shall sing with the mind also. (1)

Paul said he prayed in tongues but he also prayed with understanding. Paul taught that there was a difference in praying in the spirit (tongues) and praying with understanding.

Did Paul know what he was saying when he spoke in tongues?

Paul admitted that he did not know what he was saying when he spoke in tongues.

> I Corinthians 14:6, 9-11: Just suppose, brothers, that I should come to you speaking in tongues. What good will I do you if my speech does not have some revelation, or knowledge, or prophecy, or instruction for you?... Similarly if you do not utter intelligible speech because you are speaking in a tongue, how will anyone know what you are saying? You will be talking to the air. There are many different languages in the world and all are marked by sound; but if I do not know the meaning, I shall be a foreigner to the speaker and he a foreigner to me. (3)

Paul did not use tongues to preach the gospel. Paul said,

> I Corinthians 14:18-19: Thank God, I speak in tongues more than any of you, but in the church I would rather say five intelligible words to instruct others than ten thousands words in a tongue (3).

Why would Paul waste his time making sounds with his mouth that he or no one else could understand? Yet, Paul thanked the Lord that he did this more than any of the Corinthians. In church or an assembly, Paul said he would rather speak five intelligible words to the people than ten thousands words in a tongue. This shows that tongues were not used to preach the gospel, because when one speaks in a tongue he does not know what he is saying. How can one preach the gospel if he does not know or understand what he is saying?

Did the Apostles know what they were saying on the day of Pentecost?

> Acts 2:1,4-8,11: And when the day of Pentecost had come, they were all together in one place....And they were all filled with the Holy Spirit and began to speak with other

tongues, as the Spirit was giving them utterance. Now there were Jews living in Jerusalem, devout men, from every nation under heaven. And when this sound occurred, the multitude came together, and were bewildered, because they were each one hearing them speak in his own language. And they were amazed and marveled, saying, "Why, are not all these who are speaking Galileans? And how is it that we each hear them in our own language to which we were born?…we hear them in our own tongues speaking of the mighty deeds of God. (1)

These Apostles were Galileans. They were unlearned and uneducated men. They did not know all the languages of the world that they were speaking. They were simply speaking in the spirit by the Holy Spirit. The Jews from every nation of the world who were living in Jerusalem heard different apostles speaking in their native language about the Lord. The apostles had no idea what they were saying. The Jews were amazed that these unlearned and uneducated Galileans were speaking in their native language about the Lord. How were these uneducated Galileans able to speak all the languages of the known world? Then some of the Jews began to mock them, saying they were drunk. Now notice that Peter spoke up and began to preach the gospel to the three thousand Jews who had gathered (Acts 2:14-42). Peter spoke the gospel in the language which he and they understood. The gift of tongues was not used to preach the gospel.

The gift of tongues is used as a sign for the unbelievers.

I Corinthians 14:21-22: In the Law it is written, "By men of strange tongues and by the lips of strangers I will speak to this people, and even so they will not listen to Me," says the Lord. So then tongues are for a sign, not to those who believe, but to unbelievers; (1)

The gift of tongues was used as a sign to all the Jews in Jerusalem. These Jews knew that these Galileans were uneducated Jews and that they were speaking all the languages of the world by the Spirit of God. If the Jews in Jerusalem wanted to find out whether these apostles knew their native language, all they had to do was ask the apostles some questions in their native language. If they did, chances are they would have found that the apostles did not know their native language or understand what they were saying, unless the Lord gave them the gift to understand what they were saying. St. Vincent Ferrier, who lived in the 14th century, traveled all over Europe preaching the gospel, speaking only in his native language, yet people of other languages understood what he was saying.

What language was St. Vincent using, for all were ready to swear that he was using their native tongue?

> "You are all wrong and all right, my friends," said the friar with a smile, "I am speaking Valencian, my mother tongue; for, except for Latin and a little Hebrew, I know no other Spanish. It is the good God who had rendered this intelligible to you."

Distance made no difference. Those on the outskirts of huge crowd could hear as distinctly as those close to the pulpit.

St. Vincent Ferrier was not speaking in tongues, for he knew what he was saying. The apostles surely had this gift where people of other nations and languages understood what they were saying even though they were speaking in their native language. (37, 38)

On the day of Pentecost, the gift of tongues was used as it was intended to be used, i.e. as a sign to the unbelievers. The gospel was not preached in tongues. Peter preached the gospel in a language that he and all the Jews understood. As a result three thousand Jews repented of their sins, were baptized and accepted Jesus Christ as their Lord and Savior.

Speaking in tongues is used primarily for private, personal prayer.

Though speaking in tongues is used in church or in an assembly as a sign to unbelievers, it is used primarily for private, personal prayer. Paul thanked the Lord that he prayed in tongues more than any of the Corinthians. Why did Paul spend all his time praying in an unintelligible language when he did not know what he was saying? Why did Paul say he wished that all the people spoke in tongues?

> I Corinthians 14:5: Now I wish that you all spoke in tongues,…(1).

Speaking in tongues is a gift from God. When one prays or sings in tongues, he is praying or singing in his spirit to the Lord.

> I Corinthians 14:2: For one who speaks in a tongue does not speak to men, but to God; for no one understands, but in his spirit he speaks mysteries (1).

Do not forbid speaking in tongues.

> 1 Corinthians 14:39: Set your hearts on prophecy, my brothers, and do not forbid those who speak in tongues, but make sure everything is done properly and in order (3).

Tongues are God's words or messages coming forth when we yield to the Spirit.

The Spirit makes intercession for the saints according to the will of God.

Romans 8:26-27 says the Spirit of God makes intercession for us according to the will of God when we do not know how to pray. Our battle is not against flesh and blood but against the unseen spiritual powers of darkness in the heavenly places.

> Ephesians 6:12: For we are not fighting against people made of flesh and blood, but against persons without bodies - the evil rulers of the unseen world, those mighty satanic beings and great evil princes of darkness who rule this world; and against huge numbers of wicked spirits in the spirit world. (16)

How do we fight a battle against the unseen enemy – the unseen ruler of the unseen world, the power of darkness?

Since our battle is against the spiritual forces of darkness in the heavenly places, we do not know how to fight this battle or how to pray. This is the reason the scripture in Ephesians 6:18, after the discussion of the unseen rulers and powers of darkness, says to pray always in the Spirit.

> Ephesians 6:18: With all prayer and petition pray at all times in the Spirit, . . (1).

When we pray in the spirit, the Holy Spirit makes intercession for us according to the will of God against the unseen forces of darkness. This is what Paul did. He prayed all the time, making foolish sounds with his mouth that neither he nor anyone else understood. Paul was praying to the Lord. "Praying in the Spirit at all times" shows that praying in the Spirit or in tongues is primarily a prayer language for an individual, personal, private prayer time. Praying in tongues is essential in exorcism and dealing with evil spirits. There is power in our prayers when we pray in the spirit. Demons hate the gift of tongues.

What is speaking in tongues or praying in the Spirit?

Praying in the spirit or speaking in tongues is like baby talk. We yield ourselves to the groaning of the Spirit within us - letting the syllables that are formed by the Spirit with our cooperation come forth. Like a baby, we have no idea what the syllables or words that come forth mean. As we yield our voices and form the syllables in cooperation with the Holy Spirit, the Spirit of God is able to intercede and pray for us according to His will when we do not know how to pray. A person has to have faith in God and be willing to make a fool of himself to pray in the spirit or pray in tongues. Praying in tongues is when the Lord speaks through you with words or a language you do not know or understand.

Bobbie Cavnar, a retired Air Force Colonel, and a leader in the Christian Community of God's Delight, was talking about speaking in tongues. He said you are making sound that is baby talk. He quoted the syllables or words he received when he first experienced the baptism in the Spirit. A man from the Philippines recognized the words and told Bobbie that he was speaking Filipino: "Father, father makes me a teacher." The Holy Spirit gave Bobbie the words asking God the Father to make him a teacher. Bobbie actually became a spiritual teacher to community members.

Praying in the Spirit helps us to pray for our infirmities.

After I was angry and having hurt feelings and resentments against some of the brothers in the Lord because I felt they had rejected and mistreated me, the Lord started dealing with me. Over a three-year period, after many promptings from the Lord, I would repent and ask the Lord for forgiveness. Then these thoughts about how I was rejected and mistreated would creep in again. I would cultivate these thoughts. I repented many times but always ended up having angry, hurt feelings over and over again. Because I had a hard time turning loose of these resentments, the Lord started dealing with me by allowing an arthritic condition to develop in my neck, causing severe muscular tensions and spasms from which it was difficult to get any relief. My neck became so stiff that I had to turn my body, as I could not turn my neck. I finally repented of my anger, hurt feelings and resentments and made a decision not to cultivate these thoughts again. My neck was so stiff, I could not turn it and the pain was always there. I went to a chiropractor, who treated me twice a week for a month with no relief. He took some x-rays and told me that I had a hereditary condition. He said there was nothing that could be done. This was something I was going to have to learn to live with. I knew then that this was something that I was going to have to take to the Lord in prayer. The scripture Romans 8:26 came to me about praying in the Spirit for our infirmities.

Romans 8:26 -27: Likewise the Spirit also helpeth our infirmities: for we know not what we should pray for as we ought: but the Spirit itself maketh intercession for us with groanings which cannot be uttered. And he that searcheth the hearts knoweth what is the mind of the Spirit, because he maketh intercession for the saints according to the will of God. (35)

Father Bob Hilz received the following message from the Lord in a prayer meeting in our home:

You do not know what a great gift I have given you to pray in tongues.

I made a list of 20 intentions for which to pray in the spirit for each day. This was in addition to my regular prayer time and going to Mass every day. My neck was one of the intentions for which I prayed five minutes in the spirit each day. After praying in the spirit, I would put a check mark on my list for that intention for that day. After a month and a half, I was able to freely turn my head and neck without much discomfort. I no longer had severe muscular spasms or cried out with a sharp pain as I lay down or tried to turn over in bed.

Because the pain or discomfort was bearable and I was tired of praying five minutes in the spirit for so many intentions above my regular prayer time, I quit praying in the spirit for all the intentions. Almost a year went by before I started praying again in the spirit for the different intentions including my neck. After another month and a half of praying daily in the spirit, the discomfort left my neck. I was able to freely turn my neck without any pain or discomfort. It is interesting that even though I went to Mass daily and spent two hours in prayer each day plus fasting three or more days each week and thanking the Lord daily for the healing of my neck, the Holy Spirit did not continue to intercede for me until I started and continued to pray in tongues daily for another month and a half. In this case the Holy Spirit only interceded for me while I prayed in tongues.

When we pray in the spirit, the Spirit makes intercession for our infirmities. If our infirmity is due to sin, we must first deal with that sin before we can expect the Lord to answer our prayer. If we have any resentment or cultivate thoughts about how we have been hurt, mistreated or taken advantage of by others, we need to repent and ask the Lord to forgive us.

Sirach 28:3-5: Should a man nourish anger against his fellows and expect healing from the Lord? Should a man refuse mercy to his fellows, yet seek pardon for his own sins? If he who is but flesh cherishes wrath, who will forgive his sins? (3)

Did Jesus pray in the Spirit?

Paul taught that praying in the spirit is the same as praying in tongues.

I Corinthians 14:2,14-15: For one who speaks in a tongue does not speak to men, but to God; for no one understands, but in his spirit he speaks mysteries... For if I pray in a tongue, my spirit prays, but my mind is unfruitful. What is the outcome then? I shall pray with the spirit and I shall pray with the mind also. (1)

When one prays in the spirit, he speaks mysteries that no one understands except God. Romans 8:26 shows that the Spirit intercedes for us speaking mysteries with groanings too deep for words.

Roman 8:26:...the Spirit also helps our weakness; for we do not know how to pray as we should, but the Spirit Himself intercedes for us with groanings too deep for words; and He who searches the hearts, knows what the mind of the Spirit is, because He intercedes for the saints according to the will of God. (1)

When we pray in the spirit, the Spirit prays with groanings that comes from deep within us. This groaning is the Spirit of God making intercession for us according to the will of God, when we do not know how to pray. Some say that groaning in the Spirit is not the same as praying in tongues. Whether we groan or speak, there are sounds or words coming forth, which are the languages of the Spirit. I do not know how to take advantage of Roman 8:26 except to pray in tongues.

The Scripture teaches that Jesus groaned in the Spirit.

> John 11:32-33,38: When, therefore, Mary came where Jesus was, and saw him, she fell at his feet, and said to him, "Lord, if thou hadst been here, my brother would not have died." When, therefore, Jesus saw her weeping, and the Jews who had come with her weeping, he groaned in the spirit and was troubled,....Jesus therefore, again groaning in himself, came to the tomb. (20A)

Jesus groaned in the spirit. This shows that Jesus prayed in the spirit, which is the same as praying in tongues. This shouldn't be so puzzling. We have shown that Jesus is the Son of God incarnated into a human body. Jesus emptied himself of His divine nature and became like man in every respect except sin. Jesus did not know everything. He grew in wisdom, knowledge and understanding. At His baptism by John the Baptist, the Holy Spirit came upon Him in the form of a dove. The scripture says that Jesus was led and guided by the Spirit from that point on. He did not do what he wanted to do, but what His Father wanted Him to do.

Jesus was a man of prayer. Jesus had both a human and a divine nature. Since the divine nature of God was not manifested in Jesus, Jesus did not know everything. Jesus grew in wisdom and knowledge. Certainly, there were times when Jesus did not know how to pray. If Jesus knew everything, why was He led or guided by the Spirit? If Jesus was led and guided by the Spirit, is there any reason why He should not pray by the Spirit?

When we pray in the spirit, the Holy Spirit makes intercession for us in fighting spiritual battles, praying for our needs and our infirmities when we do not know how to pray. The Holy Spirit comes to our aid, making intercession with unspeakable yearning and groaning too deep for utterance.

Paul said that he wished all the people prayed in tongues. Ephesians 6:18 says to pray at all times in the Spirit. When a person prays, he is talking to God. Praying in tongues is primarily for our private prayer time with the Lord. Speaking in tongues is a gift from God. If you do not have this prayer language, you should seek the Lord with everything within you for this gift. Praying in the spirit or praying in tongues is a very powerful means of prayer.

When there is someone, or something, or a need, or an infirmity for which we need to pray but don't know how, we should pray in the spirit. The Holy Spirit will make intercession for us according to God's will. When the Lord wakes me up in the middle of the night to pray, I pray in tongues.

Praying in the spirit will do wonders when praying for our intentions and needs. To help me pray regularly in the spirit, I made a list of intentions with all the days of the month. When I am through praying for that intention, I made a slanting line as a check for that day. The next day, I will cross the line to make an X. In a month, you can grade yourself and see how faithful you have been to praying each day.

You can determine the length of time you want to pray for each intention. It is not a good idea to have too many intentions or pray too long for each intention. You will have a hard time praying for all the intentions and the other needs will suffer. I tried to pray five minutes for each intention while driving to work or any time during the day when my mind is not needed for work or any other activities. You can pray one or two or three minutes for each intention whatever suits you best. Remember that one should have a balanced prayer life. We need to have time each day to read and study the scripture, to sing and to praise him, and to be quiet and let him speak to us.

Month-July	1 & 2	3 & 4	5 & 6	7 & 8	9 & 10	11 & 12	13 & 14	15 & 16	17 & 18	19 & 20	21 & 22	23 & 24	25 & 26	27 & 28	29 & 30	31
Divine protection for us, our family and parents	X	X	X	X	X	X	X	X	/	X	X	X	X	X	/	
Our Nation	X	X	X	X	X	X	X	X	/	X	X	X	/	X	/	
Mom	X	X	X	X	X	X	X	X	/	X	X	X	/	X	/	
Dad	X	X	X	X	X	X	X	X	/	X	X	X	/	X	/	
Brother and Sister	X	X	X	X	X	X	X	X	/	X	X	X	/	X	/	
Aunt and Uncle	X	/	X	X	X	X	X	X	/	X	X	X	/	X	/	
Laborer for Harvest	X	/	X	X	X	X	X			X	X	X	X	/	X	/
Spiritual revival among the Priests and Clergy	X	/	X	/	X	X	X	X		X	X	/	X	/	X	/
Any infirmity	X	/	X		X	/	X	/		X	X	/	X	/	X	/
Special intentions	X	/	X		X	/	X	/		X	X	/	X	/	X	/

131

For successful encounters against the adversary

It is essential that we study the scriptures with an open mind and a contrite heart with diligence for the truth. We need to be firmly rooted in God's Word for it is the embodiment of all truth. The scripture says to study the Word so that you will know the truth and the truth will set you free. Knowing the scriptures will increase our faith and aid us in our fight against the enemy.

Vigilant, persistent prayer and self-denial are the necessary ingredients for successful and victorious encounters against the adversary. One should be sensitive to the prompting and leading of the Holy Spirit. Pray at all times in the spirit as the Holy Spirit will make intercession for the saints according to God's will when we do not know how to pray.

Why do we have to pray? Four reasons:

1. It's in God's words.

   James 4:2: You do not have because you do not ask (1).

   Philippians 4:6: Have no anxiety about anything but in everything by prayer and supplication with thanksgiving let your requests be made known to God (31).

2. One must be obedient to God's words. Praying is a step in obedience to God.

3. Prayer is an act of humiliation - humbling one-self before God saying, "I cannot do this on my own. I need your help."

   Prayer is a means of communication with God. Prayer conveys a thought, desire or intercession and expresses those concepts into words. These mere words are the representation in our physical world or "reality in a physical sense" of what was merely nothing before or "did not exist."

   Hebrews 11:3: By faith we understand that the worlds

were prepared by the word of God, so that what is seen was not made out of things which were visible (1).

In other words, just the words of prayer bring forth a new significance to what were basically just mental concepts. Prayer brings substance to our desires and thoughts, and makes them real in a spiritual sense to God. Out of God's words came the existence of the whole universe. If we are part of Christ's Body and act on the power that creates something out of words, this power will be manifested in our prayers to give substances to our intentions, desires, and intercessions, making them a reality.

The scripture says that faith is the substance of the things hoped for and the evidence of the things not seen. The key to praying with creative and expectant faith is abiding in Christ and in His words.

John 15:7: If you abide in Me and My words in you, ask whatever you wish and it shall be done for you (1).

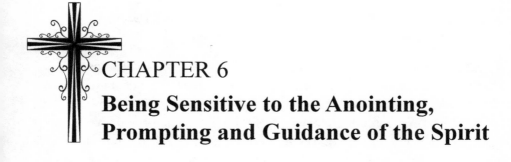

CHAPTER 6

Being Sensitive to the Anointing, Prompting and Guidance of the Spirit

God's Spirit will dwell within us.

Before Jesus ascended into heaven, He told His disciples that God the Father would send His Spirit to be with them, to comfort them, and to help direct and guide them. His Spirit would dwell within them and they would know Him but the people of the world would not.

> John 14:16-17 And I will ask the Father, and He will give you another Helper, that He may be with you forever; that is the Spirit of truth, whom the world cannot receive, because it does not behold Him or know Him, but you know Him because He abides with you, and will be in you. (1)

The Spirit will be a personal teacher.

> John 14:26: But the Helper, the Holy Spirit, whom the Father will send in my name, He will teach you all things, and bring to your remembrance all that I said to you (1).

> I John 2:27: And as for you, the anointing which you received from Him abides in you, and you have no need for any one to teach you; but as His anointing teaches you about all things, and is true and is not a lie, and just as it has taught you, you abide in Him. (1)

The Holy Spirit will teach us, comfort us, direct us and guide us through His anointing. There are many different kinds of anointing.

Some which I have experience will be discussed in this chapter

The Spirit gives wisdom and understanding that does not come from man.

> I Corinthians 2:9-16:...Eye has not seen, ear has not heard, nor has it so much as dawned on man what God has prepared for those who love Him. Yet God has revealed this wisdom to us through the Spirit. The Spirit scrutinizes all matters, even the deep things of God. Who, for example, knows man's innermost self but the man's own spirit within him? Similarly, no one knows what lies at the depths of God but the Spirit of God. The Spirit we have received is not the world's spirit but God's Spirit, helping us to recognize the gifts he has given us. We speak of these, not in words of human wisdom but in words taught by the Spirit, thus interpreting spiritual things in spiritual terms. The natural man does not accept what is taught by the Spirit of God. For him, that is absurdity. He cannot come to know such teaching because it must be appraised in a spiritual way. The spiritual man, on the other hand, can appraise everything, though he himself can be appraised by no one. For, "Who has known the mind of the Lord so as to instruct him?" But we have the mind of Christ. (3)

Discerning the voice of the Lord

The Lord spoke to Elijah in a cave and told him to go and stand outside the cave on the mountain as He (the Lord) was going to be passing by.

> I Kings 19:11-13: Then the Lord said, "Go outside and stand on the mountain before the Lord; the Lord will be passing by." A strong and heavy wind was rending the mountains and crushing rocks before the Lord - but the Lord was not in the wind. After the wind there was an

earthquake - but the Lord was not in the earthquake. After the earthquake there was a fire - but the Lord was not in the fire. After the fire there was a tiny whispering sound. When he heard this, Elijah hid his face in his cloak and went and stood at the entrance of the cave. (3)

Elijah did not move when the terrible storm, the earthquake or the fire went by. Was Elijah being disobedient to the Lord? It would be easy to assume that the Lord was in the storm, or in the earthquake or the raging fire; however, Elijah did not move. Elijah knew the voice of the Lord. If Elijah had come out of the cave at the wrong time, he could have easily been killed. After all the drama of the roaring thunder, lightning, wind, loud noise, earthquake, fire and smoke, Elijah heard a tiny soft quiet voice. Elijah immediately wrapped his cloak around his face, went out and stood in front of his cave for he knew the Lord would be passing by.

When the Lord asks us to do something, we must discern when, as it is not always immediately. The Lord speaks in a tiny voice that is inaudible to any one except the person to whom he is speaking.

Psalm 46:10 says, "Be still, and know that I am God." (2)

If a person is talking, moving around or doing something, it will be difficult to hear the voice or detect the anointing of the Lord. If Elijah had not listened for the Lord's signal and timing, and had come out of the cave at the wrong time, he could have been killed.

The Lord has a plan and a purpose for each one of us and our life. We need to spend time in prayer, study His words, be still and quiet, and listen to His Spirit to discern His plan and purpose for us. The Lord does not lay out a blueprint for us to follow. We must come before the Lord daily to discern His intentions for us.

Being sensitive to the anointing, prompting, teaching, and guidance of the Spirit.

When a person accepts Jesus Christ as his personal Lord and Savior, or is baptized with water or is prayed with for the infilling of the Holy

Spirit, he will often feel an anointing from the Lord. There are many gifts of the Holy Spirit. The Lord gives different gifts and anointing to different people. Each person has a different calling. The Lord speaks, touches, and teaches His people with different kinds of anointing and in many different ways.

Joel, the prophet, foretold that in the last days, before the coming of the day of the Lord, God would pour out His Spirit upon all flesh and He would speak to His people through visions, dreams and prophecies. This scripture is also quoted in Acts.

> Acts 2:17-18: This is what I will do in the last days, God says: I will pour out my Spirit upon all men. Your sons and your daughters will prophesy; your young men will see visions, and your old men will dream dreams. Yes, even on my slaves, both men and women, I will pour out my Spirit in those days, and they will prophesy. (17)

The Lord has always spoken to His people through dreams, visions and prophecies.

How does the Lord speak to us and teach us by His Spirit?

I cannot speak for anyone else so I will discuss my own personal experiences.

Dreaming in color

For the first thirty-six years of my life, I never dreamed in color. While attending a church service one night, I felt unusual movement of the Spirit within the back top part of my head. This was a strange feeling as I never felt this before or since. That night I had my first dream in color. The next day, I asked my wife, who is a science teacher, what was the function of the top back part of the brain. She replied that it had to do with sight. Something happened that enabled me to dream in color. I also see visions or pictures in colors when my eyes are closed.

Baptism of the Holy Spirit

I sought the Baptism of the Holy Spirit for about five months before I experienced the power and the presence of God. I was angry with the Lord because I had not experienced the Baptism of the Holy Spirit or received tongues. I asked the Lord to forgive me for this. On Tuesday evening, the third week of September 1970, a friend laid hands on me and prayed with me for the Baptism of the Holy Spirit. The only thing I felt was a ring of electricity around the top part of my head. Later, as I went home and to bed, I felt electricity going through my feet and legs. This continued all night with the electricity getting stronger, going all over my body. I slept very little that night. It had been raining and misting all night. It was pitch-dark outside.

About four o'clock in the morning, I found myself in the center of a strong, roaring wind whipping around my body, penetrating into my flesh at a thousand miles an hour. This wind whipped around inside my ears so strong that my inner ears were bruised and tender for several days afterward. My lips started moving a hundred miles an hour the moment the wind started. I was frightened and very tense. While this was going on, I had an apparition of our Lord Jesus Christ, face to face. His eyebrows and nose were flush against my eyebrows and nose. His eyes were looking directly into my eyes. The vision was as in a bright, soft light in clear colors and details. Our eyes were so close; I could see the blood pumping in the blood vessels in His eyes. I could see traces of a yellow mucous coating on the white of each eye. His eyes were blue and crystal clear. I could see parts of His cheek and face. His skin was an olive complexion. The Lord's eyes were very peaceful and calm. The vision lasted about a minute. The strong wind continued around my body and my ears and lips for another thirty seconds after the vision. The electricity continued afterward in my legs for about a week. The bright daylight encounter with the Lord was a great contrast to the pitch-black darkness, rain and drizzle at four o'clock in the morning. The thoughts that went through my mind afterward were how easy it would be for the Lord to flash every detail of our life before us in color and how insignificant we really are. We exist only because of His love for us. I did not receive tongues or a personal prayer language until several months later. The Holy Spirit also came as a mighty roaring wind on the 120 disciples on the day of Pentecost.

An anointing electrical sensation

I first felt an electric anointing on my lower legs and feet before I experienced the Baptism of the Holy Spirit. I do not know what this anointing means other than the presence of God. I used the term, "an electrical anointing" due to the lack of a better description or explanation.

I asked my prayer partner to pray about an electricity-type anointing:

> Just as a generator produces power, so do I. The electricity you are feeling comes from what is being produced inside. Look inside yourself and see what I have done and am doing with you. Spend time in solitude and reflecting on Me and what I want to do through you. It must be you and Me. Make time to come to be with Me alone, not for others, but just be with Me.

Healing type of anointing

One day a friend called asking me to pray for a mutual friend who had fallen against the edge of a counter-top cutting a deep gash on the upper base of his lip under his nose. The doctor put stitches both on the outside and inside of his lip, but told him he would have to have plastic surgery. When I turned to the Lord in prayer, a very heavy surge of mild electricity, goose bumps and chills went through my head and body. I did not know what was going on. I later learned that my friend's lip was instantaneously healed, and he did not have to have plastic surgery. This heavy surge of electricity going through my head and body is an anointing which I usually experience when a healing has been manifested.

Jesus felt healing power leaving His body.

In Mark 5:25-34, a woman with hemorrhage touched Jesus' garment and was healed. Jesus turned around and asked "Who touched my clothes?" as He felt healing power leaving Him.

> Mark 5: 25, 28 –34: There was a woman afflicted with hemorrhages for twelve years....She said, "If I but touch his clothes, I shall be cured." Immediately her flow of blood dried up. She felt in her body that she was healed of her affliction. Jesus aware at once that power had gone out from him, turned around in the crowd and asked, "Who has touched my clothes?"...The woman realizing what had happened to her, approached in fear and trembling. She fell down before Jesus and told him the whole truth. He said to her, "Daughter, your faith has saved you. Go in peace and be cured of your affliction." (3A)

Healing power leaving Jesus is one of the manifestations of the Spirit. Jesus walking through a crowd was touched by many people but He felt healing power leaving His body. He knew that someone specifically was healed. Jesus had to ask who touched Him. All He knew was healing power had left him. The woman felt healing power in her body and knew she was healed. With fear and trembling, she identified herself as the one who had touched Him.

Jesus wants us to be filled, anointed, led and guided by the Spirit just as He was. I have felt a strong surge of power pass through my body, when I prayed for people and a healing was manifested. There are times when one prays, one will feels a light anointing of the Spirit. This is the Lord saying, "I have heard your prayer. Stand firm, believe, and fight the fight of faith until your prayer is manifested. You are doing what I want you to do.".

Heat

When a group of people laid hands on me and prayed for my hearing, the top center of my head got very hot. It was so hot that I felt I had been burned. That spot, the size of a silver dollar, was sensitive to the heat of the sun for several months afterward. I have no explanation for this. The healing of my ears was not manifested at that time.

Heat in my feet and legs

From time to time, I feel heat in my feet and lower legs. Though this heat is hot, it is not a burnt feeling as it was in my head. There are times when the heat is so intense, I have to take my shoes off. To me, this heat is the presence of God. Sometimes, this heat will stop immediately and a cool sensation will prevail. This heat will often manifest itself when I walk into a prayer meeting or when I am in prayer. There are times when this heat will be present for a week or more. This has been going on for years.

After describing the electricity and heat in my feet and legs, the thought occurred that the electricity and heat are anointing of the Holy Spirit and obviously have a meaning and a purpose. I asked a friend to pray with me to ask the Lord to give us the meaning of the electricity and heat. While in prayer the following words came to us.

> Electricity is a discharge of ions in the physical world, a physical force of ionic exchange within matter. Electricity within the body is salvation of the soul, which has been brought up to God, an exchange or gravitation of one's spirit into God's hands.

> How God relates to His people: When a man prays for an unsaved person, this prayer is "POWER." Power in the physical world, as seen in electricity, is an outburst of ionic exchange. Charges are built up and stored in clouds and when the imbalance of charges becomes overwhelming, a burst of electricity is sent forth.

> Electricity represents the salvation of one's soul. A soul is sent to heaven into God's hands. It becomes a part of the Light for evermore. When one prays, this prayer in effect is symbolic of ionic storage that is occurring in the heavens. The ionic storage is deposited and accrues to the point where an outburst of electricity is likely to occur at any time. When the electricity bursts, it means a soul is now in God's hands.

The heat within your body relates to the ionic storage. A soul is climbing its way into God's care and control each time a prayer is sent forth. Once a soul reaches the highest step of the stairway, the harvest is near and at any point in time a soul is likely to be saved.

Heat in the palm of my hands

When this heat was first manifested in the palm of my right hand, I quickly jerked my hand as I thought I had touched something hot. When I saw that I had not touched anything hot and the heat continued to be manifested, I knew this was spiritual heat. This heat was manifested on about one-third of the palm of my hand in the area next to my little finger. The heat lasted about ten minutes. Five minutes later, the heat was manifested in the same area of the left hand. About twenty minutes later, as I was taking a walk and praying, this heat was manifested in both hands at the same time.

As I sought the Lord for the meaning of this heat, He revealed that the physical presence of the Holy Spirit in a human body is often manifested through the senses. Heat is one of the means through which the Holy Spirit manifests His presence in a human body.

Jesus, after His resurrection from the dead, was walking with two disciples on the road to Emmaus. After the breaking of the bread, they recognized Jesus. The disciples immediately walked back to Jerusalem to tell the apostles that Jesus has truly been raised from the dead. They said, "Did not our heart burn within us while He explained the scriptures to us on the road to Emmaus?"

> Luke 24:32 They began telling each other how their hearts had felt strangely warm as he talked with them and explained the Scriptures during the walk down the road (16).

Heat is one of the manifestations of the Holy Spirit.

Colors

During my prayer time or when I am just resting with my eyes closed, I will see continuous flashing or moving of colors of purple or green or purple and green. Through discernment of another person, I learned that purple was a call to repentance. When I have done something wrong such as having an angry thought or looked at a woman in a tight sweater, the Lord will sometime flash a purple color or a purple image of what I glanced at. I know this means to repent. Green means new life after repenting.

At times, the Lord will flash a red color. For instance, if I was thinking about something or was going to do something that the Lord did not approve of, I may see a flash of either red or purple which I know means to take another look at what I was thinking about or what I was going to do.

Purple and yellow

Though I have seen the colors of purple and green for over ten years, it was just recently (in the early 1980s) that I saw the colors of purple then yellow, purple then yellow over and over. While in prayer, the Lord revealed that:

Purple is symbolic of sin.

Yellow is symbolic of the Light of the Lord.

Purple that remains with yellow signifies that a person, who has walked close with the Lord, has chosen to retain certain sins in his life. This sin needs to be repented of so that the Lord may continue to bless this person.

The Lord was asking me to pray for this person. He did not reveal who this person was. The Lord wanted me to pray in the spirit so He could deal with this person about this sin through the Spirit.

Check in the Spirit is like a check in your conscience.

A check in the spirit is when your spirit or conscience has an uneasy feeling about something or about doing something. It does not seem right, or you should not do it.

Seeking the Lord for an answer

Sometimes, we have to fast to get an answer from the Lord. When my mother came down with the painful nerve disease, shingles, I started fasting, seeking, and asking the Lord if I should fast for my mother. In a dream during the night of the sixth day of my fast, I saw a picture of myself laying hands on someone and a voice spoke and said,

"Prayer, without fasting, has no authority."

I knew the Lord was telling me to continue my fast. On the fifteenth day of my fast of no food, my mother was healed.

Sometimes, it is essential to fast to get an answer from the Lord just as Daniel had to fast for 21 days to receive wisdom and understanding from the Lord (Daniel 10:2-3).

Buzzing type sound

When I first came into the Spirit, I would hear a buzzing that sounded like there was an insect buzzing in both of my ears at the same time. The first time I had this experience, I talked with a friend about it. He asked me what time it happened. I told him about nine o'clock the night before. He said he had an anointing at the same time to pray for our friend, Bill. Bill was on vacation. When Bill came back, we asked him about it. Bill said he was crossing a narrow bridge on the Mississippi River at Vicksburg in a Volkswagen at nine o'clock. A big 18-wheeler coming in the opposite direction had misjudged the passing room between them and was coming too fast. He said he rolled his window down and told his wife to do the same. While they were passing, they were almost pulled into the path of the truck by the vacuum of air created by the truck.

Through the discernment of another person, I learned that this buzzing sound was an anointing from the Lord, prompting me to pray. When I do not know what, how or for whom I should pray, I pray in the spirit.

This buzzing sound came on me a little after 12 o'clock one Sunday night. I could hardly wake up. I managed to get up and pray. A week later, I learned that my father-in-law was having great difficulty breathing. My mother-in-law said, "Let's go to the hospital." He said, "There is not enough time, just pray." After they prayed, he began to breathe easier. The Spirit gave me an anointing to pray for him at that moment even though I did not know for whom or what I was praying for.

Voices

I have heard audible voices but usually they are inaudible. The first time I heard an audible voice was when I had some doubts about praying in tongues or in the spirit. A person has a tendency to think that he is making up the syllables or sounds he speaks. I had spent the night upstairs at my mother and dad's house. My mother and dad were downstairs but there was no one upstairs. It was after daybreak and the sun was up. I had just awakened but had not yet opened my eyes. I heard an audible voice that was identical to my voice, speaking the identical sounds and the syllables with which I pray in the spirit. I listened to the voice for about 45 seconds before I opened my eyes. When I opened my eyes, the voice stopped. There was no one in the room. The door was shut. I have never heard anyone before or since pray with the same voice, sounds and syllables that I have been given. My voice, sounds and syllables are unusual as I have a severe speech impediment due to a severe hearing loss. I knew the Lord was telling me to have no doubts about the prayer language He had given me.

I have heard inaudible voices of my mother, dad, wife, sons, brother, sisters and others on different occasions calling my name or nickname. I recognize this as a prompting of the Spirit to pray for them. Once, while I was sitting quietly in my office, I heard my wife's inaudible voice saying, "I need help." I simply prayed in the Spirit and asked the Lord to watch over her and to put his angels around her to protect her. I pray in the spirit when I do not know how to pray or know what the need is. Sometimes that person will not know what the need is.

When my wife was home with our last son, she would drive to school and pick up our other two sons to bring them home. One morning, a friend had a prompting from the Spirit to pray for my wife. The friend did not know why but she prayed all day. That day my wife did not come straight home from school but stopped at a store, which she seldom did. When she got home our house had been burglarized. The men that burglarized our home were caught in an armed robbery two weeks later and confessed to the burglary. If my wife and children had come straight home as they usually do, they would have surprised the burglars and could have been seriously harmed. We found out that our friend had prayed all day for my wife on the day of the burglary. We were thankful that our friend was sensitive to the prompting of the Spirit to pray for my wife's and sons' protection.

For years the Lord woke me up in the middle of the night to pray for an hour or two.

Most of the time, I would feel someone (probably my angel) touching me to wake me to pray. When I was very tired or in a deep sleep and had trouble waking up, I would experience intense chest pain. The moment I got up to pray, the pain would stop. Sometimes this intense pain would happen in the middle of the day. This is an unusual type of pain, which I recognize as the Lord asking me to pray.

A man was drilling a water well on our property. He had taken an old cable of fiber wires off of his drilling rig and put a new cable on the rig. While he was rolling up the old cable, I felt pain in my chest. The pain stayed with me indicating the Lord did not want me to just shoot up a quick prayer but to continue to pray. I kept praying in the spirit for about 30 minutes as I did not know for what I was praying. As the driller threw coiled cable on to his pickup, part of the cable with loose fiber wires broke and quickly slapped him across the face. His face, nose and mouth were bleeding. I knew then the Lord had me praying for the protection of his eyes. The pain in my chest stopped after the accident. The loose fiber cable wires could have easily put his eyes out.

Once as I was catnapping in middle of the afternoon in a reclining

146

swivel chair, someone slapped my foot. There was no one in the room. I knew that the Lord or an angel of the Lord was asking me to pray. I have had many experiences of an angel touching me to get my attention.

Another example of the Spirit giving us wisdom and understanding

As I was writing in Chapter 4 in the book *Lifting the Veil of Revelation* (29), I was seeking the Lord for an understanding of the kingdom of iron and clay in Daniel 2. I was trying to comprehend this kingdom being a mixture of iron and clay; how was the iron stronger than clay; and how they will come together in the seed of men but will not adhere to one another. As I was seeking the Lord for an understanding, a voice spoke in a dream and said, "Clay is another element like iron, gold, silver, bronze and stone. Clay is another kingdom that will combine with the kingdom of iron to form one kingdom." I could visualize ten nations of iron and ten nations of clay making a covenant with each other to become one mighty kingdom. At the end they will break the covenant as they will not adhere to one another. This is another example of how the Spirit teaches us, giving us wisdom and understanding.

Seeking the Lord for an understanding

Many theologians believe that the invasion of the army of the north described in Ezekiel 38 and the battle of Armageddon mentioned in Revelation 16 are two separate battles. While comparing Ezekiel and Revelation, the events are same:

1. There is a great earthquake in Israel.
2. The mountains and cities of Israel are leveled.
3. Huge hailstones of a hundred pounds fell causing great destruction.
4. Call for the fowls of the air to feed on the great supper of our God.
5. The Lord fights for Israel. The rest of the people are killed by the sword of the Lord.

I said Lord, "The events are identical in both battles. How can I show that these two battles are one and the same?" I prayed for three days

147

asking the Lord for an understanding. While I was pacing the floor at 5 am praying and praising the Lord, words came to me that the mountains of Israel can be leveled only one time. If the battles are two separate events, where are the mountains to be leveled in the second battle? Since the mountains can be level only once, this proves that the battle in Ezekiel and Revelation are one and the same.

Visions or pictures

When the Lord wants me to pray for someone, most of the time, he will show me a picture of that person. I have these visions or pictures when my eyes are closed. Though some pictures are without color or are blurred, most of the pictures are in color and in sharp details just as if you are actually there in person seeing everything with your natural eyes.

At times, I will be praying with a blank mind and a picture or movie-type scene will come floating by and will be almost gone before I am aware of it.

Parables or symbols

The Lord has always spoken to His people in parables or in symbols. The Lord continues to speak to His people in parables or symbols, just as He spoke to Joseph about the seven lean ears of corn swallowing the seven fat ears of corn and seven lean cows swallowing the seven fat cows. Or the man in Nebuchadnezzar's dream with the head of gold, breast and arms of silver, belly and upper thighs of bronze, two legs of iron, and feet and ten toes of clay and iron (Daniel 2). Or to Peter about the unclean animals coming down out of heaven (Acts 10:9-16).

When the Lord speaks to us in parables or symbols, we have to pray and seek the Lord for an interpretation and understanding. For an example, I had a vision of two blue eyes looking at me. Blue is symbolic of holiness but for some reason, I knew these eyes were evil. I asked a friend to pray with me for discernment and meaning of the vision. After praying, the following words were spoken to me.

Do not be deceived by those who would appear in the eyes of men to be holy. For not all holiness is of God. The Pharisees appeared to be holy. However, they were empty shells and dead inside as Pharaoh of ancient Egypt. Be cautious in trusting yourself to those who appear to be holy. Trust the Spirit of God that seems to be present in them. Not all of the men that came to me were of God, My Father. There were those who wanted to use Me for themselves and for the benefit of others, such as Judas Iscariot. Know this My son, I have given you all wisdom and knowledge to discern the intentions of those who would come in the appearance as holy men. I am in charge. Trust in Me, for this is the Lord God Yahweh Who speaks.

This is an example how the Lord continues to speak to His people in visions, dreams and symbols with an interpretation.

The Spirit gives guidance

When my son, Michael, was twelve years old, he went with a youth group to Six Flags over Texas. He wore a tank-top shirt with straps over the shoulders. He was really sunburned after being in the sun all day. He could not stand to be touched or washed with a wet washcloth.

We turned to the Lord and rejected the sunburn. We asked the Lord to heal him completely and asked that his skin would not peel. In the middle of the night, while I was asleep, I heard my son's voice saying, "Dad." I replied "Yes, Mike," but when I opened my eyes, he was not there. I went to his bedroom and he was sound asleep. I knew the Lord was asking me to pray. I went to the front room to rejoice and dance before the Lord, thanking him for healing my son. I did this for about thirty minutes and then went back to bed. As I got in bed, I saw a vision of my son so I knew the Lord was asking me to continue to pray. I prayed a little while longer, then I saw another vision of my son, but somehow I knew the angel of the Lord had gotten through and he was healed. The next morning, Michael did not have a sunburn. He was completely healed. His skin did not peel. This is an example of how the Spirit gives us guidance in praying and fighting a spiritual battle.

The Spirit helped us to witness to people.

I had just returned from a noon-hour church service and was having a quiet time with the Lord before I had to start to work. During this quiet time, a word "ablux" was spoken to me, then a flash of purple, which I knew meant to repent. I did not know what this word meant. I called a friend to see if it might be Hebrew word. She said, she thought the word was French. There was a woman in our company that knew French. When I called her, she said she didn't have a dictionary with her but to check with a person in my building. I did not know this person in my building knew French. I asked her if she knew what this word meant. She said she would get her dictionary and come to my office. She looked up this word and said it meant to wash, to purify or to clean. Then she said, "Where did you get this word?" I told her I was going to be honest with her. While I was having a quiet time with the Lord, this word was spoken to me, then the Lord said to repent. She said, "Mike, I believe you," then tears started flowing down her cheeks. She said I did not have the word spelled right but it was spelled as it was pronounced. I talked to her about the Lord. I had only a casual relationship with her and did not know she knew French. I do not know French, yet, the Spirit used this to enable me to witness to her.

The Lord's anointing witness to our spirit that the Lord heard our prayer

Oftentimes, when I turn to the Lord in prayer asking for a request or when I lay hands on someone and pray, an anointing of chills and goose bumps will come upon me. I interpret this as the Lord saying, "I have heard your prayer. Just have faith and believe that it will come to pass."

A belt in a pair of trousers

A friend and I were praying about this chapter, as I had just finished "Being sensitive to the anointing, prompting and guidance of the Spirit."

As we were praying, the Lord showed us a picture of someone wearing blue trousers with a belt. The belt was loose and the trousers kept slipping down until he tightened his belt to keep his trousers up. We turned to the Lord for an interpretation and an understanding of this picture. The following words came to us:

> The anointing of the Holy Spirit is for a purpose. It keeps you in tune with God and in line with His Word just as a belt keeps your trousers up. You must have the support of the Holy Spirit to keep in line with God's will.

All of these things, which have been revealed to me, are mentioned to give glory to God and to bear witness to the working of God's Spirit, who is quiet and gentle in speaking to us, teaching us, comforting us, strengthening us, directing us and guiding us.

Being sensitive to the anointing, prompting and guidance of the Spirit as our life or lives could depend on it.

Prior to leaving for a vacation trip into Mexico, I had a vision of a sign on the edge of town that gives the name and population of the town. I was not able to read the sign. The Lord said, "Do not be concerned about the sign. Be concerned about your driving and keeping your eyes on the road." My prayer partner saw an oncoming curve on the road.

While my wife and I and another couple were in Villadama, Mexico, I woke up in the middle of the night with a strong check about driving on to Mexico City. I got up and prayed for an hour. Afterward, I received peace about going on. While we were driving in central Mexico the next day, two big 18-wheelers were rounding a curve toward us. A car was passing the 18-wheelers in our lane. This was a narrow, two-lane road with posts and wire guards on the roadsides to protect us from the big slope off our side of the road. There was no room to get off the road. Our driver pulled over as far as he could. The car miraculously passed between the eighteen-wheelers and us. I know this was the Lord and his angels protecting us.

This was the oncoming curve and danger the Lord warned us about prior to the trip. This was the reason for the strong check in the middle of the night. If I had not prayed and received an OK from the Lord to continue on to Mexico City, we could have easily been killed in a head-on collision. It is imperative that we are sensitive and obedient to the Lord's voice as our lives could depend on it.

Years earlier, my son, Michael received understanding that he needed to be sensitive to the Lord's voice as the day was coming when his life would depend on it. This was definitely a life threaten situation for his mother and dad.

Discernment

When we see a picture or vision, have a dream, receive a thought or hear an audible or inaudible voice, we need to discern whether the source is God, self, or Satan and his angels. Satan and his angels can manifest their presence and speak to us in the same manner as the Holy Spirit.

> 2 Corinthians 11:14:...For even Satan disguises himself as an angel of light (3).

> Galatians 1:8: For even if we, or an angel from heaven, should preach to you a gospel not in accord with the one we delivered to you, let a curse be upon him! (3).

> 2 Thessalonians 2:1-2: Now we request you, brethren,... that you may not be quickly shaken from your composure or be disturbed either by a spirit or a message or a letter as if from us,...(1).

> Jeremiah 29:8-9: For thus says the Lord of hosts, the God of Israel, "Do not let your prophets who are in your midst and your diviners deceive you, and do not listen to the dreams which they dream. For they prophesy falsely to you in My name; I have not sent them," declares the Lord. (1)

Always ask the Lord, "Is this vision, dream, thought, voice or person speaking to me from Him?" Otherwise, you can get all kinds of interpretations and answers. Even a person with the gift of discernment can be deceived. I was concerned because one person with the gift of discernment would say this is not of the Lord. Another person would get a powerful message. I asked the Lord about this. This is the message I received:

> When you pray for discernment and hear from one prayer partner that the message is not from God and another says plainly and powerfully, that it is, you are to realize that you are under constant spiritual attack. God has given you many ears and prayer partners because all men are imperfect and Satan can get through in some way in each of them. That is, each man has some weakness in his spiritual defenses. Do not worry about this situation. God's words to you are so powerful that it will get through. Each prayer partner is called to feel God's anointing in some area because he wants to minister to them. That area is usually where they are strong.

There are times when a prayer partner will say something is from the Lord when it is not or he will give the wrong interpretation. There are times when two different prayer partners will give two different messages, yet both are from the Lord. One should always seek the Lord for more than one discernment or confirmation on whether a message or a vision is from Him. When we continue to seek the Lord for understanding, His message will always come through.

Distinguishing the spirits

Discernment is one of the gifts of the Holy Spirit that God gives to help us to distinguish the spirits.

> I Corinthians 12:4-5, 7-8, 10: Now there are varieties of gifts, but the same Spirit. And there are varieties of ministries, and the same Lord....But to each one is given the manifestation of the Spirit for a common good. For to one

153

is given the word of wisdom through the Spirit, to another the word of knowledge according to the same Spirit;...;... to another the distinguishing of the spirits,...(1)

Test the spirits

John tells us not to believe every spirit but to test the spirits that speak to us to see if they are of God.

> I John 4:1-3, 6: Beloved, do not trust every spirit but put the spirits to a test to see if they belong to God, because many false prophets have appeared in the world. This is how you can recognize God's Spirit: every spirit that acknowledges Jesus Christ come in the flesh belongs to God, while every spirit that fails to acknowledge him does not belong to God. Such is the spirit of the antichrist which, as you have heard, is to come; in fact, it is in the world already....We belong to God and anyone who has knowledge of God gives us a hearing, while anyone who is not of God refuses to hear us. Thus do we distinguish the spirit of truth from the spirit of deception. (3)

> I Corinthians 14:29: And let two or three prophets speak, and let the others pass judgment (1).

> I Thessalonians 5:19-22: Do not quench the Spirit; do not despise prophetic utterances. But examine everything carefully; hold fast to that which is good; abstain from every form of evil (1).

How do we test the Spirit?

1. Do you have a peace about what you saw or heard (pictures, dreams, voices, etc.)?
2. If it is a voice, does it acknowledge Jesus Christ as Lord?
3. If the spirit teaches anything contrary to scripture, have nothing to do with it. This is where it is essential to know God's Word.

4. Counseling - check it out with someone who has the gift of discernment.
5. Circumstances - does everything fall into place smoothly? Does everything fit together like pieces into a jig-saw puzzle or are there some questions?
6. If it is from the Lord, He will confirm it in two or more ways.

In praying for insight and understanding, it is essential to bind Satan and all lying and deceiving spirits each time we pray. When we do receive understanding, we need to discern if the message is from the Lord. The scriptures encourage us to test everything to see if it is of God. If it is of God, He will confirm it and you will have a peace about it.

Cutting the Bible to get a message from the Lord

Some people open the Bible at random to get a message from the Lord. There are times when the Lord does speak to us when we cut the scriptures at random. Two examples are discussed in the next chapter. Nevertheless, we know that the Lord does not speak to us each or every time we cut the Bible.

The Lord has given us an intellect to make intelligent decisions. We do not cut the Bible to determine if the Lord wants us to put salt and pepper on our eggs. If one cuts the Bible to where it says, "Judas went out and hanged himself," we need to understand that this certainly is not a message from the Lord to go out and hang oneself.

A humiliating experience

After experiencing the baptism of the Holy Spirit, I was really on fire for the Lord. I had witnessed the Lord healing a lady at the Full Gospel Business Men's Convention. The lady wore a three-inch lift on one shoe. Her leg grew three inches right before my eyes. She had to take both shoes off to walk evenly.

Some of my friends had talked to me about being bold, standing on faith and believing, and that the Lord would answer my prayers if I did not waver. My wife was completely turned off by my experience and was not having anything to do with my excitement. A short time afterward, we found out that my wife was expecting. After the prayer meeting, I went to the prayer room and asked for prayers that my wife would start coming to the prayer meetings and since she was expecting that we would have twins. One of the ladies who were praying with me had a vision of two ears of corn. I immediately interpreted this to mean that my wife was going to have twins.

I was bold. I told everyone that my wife was going to have twins even the doctor. It was a very humiliating experience when my wife did not have twins. My actions of standing boldly on faith, fighting all doubts for seven months were very embarrassing to my wife and certainly did not draw her closer to the Lord.

Shortly after the birth of our son, the lady that had the vision of two ears of corn turned to the Lord in prayer to learn the meaning of the two ears of corn. The Lord revealed that the two ears of corn were my wife and I. The following words were spoken to us.

> "My ways are not your ways," saith the Lord. "Look neither to the right nor to left for the Son of Man has need of you in the kingdom. No man having set his hand to the plow should look back. The Master has a plan and a purpose for your life and knows every hair on your head. He has need for your family so give them to Him. Two are better than one, and when bound together in mind and will, they will bear much fruit. Seek My will, know My will, do My will and great shall be the blessing on your house."

If I had turned to the Lord to determine the meaning of the vision of the two ears of corn, it would have spared my family a lot of embarrassment. Though my wife was very embarrassed and I would have liked to drop out of sight, I knew the Lord was saying that once you have set your hand to the plow you cannot look back. You have to accept the humiliating experience as a lesson and move forward.

When the Lord shows me a picture of someone I know, I understand that he is asking me to pray for this person. From time to time I have seen a picture of my boss. In my heart, I said, "Oh no! Lord, what have I done now?" not realizing at the time that the Lord was just asking me to pray for my boss.

It is easy to get the wrong impression or meaning of a picture or vision or a dream. There are many books on interpreting dreams and visions. There is great danger of getting the wrong interpretation when using these books to interpret dreams and visions.

When one has a dream or a vision, he needs to ask the Lord if the dream or vision is from him. If it is, one needs to continue praying for an understanding.

On several occasions, I have let a friend interpret my dreams or visions according to his book on dreams. At the same time, I asked another friend to pray with me seeking the Lord for an understanding. The understanding received in prayer was entirely different from the interpretation coming from the book. The interpretations by prayer made more sense, and I had a peace concerning the interpretation.

Pharaoh's wise men could not interpret Pharaoh's dream of seven fat ears of corn being swallowed by seven lean ears of corn and seven fat cows being swallowed by seven lean cows. Joseph was able to interpret Pharaoh's dream only by a revelation from the Lord.

It is very important that we ask the Lord if the dream or vision is from Him and seek Him for an interpretation and understanding to keep from being deceived.

To determine God's will and direction for our lives, it is essential that we spend time in prayer, study and read His words daily, keep a notebook and be attentive and sensitive to the prompting and guidance of the His Spirit. The Lord has a great love for each of us. He wants to be the center of our life. He wants us to come to Him daily and seek His purpose, plan, directions, and guidance that He has for each of us.

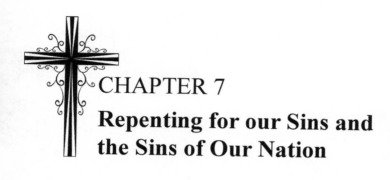

CHAPTER 7

Repenting for our Sins and the Sins of Our Nation

While in prayer early in the morning of January 19, 1984, somehow in a vision, I was walking on the grounds of the U.S. Capitol with some of the national monuments in the background. As I walked on the sidewalk through the park, I saw a soft white moon-like light in the sky in the form of a long trumpet. The sky was purple.

The Lord had previously revealed to me that purple was a call for repentance. In the Old Testament, the trumpet was an instrument used to give certain signals or calls to the people. In Matthew 24:31, the Lord sends His angels with a loud trumpet call prior to the gathering of His elect. Because the moon-like trumpet was in a purple sky in the presence of the U.S. Capitol, I felt the Lord wanted to sound a trumpet call to the people of this nation to repent for their sins and for the sins of their leaders and their nation. The Lord is asking the people to repent and turn from their sins and their wicked ways, and to pray for a spiritual revival so that this nation may be restored as one nation under God.

As I continued to seek the Lord about the meaning of this vision, the following words were spoken to me:

> The pen is mightier than the sword and
>
> My sword is the sharpest pen known to mankind.
>
> Take up My pen which is My Word and
>
> write about the need for national repentance.
>
> Do this now in order that
>
> you will be ready to publish it at the appropriate time.

All that is important for you to know at this time is that

I would have you to write about the need for repentance
in your nation.

Trust in Me for the message of repentance in your land
must come forth.

I believe the Lord wants me to share what He has taught me about
repentance. In 1970, the Lord started speaking to me about repenting
for my sins. I started confessing every possible sin I could think of. The
Lord started bringing to my attention sins committed in my youth and
teenage years.

I was born two and one-half months prematurely with a severe
hearing loss resulting in a severe speech impediment. I could hear the
vowels but not the consonants. I talked with the back of my throat. There
was no speech therapy in grade or high school. I did not have any speech
therapy until I started to college. This was when I learned to move my
lips and tongue to form the correct syllables and to learn to talk. Though
I learned to talk so people could understand me, I still had a severe
speech impediment, as there were many consonants I was never able to
pronounce correctly.

Because of my hearing loss and speech impediment, some of the
children would mock me or make fun of the way I talked. I had deep
anger against some of these kids. The Lord started speaking to me about
repenting for my anger and frustration and to forgive these children and
teenagers for they truly did not know what they were doing. I had to
forgive people who had hurt me. I had to ask for forgiveness from the
people I had hurt.

Even after two years of repenting for everything I could think of, the
Lord kept telling me to repent. Finally one night at a prayer meeting a
scripture was read where Jesus said, "Anything asked of the Father in
His name, He will do it." I said, "OK Lord, you keep telling me to repent
and I can not find anything in my life at this time to repent for. Please tell
me for what you want me to repent."

I do not have a habit of opening the Bible at random to get a scripture;

however, the next morning in prayer I cut the Bible to the ninth chapter of Daniel. This whole chapter shows Daniel fasting and praying, in sackcloth with ashes on his head, interceding before the Lord, repenting for his sins, the sins of his people and nation.

> Daniel 9:3-5, 19-20: So I gave my attention to the Lord God to seek Him by prayer and supplications, with fasting, sackcloth, and ashes. And I prayed to the Lord my God and confessed and said, "… we have sinned, committed iniquity, acted wickedly, and rebelled, even turning aside from Thy commandments and ordinances…O Lord, hear! O Lord, forgive! O Lord, listen and take action! For Thine own sake, O my God, do not delay, because Thy city and Thy people are called by Thy name. Now while I was speaking and praying and confessing my sin and the sin of my people Israel, and presenting my supplication before the Lord my God in behalf of the holy mountain of my God, (1)

Daniel was a righteous and holy man of God; yet, the scripture teaches that Daniel repented for his sins and the sins of his people and nation. Daniel interceded before the Lord with petitions, prayers, supplications and fasting. When I opened the Bible to the ninth chapter of Daniel, I knew the Lord was asking me to fast, pray, intercede and repent for the sins of the people and leaders of our nation so the Lord's wrath would not be poured out on us as it happened to Jerusalem and Israel during the Babylonian captivity.

Fasting

Fasting is a powerful means of prayer and a way of humbling oneself before the Lord. Since the time of Moses, fasting has been very common among the Jewish people and among the Christians in the early history of the church. Jesus began His public ministry by fasting for forty days. When Jesus was asked why His disciples did not fast, He said the days were coming when they would fast (Matthew 9:14-15). When Paul was a prisoner on a ship, everyone on the ship fasted for 14 days in fear for their lives, due to the severe storm at sea (Acts 27:33).

In the early 1970s, I heard Derek Prince give a teaching on prayer and fasting for the sins of our nation. Mr. Prince had a very simple prayer for the leaders of this nation: "Up with the righteous and down with the wicked." These words have been a part of my daily prayer ever since. Mr. Prince requested that Christians unite to fast and pray one day a week for our nation. (39)

Everyone, who can, should be encouraged to fast and pray one day a week not only for our nation, but for personal intentions and for a closer relationship with the Lord. I fasted every week from 1970 to 1998, 28 years except when I was on vacation. In the beginning, I would fast from 2 to 4 days straight on nothing but water or sometimes some coffee or tea. Unless I am on a continuous fast for a specific intention, my fast in the latter part of the 28 years has been twenty-four hours from supper to supper. I learned that it is best to abstain from coffee while fasting, as coffee tends to give you a headache and make fasting more difficult especially on a long fast.

After twenty-eight years of fasting in which at times I would go on a long fast of 5 or 7 or 10 days with nothing but water, I received knowledge from the Lord to go on a 13-day Daniel fast. I was not familiar with a Daniel fast. The scripture in Daniel 10:2-3 said Daniel did not eat any meat or food that was delightful such as dessert or wine. A Daniel fast is one where a person eats mostly vegetables. I received knowledge that I was to eat only one meal a day. This fast is certainly easier than a total fast.

Pains in lower back and right hip

After fasting every week for 28 years, I quit fasting every week in 1998. I developed pains in my lower back and right hip, making it painful getting in and out of bed and turning over in bed. After six months of great discomfort, I received understanding in a dream that this was due to a harassing spirit. I went on a three-day fast of water only. The Lord set me free with no more pain. Fasting with prayer is a very powerful tool, as it gets the Lord's attention quicker than prayer alone.

A man called my name, "Mike" three times. I did not recognize the voice or see anyone. Then purple flashed before me three times:

> The man is the Lord. He wants you to continue to repent for the sins of this nation.

Vision of an irregular purple star that starts off as a small dot that gets bigger and bigger. The purple fades then start all over again as a dot:

The Lord has revealed to me that "purple" means to repent. My prayer partner received the following words:

> You have been praying for your friends and relatives. They sin and it grows, then your prayer and petition washes away that sin. I am asking you to pray that they will pray and repent. I await your action in prayer that I may see Satan and his angels fall and My people will be set free from the weakening of repeated sin. I am excited that you now know. Don't wait! I am excited with antici-pation of your petitions.

Not acknowledging and worshipping God

One of the most serious sins is not worshipping God. It appears that very few people in America acknowledge or worship God. Most of the people who call themselves Christians do not worship or praise God for Who He is. We do not thank Him for our family, our homes, our food, our indoor plumbing facilities, our modern conveniences, our medical profession, our modern means of transportation and communication, and many other blessings. Most of all, we do not thank Him for our freedom and the privilege of living in this great nation, America.

Most Christians do not go to church or only go a few times a year, if it is convenient. We do not spend time each day in prayer or reading and studying God's words (40). We prohibit our children from praying and asking the Lord for His blessing, help and protection at schools. We discourage praying in public or displaying of religious pictures, symbols or scenes.

There is nothing we can do or give the Lord, except to worship and praise Him for Who He is, and to thank Him for everything He has done for us. The Lord desires this, and we are obligated to worship and praise Him.

Agnosticism

Some people claim to be agnostic, i.e. they do not know whether there is a God or not. This scripture teaches that there is no man that does not know that there is a God.

> Romans 1:18-21: The wrath of God is being revealed from heaven against all the godlessness and wickedness of men who suppress the truth by their wickedness, since what may be known about God is plain to them, because God has made it plain to them. For since the creation of the world God's invisible qualities - his eternal power and divine nature - have been clearly seen, being understood from what has been made, so that men are without excuse. For although they knew God, they neither glorified him as God nor gave thanks to him, but their thinking became futile and their foolish hearts were darkened. (2)

Every man knows instinctively within his heart that there is a God, therefore, there is no excuse. Everyone - atheists, agnostics, skeptics, non-believers and believers know in their hearts that there is a God, but they do not give Him honor and glory. This is a serious sin. Everything one does is recorded in the book of life. Life is like a vapor of smoke, here one second and gone the next. All men, who do not honor and worship God, will be without excuse on the Day of Judgment.

Turning from sin is a decision

The sins of the flesh are an abomination to the Lord our God. Some people have a desire to look at pornographic magazines or nude pictures.

I had this problem. Although I have never bought a pornographic magazine, just glanced at some in the store, I knew this was wrong and asked the Lord to take this desire away. After struggling with this problem for several years and not turning away from it, the Lord revealed to me and taught me, through a series of events over a three-month period, the seriousness of this sin, and that turning from sin was a decision. The Lord was not going to take away my free will or desire to look at nude pictures. It was obvious to me that I had to make a decision to turn from this natural desire. Turning away from sin was a decision that had to click in my mind.

The Lord will not take away our free will, desires or natural attractions. He wants us to control our desires to please Him by striving to be pure and holy. Love and sex is lovely, beautiful and wholesome within the sacrament of marriage as designed by God. Sex is the highest expression of intimate love a man and wife can experience.

Looking at a nude picture or statue or nude work of art, itself, is not wrong unless it leads one to sin or to entertain thoughts that are sinful. Michelangelo's classical works of art in the Sistine Chapel are full of nude men and women. Nude pictures or statues that are a work of art are not usually designed to cause sexual excitement. Pornographic magazines or X-rated movies depict erotic scenes designed to cause sexual excitement. The scripture tells us that it is a sin to entertain lustful thoughts, which is what happens when one reads pornographic magazines, looks at X-rated movies or reads sex novels. Pornography and obscene videos are very destructive to a married couple as it destroys the deep, close, sacred intimacy and love between a man and his wife. While men are usually sexually excited, women are not. Women feel rejected, violated and abused, causing the normal sexual act to be repulsive.

Adultery and lust

Thou shall not commit adultery. Thou shall not look at a woman to lust for her.

> Matthew 5:27-28: You have heard that it was said, "You shall not commit adultery; but I say to you, that everyone

who looks on a woman to lust for her has committed adultery with her already in his heart." (1)

This scripture shows that we can commit sin through the thoughts we entertain.

In a dream, which I feel was from the Lord, I received knowledge that it is wrong to fantasize sexual activities that are forbidden by the scriptures. I had a strong understanding that I was to write about this. A man or a woman, when having sexual relations with the spouse, cannot fantasize that he or she is having sexual relations with another woman or man. The scriptures teach that it is wrong for a man or woman to have sexual relations with someone, who is not the spouse.

> Proverbs 6:29, 32: So it is with the man who commits adultery with another's wife. He shall not go unpunished for this sin....But the man who commits adultery is an utter fool, for he destroys his own soul. (16)

The scriptures teach it is wrong to have sex prior to marriage.

> I Corinthians 7:8-9: So I say to those who aren't married, and to widows - better to stay unmarried if you can, just as I am. But if you can't control yourselves, go ahead and marry. It is better to marry than to burn with lust. (16)

The temptations to entertain lustful thoughts will come, but if one rejects these thoughts, he does not commit a sin. However, if one entertains these thoughts, he commits a sin.

Job made a covenant not to look with lust on any woman.

> Job 31:1-4: I made a covenant with my eyes not to look with lust upon a girl. I know full well that Almighty God above sends calamity on those who do. He sees everything I do and every step I take. (16)

Homosexuality

God loves everyone, sinners and all, including those who are homosexual. It is morally wrong to attack or harm a person who is a homosexual.

I had a vision of someone whittling a long square pole, 50 feet or so long to make it round. I asked the Lord the meaning of the vision. The Lord said:

> The people who would justify their godless behavior, are like a man, who would see a long square pole and decide it is round. When he tries to use the square pole to fit a round hole, he is forced to whittle and scrape and shape the square pole to get it to fit. What you see are the lies, excuses, deceits and other devious acts of men trying to promote an illicit lifestyle, which will never fit God's plan. They are doomed to fail.

The scriptures, both Old and New Testaments teach that the homosexual act is wrong.

> Leviticus 20:13: If a man lies with a male as with a woman, both of them shall be put to death for their abominable deed: they have forfeited their lives (3).

> Judges 19:23-24: "No, my brothers; do not be so wicked. Since this man is my guest, do not commit this crime. Rather let me bring out my maiden daughter or his concubine. Ravish them, or do whatever you want with them; but against the man you must not commit this wanton crime." When the men would not listen to his host, the husband seized his concubine and thrust her outside to them. They had relations with her and abused her all night until the following dawn, when they let her go. (3A)

> Romans 1:24-28: Therefore God gave them over in the lusts of their hearts to impurity, that their bodies might

be dishonored among them. For they exchanged the truth of God for a lie,...For this reason God gave them over to degrading passions; for their women exchanged the natural function for that which is unnatural, and in the same way also the men abandoned the natural function of the women and burned in their desire towards one another, men with men committing indecent acts...And just as they did not see fit to acknowledge God any longer, God gave them over to a depraved mind, to do those things which are not proper... (1)

Second translation:

Romans 1:24-28: In consequence, God delivered them up in their lusts to unclean practices; they engage in the mutual degradation of their bodies, these men who exchanged the truth of God for a lie and worshiped and served the creature rather than the Creator – blessed be he forever, amen! God therefore delivered them up to disgraceful passions. Their women exchanged natural intercourse for unnatural, and men gave up natural intercourse with women and burned with lust for one another. Men did shameful things with men, and thus received in their own persons the penalty for their perversity. They did not see fit to acknowledge God, so God delivered them up to their own depraved sense to do what is unseemly. (3)

Another translation says

Romans 1:24-28: So God let them go ahead into every sort of sex sin, and do whatever they wanted to - yes, vile and sinful things with each other's bodies. Instead of believing what they knew was the truth about God, they deliberately chose to believe lies. So they prayed to the things God made, but wouldn't obey the blessed God who made these things. That is why God let go of them and let them do all these evil things, so that even their women turned against God's natural plan for them and indulged in sex sin with each other. And the men, instead of having a normal sex relationship with women, burned with lust for each other, men doing shameful things with other men and as a result, getting paid within their own souls with the penalty they so richly deserved. So it was that when they gave God up and would not even acknowledge him, God gave them up to doing everything their evil minds could think of. (16)

Those who condone homosexuality, saying that homosexuals have no control over their desires or are not responsible for their actions, are wrong. The scripture says they know in their heart what they are doing is wrong. A married person may have a strong desire to lust and commit adultery. This desire does not make it right. A person has to control himself and turn away from thoughts and desires that lead to sin.

The gays keep saying they are gay because they were born that way – God made them that way. I asked the Lord about this statement.

My Word is clear. It is a perversion of darkness. It is an abomination to My Spirit. It is a devious lie and a tool of Satan.

A person is not born a homosexual. It is a choice. A homosexual is a person who has chosen to be one.

John Leary received the following message .

Jesus said: "My people, I know that many of you had difficulty looking at a gay marriage which I abhor in My Church. I created man and woman to be joined in marriage and not same sexes. This is an open defiance of My institution of Marriage between a man and woman in the sacrament of Matrimony. I love all peoples, but relations between same sexes are as sinful as two of the opposite sex living together in fornication. This is not about rights, but it is against My Commandment.

Only relations under the marriage covenant are lawful." (41)

The scriptures teach that homosexuals and those involved with the sins of the flesh will not inherit the kingdom of God.

> I Corinthians 6:9-10: Or do you not know that the unrighteous shall not inherit the kingdom of God? Do not be deceived; neither fornicators, nor idolaters, nor adulters, nor effeminate, nor homosexuals,...shall inherit the kingdom of God. (1)

> Jude 7: Likewise, Sodom, Gomorrah, and the surrounding towns, which, in the same manner as they indulged in sexual promiscuity and practiced unnatural vice, serve as an example by undergoing punishment of eternal fire. (3A)

Homosexuality is one of the sins that destroyed Sodom and Gomorrah. Genesis 19 shows that when the two angels came into Sodom, the men of the town wanted to make love with them, which is the sin of homosexuality. Lot offered these men his two virgin daughters, pleading with them not to touch the two angels.

> Genesis 19:7-8: "I beg you, my brothers, not to do this wicked thing. I have two daughters who have never had intercourse with men. Let me bring them out to you, and you may do to them as you please. But don't do anything to these men." (3A)

The sins of the flesh are an abomination to the Lord our God. For this reason, God destroyed Sodom and Gomorrah.

Turning from sin is a decision. Homosexuals, who truly want to be set free from this sin, can be set free by repenting and truly turning to the Lord seeking His help and guidance. With God's grace and help, a person can be set free.

Lesbians

While praying the following prayer, the Lord gave me to pray for a lesbian's friend; I decided to include others, that I am aware of, who are lesbians.

> You can not pick and choose My words to you. It is either true or not. You either accept all of it or none of it. Do not fear about your physical health for I am a God who heals. Do not rebel. Obey and live.

While saying this prayer, I had a vision of a woman in front of me who sleepishly raise her head and open her eyes and eyebrows in a manner as to acknowledge my prayer. The Lord said:

> You are entering a world where no one is going to pray. This is a desert. There is no water here, no oasis. Those involved are lost. Some want to change. There is no one here to pray. The battle is being lost every minute. Their weakness is overshadowed by the great sin. The enemy has the high ground. She was awakened by your prayer.

Prayed for a friend who is a homosexual. The Lord speaks:

> I would have you meet my love. He knows not love. He has great hurt. He has covered his hurt with evil. He has chosen this life as a way of acceptance. These are linked to his mother and father. He is hiding his spirit and his soul. The pain is great. He will be destroyed for his decisions. It will take many great battles to have the doors opened for his salvation.

Masturbation

Masturbation is wrong as the following scriptures show that a man or a woman can not have sex alone.

I Corinthians 7:2-4:...let each man have his own wife,

and let each woman have her own husband. Let the husband fulfill his duty to his wife, and likewise also the wife to her husband. The wife does not have authority over her own body, but the husband does; and likewise also the husband does not have authority over his own body, but the wife does. (1)

I Corinthians 7:8-9: But I say to the unmarried and to the widows that it is good for them if they remain even as I (Paul never married). But if they do not have self control, let them marry; for it is better to marry than to burn. (1)

A man has no authority over his body, only his wife. A woman has no authority over her body, only her husband. If a single person cannot control himself, he should get married. It is better to get married than to disobey God and suffer the consequence. Sex alone or with any person other than one's own husband or wife is wrong as the scripture clearly states. Homosexuals do not qualify as husbands and wives, as they are of the same gender.

Abortion

When an egg and a sperm are united and conception take place, is there a child present? Let us see what the scriptures teach.

Luke 1:26-27,30-31: Now in the sixth month the angel Gabriel was sent from God to a city in Galilee, called Nazareth, to a virgin engaged to a man whose name was Joseph,...And the angel said to her, "Do not be afraid, Mary; for you have found favor with God. And behold, you will conceive in your womb, and bear a son, and you shall name Him Jesus. (1)

Mary asked the angel how this could happen since she was a virgin.

Luke 1:35-36: And the angel answered and said to her, "The Holy Spirit will come upon you, and the power of the Most High will overshadow you; and for that reason

171

the holy offspring shall be called the Son of God. And behold, even your relative Elizabeth has also conceived a son in her old age; and she who was called barren is now in her sixth month. (1)

After the angel departed, Mary left immediately for the hill country to visit her cousin, Elizabeth. The distance from Nazareth to Judah was no more than a two or three-day journey.

Luke 1:38-41:...And the angel departed from her. Now at this time Mary arose and went with haste to the hill country, to a city of Judah, and entered the house of Zacharias and greeted Elizabeth. And it came about that when Elizabeth heard Mary's greeting, the baby leaped in her womb; and Elizabeth was filled with the Holy Spirit. (1)

Now notice in the following passage that Elizabeth spoke through the utterance of the Holy Spirit. She called Mary a mother even though Mary had conceived only two or three days before. Elizabeth could not have known that Mary was a mother except through the revelation of the Holy Spirit. At this time Elizabeth still had three months to go before the birth of John the Baptist.

Luke 1:42-43: And she cried out with a loud voice, and said, "Blessed among women are you, and blessed is the fruit of your womb! And how has it happened to me that the mother of my Lord should come to me? (1)

The scriptures teach that Mary was a mother at the moment of conception. She was with child as soon as conception took place. It was at the moment of conception that the Son of God was incarnated into a human body, not nine months later. Even though there was only one cell present at the moment of conception, that one cell was the temple of the Son of God. The Son of God was present and living in that one cell at the moment of conception.

The scriptures teach that when an egg and sperm are united and conception takes place, a child, i.e. a life is present. This is shown by the fact that Elizabeth, under the anointing of the Holy Spirit, called Mary a mother within two or three days after Mary consented to the angel to be the earthly mother of God's Son. The incarnation of the Son of God (Who is Spirit) into a human body, with a human mind, took place at the moment of conception.

When a child is conceived, the spirit, soul and body are all created at the moment of conception to form a child. All the ingredients of a human being are present at the moment of conception. The body that grows and develops within the womb is only an earthen vessel or a house for the soul and spirit. Once a child is created, the soul and spirit will live forever, regardless of whether the child's life is terminated before leaving its mother's womb or whether the child lives to full maturity. When a man dies, his body returns to dust while the soul and spirit either return to the Lord or go to hell.

The child who has an opportunity to live, love, honor, worship, obey and serve God, has an opportunity to earn high rewards, honor and glory for all eternity. God wants every life that is created to have this opportunity. The child, whose life is terminated, does not have this opportunity.

The Lord knew each one of us before we were conceived in our mother's womb. He knew our personality, looks, likes and dislikes long before we were conceived and born.

> Jeremiah 1:5: Before I formed you in the womb I knew you (1).

The Lord will never forget us, regardless whether our life was terminated in the womb or whether we lived to full maturity.

> Isaiah 49:15: Can a mother forget her infant, be without tenderness for the child of her womb? Even should she forget, I will never forget you. See, upon the palms of my hands I have written your name. (3A)

The scripture called the unborn infant of the womb a child.

A friend said abortion is the sacrifice of unborn children to the gods of pleasure and convenience. To prevent the completion of the life of a child within a womb is murder.

Pope John Paul II wrote:

How can one morally accept laws that permit the killing of a human being not yet born but already alive in the mother's womb? (42)

Bishop Robert J. Herman wrote that judgment day is coming. In Matthew 25:31-46, Jesus said what you have done to the least of My brethrens, you have done to Me. To those who has had or performed an abortion, Jesus will say, "I was in your womb, My mother's womb and you took My life." (43)

Our human body is the temple of God.

> I Corinthians 3:16-17: Do you not know that you are a temple of God and that the Spirit of God dwells in you? If any man destroys the temple of God, God will destroy him, for the temple of God is holy and that is what you are. (1)

> 2 Corinthians 6:16:...For we are the temple of the living God; just as God said, "I will dwell in them and walk among them; and I will be their God and they shall be My people" (1).

The human body is the temple of God. When one destroys a human life, whether it is by abortion, suicide, or taking of another person life, one is destroying the temple of God. God said He will destroy anyone that destroys the temple of God.

Is the child within his mother's womb the temple of God?

In prayer with a friend, I asked the Lord if the child within his mother's womb, even at the moment of conception was the temple of God? The following words of knowledge came to us:

> Life itself is a vehicle for the Spirit of God. At concep-tion, a single cell is formed out of the order of God's

Divine Creation Principle, which means that a part of God's own existence is made manifest. This principle of Perfect Creation that God designed is evidence for purity, innocence and holiness with the sinful reality of the world not yet made manifest. What is created is holy and made perfect by the just and righteous hand of God. Due to the nature of man's sinful fall out of perfect holiness in the beginning, however, makes him subject to the spirit of darkness rather than that of Light. This is the reason for the commandments to guide thy son or daughter immediately at the time of physical development within the womb. Guide him steadfastly in the ways of the Lord so that he may spiritually develop a sturdy shield of protection from the Evil One.

I asked the Lord a question and he gave me a deep teaching. I had no intention of putting this teaching into this book. Several days later, the Lord revealed to me that He definitely wanted this teaching in the book.

It is obvious from the words received in prayer that the Lord wanted me to discuss the human body, not only as the temple of God, but as a habitation for the spirits of darkness. I want it understood that I am not talking about the sin of a child, for a child within the womb is not capable of committing a sin.

The Lord revealed that life itself is a vehicle for the Spirit of God. Without God, life cannot exist. The human body was created as the temple of God. A child at the moment of conception is the temple of God. God is dwelling in the temple of that one cell at the moment of conception. That one cell contains all the genes or the keys for the full development of a perfect human body.

God created the human body perfect and holy. However, when man sinned, the body became subject to the habitation of spirits. The following scriptures confirm the presence of evil spirits in human bodies:

> Matthew 9:32-33:...behold, a dumb man, demon possessed, was brought to Him. And after the demon was

cast out, the dumb man spoke;…(1).

Matthew 17:18: And Jesus rebuked him and the demon came out of him and the boy was cured at once (1).

Mark 9:25: And when Jesus saw that a crowd was rapidly gathering, He rebuked the unclean spirit, saying to it, "You deaf and dumb spirit, I command you, come out of him and do not enter him again" (1).

Luke 8:29-30: For He had been commanding the unclean spirit to come out of the man. For it had seized him many times;…And Jesus asked him, "What is your name?" And he said, "Legion"; for many demons had entered him. (1)

A child within its mother's womb is defenseless, helpless and subject more to the spirit of darkness rather than to the light because of man's sinful nature. If a woman finds herself pregnant and rejects the child, a spirit of rejection can enter into the child. A mother with a spirit of fear can impart a spirit of fear into her child. Spirits can be passed from generation to generation from parents, grandparents and great grandparents or spirits can enter into a child through the sins of his or her parents. The following scripture confirms this.

Numbers 14:18: The Lord is slow to anger and abundant in loving kindness, forgiving iniquity and transgression; but He will by no means clear the guilty, visiting the iniquity of the fathers on the children to the third and fourth generations. (1)

God created the human body perfectly with no sickness, diseases or defects. However, through sin and the fall of man, the spirits of darkness get in and try to disrupt the Spirit of Life, bringing forth sickness, diseases, birth defects and death.

Health problems and birth defects that are spoken of as being hereditary are in reality caused by the curse of the spirits that were in our parents or ancestors and passed from generation to generation. The fact that spirits try to disrupt the Spirit of Life by causing birth defects, diseases and health problems is demonstrated in the gospels, when Christ healed people by casting out spirits. The scriptures teach that serious sin can lead to serious sickness. This was discussed in Chapter 5.

I am not saying that all sickness is due to spirits. Our bodies need proper food, sleep and rest for proper nourishment and health. If we do not take care of our bodies by eating improper food, wearing improper clothes, not getting the proper amount of sleep and rest or working too hard, we can bring on sickness.

Sin opens the door for evils to attack us.

Spirits can enter into a person when a sin is committed. In the early 1970s, I was attending a convention in New Orleans. I purposely avoided Bourbon Street. While I was walking down another street sightseeing, two topless girls opened two swinging doors and stood at the entrance, just as I walked by. Naturally, being curious as any human being, I turned around to look. The second I turned around, I received a very hard impact against my face and chest, which went through my nostrils down into my lungs, momentarily, taking my breath away. The impact was like a slap in the face and chest. I knew immediately what had happened. When I committed the sin of turning around to look at the topless girls, an evil spirit hit me with a heavy impact entering my body through my nostrils. I immediately repented for that sin and went to confession the next morning. The Lord allowed me to experience the result of sin and an evil spirit entering into my body.

When one commits a sin the door is open for spirits to get in. Fear also opens the door for spirits to get in. Usually one does not feel anything when a spirit enters into his body. The Lord allowed me to feel the impact of the spirit to teach me what was going on.

When the Legion of spirits left the demoniac man at Gerasenes and went into the pigs, the pigs were frightened and ran off the cliff into the sea and downed. The pigs were frightened because they knew something had entered into them. If demon spirits cannot have a human habitation, they will accept an animal habitation (Luke 8:26-39).

The Lord spoke of a commandment to put a shield of protection around thy child from the moment of conception on to guard and protect the infant from the Evil One. I asked the Lord where this commandment was found. He said this commandment is implied rather than stated. After a week of searching and not being able to find it, I turned to the Lord in prayer. After praying, my friend called saying that he felt the Lord wanted him to call me. I told him I was still looking for the commandment to pray for the protection of the unborn infant in the womb. As we began to pray, the Lord told my friend to randomly open the Bible. The Bible was opened to the following scripture.

> Psalm 51:5: But I was born a sinner, yes, from the moment my mother conceived me (16).

This scripture along with Numbers 14:18, shows that unclean spirits can get into a child at the moment of conception. The temple of a child can be defiled by the passing of spirits that are the result of the curse of the sins of his parents or ancestors

> Number 14:18: The Lord is slow to anger, abounding in love and forgiving sin and rebellion. Yet he does not leave the guilty unpunished; he punishes the children for the sin of the fathers to the third and fourth generation. (2)

This is the reason for the Lord's commandment to put a hedge of protection around thy child within the womb. This hedge needs to be put around the child each day to protect the infant from the Evil One. Ephesians 6 speaks of putting on the armor of God each day for protection against the power of darkness. It is essential to keep a hedge of protection around the child, not only at the moment of conception, but throughout his life.

Our battle is not against flesh and blood but against the principalities, powers and unseen rulers of darkness. The reason for discussing this subject is so that one will be aware of the danger and pitfalls, and take steps to protect oneself and the family as one walks down the road of life.

Bill Gothard, in his book, "Institute in Basic Youth Conflicts" gives an excellent case history of how the curse of the sin of rebellion in the grandmother was passed to the daughter and also on to the granddaughter before the bondage was broken. (44) The curse can be broken by repenting for the sin, asking for forgiveness and then breaking the bondage in Jesus' name.

We need to understand the curse and bondage that result from sin so that we do not deliberately commit a sin. Sin destroys our hedge of protection. Usually when one turns from sin, the spirits become restricted in their mode of action, and our hedge of protection is restored.

We need to be aware of the unseen rulers and powers of darkness so that we can take steps to protect ourselves, when necessary. However, we should be very cautious in discussing Satan, his angels and demons, and not focus on them. Once we start talking on the subject of demonic activity, it is difficult to stop.

When I first came to an understanding of demons and fallen angels, they had my full attention. As a consequence, I experienced many kinds of satanic spiritual manifestations. Because of these problems, I asked a deacon to bless my house. He told me not to focus on demons but to keep my eyes on the Lord. These manifestations left when I quit talking and thinking about them. As long as we talk about demons, Satan, instead of the Lord, is getting all the attention and glory.

The Lord gave me road signs as an example in dealing with evil spirits.

Dealing with demons and fallen angels is like driving a car down the road. Road signs are placed along the side of the road or highway to warn the driver of oncoming curves, slopes, road conditions, etc. The Christian walk with God is the same way. The Lord wants us to be aware of the enemy as He gives us signs to foretell us of impending danger or attacks from the enemy. However, just as we do not focus our attention on the road signs depicting dangerous curves that would incline us to take our eyes off the road and cause us to have an accident; we should not focus on unclean spirits that might hinder us from a true Christian walk with the Lord.

We need to be aware of unclean spirits so that we can deal with them to protect ourselves. However, when this is done, we need to turn our eyes to the Lord, so that we can continue our Christian walk.

> Luke 9:49-50: It was John who said, "Master, we saw a man using your name to expel demons, and we tried to stop him because he is not of our company." Jesus told him in reply, "Do not stop him, for any man who is not against you is on your side." (3)

If the Lord did not intend for us to be involved in exorcism why did the Lord give me the example of road signs above.

Camping trailer, electrical problems and evil spirits

We had used our 16-foot camping trailer a number of times with no problem with the trailer lights. We were leaving on a Friday night in the 1970s to go on a vacation. When we hooked the trailer lights to a trailer socket on the car, the lights were all messed up. When the left turn signal was turned on, the brake light came on. When the right turn signal was turned on, the left turn signal light came on. When the brake was pushed, the right turn signal light came on. All the lights on the trailer were functioning incorrectly. The next morning, we took the trailer to a dealership. I attempted to demonstrate what had happened the night before. However, when I turned the right turn signal on, the brake lights came on. This was entirely different from the night before. The trailer people said this could take all day to fix. When the lights performed differently from the night before, I knew this was spiritual attack. We took the trailer home. After reading the prayer of exorcism from the Roman ritual, all the lights functioned correctly. The trailer lights were working properly on previous trips. There was no reason for the trailer lights to function improperly, if they had functioned correctly before, as we were just connecting two sockets together. This demonstration taught me that evil spirits can get into electrical equipment.

Deep freeze and icemaker in the refrigerator

When our freezer quit working, we called the repairman two times. After repairing the freezer for the second time, it quit working again a week or so later. I asked my wife to turn to the Lord and find out why we could not get the freezer fixed. She lay on the floor before the freezer praying. When our two sons came home from elementary school they said, "Mommy what are you doing?" She told them she was asking the Lord why we have not been able to get the freezer fixed. She asked our two boys to pray with her for understanding. The boys said, "Mommy, there is something in this house the Lord wants you to get rid of." She told the boys to go out and play. Ann sat down on the couch in the living room in front of the library. The Lord made known to her the books on the bookshelves that he wanted her to get rid of. My wife filled a large laundry basket full of books. Ann had not read these books. When she finished college, her girl-friend gave her all of these books. These books involved the occult, witchcraft, false religions, and things that were not of the Lord. Ann had merely wanted a pretty library. My wife bought a few books because the covers were at-tractive; she had no idea what the books were about. After we destroyed these books, the repairman was able to fix the freezer. The icemaker in the refrigerator had not made ice in over a year. The moment we destroyed the books, the icemaker started working on it own. This shows that evil spirits can manifest themselves in electrical equip-ment. The Lord does not want us to have books on magic and witchcraft in our home.

Those who practiced magic brought their books together and burned them.

Seven sons of a Jewish chief priest attempted an exorcism in Jesus' name. The evil spirit said he knows Jesus and Paul but who are you? The man with the evil spirit viciously attacked the seven sons who left the house wounded and naked. Those who practice magic were frightened and brought all of their books on magic together to be burned.

> Acts 19:19: And many of those who practice magic brought their books together and began burning them in the sight of all; and they counted up the price of them and found it fifty thousand pieces of silver. (1)

Can Satan read our mind?

A friend told me Satan could not read our minds. For several months I thought about this, trying to think of a way to put Satan to the test. When I pray in tongues, Satan harasses me pretty quick, usually with pictures or other thoughts to distract me. I made the decision to lie down really still, pretending that I was asleep with my eyes closed. I was going to pray in tongues with my mind without moving my lips or tongue. Thirty minutes went by before I was physically slapped on the leg and heard a loud horrible scream, as if someone had been burned or severely hurt. I knew then that Satan could not read my mind. Satan knew someone was praying, but he did not know where the prayers were coming from. Finally, he figured that they had to be coming from me. When my prayer partner and I prayed for an understanding about the horrible scream, the Lord said that while I was praying in tongues, my spirit was praising God. Satan cannot stand for us to praise God. Satan knew someone was praying due to the activity of the angels. For Satan to hear, we must rebuke him with a voice. We can silently ask the Lord to put a hedge of protection around us.

How does Satan know when we commit a sin with our mind or thought?

Once I allowed my feelings to be hurt and some resentment to come in. Suddenly, I had a crick in my neck. I thought to myself, if Satan cannot read our minds, how did he know that I had committed that sin. So I asked my prayer partner to pray with me for an understanding. This is what the Lord said: There is a hedge of protection around you. Satan and his angels try to attack you at all times. When you commit a sin, your hedge of protection falls down and Satan and his angels can get through. Satan does not know we commit a sin until our hedge or wall of protection falls down.

Dealing with spirits

When I pray for someone with a serious illness, I have someone with the gift of discernment to pray with me to discern what is going on. I ask the Lord if there is a spirit or spirits involved and if he wants me to cast them out. If yes, the Roman Ritual tells us:

1. to commands the spirits to identify themselves,
2. to tell us when they got in,
3. to tell us by what authority they are in.

The spirit will identify itself by its name such as fear or the name of the sin that was committed. A frightening experience will open the door for fear, and allow other spirits to get in. In praying for a person with fear, I ask the Lord to go back to that moment and time the spirit got in and to heal this person. I rebuke the spirit of fear in Jesus' name and quote the scripture II Timothy 1:7 "For God hath not given us the spirit of fear; but of power, and of love, and of a sound mind." (35) Then I call forth a spirit of peace. Then I ask the Lord if there are any other spirits involved.

If a spirit identifies itself by naming a sin, I ask when it entered the person. This tells me if the person committed the sin or if it came down through the ancestors. I repent for the sin to break the bondage and then cast the spirit out. The person with the gift of discernment will discern if the spirit has been cast out. There are times when one has to do a lot of praying and fasting to get the victory. For an example, if the sin is unforgiveness, I will repent for the sin, then command the spirit of unforgiveness to come out in Jesus' name, then I call forth a spirit of forgiveness to come in and fill the void.

SEVEN VITAL TRUTHS FOR GOD'S CHILDREN

Recently we prayed for a young man suffering from high blood pressure, who has had this problem for several years. He spent five days in the hospital as they had trouble getting his blood pressure down. My prayer partner discerned that this high blood pressure was due to sins committed by the young man's great grandparent. Another prayer partner confirmed this. I repented for each of the sins as they were identified by quoting I John 5:16 "If you see a brother or sister commits a sin which is not into death, you shall pray, and it shall be forgiven them (paraphrase)." The Lord revealed that my friend and I were to go on a three days fast to seal the victory. The young man was not present when we prayed for him, but he said that he was not having any more problems.

> I John 5:16-18 If anyone sees his brother commit a sin that does not lead to death, he should pray and God will give him life. I refer to those whose sin does not lead to death. There is a sin that leads to death. I am not saying that he should pray about that. All wrong doing is sin, and there is sin that does not lead to death. We know anyone born of God does not continue to sin. (2)

A spirit in the chamber of my heart.

While in prayer with a friend seeking an interpretation of a vision I had, my friend received knowledge that some brothers in the Lord had mistreated me. This was discussed in Chapter 5. My friend was not aware of this. Though this knowledge was related to the interpretation of the vision, this knowledge, itself, was not the interpretation of the vision.

It has been at least two years since I repented of my anger, bitterness, and resentment toward my brothers and made the decision not to cultivate these thoughts again. I thought this was strange that the Lord brought this up or that my friend was even aware of this mistreatment. Nevertheless, I thought about this, off and on, for the next three weeks, and anger flashed through my mind a couple of times.

One morning, as I was driving to work, a crick came upon my neck making it uncomfortable to turn my head in one direction. I did not pay much attention to this, thinking that it was the way I slept or something. During the noon hour, when I was having a quiet time with the Lord, an inner voice spoke and said, "As you aged for three years, I grew in the chamber of your heart."

I asked another friend to pray with me for discernment. My friend believed that this was a voice of an evil spirit. For the next three days I sought the Lord for an understanding of what was going on. After spending two hours on my daily prayers one Saturday night, I started trying to figure what sin I had committed that would open the door for the spirit to get in. I began putting two and two together. My neck was uncomfortable. I remembered that I had a problem with my neck when I had some anger and bitterness against my brothers. I knew I had cultivated thoughts on this mistreatment, off and on, for the last three weeks. I remembered that the Lord had dealt with me on this bitterness for three years before I turned from it. Suddenly, I knew this inner voice was the spirit of anger and bitterness and he was saying that as I aged with anger and bitterness in my heart for three years, he grew in the chamber of my heart for three years. Even though I had repented for this sin two years ago, the spirit was still within me. I immediately repented for my thoughts of anger and bitterness. The next morning while I was in Church, my neck was still stiff. The thought came to me to pray in the spirit for my neck. I prayed briefly for a minute or two. After church, the stiffness in my neck was gone.

Dealing with anger

A week after getting rid of the stiffness and tightness in my neck and shoulder, it came back again. I began to examine myself to seek an understanding of what was going on. I had just had a dream in which the Lord gave me the freedom to act and make decisions as if I were awake.

In the dream someone got upset with me over something for which I was responsible but had no control over. Even though I told this person I would make everything right, this person continued to be upset with me. Eventually, I got angry, though it was not an outward expression of anger. It was anger within. I knew from the dream that the Lord was dealing with me about anger.

My wife and I have had a happy and blessed marriage. However, as in all marriages, there are times of frustration when things do not go right or we cannot have our way. My wife was fussing at me because I have been repairing, building and adding on to our house for most of our married life and never seemed to get everything completed. While on a long walk with my wife one afternoon, she became critical of me for not getting the house finished. I understood her frustration. I should have hired someone to help me to do part of the work, instead of trying to do it all myself. As she got angry with me, I continued to listen but got angry within and tried not to focus on it. I never thought of this as being anger, as the subject was soon dropped and this sort of thing had been going on all of our married life. It was part of being married. When we got home my neck and shoulders were tight and stiff. As I prayed about my neck and shoulder, the Lord told me to repent for my anger. I told the Lord I would repent, but He was going to have deal with my wife about being fussy and grumpy. Immediately, I had a vision of a rainbow. The rainbow was a sign of the covenant God made with Noah to never destroy the world by flood again. I knew the Lord was saying if I will control my feelings of anger, He would deal with my wife. Two years later to the day of the vision of the rainbow, the Lord showed me a picture of the bride and groom figurine that was on our wedding cake. He told me that He had fulfilled the covenant He had made with me. He had truly dealt with my wife. This took place in the early 1980s.

When we have anger, bitterness or resentment in our heart against our spouse, family, friends or business associates, regardless of how justified we are, we are offending God, our Father. This anger hurts us more than the person with whom we are angry, for it will eat us up inside, eventually making us sick.

As long as we hold a grudge against another person, we keep ourselves as well as the other person in bondage. It is foolish to have and to hold on to anger, frustration and resentment on things over which we have no control. If we will control our anger and forgive the other person for what has happened, then we are set free, and the Lord will deal with the other person.

There is a time for righteous anger such as when Christ drove the money changers and merchants out of the temple, overturning their tables, scattering their coins and animals (John 2:14-16). However, Christ did not continue to nurse or hold a grudge against these people. He was angry at the moment for what they were doing.

Pride

Pride is the beginning and the root of all sins with its focus being self-centeredness.

> Sirach 10:12-18: The beginning of pride is man's stubbornness in withdrawing his heart from his Maker; For pride is the reservoir of sin, a source which runs over with vice; Because of it God sends unheard-of afflictions and brings men to utter ruin. The thrones of the arrogant God overturns and establishes the lowly in their stead. The roots of the proud God plucks up, to plant the humble in their place; He breaks down their stem to the level of the ground, then digs their roots from the earth. The traces of the proud God sweeps away and effaces the memory of them from the earth. Insolence is not allotted to a man, nor stubborn anger to one born of woman. (3)

Pride was the sin that led to Lucifer's rebellion against God. It led to Adam and Eve's desire to be like God and know the difference from good and evil. Disobedience and rebellion are the results of the sin of pride. There are many types and degrees of the sin of pride. The most serious is when one turns completely away from God, putting all of his trust, and confidence in oneself. The sin of pride also involves those who have faith, trust and belief in God but focus their attention on themselves, having an inordinate love of self. Pride includes self-exaltation; having an excessively high opinion of one's importance, ability or superiority; or trying to overwhelm others with things one has, has done or has accomplished. A person can have too much pride in his birth, wealth, physical qualities, knowledge, education, position, rank, etc.

Pride is not giving God the credit or glory for who and what we are, and for our accomplishments. Man must remember that he is dust, from dust he was created. All that a man is, his abilities, accomplishments, and everything he has, is a gift from God. (45)

Pride is when we get our feelings hurt.

Gordon Lindsay told a story of a young lady who did not understand the sin of pride. She asked a minister for an understanding of the sin of pride. The minister looked at the young lady and said, "How can you ask such a stupid question?" The young lady turned red in the face, as her feelings were hurt. Then the minister said, "That is pride!" Pride is when we get our feelings hurt. There is no one who has not had his feelings hurt at one time or another.

Pride is a subtle sin, of which most of us are not aware, and it is the cause of many sins and problems. When we get our feelings hurt, then come anger, unforgiveness, resentment, bitterness, hatred, rage, murder, etc. Pride is the root of all sin, and it opens the door for serious sins and sickness.

Pride is a complex sin, which lies deep down, half-hidden as the seed. It foments many sins, of which we rarely suspect the origin. Pride is self-centered, feeding and growing on self-gratification.

Pride is something that all of us, even those who have a close walk with the Lord, have to work to keep under control. Pride is the biggest obstacle and hindrance to spiritual growth and perfection. Scripture says, "God resists the proud but gives grace to the humble". Man needs grace, which is God's help to be humble. (46)

We need to control our tongue.

James 3:1-10: Dear brothers, don't be too eager to tell others their faults, for we all make many mistakes; and when we teachers of religion, who should know better, do wrong, our punishment will be greater than it would be for others. If anyone can control his tongue, it proves that he has perfect control over himself in every other way. We can make a large horse turn around and go wherever we want by means of a small bit in his mouth. And a tiny rudder makes a huge ship turn wherever the pilot wants it to go, even though the winds are strong. So also the tongue is a small thing, but what enormous damage it can do. A great forest can be set on fire by one tiny spark. And the tongue is a flame of fire. It is full of wickedness, and poisons every part of the body. And the tongue is set on fire by hell itself, and can turn our whole lives into a blazing flame of destruction and disaster. Men have trained, or can train every kind of animal or bird that lives and every kind of reptile and fish, but no human being can tame the tongue. It is always ready to pour out its deadly poison. Sometimes it praises our heavenly Father, and sometimes it breaks out into curses against men who are made like God. And so blessing and cursing come pouring out of the same mouth. Dear brothers, surely this is not right! (16)

The tongue is a flame of fire, full of wickedness and poison that can literally destroy another person. When we speak against a person, we not only hurt, harm or destroy that person, but we are offending God, bringing judgment on ourselves.

I had a vision of a man sitting on the floor with a long tongue hanging out of his mouth full of red sores. I asked a friend to pray with me for understanding. These are the words that my friend received.

Beware the sins of the tongue. They will come back to haunt you. Beware how you talk about anyone; politician, professional, enemy, lost soul or friend. If you speak ill of anyone, your words are like daggers. They damage those who hear them and those of whom you speak. My people must speak a positive message or they will become sick from their words. Make it your special work not to speak ill of anyone.

Forgiving another person

If we cannot forgive another person how can the heavenly Father forgive us?

> Matthew 6:15: But if you do not forgive others their trespasses, their reckless and willful sins, leaving them, letting them go and giving up resentment – neither will your Father forgive you your trespasses (sins). (5)

There are times when we have been hurt to the extent that we cannot forgive someone for what has happened. If we cannot forgive that person for their sake, we need to forgive that person for Christ's sake because that is what Christ asked of us. We need to forgive that person for our sake, for resentment, bitterness and unforgiveness will bring on serious sickness and destroy us, if we do not forgive and ask the heavenly Father for his forgiveness. When we forgive someone, this means we are willing to turn loose of our bitterness and resentment, and forget about what has happened. We do not bring up the subject again. It is difficult for us to forgive someone on our own. We need to ask the Lord to help us to forgive that person.

While praying for discernment for someone who would not forgive the spouse, we received these words:

> Unless my people forgive each other as I forgive them,
>
> there will be no peace between them.
>
> Are you perfect?
>
> Are your thoughts always pure?
>
> Have you never sinned against me?
>
> Who are you to hold a grudge?
>
> Behold, if you do not forgive, and
>
> if you do not try to heal the hurt you have caused,
>
> then I will not forgive you.
>
> I will not heal you.

The Lord chastises those whom he loves.

Hebrew 12:5-11: Have you forgotten the encouraging words which God speaks to you as his sons?

"My son, pay attention when the Lord punishes you, and do not be discouraged when he rebukes you. Because the Lord punishes everyone he loves, and chastises everyone he accepts as a son."

Endure what you suffer as being a father's punishment; because your suffering shows that God is treating you as his sons. Was there ever a son who was not punished by his father? If you are not punished as all his sons are, it means you are not real sons but bastards. In the case of our human fathers, they punished us, and we respected them. How much more, then, should we submit to our spiritual Father and live! Our human fathers punished us for a short time, as it seemed right to them. But God does it for our own good, so that we may share his holiness. When we are punished, it seems to us at the time something to make us sad, not glad. Later, however, those who have been disciplined by such punishment reap the peaceful reward of a righteous life. (17)

Sometime this chastisement is in the form of sickness. Once in praying for a person we received knowledge that his sickness was due to anger, bitterness, resentment and unforgiveness.

Not all sicknesses or afflictions are due to sin. While I was asleep, I clamped down so hard on my left teeth, that I broke one tooth, unknowingly snapped the nerve on the tooth next to it and severely bruised a third tooth. The pain was very intense. I did not get much sleep from Wednesday through Monday. On Monday the dentist did a root canal. I asked the Lord, why He permitted this to happen. Had I committed a sin or done something wrong? He said,

"No! This is so you can share a little in My suffering."

Greed and covetousness

Many people have an avid desire for money, material goods, power and wealth. Some people will do almost anything to get these things. The love of money is the root of all evil.

> I Timothy 6:10: For the love of money is the root of all evil: which while some coveted after, they have erred from faith, and pierced themselves through with many sorrows (35).

Money itself is not evil. It is the love and desire for money that is evil. A person who has no money can be guilty of this sin.

Man did not bring money into the world, and he will not be able to take money with him when he leaves.

> I Timothy 6:7: For we brought nothing into the world, and obviously we cannot take anything out of the world (5).

Yet, man pursues money, material goods, power and wealth as though it is the only means of security. People conduct themselves as though they will live forever, giving little or no thought as to where they might spend eternity. Jesus gave an example of this in a parable of a rich man.

> Luke 12:16-21:...The ground of a certain rich man pro-duced a good crop. He thought to himself, 'What shall I do? I have no place to store my crops.' Then he said, 'This is what I'll do. I will tear down my barn and build bigger ones, and there I will store all my grain and my goods.' And I'll say to myself, 'You have plenty of good things laid up for many years. Take life easy, eat, drink and be merry.' But God said to him, "You fool! This very night your life will be demanded from you. Then who will get what you have prepared for yourself?" This is how it will be with anyone who stores up things for himself but is not

rich toward God." (2)

The rich man had enough money to live several years without having to work. His only thoughts were his comfort, pleasure and security at this moment. His desires were to enjoy the leisure of life, without any thoughts about God or life after death.

The Lord called the rich man a fool and said that his life would be taken from him that night. The rich man was not able to enjoy the wealth he had accumulated nor was he able to take it with him.

Life on this earth is not even one second in contrast to eternity. Yet, the rich man had not given any thought to God or where he might spend eternity. The rich man lived as though he was going to live forever. Unaware and unexpectedly, the rich man's life was taken from him.

Lay up treasures in heaven

Rewards on earth are temporary, while rewards in heaven are for all eternity.

> Matthew 6:19-21: Do not store up for yourself treasures on earth, where moth and rust destroy, and where thieves break in and steal. But store up for yourselves treasures in heaven, where moth and rust do not destroy, and where thieves do not break in and steal. For where your treasures is, there your heart will be also. (2)

Taxes

The scripture teaches that we are obligated to pay taxes.

> Romans 13:5-7: For this reason you must obey the authorities - not just because of God's wrath, but also as a matter of conscience. This is also the reason that you pay taxes; because the authorities are working for God when they fulfill their duties. Pay, then, what you owe them; pay them your personal and property taxes, and show respect and honor for them all. (17)

Those that connive, deceive, and cheat the government out of money by not paying their taxes are stealing. If everyone paid his taxes then the few who are paying their taxes would not have to carry the whole load.

Those that are in position of authority and are responsible for the use of taxpayers' money are obligated to use this money wisely. Fraud, bribes, kickbacks in business or the misuse of taxpayers' money is morally wrong.

Lack of justice

One of the serious sins of this nation is the lack of justice. Today, criminals have more rights than the victims of crime. Criminals should be promptly punished for their crimes to serve as deterrence to crime.

God has given those who rule over us the rights to punish those who commit crime.

> Romans 13:1-5: Everyone must obey the state authorities; because no authority exists without God's permission, and the existing authorities have been put there by God. Whoever opposes the existing authority opposes what God has ordered; and anyone who does so will bring judgment on himself. For rulers are not to be feared by those who do good but by those who do evil. Would you like to be unafraid of the man in authority? Then do what is good, and he will praise you. For he is God's servant working for your own good. But if you do evil, be afraid of him, because his power to punish is real. He is God's servant and carries out God's wrath on those who do evil. For this reason you must obey the authorities - not just because of God's wrath, but also as a matter of conscience. (17)

Capital punishment

The scripture teaches that murder is wrong. If a man unjustly takes another man's life, he shall also be killed.

Genesis 9:5-6: And murder is forbidden....and any man who murders shall be killed; for to kill a man is to kill one made like God (16).

Another translation says,

If anyone takes human life, he will be punished....Man was made like God, so whoever murders a man will himself be killed by his fellowman (17).

Matthew 5:21: Under the laws of Moses the rule was, "If you kill, you must die" (16).

When a man unjustly takes another man's life, he forfeits his right to life. The Lord expects those in authority to carry out this justice.

When Pope John Paul II came out against capital punishment, I asked two different prayer partners on two separate occasions to pray with me and ask the Lord if I should change what I had written about capital punishment. Both prayer partners said I was not to make any changes. A friend said Pope John Paul II taught that capital punishment is just only if all "bloodless alternatives" are dangerous or unavailable.

The Lord wants justice

The Lord wants those who commit a crime to be promptly punished. The Lord despises the innocent being punished or the guilty being set free.

Proverbs 17:15: Acquitting the guilty and condemning the innocent - the Lord detests them both (2).

Only when justice is dealt promptly and quickly, and criminals are required to make restitution to the victims, will crime be deterred.

Violence

The permissiveness, infidelity, rapes, beatings, murders, profanity, violence and destruction shown on videos, TV and movies today have hardened the hearts of the people, especially the children, making them insensitive and encouraging them to violence, cruelty and destruction. If a frog is placed into a pan of hot water, the frog immediately senses the danger and will jump out. If a frog is placed in cold water, which is slowly heated to a boil, the frog fails to recognize the danger and is boiled to death. Our society is like the frog being boiled to death in water. The immoral movies and talk-shows are a parade of dysfunctional, sinful, and immoral lifestyles which are desensitizing the people, especially the children, from being able to differentiate between right and wrong, leading the family and nation down a path of moral decay and destruction.

The immorality and violence are destroying the moral fiber of the family and the nation. Shootings on the freeways and into homes, killing innocent people just for the thrill of it, or the insensitive killing of a person to take his gold or silver chrome car wheels has been encouraged by the murders, beating and violence seen on videos, movies and TV.

The Lord calls us to focus on all that is pure, all that is holy, and all that is righteous. As parents, we must turn off the TV on illicit programs. We must take an active role in deciding what our children watch. We cannot afford to let the TV be a babysitter.

Our nation, America

Though there are many religious beliefs in America, this country was founded as one nation under God. Our nation has been greatly blessed because our forefathers upheld the belief in the principles of the Bible. Our nation is a nation composed of people from many nations, languages, customs, heritages and beliefs standing united as one nation under God.

America was a strong nation because of its strong family and religious ties. Families encouraged their children to go to church, to worship God and to obey his commandments. Children were taught to be honest, loyal, trustworthy, helpful, hard working Americans that were obedient and respectful to their parents, to God and to their nation. The families were proud of their national heritage and were proud to be Americans. Strong families were the backbone of our nation.

The best way to destroy our nation is to destroy the family. This is exactly what is happening in America today. In the 1950s and 1960s, divorce was a rarity. Today, divorce and destruction of the families and homes is rampant. Pornography, X-rated movies, nudity and violence encourage promiscuity, adultery, incest, rape, homosexuality, dishonesty, and lack of trust, which not only destroys the family and the home but affects the community, and nation.

Today, the leaders of this nation are acting and ruling contrary to the principles upon which this nation was founded. The Supreme Court has banned school prayer; thus preventing our children from praying to the Lord, asking for his help, blessing, protection and guidance. They have given a woman the right to abort and murder her child. Most of the leading candidates for president in recent years have endorsed the gay bill of rights and support a woman's right to terminate the life of her child.

Is there any reason why our nation is in such a state of trepidation and moral decay? When one's moral principles are gone, then lying, cheating, stealing and drugs also become prevalent. The Roman Empire was not destroyed by outside forces but by the destruction of moral values. Divorce, destruction of homes and moral decay were rampant at the fall of the Roman Empire, as they are today in America.

America has been the most blessed and prosperous nation in the world because it was founded as one nation under God. Now America has turned from the Lord by stopping school prayer, permitting abortion, murder, pornography, homosexuality, lust, sins of the flesh, greed, etc. to pollute the land.

Our nation is on a course of rapid destruction. Unless we, the people and the leaders of this nation, repent for our sins and turn from our wicked ways and return to the Lord and to the moral principles upon which our nation was founded, we will be destroyed.

The people and the leaders of this nation cannot act, govern and rule contrary to the principles of God's laws and survive. Unless we return to the moral principles of the Bible, which produce strong families, our nation cannot survive. Strong families are the backbone of a strong nation. The restoration of this nation must begin with the restoration of the families. It is imperative that the family be protected and unified under God, as outlined in the scriptures in order to have a healthy nation.

The Sacrament of Marriage

What God has joined together let no man put asunder.

> Mark 10:6-9: But from the beginning of creation God made them male and female. For this reason a man shall leave his father and his mother and be joined to his wife, and cleave closely to her. And the two shall become one flesh, so that they are no longer two but one flesh. What therefore God has united - joined together - let not man separate or divide. (5)

When a man and a woman get married, they make a covenant with each other before God to honor, to love, to care and to be faithful to one another for better or for worse, in sickness or in health, in riches or in poverty until death separate them. This covenant is a commitment to be faithful and loyal to each other and to work together to make the marriage work in spite of any hardship, inconvenience, difficulties or storms that may come forth on their journey through life. A marriage is not a 50 –50 proposition. In a marriage both the husband and wife must be willing to give a hundred percent on their part, especially under circumstances such as sickness. A stable marriage is one in which both husband and wife work hard to make their marriage successful. If a man and a woman get angry at the other, they should forgive and make up and be reconciled with each other before going to sleep.

> Ephesians 4:26-27: If you are angry, don't sin by nursing your grudge. Don't let the sun go down with you still an-gry - get over it quickly; for when you are angry you give a mighty foothold to the devil (16).

A family that works together and prays together will stay together.

That a man is the head of the household does not mean that he is to dominate his wife and family or mistreat them. A man and a woman are equal partners. A man is to listen to, consider and respect his wife's opinion and discernment before making any decision in any matter which involves and affects the family.

Divorce

I do not wish to bring any condemnation on anyone who has gone through a divorce or has remarried. God is a loving, kind and forgiving Father. Those that have gone through a divorce or have remarried need to seek counseling and God's guidance in rebuilding their lives.

Nevertheless, the scriptures teach that God hates divorce. Divorce destroys the family. Divorce destroys the covenant relationship between a man and his wife and it hurts their children.

> Malachi 2:14-16:...It is because the Lord is acting as the witness between you and the wife of your youth, because you have broken faith with her, though she is your partner, the wife of your marriage covenant. Has not the Lord made them one? In flesh and spirit they are his. And why one? Because he was seeking godly offspring. So guard yourself in your spirit, and do not break faith with the wife of your youth. "I hate divorce," says the Lord God of Israel, "and I hate a man's covering himself with violence as well as with his garment," says the Lord Almighty....(2)

> Matthew 5:31-32: It was also said, "Anyone who divorces his wife must give her a written notice of divorce." But now I tell you: if a man divorces his wife, and she has not been unfaithful, then he is guilty of making her commit adultery if she marries again; and the man who marries her also commits adultery. (17)

Most divorces are the result of the sin of selfishness, pride and unwillingness to remain faithful and committed to their marriage covenant of remaining together in spite of all the storms and difficulties encountered in life.

God does not bring condemnation on a person's state in life. God does bring conviction on a person to put his life in order. It is difficult for a man to make these corrections on his own effort. However, a person repenting for his sins and asking God's help with the power of the Holy Spirit operating through Christian counseling and other avenues and with the sanctification of God's grace, reconciliation with God is made easy. A person has the option of making many choices in life. However, our relationship with God is not optional.

The restoration of our nation must begin with the family. The lawmakers of this land have a responsibility to make laws to protect the family. Laws must be passed to make it difficult for a family to get a divorce. Counseling needs to be provided to help families solve their problems, especially before it gets out of hand. Pastors, lawyers and judges have a moral responsibility to try to save the marriage and the family.

Laws must be passed to protect the lives of unborn children and to protect families from pornography, X-rated movies and detrimental TV shows that encourage lust, unfaithfulness and sin, which destroy the family. The lawmakers and rulers in this nation must let God's laws and the principles of the Bible guide their conscience in making decisions, which affect the family and the people of this nation. It is essential that a period of courtship be required with counseling so that a man and a woman know each other and their likes, dislikes, faults and their compatibility, before making a serious lifetime, binding commitment to be husband and wife.

A man and a woman need to have some mutual interests and some things in common before getting married. Sex and children will not hold a marriage together. Sex is only a physical expression of love between a man and his wife. It takes a commitment on the part of both the man and the woman, working together, to hold a marriage together.

The restoration of our nation must begin with a change in the heart of the people to worship God, to protect the family and the lives of the children.

The Women's Liberation Movement and Equal Rights.

I want it clearly understood that I am not against women or women working outside the home. My wife is a school teacher. Most of us are sympathetic and understanding, when we speak of equal rights for women. We feel that a woman that does the same quality and quantity of work as a man should receive equal pay and benefits. However, the term Equal Rights is deceiving as the women leaders the Women's Liberation Movement all appear to be anti-family and anti-God.

I do not intend to discuss the Women's Liberation Movement and how they are attempting to destroy the family. There are a number of good books on this subject. Two such books are *Attack on the Family* by James Robinson and *The Assault on the Family* by Dr. James M. Parsons. My intentions are to cite a few public and written quotes and utterances by the main leaders of the Women's Liberation Movement and movement supporting The Equal Rights Amendment to show that they are anti-family and anti-God.

In a speech at Southern Methodist University in Dallas in 1979, Gloria Steinem, one of the foremost leaders in the Women's Liberation Movement, said,

> You find the same forces that are anti-abortion are also behind laws on the books prohibiting various sexual acts between heterosexuals, and prohibiting sex between people of the same gender.

She also said,

> The women's movement should not separate itself from the homosexual rights movement as the gays were fighting the same oppression as the women's libbers (46).

Gloria Steinem, editor of *MS magazine* said,

> For the sake of those who wish to live in equal partnership, we have to abolish and reform the institution of marriage (46).

In *Saturday Review of Education* in March 1973, Gloria Steinem said,

> By the year 2000 we will, I hope, raise our children to believe in human potential, not God.

Betty Friedan, the founder of the National Organization of Women, signed the *Humanist Manifesto II* in which is stated:

> No deity will save us; we must save ourselves. Promises of immortal salvation or fear of eternal damnation are both illusory and harmful (47).

At the International Women Year meeting held in Houston on November 1977, Betty Friedan publicly announced that she was willing to include the fight for lesbian rights in the Women's Movement (46).

In regard to raising children, Dr. Mary Jo Bane in the Associated Press in the *Tulsa World* on August 21, 1977 said,

> What happens to children depends not only on what happens in the homes, but what happens in the outside world. We really don't know how to raise children. If we want to talk about equality of opportunity for the children, then the fact that children are raised in families means there is no equality. It is a dilemma. In order to raise children with equality, we must take them away from families and communally raise them. (46)

These statements and utterances by these foremost leaders of the Women's Liberation Movement and the National Organization for Women (N.O.W.) show that they are anti-family and anti-God. James Robison and Dr. James M. Parsons have many more quotes by these women and other leaders in their books.

Dr. Jonathan H. Pincus, a professor at Yale Medical School made the following comment in the *New York Times* on October 24, 1971.

If family stability plays an important role in the well

being of our nation, it is hard to envision the Equal Rights Amendment…as a constructive act. One must agree with the women's liberation groups that the liberating effect of the Equal Rights will apply to men as well to women. What they are both being liberated from is nothing less than the restrictions of traditional roles in a family structure. (46)

I was troubled as to why Gloria Steinem was making such strong statements against the family and God. As I was talking to a friend, he said Paul Harvey in "*The Rest of the Story*" on his radio program had just told an interesting story. This was a story of a family in which the father deserted his wife and very young daughter causing the wife to lose her mind. This daughter grew up having to take care of her mother. This daughter turned out to be Gloria Steinem.

My heart aches for Gloria and her mother, for I fully understand the devastating effect the father's desertion had upon the family. I understand from where Gloria is coming and why she made the statements against the family and God.

Gloria's father did not keep the covenant he made before God to Gloria's mother to honor, to love, to care for and to protect his wife and family, regardless of the storms they encounter in life, until death does them part. Mr. Steinem's actions not only devastated the family, but also destroyed the mother, causing her to lose her mind. Gloria did not have a happy home or a happy childhood. She grew up without the love, care, concern, understanding, supervision and guidance of a mother and a father that every child needs. I fully understand the deep bitterness, resentment, anger, hurt and frustration Gloria experienced because her father disobeyed God's ordained responsibility of a man to honor, love and care for his wife and family. However, these are his sins, and she is encouraging others to commit sins likewise.

I have a friend whose father deserted his mother at the beginning of the depression of the 1930's. My friend was five years old at the time. It was a great stigma to be divorced at that time. My friend and his mother were asked to leave the house in which they were living because they could not pay the rent. The father never once provided any money or help to the family. The mother finally got a job as a cashier in an all-night restaurant, by working from 11PM to 7 AM. The son remembers sleeping at home alone at night as a five-year-old, while his mother worked. He said he tried to stay awake hoping his mother would stay at home, instead of going to work. He recalls living on only one meal a day. The mother kept her sanity with her trust and faith in God. The son is a strong Christian, in spite of what his father did. The son was later reconciled with his father before his father died.

Separation and divorce can have a devastating effect upon the family. God never intended it to be this way. Men have a moral responsibility to honor, love and care for their wives and families. Mistreatment of women and families or women mistreating their husbands and families are not Christian principles.

The men are to blame for the Women's Liberation Movement. If men had respected and treated their wives and other women fairly, there would have been no need for the Women's Liberation Movement. The scripture teaches that men are to love their wives as Christ loves the Church.

> Ephesians 5:25, 28: Husbands, love your wives in the same way that Christ loved the Church and gave his life for it....Men ought to love their wives just as they love their own bodies. A man who loves his wife loves himself. (17)

It is my opinion that if Gloria Steinem had grown up in a loving Christian home and had developed a personal relationship with the Lord, she would have had a completely different attitude toward God and the family. It is ironic that Gloria Steinem with the Women's Liberation Movement is knowingly or unknowingly encouraging the same dysfunctional family environment in which she grew up. This environment is devastating to the family.

James Robinson summed up the Women's Liberation Movement by saying,

Women's Liberation Movement teaches women to be irresponsible in their God assigned roles in the home. It educates them to consider their husbands at best as excess baggage, at worst cruel oppressors depriving them of their "human rights". It coaches them to regard children as problems to be avoided - by abortion where necessary - or if unavoidable to be shunted aside in favor of careers and "self-realization" projects. (46)

The scriptures tell women to be submissive to their husbands and to live godly lives. Husbands are to honor, love and care for their women.

I Peter 3:1-4, 7-12: Wives, fit in with your husband's plans; for then if they refuse to listen when you talk to them about the Lord, they will be won by your respectful, pure behavior. Your godly lives will speak to them better than any words. Don't be concerned about the outward beauty that depends on jewelry, or beautiful clothes, or hair arrangement. Be beautiful inside, in your hearts, with the lasting charm of a gentle and quiet spirit which is so precious to God... You husbands must be careful of your wives, being thoughtful of their needs and honoring them as the weaker sex. Remember that you and your wife are partners in receiving God's blessings, and if you don't treat her as you should, your prayers will not get ready answers. And now this word to all of you: You should be like one big happy family, full of sympathy toward each other, loving one another with tender hearts and humble minds. Don't repay evil for evil. Don't snap back at those who say unkind things about you. Instead, pray for God's help for them, for we are to be kind to others, and God will bless us for it. If you want a happy, good life, keep control of your tongue, and guard your lips from telling lies. Turn away from evil and do good. Try to live in peace...For the Lord is watching his children, listening to their prayers; but the Lord's face is hard against those who do evil. (16)

Men, just because you are the head of the household, and women are to be submissive to you, does not mean that you are to lord it over them, to abuse and mistreat them or the children. Men, the rebuilding of the family and the restoration of this nation must begin with you. The Lord is telling you to stand up and assume your responsibility to be faithful, to honor, to love, to care for, to respect and to protect your wife and family. The men are to take their wives and children to church to worship God. The family is to study the scriptures and teach the children the way of the Lord. The family that worships and prays together will stay together.

The leaders of this nation have a moral responsibility before God and the people to protect the family as ordained by God and to prevent the devastating effects of the environment encouraged by the Women's Liberation Movement, the Equal Rights Amendment and same sex union.

The following visions and messages I received from the Lord pertain to the women's liberation movement:

Vision of a woman with two small girls, ages four and six years, dressed in their Sunday best, with bonnets on:

> The Lord will bring His children back to Himself. The girls especially will come back; led away from the errors of the feminist movement by their mothers, who will see the errors, they have made. God will save His children.

Vision of a woman walking out of church at communion:

> Many people are receiving communion who should not. Many women are confused about communion because they have heard and believed the lies of the militant feminists. Pray for clarity of truth in the Church and a return to holiness at communion.

While at church, I had an image of an attractive, smiling, young lady, whose smile faded. My prayer partner received the following words:

> The attractive lady, whose smile fades, stands for the mis-led women of our Church, who have bought the lies of the feminists and who cannot now finds joy in Jesus and His promises or Church. They are confused.

Vision of a girl in a purple sweater. The Lord said:

> The girl in the purple sweater represents the feminist movement, which is in error. The purple denotes a need for repentance. We must pray that women reject the errors being taught and that the godless leaders doing the teaching may repent. This is a real heartache to God.

Vision of a woman, then a picture of lips, then a picture of an ear:

> Women are speaking more and listening more to women. They have fallen into error because of their sexist inclinations. They are not seeking the leadership of men as God planned. They are bound in the cords of willful neglect of God's leading. Pray for them. Lead your wife and daughter away from error.

Vision of a woman in blue jeans walking toward me with a smile. I had knowledge she was a supervisor.

> Woman has taken a godly role that was originally intended for her husband. The smile is actually deceit, which represents a false security in this role.

School Prayer

Our nation was founded as "one nation under God." Most everyone, who has ever held public office, starting with George Washington, has taken an oath of office with his or her hand on the Bible. Our money, the bills and coins, have an inscription, which says, "In God we trust." In the Pledge of Allegiance to the Flag of the United States of America, we profess to be "one nation under God."

In our National Capitol, the chaplain of the House or the Senate opens the meetings of the House of Representatives and the Senate with public prayer. Though, there are many religious beliefs in America, our nation has flourished and became a strong nation, because we acknowledge God and live by His laws and the moral principles of the Bible.

After almost 200 years of existence, the Supreme Court has ruled that children no longer had the right to begin the day by praying together, asking God for His help, blessing, guidance and protection. This is morally wrong. This is an injustice that needs to be corrected. Our children, who are tomorrow's leaders, need to have the right to stand together and ask God for His help, protection and guidance, just as our leaders in Congress do.

The question most often asked is what prayer we can say. America is a nation of Judeo - Christian heritage. Though we are of many faiths, most of us worship the same God. Any prayer to God our Father and Creator should not offend anyone. The twenty-third Psalm or the Lord's Prayer is prayer to God our Father. There is nothing in any of these prayers that should be offensive to anyone. Regardless of the prayer said, it is most important that we pray and acknowledge God and ask for His guidance and protection each day.

National defense

It is imperative that we maintain a strong defense for our nation. This is the only way to protect our nation and reduce the chances of war.

When the Israelites came out of Egypt into the Promised Land, God commanded the Israelites to destroy all the inhabitants in the land of Canaan (Israel). King David was a man after God's own heart. Yet, King David was a man of war. As a young boy, David took on the Philistine's giant and killed him with a sling. King David fought many battles under the direction of the Lord. God is the same, yesterday, today and forever.

God did not change with the New Testament. The New Testament did not do away with the law - it fulfilled the law.

The Lord taught that there would always be war.

When the apostles asked the Lord what would be the signs of his Second Coming, he said,

> Matthew 24:6-9: You will hear of wars and rumors of wars....For nation will fight against nation, and kingdom against kingdom....Then they will hand you over to be tortured and put to death; and you will be hated by all the nations on account of my name. (18)

The Lord taught that there would always be wars and rumors of war. Christ never taught that there would be peace on earth, prior to His Second Coming. Paul said,

> I Thessalonians 5:3: Just when people are saying, "Peace and security," ruin will fall on them with the suddenness of pains overtaking a woman in labor, and there will be no escape (3).

Nuclear warfare will happen at the Second Coming of the Lord.

Zechariah in the Old Testament speaks of a plague that is similar to a nuclear explosion that occurs at the Second Coming of Christ.

> Zechariah 14:3-4, 12, 15: Then the Lord shall go forth and fight against those nations, fighting as on a day of battle. That day his feet shall rest upon the Mount of Olives, which is opposite Jerusalem to the east....And this shall be the plague with which the Lord shall strike all the nations that have fought against Jerusalem: their flesh shall rot while they stand upon their feet, and their eyes shall rot in their sockets, and their tongues shall rot in their mouths....Similar to this plague shall be the plague upon the horses, mules, camels, asses, and upon all the beasts

that are in those camps. (3)

This is similar to what happens in a nuclear explosion.

Revelation 18 speaks of the destruction of the city of Babylon in one hour. The kings of the earth, every sea captain, sailors and seafaring men will mourn at the destruction of this great city and fear the torment of the smoke that goes up. They will keep their distance from this great city in fear of the punishment that was inflicted upon her. The description of the events described in Zechariah and Revelation are similar to what happens in a nuclear explosion. The thing which the kings, the captains and the sailors feared was the nuclear radiation and fallout from the explosion.

Nuclear arms are going to be around until the Second Coming of Christ. If we, the Christians or anyone else, seek to have peace through a ban on nuclear weapons and disarmament, we are being deceived. The scriptures teach that there will be no peace on earth until the Second Coming of Christ. The scriptures teach that there will be war and rumors of wars; nation will fight against nation and kingdom and against kingdom.

There is no way anyone can win in a nuclear war. However, if we do not have nuclear arms and a strong national defense, we cannot protect ourselves or prevent a war with Russia or any other nation. Do not be deceived by the peace and freedom in Russia and other Communist nations at this time. Communism is not dead. All of this could change overnight. Russia is a godless superpower that has no morals. It is no secret that their goal is to conquer the world and enslave the people. Dimitri L. Manuilski, former Deputy Editor of *Pravda* and past Soviet-Ukrainian Ambassador to the United Nations said:

> War to the hilt between Communism and Capitalism is inevitable. To win, we shall need the element of surprise. The bourgeoisie will have to be put to sleep. So we shall begin by launching the most spectacular peace movement on record. There will be electrifying overtures and un-heard of concessions. As soon as their guard is down, we will smash them with our clenched fist. (48)

We must be very cautious in any dealing with Russia, China, North Korea, Iraq, Libya, or Iran because they will lie, steal, cheat and kill to achieve their goal. A treaty will bind us but it will not bind them. Security must be taken to protect our secrets, our personnel and our nation. Those protesting nuclear arms need to protest to Russia, China, North Korea, Pakistan, India, Iran and other nations with nuclear arms. The minute other nations feel that they can start something with us or defeat us without an excessive cost they will attempt it.

America was proclaimed by her fathers to be one nation under God and a land of freedom. America has had to fight for or defend her beliefs and freedom on an average of every seventeen years throughout her history. (49) Not all America's wars were not to defend freedom. Some were outright aggression for territorial gain while some conflicts were to force our will on others.

America has been the light, the hope, and the envy of the nations of the world. Most of the nations of the world do not have the peace and freedom that we have. This peace and freedom came by the sweat, blood and lives of her young men and women, who fought for her freedom. This peace and freedom we enjoy today, to worship God, to say, to do, and to come and go as we please, did not come via laying down of our arms and not fighting for our rights.

Jesus said,

> Matthew 12:29: How can anyone enter a strong man's house and make off with his property unless he first ties him securely? Only then can he rob his house (3).

America is the strong man and the champion of world peace. America is strong because of her weapons of defense. There are nations in the world that would love to take possession of America. The only way America can keep that from happening is to be the strong man that Christ spoke of. Sure, we are to seek peace. However, we must be ready at all times to defend ourselves against anyone who would seek to destroy us.

It is plain from the scriptures that we will always have war and there will never be peace throughout the world until Christ comes for the second time. Most nations of the world do not live in peace and freedom that we are privileged to have and enjoy in America because they were taken over by a stronger nation that wanted to dominate and control them. The Communists have taken over ten nations in Eastern Europe, most of Asia, parts of Africa, Cuba and Nicaragua.

According to an article by the Associated Press, published in the *Dallas Morning News* on June 5, 1986, a group of thirty Soviet scientists, most of whom have defected or moved to the United States in recent years, have written a letter to the U.S. House and Senate urging them not to make any cuts in the U.S. Star Wars anti-missile program. They stated that the Soviets are hard at work developing an anti-missile program, as part of their quest for global domination.

> Development and deployment of Soviet "Star Wars" system is part of the Soviet Union's global strategy against the non-communist world, which seeks by coercion to usher in the final historical era "of world wide communism and peace" maintained by the Soviet military power. The Soviet scientists urged a continuation of the Star Wars program saying that a strong strategic defense combined with mutual reductions in offensive nuclear weapons offers the greatest hope to the peoples of the world for a stable and enduring peace.

If America disarms herself, while knowing full well that the other nations and her allies will not stop producing arms but will lie, steal, cheat, deceive and kill at any reasonable cost to destroy and take over America, then we are not using the wisdom that God gave us and our forefathers that made us a strong nation and a champion of world peace.

Just as a weak man will never try to rob a strong man without first binding the strong man, a weak nation will never try to take over or destroy a strong nation, without first taking away her weapons. Keep America's defense strong so we do not have to use weapons of war. Jesus said,

Luke 14:31-32: If a king goes out with ten thousand men

to fight another king, who comes against him with twenty thousand men, he will sit down first and decide if he is strong enough to face the other king. If he isn't, he will send messengers to meet the other king, while he is still a long way off to ask for terms of peace. (17)

America is the king with ten thousand men, while Russia, China, North Korea, Iran or any combination of nations, is the king with twenty thousand men. America is at the crossroad of survival. Does America lay down her arms and surrender, allowing her people to become slaves to do forced labor, to be tortured for their religious belief and perhaps to be sent to Siberia with no hope of returning or seeing their loved ones; or, does America take steps to defend her precious and priceless freedom?

Prayer against terrorism

Father God, we recognize that You are in charge of everything that happens, including this terrible war against terrorism. We acknowledge that our victory is not in our might, but in our humility before You. As such, we pray that You will bring our nation into a season of repentance and ultimately revival. We also pray for all those who suffer from the violence brought about by terrorism. Lord, protect our military men and women, police and fire personnel and all those responsible for our safety, and bring righteousness to our world. Through Your Name and through the Blood of Your precious Son, Jesus Christ, we come against our common enemy, Satan and his evil demons and their emissaries. We say, "Begone! Cease and desist your attack against us and all humanity." Oh, gracious Father, hear the prayers of Your people. Protect us, and those we love. We pray for Your victory and justice. May Your Name be honored and glorified by all peoples until the end of time. Amen. (50)

The American people have an obligation to vote for moral and righteous leaders.

The people in America are blessed by having the honor and privilege of voting for and choosing their leaders and representatives every few years. Every American old enough to vote has a moral obligation:

1. to register to be eligible to vote
2. to question and study the moral beliefs and principles of their political candidates
3. to then vote for the most righteous candidate for office, regardless of their party affiliation.

Some people vote for a party rather than for the best and most righteous candidate. There are righteous as well as unrighteous leaders in both major parties.

A very small percentage of the eligible voters do their duty and vote. As a consequence, small minority groups, such as pro abortionists and homosexuals, carry a lot of weight in influencing political candidates to vote in their favor after being elected to office. If the American people would question the moral beliefs and principles of their candidates and vote for the most righteous candidate then we would have righteous leaders in office.

The people also have an obligation to write and inform their leaders and representatives how they feel about certain issues being voted on in the House and in the Senate at both the state and the national levels. Only when each person does his part, shall we have righteous leaders making righteous decisions, with a righteous government for all the people.

We must pray for our nation, its leaders and all of those in authority.

Paul in Timothy, urged us to intercede and pray for all men, especially the leaders of our nation and those in authority so that we may live in peace and prosperity.

> I Timothy 2:1-3: I urge, then, first of all, that requests, prayers, intercession and thanksgiving be made for everyone - for kings and all those in authority, that we may live peaceful and quiet lives in all godliness and holiness. This is good, and pleases God our Savior,...(2)

When the national debt is overwhelming, interest rates are too high, people are out of work, costs of homes are prohibitive and chaos is reigning in the land, then the nation is out of order. The people are not praying for the nation, its leaders and all those in authority.

We need to repent and pray not only for our sins but the sins of our nation. We need to ask the Lord to forgive our brothers of their sins.

This scripture says if we see a brother commit a sin, which is not unto death, we shall pray, and his sins shall be forgiven him.

> I John 5:16-18: If anyone sees his brother commit a sin that does not lead to death, he should pray and God will give him life. I refer to those whose sin does not lead to death. There is a sin that leads to death. I am not saying that he should pray about that. All wrong doing is sin, and there is sin that does not lead to death. We know anyone born of God does not continue to sin. (2)

The scriptures teach that Daniel fasted, prayed and repented for his sins, and the sins of his people and nation. Timothy tells us to pray for our nation and its leaders, and for all men, so that we may live in peace and prosperity. The first book of John shows that we can pray and ask the Lord to forgive our brothers and sisters of their sins.

Because of the wickedness and the abominations that are being committed by our nation and the nations of the world, we need to pray, fast and repent for our sins and the sins of our nation, so that our nation may be restored as one nation, under God, as it was when it was first founded by our forefathers. We need to pray that Russia will turn to the Lord and the forces of Communism will be wiped off the face of the earth, so that we can live in peace and prosperity.

Our sins continue to crucify our Lord Jesus Christ.

On July 10, 1986 Louise Tomkiel received the following message from the Lord.

> Jesus said: Today you aborted an unwanted, unborn baby. You said it had no life yet I live in that innocent body and you killed Me. Today you beat your spouse or your child in your rage of anger and you scourged Me. Today an innocent animal was in your path so you tortured it, hit it with your car, drowned it, for this is only an animal, yet you've shed innocent blood, glorified in seeing suffering and torture and you've broken My commandments. All creation is Mine and all life comes from Me. Only I have a right to take a life. Today you dumped toxic waste and poisoned the earth and the atmosphere and you have poisoned Me. Today you were immoral in dress and in words and you mocked Me. Today you refused to lend a helping hand and you ignored Me. Today was a new beginning in life yet you refused to change, to start anew, and you were ungrateful to Me. Tonight I will come for you and you'll expect a bright tomorrow, and I won't know you. The blood of innocents is sacred and all creation, person and animals must answer to Me. (Genesis 9:5) Everything I created, I made good for My honor and glory and for your happiness. Mankind spilled all My Blood on Calvary and every day when murder occurs, and My commandments are broken, more innocent blood is spilled; therefore mankind crucifies Me daily. (51)

Let Us Pray

Heavenly Father, we come before you through your Son, Jesus Christ of Nazareth, asking that you forgive us of our sins, the sins of our nation and of the nations throughout the world. We repent for all the abominations and wickedness that are prevalent in our land. We repent for the abortion, murder, lying, stealing, fraud, cheating, resentment, and the sins of the flesh - lust, homosexuality, pornography, adultery, and all the sins of Sodom and Gomorrah. Lord we repent for the pride, unbelief, greed, bitterness, hatred, drugs, occult practices, astrology, horoscope reading and everything that is going on that is not of you. We ask that you send forth a Spirit of repentance throughout this land and throughout the nations of the world. Touch the hearts of the people and draw them to your Son, Jesus Christ of Nazareth. Let the people repent of their sins and return to you. Touch the leaders of this nation and the nations throughout the world; up with the righteous and down with the wicked. Be with our President in a deep and powerful way. Direct him in the path you want us to go. Lord, you told us that the prayer of one would put a thousand to flight, while the prayers of two would put ten thousand to flight.

> Deuteronomy 32:30: How could one have chased 1,000 and two put 10,000 to flight, except their rock had sold them, and the Lord had delivered them up? (5)

Lord, we are united with our brothers and sisters throughout this nation and the nations throughout the world. Lord, we ask that you multiply the power of our prayer as we bind back the forces of darkness. We bind Satan and all principalities, powers and rulers of darkness. We bind the spirits of abortion, murder, homosexuality, lust and all sins of the flesh. We hand the people involved in these things over to you for correction so that their spirits may be saved on the day of the Lord.

Lord, we pray that you will send laborers into the field to gather the harvest. Send forth a spiritual revival among the priests and the clergy that they will preach the truth and righteousness to your people. We ask that you put your armor on us and put your hedge of protection around us and that you protect our families and especially the children. Protect our homes, our jobs and all the people for whom we are praying. We asked that you remove the wickedness and evil from our land, and restore our nation as one nation under God. Lord, we ask that you restore our nation with strong Christian families, and give us strong Christian leaders. Lord, take away those things within us that are not of you and fill us with your love, your wisdom, your knowledge, understanding and your discernment. Direct us to the center of your most perfect will. Amen.

Words received while in prayer:

> My people have forgotten how to pray. My people have forgotten how to stand firm. Beware of your lukewarm nature. If you do not stand firm, you are open to all diseases; all attacks of the enemy. If My people will pray daily, if they will surrender unconditionally to Me, I will protect them from all harm – even if it is the worst plague known. What I want are hearts given to Me in truth. The world has forgotten Me. Words will not be enough. I want your hearts.

The trumpet call

On January 19, 1984, the Lord showed me a moon-like trumpet in a purple sky in the presence of the National Capitol. I knew the Lord wanted to sound a trumpet call to the people of this nation to repent for their sins. As I wrote about repentance, the main theme centered on the sins that destroy the family. With divorce and destruction of the family running rampant in our nation, it is interesting that the vision occurred on my mother's and dad fifty-eighth wedding anniversary (My mother and dad were married 68 years before she passed on).

Long and stable marriages are still prevalent in our nation. The Lord wants us to return to the strong, stable, God-fearing families that made our nation strong.

I was praying and seeking the Lord about how he wanted to end this paper on repentance. Since the Lord began by showing me a vision when I was walking on the grounds of the National Capitol with a trumpet in the sky, asking me to write about repentance in this land, it is only appropriate that the Lord would close with the following words:

> The call that goes forth from My trumpet at this time is one of repentance.
>
> Are you hearing My call?
>
> Have you made your confession of repentance?

Or are you hearing the trumpet of self, the world and darkness calling you to death and destruction?

It is time for a choice: one that will bring light, truth and life

or one that will bring darkness, falsehood and death.

This call of Mine is for your benefit and the benefit of your nation.

I urged you to follow this call of Mine.

The words Moses spoke to the Israelites, are for us today.

> Deuteronomy 30:15-18: See, I set before you today life and prosperity, death and destruction. For I command you to love the Lord your God, to walk in his ways and to keep his commands, decrees and laws; then you will live and increase, and the Lord your God will bless you in the land....But if your heart turns away and you are not obedient, and if you are drawn away to bow down to other gods and worship them, I declare to you this day that you will certainly be destroyed. (2)

While praying, I had a vision of a small village on a hillside. There was a very tall pointed church steeple rising high above the homes. There were two golden crucifixes just like the one I pray with in the night, extending high above the village from the ground. One crucifix was higher than the other. My prayer partner spoke the following words:

> The little village represents all the small and big towns of America. The cross above the town means that as long as My people will seek Me and My cross, I will hear them and visit their land and bring them back to Me. I will heal their land.

Unless we fast, pray, repent and turn from our wicked ways, the Lord will pour out His wrath on us, just as He did on the Israelites during the Assyrian and Babylonian captivities.

Turning from sin is a decision. The path of life and prosperity or death and destruction has been set before you. "Choose this day whom you shall serve." But as Joshua said, "for me and my household, we shall serve the Lord" (Joshua 24:15).

Vision of a nuclear explosion shape as a mushroom cloud that was purple in color. Purple means to repent.

As we began to pray my prayer partner received:

> II Chronicles 7:14 If my people who are called by my name, will humble themselves, and pray and seek my face, and turn from their wicked ways, then will I hear from heaven, and will forgive their sin and heal their land (2).

The Lord said in 2 Chronicles that if we, His people, would repent and turn from our sins and seek Him, He would forgive us of our sins and heal our nation. If not, the Lord will bring severe judgment on the land.

Words from the Lord

This generation cannot receive for their hearts are of stone. Only those who want their eyes open to Me and follow Me can receive. Stand firm! Stand on the Rock! Confess on this earth to this land that it shall lay waste and be of want. I will not open the heavens for blessings on them but those who seek after Me and My blood to keep them cleansed. I tell you to take My Word and pronounce judgment to this land, then they will seek My Words and My ways. I shall blind My Words of My prophets and seers. They will say, Woe unto me and beg for mercy. They will seek those for My blessings to take from them and kill them. Yeah, I have sealed mine and I keep them from the slayers of My people. You have been given safe passage to My place of joy and rest for you and yours. There I will continue to use you to teach My ways and My mercy.

CHAPTER 8

Revelations of the
Holy Spirit to His People

After I started receiving visions and messages from the Lord, the Lord indicated I was to use caution with whom I shared these.

> Do not distribute what is holy and of God to the dogs. It's like giving away treasures that are bestowed upon you. The Holy Spirit directs writings among people, but such writings cannot be disclaimed or criticized too harshly for it is the same nature as grieving the Holy Spirit's works. Just be very careful to whom you issue holy writings and make sure that nothing is said to destroy anything that is of the Lord.

Now, I have received knowledge that I am to share the messages I have received in regard to visions or pictures, words spoken or of knowledge received, even those that are very personal. I have a great reluctance to share many of the personal messages as I feel I am vulnerable, opening myself up to much criticism. A prayer partner said these messages would be a source of comfort to those who receive them. I asked the Lord if this was to be another chapter. I received an understanding this was to be Chapter 8, but I was not to change the title of the book. When I asked the Lord what was to be the title of this chapter, he said, "Revelations of the Holy Spirit to His people." The Lord wants us to know that He wants a warm, individual, close personal relationship with each one of us. The Lord is bountiful in His gifts to those who are open to receive His treasures and understandings. He manifests these gifts differently in each individual. **I did not receive**

221

any of the messages directly. Each of the messages was spoken to me through one of the many prayer partners while we were in prayer. Each message was related to a vision or a picture, a word of knowledge, a word, or words that were spoken to me, or a question that I asked the Lord. I did not choose my prayer partners. The Lord said He selected my prayer partners. The Lord obviously spoke to me through prayer partners so the messages would not be contaminated with my words or thoughts. These visions and messages were received over a period of thirty something years.

Vision - a young black boy standing before me wanting to know if he can pray with me. When I told him yes, he had a big happy smile. The Lord said:

> You have not chosen your prayer partners. You have allowed Me to choose for you. You are free.

I am going to share some of the things I have received in prayer: Whenever I have a vision, a picture or have received a word, I ask a prayer partner to discern if this is from the Lord. If so, does the Lord have a message? A vision or a picture is really the same. The messages my prayer partners received are quoted after the description of each vision, dream or question I asked the Lord:

What you have written

A prayer partner spokes the following words to me.

> My son, what you have written, I give to you so that you might learn more deeply Who I am. I give you this knowledge so that you will grow in faith and trust so that you will know without a doubt the tremendous, loving, limitless God I am. To share this knowledge with others who do not have your spiritual light will bring difficulties. They will not understand but you must share it.

222

Vision of my prayer partner carrying a brown grocery bag:

A prayer partner spokes the following words to me.

> The bag contains the fruits of knowledge, wisdom, understanding, love and peace, which were present in the Garden of Eden at the time of Adam and Eve. By prayer and faith you are to continue in love for Me as I have loved you. I will reveal many things to you by means of visions to impart truth to you individually and for which you will be responsible for delivering to others in need of spiritual guidance. My words are given to you freely so you must give them freely to others in return. Be not selfish but give with concern and love for others in need. Be not alarmed by the words, which I give. They are words not comprehended easily by mortal man, if not received by the help of My Spirit. Deliver My words with courage and be always certain in your spirit that you are hearing from Me. Your Adversary is strong, stronger than you are, if you do not pray for My protection first.

Vision of a small blue flame (similar to a pilot light) in a small white stove:

> A small effort on your part is like a pilot light for a great fire of results. When you are faithful in prayer and sacrifice, great things happen.

Visions and messages from the Father, Son and the Holy Spirit

Vision of a white dove flying and suddenly one his wings was clipped.

The dove is a symbol of the Holy Spirit. After becoming aware of the gifts of the Holy Spirit in 1969 and 1970, I really started seeking the Holy Spirit. My focus was on Holy Spirit instead of Jesus. The meaning of this vision is that we are to keep our eyes on Jesus. We are to pray to and for the Holy Spirit realizing Jesus is the one Who baptizes with the Holy Spirit.

Vision of the Lord Jesus Christ standing before me wearing a white garment and a bright red robe.

> Behold I come soon. I have urgency in My voice. Be prepared. I come quickly, sooner than they know. You must be prepared. Many people are wasting their lives. They are scattered in their thinking. They do not call upon Me. They draw back without care. They are about foolishness and trivia. They are not serious about Me and My Father, but I tell you those that are prepared shall reap a great reward with Me, for I shall use them. I shall set them upon a high mountain to be used by Me and for all to see. Many will not come and many will not follow. Join yourself with those who follow after Me.

Vision of Jesus lying down with His eyes closed:

> I choose to close My eyes to the iniquities of My people now. Repent My children. Make reparation to Me for your sins, while you have time. Come back to Me before I open My eyes to your wrongdoing and bring My wrath upon the world. Now is the time to turn back. Tomorrow may be too late.

Vision of the Lord Jesus Christ from the waist up. He was wearing a white garment and He was looking straight at me. His red heart was exposed:

> The Sacred Heart of the Lord is a symbol of His love for mankind. The Lord gave His holy blood for what represented the most important and triumphant victory in the history of the world. Believe in what is holy and let faith

unite your soul and body with God by resting your cares and worries in the Lord Jesus Christ. Nothing can please God but faith. It is this faith in Jesus Christ's holy, sacred blood that has been shed so long ago that keeps us in line with God's will.

Vision of a picture of the Sacred Heart of Jesus:

Many people have a picture of the Sacred Heart of Jesus in their homes, yet they do not pray to the Sacred Heart. Therefore they do not receive the blessing.

Vision of a picture of the Sacred Heart of Jesus in the middle and front of many trophies:

I am blessing those who are displaying My Sacred Heart in their homes. This is a promise and I will keep it until the end. My joy is present in their hearts. Jesus is the greatest trophy we can strive for.

Message after I decided to go on five day water only fast for whatever were the Lord's intentions:

My son, I am pleased that you have decided to fast in My name. I would have you follow Me along My path to Calvary. Start your fast with a reading of My baptism by John, follow Me through the desert, then on to the shore of Galilee. Pray with Me at the Sermon on the Mount. Come with Me to Capernaum on into Jerusalem. Spend the night with Me at Gethsemane. Help Me as Simon, the Cyrenian, did on My way to Calvary. Stand at the foot of My cross, as John, My disciple did. Come to the tomb like John did on that first Easter Sunday morning. Let Me take you to the Mount of Olives in order that you might experience My ascension. I love you very much because you are faithful to your work as John was faithful to his.

The Lord showed me several visions while I was on this fast:

Vision of Jesus with a crown of thorns:

While attending Mass, I saw a circle of light. After a few seconds, the light turned into a picture of Jesus with His head hanging down from the cross. Jesus had a crown of thorns on His head. I could not see the cross or His body.

Vision of Jesus with His disciples:

I could see the back of Jesus as He was standing at a U-shaped table, talking to His disciples. The disciples were sitting at the table. Some were leaning back in their chairs; other had their heads on their hand with their elbows on the table facing Jesus. All had colorful robes. Jesus was wearing a bright red and blue robe.

Vision of side view of Jesus:

After attending Mass, I saw a full-length side view of Jesus standing before me looking to my right. He was wearing a white robe. His hair and beard were dark in color.

Vision - a heavenly view looking down on Jesus on the cross:

While praying before going to bed, I had knowledge that I was standing at the foot of the cross. Then I had a vision in which I was high in the air, directly above the cross looking down with a heavenly view. I could see Jesus hanging limp from the cross. There were people all around the cross, the Roman soldiers, the men and women wearing biblical clothes. The whole area was filled with people.

I asked the Lord for an understanding of the visions He showed me.

My face is so that you would know Me by sight as I know you by heart.

My table is to include you in My supper of life at Passover.

My cross is to show you the great multitude for whom I died.

You are a part of all that I am. Every breath you take enriches My body.

Every breath I took made your breath special. You are Mine.

I am yours. You are afflicted with Me, to be part of Me, to share in My victory.

Hold fast My son. I am carrying you.

My prayer partner understood that part of my afflictions were my deafness, speech impediment and now my eyesight. I need glasses to read.

A very close, colorful vision of the Lord Jesus Christ from the waist up with a crown of thorns on His head. His body was bloody.

Jesus said He will be sending this vision to me many times in my life time as He wants me to truly realize the suffering He experienced on the cross.

Vision of the Jesus:

Draw near to Me, and I will draw nearer to you. Satan cannot put a muzzle on My Word. It will come forth, no matter what he does to prevent it.

Vision of Jesus dead in a casket:

This is from the Lord. It is symbolic. Jesus is dead in the hearts and minds of the people.

Vision of the face of Jesus looking up:

My purpose is always to point up to My Father. I am always about My Father's business.

Vision of Jesus with a staff in His hand. There was yellow around His head:

> Follow Me as the sheep follow the shepherd. Know My voice and believe in My all-consuming power. The power of My presence is within you.

I was awakened from a deep sleep at 2 am to pray. Later that morning, I asked my prayer partner to pray with me for understanding why the Lord woke me up to pray. We received the following message:

> When Christ went to a certain town, He was unable to heal certain afflicted people because of their unbelief. Today, there stands no one even measurable to the stature of Jesus Christ, so there can be no real substitute for lack of faith. With faith everything is possible. Without faith, nothing is possible, not even to those that are in the Body of Christ.

Rain drops, the Lord's tears: About 4:30 in the morning I felt raindrops on my face. I asked my wife, Ann, if it was raining. She said, "No!" The next morning the same thing happened. I asked Ann if it was raining. She said "No!" Then I felt raindrops on my legs, which were under the bed sheet. Then I knew these raindrops were spiritual.

> Discernment - my prayer partner could see my bed at the foot of the cross. The Lord was on the cross weeping for His Church. These raindrops were the Lord's tears for His Church.

Vision of the Lord in the form of a fog or mist or smoke with a wide silver bracelet on His arm: The silver bracelet was a solid substance while His image was not.

> The silver has two meanings: It stands for purity - pure judgment. It stands for power. The mighty right hand of the Lord will fall.

Vision of Jesus kneeling by a large rock:

> When My Son, Jesus, walked the face of the earth, He prayed without ceasing.

While at Mass, I was thinking about the bruise on Jesus' shoulder from carrying the cross. Suddenly, I had a picture of Jesus carrying the cross looking back at me. He had a beard and was wearing a red robe:

> The vision of Jesus carrying the cross, is Jesus telling you that what He did, He did for you, and that He would do it again for you.

I asked God, the Father, to take care of a relative and his family. Immediately, I had a vision of an older man. He looked sideways for a few seconds then he turned to me and nodded his head OK. I had a sense this man was God the Father:

> My prayer partner said, "Yes, this was God the Father."

Vision of Jesus lying inside a long narrow cardboard box, as if He were dead:

> I am the mighty God. I am the mighty Lord. I cannot and will not be put into a box. There is no box that can contain Me.

Christ, in a box, is symbolic of men who know Christ, yet have turned from doing what He wants. They act as if Christ is dead and His message has no meaning. They buy into the world.

Vision of Jesus alive, hanging on the cross in front of some old, odd-shaped, unpainted, weathered, rundown buildings and shacks:

The cross with Jesus in front of the buildings signifies that we, who seek God in truth, live drab and unattractive lives in the eyes of those who seek wealth and position. As we have taken on the poverty of death, with Jesus, we shall also take on the glory of His resurrection. The drab houses will be palaces.

Vision of a round blue cloth with an orange striped circle in the middle of the cloth. In the center of the circle were orange letters IHS, the Greek word for Jesus. This cloth was seen slipping off the altar, onto the floor:

Prepare for the desecration of the temple. Jesus is no longer on the altar in many churches.

Vision of the Lord on the cross. The Lord's body was colored with green and white stripes from left to right at a 45 degree angle down. The Lord was colored similar to a green and white peppermint stick. Green signifies new life while white signifies purity:

I am the way, the truth and the life. Purity will lead you to new life.

Vision of a man wearing a white apron at a restaurant. He stood in the doorway, looking up into the sky then walked back in:

I am the head chef. I am the head maitre d'. I have gone

to prepare a feast, a table before you. I have prepared a banquet table for My faithful and for all those that received Me.

Vision of Jesus on a wide golden cross, which was high in the air: His image was not clear:

Keep Me high and lifted up.

Vision of hundreds of people walking by in both directions on a sidewalk. A mother and a child of 4, 5 or 6 years of age were walking among them. Suddenly, they sat down in the middle of the sidewalk to have lunch. After the child had taken a bite, he leaned sideways and looked at me as people continued to walk by. The child had a very peaceful and calm expression:

I am the Christ-child. I give peace in this hustling, bustling world of confusion and turmoil. Stay close to Me, as I am to you. The woman is My mother.

Vision of a tall priest, with a dark bearded goatee, walked to where I was sitting and took something from my hand and walked to the podium to talk. He had priest's vestments on:

This priest is Jesus Christ.

Vision of a head and crown of a male lion:

I am the Lion of the Tribe of Judah. I take care of My own. Not a single one will be lost. I call all of those I love by name. I am calling you by name to do all that I tell you to do. It is time to move. It will be made clear as to what you are to do.

Vision – the face of Jesus on the cross, jerking his head from side to side, because of the pain:

> No matter how we suffer in this life, Christ has already paid the price. He has broken the bonds of sin and death. Do not be afraid.

Vision of a white lily with reddish, speckled, five pointed star on the side:

> The white lily is Jesus Christ. The five-pointed star is symbolic of His kingship over the Jews and us.

Vision of Jesus dead in a casket:

This is a different picture from the vision I had several years ago, when the Lord said, Jesus is dead in the minds and hearts of the people. Two visions of the same thing mean that the Lord is putting strong emphasis on the message he is speaking. The Lord says:

> My children see Me as dead. They do not know that I am alive, and I have come to bring them joy, peace and happiness. They lived as if I will not return. They sin against themselves and against My Father. They do not know about the punishment they will endure for their sins.

Vision of the Lord Jesus Christ from the waist up. He was clean-shaven with a yellowish-orange-tan light reflecting off of His face:

I want to personally reveal to you My Father's glory.

Vision of God the Father, the Blessed Mother and Jesus standing between two tall and massive pillars that were 10 to 15 feet in diameter. The colors behind them were magnificent. I asked my prayer partner to pray for an understanding. As we began to pray, he saw the same picture with the Holy Spirit and all the saints

behind them:

> The Lord said, "This is My family. We are coming back to our home on earth."

Vision of a small, wide, reddish flower only a few inches off the ground. The plant became a blinding light:

> Jesus is like a lovely flower. As He draws closer to the Father through His resurrection, He is transformed into the Light of the world. As He is lifted up, He draws all men to Himself.

Vision of Jesus standing at a white stone altar. There was nothing on the altar. The colors behind Jesus and the altar were magnificent as in the vision above:

> Jesus said, "I sacrifice Myself on this altar for all those who will accept Me that I may set them free from their sin. There are many that will not come and will bring destruction on themselves.

Vision of a man standing beside his pickup loaded with many different fruits and vegetables:

> The man at the truck is Jesus. The produce is the bounty of the Lord. "Come to Me," He says, "Ask and you shall receive. Expect to get what you ask for. All that I have is yours for asking!" He wants to encourage us, to keep trying for the prize. He is giving us what we need.

Vision of a man in the form of a mist or fog, high in the distance between two large rocks:

> The hill represents Calvary. The rocks are My Church for

which I died. The man in the mist is the Lord Himself. The reason for the mist is that the way the world sees Him is through a mist. It will not be long before they will see Him clearly.

Vision of an old man with his long hair blowing in the wind. I had knowledge that this man was a spirit:

Seek Me first, and all things will be added unto you.

Though it was not raining, clear water was everywhere. I could see lawns with tips of grass just sticking out of the water. Water was flowing down the street from the top of the hill.

Have I not said with streams of living water I will pour out on mankind? This living water will wash away sins. It will fill the thirst of the world if they will drink of it. This water is also the water of baptism that cleans us from sin.

Vision of two tablets of stone in a cloud or fog before me. The cloud or fog was as a blinding light:

The Word is My glory. It goes forth from Zion, My mountain. It overcomes. It heals. It sets all the captives free. It is My Word that will set this hurting world free. My glory is around My Word, as it comes forth.

Vision of a man standing a few feet away, smiling, walked over and put his cheek against my cheek, still smiling:

My prayer partner discerned that this person was the Holy Spirit.

Vision of a blinding light:

I am the Light of the world.

In reading a book about the Mass, a number of statements were made by different priests that the Lord Jesus is born on the altar every time Mass is said. I asked the Lord for an understanding:

> The Lord said, "I am born on the altar spiritually in the flesh through the Holy Spirit operating through the ordained priestly order."

Vision of a shoot of St. Augustine grass extending a long way from the base of its root:

> I am the root of Jesse from where all life comes. Salvation comes through this root to all that will accept it.

Vision of a large glass plate, with Jesus in the center, holding the world above His head, with angels all around Him:

> Jesus lifts the whole world to His Father and continues to do so, even when so many do not recognize Him. Pray that more will be saved.

Second prayer partner -

> I carry the world. I am about to send the world whirling. I am about to do things to the earth that have no history. Be ready, be prepared, be awake. Keep your house ready to go.

Vision of a freight train locomotive with two low headlights, one on each side:

> My light shines brightly in darkness. Nothing can put it out, not even a speeding locomotive.

Vision of a cloud that was shaped like a fully open rose with many petals. I was looking directly into the center of the rose:

> As you saw the vision looking into the center of the rose, Jesus said, "I am the center of the universe. All things are created through Me, for I am the center of life. All life proceeds from Me." He opens Himself to you just as a petal of the rose opens and releases the sweet smelling fragrance of new life.

Vision of a long-haired, blond woman standing on a hill with a strong wind blowing her hair straight back:

> The hill is God's hill. God is present with His people. The woman represents My body. The wind is My Holy Spirit. The Holy Spirit blows powerfully. My Spirit will blow so that the world will see and feel its presence.

Vision – I saw a ball of light, with white wings flying, in my bedroom, while I was lying in bed:

> The ball of light with wings represents the Spirit of the Lord coming upon this nation and on you, revealing the light that is the Lord's truth.

Vision of a large open biscuit with stacks of nickels, dimes, and pennies on the biscuit:

> I am the Bread of Life and can only be bought with a price. That price is growing, for the prayers of many are not with life. They do not have My life in them. (Jesus paid a price for our salvation. As more people are lost, the price He paid goes up.)

Vision of the moon shining through the clouds with animal's hairs streaking all through the clouds:

> The animal's hairs in the clouds symbolize the sacrifices made to God, thousands of years ago. They passed away, just like the clouds pass. The sacrifice of Jesus is everlasting, washing clean, lifting up, redeeming mankind forever.

Vision of a white stone altar with a thick, square silver bowl and a small white porcelain pitcher with gold metal rim. Both were expensive:

> The Lord is saying that the Mass is precious, and all that happens on the altar is precious. We don't know how valuable it is to us. We must revere the Mass.

Vision of a man holding a small boy 1½ or 2 years old: The little boy was stroking or feeling his daddy's face and chin with both hands:

> The man is St. Joseph. The child is Jesus. We need the support of St. Joseph, when we face problems as fathers and husbands. Jesus is reminding us to speak with St. Joseph.

Vision in the middle of the night of a twinkling star:

> "I am the Light of the world."

Vision of maize, which I feed my birds in the backyard, on the ground:

> Is not My Word like seed that, when it is thrown on fertile ground will bring forth fruit one hundred fold.

237

The word "Blessed Sacrament" came to me:

The Blessed Sacrament is the center of My Church.

Vision – I could see the nose and forehead of the Lord's face. I could not see His eyes, as it was dark. His face was close to my face:

The Lord was asking us if we would watch and pray with Him.

Vision of Jesus alive on the cross just below and in front a pulpit.

Paul said he was going to preach Jesus and Jesus crucified. We are to preach Jesus crucified.

Vision of a tiny red dot:

If this red dot were the only drop of blood I spilt for the world, it would be enough. But I poured out My mercy on you. Every drop of blood in My body, I let fall, including the last drops mixed with water in My heart. You are truly redeemed. My mercy is on you. Receive it.

Vision of a man's feet and lower part of a white garment like those worn in the Biblical days:

These are the Lord's feet. We are to follow in His footsteps.

Vision of a cross section of a volcano with knowledge of how powerful they are:

This volcano is very powerful, but I am more powerful.

Visions and messages from Blessed Mother

Dream of an intense devotion to the Blessed Mother:

Those seeking to be close to My mother are really pursuing Me. They do not always know and recognize this. It is not for you to do anything but to know that I love them very much. Many of these beautiful children do not have salvation as you have seen and experienced. They have the baptism of desire. They are confused by doctrine and poor teachings. However, they are led to Me through My mother. She loves their devotion for Me although at times it is misguided. I want them to experience more of the promises from Me by coming to Me and seeking My words. These people are Mine without the extra blessings that you are aware of in your life. Do not turn your back on them. When you speak with them, speak in love and let your words be Mine to enrich their spirits. The anointing I have poured on you shall fall on them as you yourself honor My mother. Expose your heart to them that their hunger will increase. Only those who are willing to step out of the boat, will experience this blessing.

Vision of the Blessed Mother, very beautiful, and wearing a white garment and light blue cape bordered with a wide yellow ribbon. There were beautiful red roses embroidered on the cape:

Your heart is so full of love for my Son. I would wish that you would come to me in your prayers more often, that I might intercede with you in your daily prayers. I want to add whatever I can so that your requests may be answered more quickly and I will not have to put forth as much effort each time. The time has come that many of your previous prayers will be answered. Seek me out that I may stand with you in your hour before the throne. My Son's glory is to be shown through your constant efforts.

Your name is known in heaven and well known before the Father. Thank you for listening and seeking my message. My purpose is to lead my saints to my Son, Jesus.

Vision - I was standing under an archway on a porch of a church. Outside was a man whose image I could only just make out because it was dark. Just under the peak of the roof of the archway was the Blessed Mother. The man said, "My own mother":

The Blessed Mother is bringing light to the Catholics living in religious darkness due to a lack of knowledge. The man is Jesus Christ. He confirms that He has raised Mary above all of us to be His mother. He wants her respected, loved and recognized as a means to come to Him.

Vision of a woman crying. It is the Blessed Mother:

My tears are for this stubborn world. In spite of all the signs many people will not turn back to my Son. Unless they turn back, they will be lost. The time is very short.

Vision of the Blessed Mother wearing a long red dress and a white cape down to her waist: Her head was bowed downward.

I asked the Blessed Mother why her head was bowed down. She said she was mourning for the sins of our nation. She asked that we pray fervently for our nation: for abortion, murder, lying, sins of the flesh, cheating and all the injustice and abominations that are going on. The red you see is from all the slain children of abortion. This technology is not from our Father. This evil is from the god of pleasure and comfort, as a result of a cold heart. My children have been and are being slaughtered every day. We must pray that the women's hearts be made soft and that they hunger for their children. The free countries are in great sin. The women are going to their way of freedom in the wrong direction. Our Father set them free by allowing them to be the ones to carry and care for life. Pray that their hearts hunger and pine for their children. Pray that the fruit of their wombs be dedicated to God, our Father. Let their births be multiplied and their children be given back to my Father and your Father.

Image of the Blessed Mother with the image turning into a cross:

To come to Jesus is to come to the cross. To come to the Blessed Mother is to be led to the cross.

A message from the Blessed Mother:

I stand before the earth. The Lord's hand has moved against it. The destruction is about to begin. I have spoken about it many times. It is now about to happen.

Vision – I was reading a sentence in a book. When the vision was over, the only word I could recall was "Mary".

I gave My mother, Mary, to the world to bring many to Me, who could come to Me through no other vessel. She is to be honored and recognized above all others.

Vision of the Blessed Mother and then Elijah. A month later on Good Friday, I had another vision of the Blessed Mother then Elijah:

Jesus said: "I will honor My mother. I will answer her prayers. I will raise up men of the same caliber as Elijah in these last days.

Vision of a small statue of the Blessed Mother with a rosary in her hands. Her cape was blue and her rosary was flexible:

> The Blessed Mother wants us to pray for the suffering Body of Christ. Pray for conversion, reconciliation, peace and unity in the Body. Have faith even when things don't go well. The rosary is a living link with Christ through His mother. We need to use it.

Vision of the Blessed Mother standing beside me, as I was lying in bed. I could see her blue cloak and a reddish area over her heart. She was wearing a white dress:

> My crowned prince, it is my joy to be here with you. I am excited for you and yours and about what you will do. Here is my heart to you. You have kept many safe from harm's way. I look forward to the same from you; also, as the battle goes on so do you, young prince. Your prayers and sacrifices are heard all over heaven. Did you know this? Be sure that many wait to see you before the throne. You are like no other. Tell Bob of the joy in my heart for him and his perseverance. I cannot express more greatly than I have about the great words spoken of you both. I will come again. Your sons are kept.

Dream – I saw the front page of the *"Dallas Morning News."* In the lower left hand corner was a pad, with many leaflets, of a picture of the Blessed Mother. I had knowledge that this picture was on the front page of the "Dallas Morning News." Above the head of the Blessed Mother was a red ball, where the leaflets were bound together. The Blessed Mother had a blue cape on. As I lifted up the leaflet, the picture of the Blessed Mother changed into a life size picture of an angel. As I tore the angel from the pad, to hang up in my room to rebuke Satan, the picture became the Lord Jesus Christ:

The "Morning News" signifies that the vision is for all to know. The multiple layers of Mary's image, succeeded by the image of an angel, indicate that God uses Mary and angels and other individuals to bring us to Himself. The message is that unless those things, which we pursue, lead us to Jesus, they are not to be followed. Jesus is the goal and purpose of our efforts.

Vision, I was in the driver's seat in a van. A small child about 11/2 years old climbs into the front seat. A woman, I assumed to be his mother also sat in the front seat and smiled at me:

The child climbing into the seat and His mother getting into it with Him and smiling at you signify Jesus and His mother, who wants you to remember that wherever you go, they are with you.

As I started praying the rosary, I had a vision of the Blessed Mother with a light where her head was. The light formed a round ball, which shrunk into a small blue ball with white wings flying:

The bright light in Mary's face was the presence of Jesus around her. The blue ball was the earth. The white wings were the Holy Spirit carrying the earth through the trials which the enemy causes.

I asked the Lord about someone who is supposedly receiving messages from the Blessed Mother that are contrary to the teaching of the scriptures:

He believed what he was receiving is from the Blessed Mother; however, he is walking by the amount of light that he has.

Vision - I saw a room with a few people who were saying the rosary. I heard the words, "Hail Mary, full of grace":

> My prayer partner had a side view of the Blessed Mother kneeling, with her head tilted down, and her hands together and extended out as in prayer. He hears the words, "Keep praying."

Vision of the face and shoulder of the Blessed Mother:

> The Blessed Mother wants you to specifically ask her to intercede for Paul (my son) to come to a full knowledge and understanding of Jesus Christ.

Vision of a small, oblong, circular, bluish, image in which I sensed the presence of the Blessed Mother:

> This picture is of the Blessed Mother, kneeling, with her head tilted and her hands together in prayer. She said, "Keep honoring me!"

Vision of a vigil candle with the Blessed Mother's image on it (Our Lady of Guadalupe):

> The world is going to know My mother more and more. She will visit the world more and more in these last days.

Vision of a bluish cloud in the sky that looked like an explosion:

> This cloud holds My mother's presence. She has a battle going on around her. She is doing My work about the world. Know that I am about a great thing and as she moves, this cloud covers and protects her.

Vision of the Blessed Mother. Then, as I blinked my eyes and took a second look, a phosphorescent glow or light surrounded her:

> The world is in decay. The world can no longer distinguish between righteousness and sin. It is just as my Son has said, His return is imminent.

While praying the rosary, I had a vision of the Blessed Mother with her eyes closed:

> The Blessed Mother was relaxing, listening and enjoying the prayer.

Vision of some pretty roses:

> These roses were a gift to Mary. She, in turn, gives them to you in gratefulness for your devotion to her Son. As you pray for others, she will reveal herself to you in powerful new ways.

Vision – people in church were standing in their pews, looking toward the back of the church at a woman as she turned into the aisle and started toward the altar. I knew that this woman was someone special but I did not know who she was. I had knowledge that there was a lesbian in the pew across the aisle from me. I also had knowledge that the woman walking toward the altar was not going to acknowledge the presence of the woman that was a lesbian. However, when she reached the pew where the lesbian was standing, she turned to the lesbian and told her something. The lesbian had a big grin on her face afterward:

> This woman was the Blessed Mother. She said to the lesbian, "There is nothing too great that my Son will not forgive."

(Note - The Blessed Mother was not dressed in her traditional biblical clothes. She was dressed in modern clothes. I have had a number of pictures of a woman, which my prayer partner later identified as the Blessed Mother, wearing a dress.)

While my prayer partner and I were praying, he had a vision of the Blessed Mother. She spoke the following words to us:

My children, my Son is well pleased with your faithfulness to prayer. I come to you as a mediator between my Son and you. Anything that you want for your family and for yourself, I will present to Him for you. It is only because of my effort of asking for additional time for mankind to repent of their sins that my Son has not been sent back by the Father. The world is in trepidation and decay because of its sinfulness. Pray that the world will have an attitude of repentance, for the sins of the flesh are an abomination to God Almighty. A time of disaster is upon your world. Pray for a spiritual revival of priests that they may lead their flocks in righteousness and truth. I love you very much. Always remember that my Son loves you too. Plead mercy for your world, and pray for repentance of heart of its people in order that they may survive. Make your prayers the same as mine in order that His (Christ's) work will come to completion. Remain committed to your first Love (Christ), and your reward will be great in heaven.

Vision– while sitting in a chair, I saw a single white string go around the left side and front of my chair. Then a voice said, "When she did this, she made a gold metal." I did not see anyone:

The Word of the Lord came into My daughter, Mary. She obeyed, and she labored and worked to raise My Son, which was pure gold and My answer for a sinful world.

Vision of a woman holding either flowers or a trophy: She said, "You have won":

> This woman is the Blessed Mother. This is a spiritual prize, a spiritual race of faith that has been won.

Visions and messages of Rosaries

Vision of a rosary:

> The Rosary is a call for constant prayer. We, Christians, must be very aware today that we cannot do it all alone. God is calling us to constant and repetitive prayer, so He can increase our trust in Him.

Vision of a rosary glowing in the dark and hanging from a bedpost:

> Pray that husbands and wives will pray the rosary together, for there is much healing power there. The rosary has the power to heal relationships, to strengthen marriages and to restore family relationships. This is important in a day and age when families are disintegrating. Pray for strong families.

While saying the rosary, I had a vision of a flowerbed early in the year with fruit jars over some of the young plants.

> A fruit jar was a means of protection for the plants; the rosary is a means of protection for us.

While saying the rosary, I had a vision of a man from the Middle East with a high cloth wrapped hat. The picture was all purple:

> The Blessed Mother wants me to pray for peace in Jerusalem and Israel.

Vision – I was in the vestibule at what looked like St. Luke's Catholic Church in Irving, with a rosary in my hand to get it blessed. There were two men walking toward the church that were priests but were not dressed as priests. Next, I saw a large wide chalice filled with holy water and my rosary:

> Contemplate the mysteries of the rosary, for out of them, you will receive the water of life. I am working in your life, My son. I am opening mysteries to you, revealing their deeper meaning in your own life.

Vision – I took three 3-feet long strings of dark colored beads off of a wall and was holding the beads in my hand. Suddenly, the beads turned into a beautiful, clear crystal rosary with a silver crucifix in my hand:

> I can take something ordinary and make it beautiful. When I made these beads beautiful, they reflected My beauty. My beauty is transparent. They are like the beauty of My mother, pure, wholesome, righteous and holy. This is what the rosary is a symbol of.

Vision of four people kneeling in a circle, facing each other, praying the rosary. I had a close view of the rosary beads which were bright, shiny crystals:

> My prayer partner saw teenagers or young adults saying the rosary. The rosary beads were dull. As they said each bead, the bead became very bright. The Lord said, "Listen and obey what Mary says, for it will lead to Me."

Visions and messages of people for whom we prayed for protection and for spiritual and physical healings

Vision of a college classmate:

My prayer partner received understanding that he is hemorrhaging. I prayed the scripture Ezekiel 16:6, And when I passed by thee, and saw thee polluted in thine own blood, I said unto thee when thou wast in thy blood, Live; yea, I said unto thee when thou wast in thy blood, Live. (35) King James translation. This is the scripture to stop bleeding or pray for blood clots. My prayer partner received knowledge that the bleeding had stopped.

Vision of an extremely large, young, light sandy-haired woman:

Her name is Cecilia. She was raped, and her parents blamed her. She eats to overcome fear and to be comfortable. She wants to be set free but does not know how to break the vicious cycle. We prayed for her healing.

Vision of a woman with three patches of white on her forehead and parts of her face:

This woman has leprosy. The Lord wants to heal her. We prayed for her healing. My prayer partner saw a picture of her completely healed. Her name is Cythenia Ann from Baltimore.

Vision of a man with a flattop haircut, in his 20's with his mouth open and his teeth clenched together. His eyes were real tight and his face showed he was in pain:

This young man broke his leg between his knee and ankle playing football. The Lord wanted us to pray that his leg would heal normally and to come against any infection. As we started praying, I came against any staph infection.

My prayer partner said something happened when I came against staph.

Vision of an older, short, stocky woman with glasses:

My prayer partner received knowledge that this woman was Sister Basilea Schlink, a Lutheran sister and she was being attacked by hepatitis. We prayed for her to be healed and we put a hedge of protection around her compound.

Vision of a man with Alzheimer's disease:

I commanded the spirits in this particular man to identify themselves. My prayer partner received knowledge of self-pity and bitterness. I repented for these two sins quoting 1 John 5:16. After I repented for his sins, my prayer partner saw the man weeping, and then lifting his hands praising God.

Dream - a man wearing blue work clothes had a white sign pinned on his back saying, "I intentionally dug a well." This man, whom I did not recognize, was working in the lobby of a large building with large glass windows:

I am in the bottom of this well. I dug this well with the evil things and thoughts in my life. This well will grow deeper at my death. I have turned from my Lord. I have denied Him presence in my life. Without someone lowering a lifeline of prayers, I will surely die. The second death is to eternity. I am in your presence from time to time. You know me. I need help to get out. The line you lower must be strong to hold the weight of all my sins. There is much blackness now. I know the blood will wash me clean again. Please do not delay. I will be ever grateful for any thing you will do. Upon asking the Lord, who is this person, He said, "It is not necessary for you to know."

Vision – Ann, my wife, walked into the bedroom while I was lying in bed and said, "There is a little boy trapped in our living room." Then I saw a little boy, 6 or 7 years of age, sitting in a chair in the middle of our den:

My prayer partner had a picture of Ann's mother, dressed in a bonnet and a long pioneer type dress, embracing the little boy. It was discerned that this little boy was Ann's mother's husband, Charles Geron's great-grandson, who lived in Tennessee. This great grandson has a rare skin disease. I commanded the spirits that were attacking this little boy to identify themselves. My prayer partner received knowledge that the little boy's grandfather or great-grandfather on his mother's side of the family had been mistreated by a black man, causing him to have prejudice, hatred, and unforgiveness. He was in purgatory. He was wearing blue coveralls. When I repented for his sins, his coveralls turned white. He was taken into the kingdom. We prayed for the little boy's healing. The skin disease disappeared gradually, and within a year, the grandson was completely healed. The scripture speaks of the curse of the sins of the fathers being passed down to the children to the 3rd and 4th generations.

> Numbers 14:18: The Lord is slow to anger and abundant in loving kindness, forgiving iniquity and transgression; but He will by no means clear the guilty, visiting the iniquity of the fathers on the children to the third and fourth generations. (1)

Vision of a daughter of a friend, who is a college graduate and the mother of two teenagers:

> This woman has a cancerous lump on her breast of which she is unaware. I commanded the spirit that was causing this lump to identify itself. My prayer partner received knowledge that it was resentment against someone in high school. I repented for the sin of resentment and asked her

angel to ask her to forgive the person that caused her to have resentment. My prayer partner received knowledge that she forgave this person. I commanded the cancerous lump to leave. My prayer partner received knowledge that it had left.

A cousin who had been sick and bed-ridden for 10 to 15 years:

I asked Bill, my prayer partner, to pray with me about her situation. Bill had a picture of me besides her reading the Lord's passion and crucifixion. I told Bill that she is in a coma. Bill said her spirit would hear. I said let us read it now. She will hear it even though she is over a hundred miles away. We read a chapter on the Lord's crucifixion and death. Bill saw my cousin sitting on a curb weeping happily. There was a man standing next to her with his hand on her head. This man was the Lord. All things are possible with the Lord with faith.

Vision of a woman in a very expensive black dress with attractive silver designs that really stood out:

She is dressed for the world. She is not dressed for Me. My son, she does not know where she stands with Me. I would have you intercede for her soul. She is Mine but she does not know what she faces. Talk with her as My friend. Treat her with joy. Be very gentle and let My love flow through her. Talk with her as if she was an intimate friend. Wash yourself with prayers. Seek My heart for her. Be gentle and loving. Bath her with prayers for sinners.

Vision of a young girl 11 or 12 said, "I don't care what they say, I will not do it":

The young girl of 12 is symbolic of the rebellion of youth against truth and order. Our society has pandered and spoiled our young people to seek pleasure and diversions, which they are not mature enough to handle. They are rebelling against God's truth. We must pray for our young people or they will be lost. We must insist on the truth, even when they rebel. Young women in particular are being led into serious error by the lies of our society and the godless orientation of our leaders.

Vision of one year old child on the floor. Suddenly, the child's face was right in my face. Her eyes were very bright and clear:

The baby's name is Jan. Pray that she will be able to walk. We prayed for her. My prayer partner received knowledge that the child was healed.

Vision of a woman in her 40's standing before me looking down with a circle spotlight around her head and chest. I did not know this woman:

Ann is her name. She has been deeply hurt, and the Lord wants to minister to her and heal her. Pray for the forgiveness of her sins and that the Holy Spirit will be stirred up within her into a mighty flame.

Vision of a bare, flat chest woman:

This woman had surgery for cancer. She has fear. We prayed for her to be healed, to have no more cancer and to have peace in her body.

Vision of a man and a woman with knowledge the man was the son of an old friend of mine. I did not know the man or woman:

The Lord revealed that this couple was on a verge of a divorce. Prayed for their marriage to be healed.

Vision, my high school math teacher introducing me to her grown daughter whom I have not seen since she was a small child, 45 years ago:

The teacher wants you to pray for her daughter.

Vision of four stars on someone's bare knee:

Na Gen Mu Lin - This man is a four-star general in the Lord's army. He is about to be betrayed. Pray that the Lord will do away with those who are about to betray him.

Vision of an outline of a face of a man on a small calendar:

This is a picture of a man who has one year to live. He thinks he knows God but doesn't. The Lord wants us to pray that he will come to know Him in a more powerful way before he dies. (The Lord gave me his name)

Vision of a young boy 14 to 16 years old with a blood-shot eye:

The Lord told us the boy's name, and where he was from. He wanted us to pray for a healing. We received knowledge the eye was healed and cleared up.

Vision of my cousin driving a car with three small children:

She took care of her children while she was on earth. She can no longer do so and wants me to pray and intercede for them.

Vision of a middle age woman coming to my back door who stood there before me:

This woman was raped. The Lord gave me her name. I prayed for her healing.

Vision of an attractive, well-to-do dark-haired young woman with rouge make-up on her cheek standing before me: She was looking down. She could not look me in the eye:

> You see me, as others, as well-to-do and taken care of by my husband. Yet, on the inside, I am a wretch. My life is filled with fear and despair. I gave myself to another man long ago. I am afraid he will see me and reveal my indiscretion. I am so ashamed that I am about to do the very same thing again with another. I am no good. I am a low person. I am filled with deceit from the wrong that I did. I do not know to whom to talk that might help me change my mind. I am afraid they will reveal my past and my present thoughts. Help me! Please help me! We prayed that angels would minister to her.

Vision of a large woman standing before me with a kerchief tied around her head. One front tooth overlapped another tooth. One tooth was dark. She placed her right hand on my left shoulder:

> Discernment, this is a Russian woman who needs prayers for her husband who has cancer. I commanded the spirit of cancer to identify itself, and I received knowledge the husband had bitterness and unforgiveness toward his brother. I repented for these sins by quoting 1 John 5:16. We called forth a spirit of love and forgiveness. I commanded the cancer to leave and asked the angels to come forth with God's healing power. My prayer partner received knowledge that the man was healed of cancer. I commanded the woman's teeth to be healed. My prayer partner had a picture of the woman's tooth completely white and straightened.

A voice said, "This body belongs to Rich Clodfeller, who disappeared":

> This man has lost his memory. The Lord wanted me to pray for him. I commanded the spirits that were affecting his memory to identify themselves. I repented for the sins and commanded them to leave. My prayer partner had knowledge that the man's memory had returned. I invited the Holy Spirit to come in and prayed that some Christian would witness to him.

Vision of Father Kazimieras Zylis in a housecoat and sitting in a wheelchair:

> Father Zylis was involved in a radiation explosion in Russia. He had gone to Chicago to see, if they can help him. I prayed Ezekiel 16:6, "As I come upon thee and saw thee polluted in thy own blood, I say unto thee while thou art polluted in thy own blood live, yea, I say unto thee live". I had a strong anointing as I prayed in the early 1990's. Father Zylis was healed. He is doing great 15 years later.

Vision of my high school classmates being shown to me one after another:

> There is a great need of prayers for the members of your class. Don't forget them.

Vision of a childhood friend:

> Pray for the friend to experience the baptism of the Holy Spirit.

Vision of a man with a drinking problem:

> Pray for protection against the spirit of alcoholism.

Vision of two young men (brothers) that I know. There was a man on a hill with a flat rock a little larger than the palm of his hand. The two boys were standing on each side of the man. When the man struck the rock with another object, fire passed down in two streaks:

Just as the Word of God crushes the rock of hard hearts, the Lord wants to crush and remold the hearts of these men. As Moses struck the rock and life-giving water came forth, the Lord wants your prayers to strike the rock and send forth the power of life-giving spirit in tongues of flames on these two young men. Pray that it is so.

Vision of a woman wearing a red and white candy-striped dress like in a hospital. She was standing before me looking at me:

Claire is the name of the woman in the striped dress. She needs prayers so that she will be freed of fear, anxiety, and pride.

The last name of a family I know came to me. Members of this family have suffered serious sicknesses and some have died young:

My prayer partner received understanding that there were many serious sins committed by an ancestor long ago. The Lord wanted me to break the bondage so that living members of this family can be set free. Though discernment we repented for each sin. We asked the Lord for confirmation that the family was set free. My prayer partner saw a bright light indicating the bondage had been broken.

Vision of an Indian with a feather in the back of his head:

He runs from Me to and fro. He tries to escape My grasp,

but he cannot. I am with him because of the faith of his wife. Her faith in Me is steadfast. She does not waver. He has no rudder. His faith is in himself, what he can do, and how he can make his next deal. To save his soul and his spirit, you must pray and intercede for him. His wife does not know how to fight. Her teachings are not as you know. His whole family is strained. He causes a lot of hate, hurt, meanness, and brutality. His list goes on. His dead wife now intercedes for him. He has many spirits in him. Cover him with My blood. Care for him as you would an infant. He will begin to follow the way his ancestors did. Bring him to Me daily. Love him, and pray for him daily. (The Lord gave me his name.)

Vision of a young nice-looking woman:

Her name is Antoinette. She has not been able to conceive because her uterus was turned sideways. The Lord wanted us to pray for a healing. After praying, my prayer partner had knowledge she was healed.

Vision of an American Indian dress; then a picture of a young American Indian woman:

The young woman is about to be married. She does not know the Lord. The Lord wants me to pray for her to know Him. Her name is Nawkita, one who shines like the sun.

Vision of a young teenage girl dressed in a blue and white dress and bonnet standing or leaning against a tree in the distance:

Pray for my youth. Pray for young women. They are so misguided. Pray that they come back to Me.

Vision of a black woman dressed in a suit:

She represents a group of My people that I want to bring to a higher plane of understanding and worship. They know of the liberal free-spirited Negro. I want them to know, worship, interrelate and practice the other mysteries of My Church, not known to them. I want them to know My mother and her work. I want them to come to know Me, through the history of My Church. They are intellectuals that have not been educated about the history of My Church. They are some of My best. I want them to know Me as an intellectual. I want to send them to speak and teach My people. Their job or task will be great. I will speak into their minds and spirits. Pray that they'll have a willing heart and mind.

Vision of black bunny rabbits:

The rabbits symbolize the errors in teaching, which are multiplying daily, (like rabbits) all over the world. Their black color shows the evil this plague of errors brings to our lives. Pray against errors in teaching.

Vision of a young woman from the Far East. Her eyes were red:

This woman is Nora Lan, a missionary to China. My prayer partner saw her on her knees, weeping and praying for China. She has a real burden for China. There are parts of China into which she has not been able to get. Pray that the doors will open for her to get into all of China.

Vision of a new born baby on its mother's shoulder:

Pray for the unborn grandchildren. (We had three grandchildren born since I had this vision.)

While thinking and praying for a college classmate, I saw the color purple flashing on and off before me:

> I am putting a call on this man's life. I am calling him to turn his life over to Me. I am calling him to repent and to follow Me.

Vision of a young woman, 25 to 30 years of age, looking at me. She was a nice-looking woman; her eyes were very clear, detailed and attractive. Her eyes were the last to fade from my view:

Her name is Tina. She knows the Lord but is dying. Pray for her.

Vision of a friend who is with the Lord:

> He wants me to pray for one of his sons.

Vision of a man wearing an English-type cap. He had a trimmed mustache and appeared to be a blond:

> Prime minister of England - pray for him, as he has some very important decisions to make, which will affect other nations.

Vision of a nun in a brownish habit with white trim before me:

> Her name is Sister Miriam. She is under a spiritual attack for defending the true faith. You are to call down a spiritual hedge of protection, made of fire, to protect her.

Vision of a middle age man with a short, dark beard:

> This man is a Jewish rabbi in this area, who has come to the knowledge that Jesus Christ is the Messiah. He is reluctant to accept Jesus as his Savior. My prayer partner and I prayed for him, but he would not give in. Two days

later, when four of us were praying for him, he fell on his knees, repented and accepted Jesus as his Lord and Savior. Two of my prayer partners received confirmation.

About a week later, I had a vision of the above Jewish Rabbi sitting in the chapel at the University of Dallas, in a pew all alone, on the other side of the altar from me. This is another confirmation that he has accepted Jesus as his Lord and Savior.

Vision of a friend and his wife from high school:

Pray for their salvation.

Vision of a nice looking little boy, 7 or 8 years old, standing before me:

I have called to him in the night. He has heard My voice, but does not know it is Me. He does not know anyone to ask. Pray that I might send a messenger to him.

We prayed for a friend, who had a serious case of arthritis, and had complicated surgery on her neck:

I commanded the spirit of arthritis to identify itself. My prayer partner received knowledge that this spirit came from a grandmother who had very deep and bitter resentment against a boy friend who jilted her. I asked the Lord if this grandmother was in purgatory. We received knowledge, "Yes!" When I repented for the sin of resentment, my prayer partner saw many mice shooting like bullets from under the feet of the afflicted granddaughter. The grandmother was set free from purgatory. We prayed for a healing of the granddaughter.

Vision of an eighteen-wheeler tanker truck on Irving Heights close to Grawyler in Irving, Texas:

> My prayer partner had a picture of the driver falling asleep at the wheel. We prayed that his angel would watch over him, encourage him to rest when tired, and not let him fall asleep at the wheel.

Vision - we were someplace with other members of the Community of God's Delight. A little boy, 5 or 6 years old, was wandering around, and then suddenly I had a strong picture of this child before me:

> This child is in some kind of danger, pray for his protection. We put a hedge of protection around this child.

Vision of a beautiful young boy and girl about 14 or 15: The girl with long blond hair had a scar on her right cheek caused by a burn.

> Pray for the youth of the world. The mark on the girl's face represents the damage done through sin, which is a direct result of the distortions of God's truths by the world's messages.

Vision of a young woman wearing a cowgirl outfit and hat, sitting in a chair. She turned her head toward me with tears in her eyes:

> I represent all those who are like me. I run to concerts; I run to bars, but I am not happy. I come away empty each time. I am lost, but I know God. I follow the singing false prophets of music and song. I have no joy. There are many like me. I do not know when or how or why to stop. I am lusting for the good life. This life and these times are but fads that we follow. To me, I am lost. I do not know

what to do to help save myself. I do not want to give up my comforts. I want money, but I am not willing to give a full day's work. Truly I am lost. Help me. I am weak, I am lazy, and I do not care. Please do not leave me.

Vision of an attractive black lady in her 20's, then the word "stealing" came to me:

Her mother has been praying for her and begging her to stop stealing. She refused to do so. She has a spirit of anger and is justifying her reason for stealing. The Lord wants you to join your prayer with her mother and intercede for her. Her name is Williemaie.

Vision of an Arab man in a whitish gray business suit with hat and tie.

This man is Saudi Arabia's ambassador to the U.S. Pray for the discussions that are going on right now for the protection of the Americans in Saudi Arabia.

Vision – I was sitting in a chair. There was a black woman in a purple dress sitting in front of me, talking to me:

My prayer partner discerned that this woman was Jane Pittman, the black slave who escaped to the north to freedom, prior to the civil war between the states. This woman was an instrument in helping many black slaves to escape to freedom. She wanted me to pray against the prejudice between the races. I repented for the prejudice the whites have against the blacks and other races. I repented for the prejudice the blacks have against the whites. I asked the Lord to send peace and to heal the hostility between the races, for we are all one body in Christ.

Vision of one-half face of a child:

This child has not been born. Pray for the healing of this child in the womb. Name is Michael David of Houston, Texas.

Vision of a baby in which I had knowledge was kidnapped:

The Lord wanted me to pray for the return of the baby. The baby's name is Olaf and he lives in one of the Scandinavian countries.

Vision of an older stocky woman with braided hair:

This woman is the mother of one of my friends. She has been praying for all of her children. The Lord wanted me to pray for her to know that He has heard and answered her prayers. My prayer partner and I prayed that the Lord would speak to her in words or visions or dreams, letting her know that He has answered her prayers.

I was thinking about one of my professors in college and his wife when suddenly I had a vision of a man and a woman together like they were posing for a picture. He was wearing a white suit:

They do not care to stand in My presence. They are not interested in Me. They go as the world. I have My angels with them. The seeds have been planted in them. Some of the seeds have fallen on hard ground. Their minds are resistant to My Word and My way. Their white coat is their perceived purity. They are only pure in the world, not with Me. They are in trenches that are deep. Much prayer and fasting will be needed to get them on level ground. You may choose as you wish. Age and a life without My richness make a person hard looking. Their countenance of My life and love is not in them. I have prayed for this couple daily for years.

Vision of a woman in a cafeteria line wearing a purple dress looking at me:

I did not know her. Her name is Sandra. The Lord wants me to pray for her.

Vision of a young black lady standing before me with her eyes closed and her head slightly tilted down. She wore bright red lipstick:

> This woman was the wife of a prominent black man who was murdered. She has unforgiveness on her heart for the murder of her husband. We prayed for the bitterness, resentment, and unforgiveness. My prayer partner received knowledge that she forgave the murderer of her husband.

Dream – a group of young men were standing around and visiting, as I was holding and looking at a book that was written by one of the young men in the Community of God's Delight:

> The Lord wanted my prayer partner and me to pray that one of the young man would respond to the prompting of His Spirit to write a book. The Lord would not tell us which one of the young men it was.

Vision of a man from the chest up, with graying hair in a business suit, who appears to be in his fifties:

This man is the new Prime Minister of Israel. Keep him lifted up in prayer.

Vision of John and Jackie Kennedy when they were young. Jackie had a baby in her arms. The baby was looking directly at me:

> Jackie's death is not from Him. It is a result of strain and hurts. The baby in her arms identified the time when her

life was peaceful and OK. No one comes to power except through Me. The Kennedy family did not choose to lift Me up in their lifestyles. Even though the world reveres them, and I have mercy on them, their examples were far from what I wanted. Pray for their children.

Vision of a naked, young girl, six or seven years of age, walking out of a drug store:

The young lady is symbolic of all the young people. The Lord is saying that sins against his children are escalating. Men are not turning to God as they should, and Satan is leading them into great sin. Pray for the children. Pray for conversion. Pray for forgiveness. There is great error around us. Pray for justice.

Vision of a tall man wearing a long, curly, white hairpiece:

This man is the Prime Minister of England. We prayed for him. After praying, my prayer partner saw him talking and explaining something to his cabinet members in the Parliament.

Vision of a tall black boy, leaning back in a chair, with the palm of his hand on his right eye. His mother was standing behind the chair, with her hands on the chair:

The woman's name is Agatha. She needs prayers for her son. Gangs may be the problem.

Vision of a squirrel on the grass:

The squirrel is a symbol of life and freedom given to souls for whom you have prayed.

Vision of a husky, nice looking, young, tall man with blond hair wearing a white shirt with double green stripes:

> This young man was involved with witchcraft. The Lord asked us to cast the spirit out and set him free.

Vision of a Muslim woman wearing expensive clothes and an expensive white facemask, which covers her nose and mouth:

> This woman is the wife of a high ranking official in Kuwait. She is close to finding the Lord. Pray for her.

Dream of an Indian chief:

> Pray for a revival among the Native Americans. Their families have been decimated by poverty, alcoholism, joblessness, and abuse of every kind. Pray for them, especially the leaders, and men that they will hear Me, as I call them, for I desire their healing.

Vision of a man that I did not recognize, looking at me: I could see the white of his eyes:

> My prayer partner received knowledge that this person was a high school classmate in fear. We repented for and came against the spirit of fear, quoting 2 Timothy 1:7, "For God hath not given us the spirit of fear; but of power, and of love, and of a sound mind." My prayer partner had a sense of peace after we prayed.

I was awakened from a dead sleep when something touched me. I felt a buzzing sound; then, the word suicide came to me. I got up at 1 a.m. and prayed for an hour or so:

> I learned a few days later that a son of a friend had

threatened to commit suicide on that night, but he is OK now. This night happened to be the son's birthday.

Vision of a face of a bear then a face of a goat:

Russia is in need of a spiritual renewal. Pray that they be freed from the sins of materialism, spiritualism, and occultism. The Lord desires their conversion.

Vision of a shirtless friend, who lifted his arm to put on some deodorant. When he touched his skin several inches below the arm pit, flames appeared:

It would be a cleansing, but he is not ready for it. He is not supported spiritually. I am to pray for the person, who is to minister to my friend, at the time of his conversion.

Vision of a black man, with his head shaved, to form a ring of hair on the top of his head:

This man is Joshua. Join his mother in prayer for his salvation. Pray that he will turn away from the gang.

Vision of a young girl, 7 to 9 years of age, in a casket:

Pray for the family, so they will not reject the Lord, because of her death.

Vision of a woman, a friend walking into our bedroom, while we were asleep. When she saw we were sleeping, she turned around and left without disturbing us:

She needs prayers, and she is too timid, ashamed and embarrassed to ask for them.

I had a dream of Manning Price, my professor at Texas A&M, who is with the Lord and a mutual friend, who is still living:

> My prayer partner said Manning Price wanted me to pray for our friend's salvation. The professor also wanted me to ask him to intercede for me each day.

Vision of a small boy 2, 3 or 4 years old with greenish brown eyes:

> A child in the community for whom the Lord wanted my prayer partner and I to pray that he would dedicate his life to the Lord and be a priest.

Vision of an old photograph of two sisters, when they were teenagers:

> Pray for these sisters that their hearts may be made young with the love they had for each other. Pray that the Holy Spirit may fill them so they may be a support to each other in their last days; that they may learn the lessons they are supposed to learn and that they may be freed of all the hurts, they have experienced over their lives.

Vision of an older Mexican woman, walking out of church, wearing a big gold scarf that covered her whole body. I had knowledge she had written a letter to some drug gang in Mexico and told them she was coming down to talk with them:

> Gold indicates the presence of the Lord's anointing on this woman. We are to pray for this woman to speak the Lord's words.

Vision of a large black woman with blemish spots on her cheeks under each eye:

> This woman is encouraging you to continue to pray for the American Blacks, especially those in poverty.

Vision of a young man in a business suit standing before me.

> Pray for a renewal among the business community of this nation. Pray against the greed, avarice and other sins.

Vision of a woman with dark hair and tears in her eyes:

> This woman wants us to pray for her son, who is dying, not physically but spiritually.

Vision of an older slim woman, with many wrinkles and high cheekbones:

> She needs prayers for an alcoholic husband.

Vision of a small, old, bald-headed man with a white beard waving his hand at me with a smile. One eye was shut:

> Pray for him to see the truth before death.

Visions and messages on abortion

While I was thinking about abortion, the word "leprosy" came to me. Then a vision of a priest wearing white vestments lying down on the floor. His face was covered by part of the vestments. When I was able to see his face, his eyes were sunken and closed like a dead man:

> Abortion is leprosy in God's sight. Those who support it

are choosing to be cast out of His society. The religious leaders, who support the decision of the people to abort children, are like dead men before the Lord.

Vision of a face of a small child on the palms of two hands:

All children belong to Me. I give them life. Their innocence pleases Me. Stand strongly against any law or action, which society may choose to follow, which seeks to deny My right over life and the sacredness of that life. All is in My hands and those who would deny this are damned.

Vision of a small red light in the form of a dot:

My prayer partner saw the red dot. It became clear. Then he saw a statue of Justice waving her hand saying, "There is no justice." The blood of the babies murdered are before God. We asked why she was waving her hand. She said, "To be noticed." We asked why the color was red? My prayer partner saw a large electronic board with many clear and red dots. The red dots are those already aborted. The clear dots are those who will be aborted. This nation can be saved but you must repent for those who are in ignorance, those with hardened hearts, and those who are being led by pride and circumstances. The red dot signifies the tremendous sin in the world. Abortion is only a part. The Lord condemns the lack of respect for Himself. God abhors the lack of adoration. He remonstrates against the willful bending of His Word. A time of retribution is coming. The red dot signifies that blood will flow and fire will burn for God will cleanse the world of its apostasy.

Vision of a woman whose face is red from crying:

The crying woman is like "Rachel weeping for her children because they are no more." She is symbolic of the sorrow women will have when the fruit of their godless goals and lifestyles come back to haunt them.

Vision of a middle age man with blood on his lips:

People, who come with blood on their lips, promoting death through abortion, euthanasia, genocide or war, are people who sold themselves out to Satan. They are to be avoided. Their message is to be rebuked and refused. This is not God's will for His world.

Vision of a very large Holstein cow lying down sideways in a pasture that is covered with about six inches of muddy water trying to give birth to a calf. This cow was about 20 yards from an area not covered with water. There were several cows standing around this cow:

My son, hear Me! Know that motherhood, as we understand it, is dying. The world stands and watches it die. There is no one to care for her calf, so it is with man. Women have turned against the gift of birth and its suffering. Suffering at birth is part of their salvation.

Vision of a very beautiful black horse in a stable.

This black horse is the horse of famine. The judgment of famine is coming on this land because of abortion. Abortion is the worst holocaust the world has ever known. The black horse of famine is going to fall upon this nation if my people do not turn from their wicked ways and stop it.

Vision of a dark cloud – This picture flashed on and off several times.

We asked the Lord the meaning. He said the cloud was the leadership throughout the country that preaches not to worry, that we do not need to repent, everything is O.K. It is this lie that is the deceit, which supports abortion and the killing of the young. The cloud signifies the blocking of the truth. The purple shows the need for repentance. The flashing on and off is God's insistent love, telling us to pay attention to the truth, to repent. We need to pray for our priests and other leaders who are not giving us proper leadership.

Vision of an attractive young blond woman with her hair tucked up in a British-type cap wearing a deep red lipstick:

My nation is being deceived by those in and through the church, i.e. the acceptance of homosexuality, abortion, the ordination of woman, etc.

Visions and messages pertaining to judgment and hard times

Vision – while praying the rosary, I had a vision in which I took a book off of a library bookshelf. The title of the book was *"War Planes"*. My prayer partner said this vision was from the Lord:

It is true, My son; you shall see this come to pass. Yet, you will not see it for I have protected you. Others, you know, will see it, for they are not protected. They live in the world and in the Spirit, but the Spirit does not dominate their lives. Because of their choice of the world, these of My children will suffer. The enemy of their souls will wreak havoc in their lives. You cannot protect them or shield them from My justice and My mercy. I have chosen, for you, a different path. A path of My peace. You will have struggles, but I will be there through all of it. It is on this feast day that I give you knowledge of My love for you. I have seen and recognized your love for Me and My Father. My mother stands beside you and petitions heaven to listen to her voice proclaiming, "he is mine and under my protection. Let no evil befall him. Let justice be brought upon them that would do him harm. Yea, he is mine. Let not the sword of justice go nigh his dwelling. Your dwelling will be a tent for a period of time."

Vision of fire blight on peaches (Fire blight is not found on peaches. It is found on apples, pears, and related species.):

The blight on peaches is symbolic of strange diseases and maladies, which are about to fall on the world. God is sending signs of His displeasure upon us; signs which have not been seen before, and for which no known remedies exist. This is because the world is not seeking God first.

Vision of one-gallon paint can with nail holes in the bottom being used for a shower:

Times are going to become hard. There are going to be problems with water, electricity, and gas.

Vision of shelves in a supermarket, some empty, and some bulging with food:

Prepare for scarcity of materials and goods. Expect uneven supplies to become common. In the midst of these difficulties, do not stock up large amounts of goods. Do not yield to fear. God is the supplier. In the midst of famine, He will feed His people.

Vision of a bright white light with a tinge of orange on the bottom edge of the light:

> The bright light is Jesus, the Lord. The orange tinge signifies the vengeance of the Lord, which is coming. He means to cast a fire on earth. We are to be warned and ready for His coming. The time is not far off.

The Lord told us to expect famine and shortage of materials. Since we know, we are to prepare. I asked the Lord how we should prepare.

> You still have time. Every day you are to bring yourselves before Me and commend yourselves, your loved ones and those I have given to you for prayer. You are to specifically lift up yourselves to My protection in the time of famine and loss to come. Every day you will be enlightened more. As time goes by I will enlighten you on the next steps to take. By the time the trials come, you will be totally protected and prepared. I, Myself, will take care of your needs. Do not be anxious. Take each step day by day. There will be no rush on you.

Vision of a black baby:

> The black baby is a sign. The racial problems we know today are the baby stage of what is to come. The population of black people in the United States shall become a millstone around the neck of freedom and truth of the law and justice. We shall see great bloodshed and greed. This will be the beginning of what will become a divisive force on our nation. There will be civil unrest, war, and division because of the black demands for unjustifiable goals.

Dream, all the priests were arrested and were in prison. I recognized one priest who was stripped of all of his clothes:

This dream is symbolic of what is coming on the world. The priest, stripped of all his clothing, is symbolic of how many will be stripped of all that they have except the Lord and as they stay in Him, they will be victorious with Him.

Stay in Me, and evil will not harm you. No power of darkness will harm your spirit. You are mine. I paid the price for your souls. Yes, evil is coming on the earth. Fear not, for the gates of hell will not prevail against My Church.

Vision of soldiers wearing helmets and preparing to fight then the words came to me, "Global action":

This is the Lord's heavenly army preparing for battle.

Vision of a red-headed man with a small red sore on his cheek.

The sore on his face is symbolic of the results of his rebellion. The Lord says, "I will mark the faces of those who rebel against Me. You will see them and you will know them. Do not be marked yourselves. The time is coming when this mark will be on so many that the way the society lives will change. Only those who walk in My ways will know peace."

Vision of a swift blow of a hammer hitting a sheet of paper with a dozen or so names. I did not recognize any of the names:

The hammer is a symbol of God's judgment. The list of names symbolizes those judged. The judgment will be swift, hard, and irreversible. The names of those judged are spiritual leaders, who have misled God's people.

I was standing in front of a small circular church with glass doors and gold rails. Many people in he church were standing around waiting for Mass to begin. I recognized one of the people.

> This is the church that will survive the holocaust that is to come. These are those who have washed their clothes with the blood of the Lamb. They are a remnant of what was and now is.

I asked the Lord when this would happen.

> It shall be in your lifetime. Do not fear for I have made all the necessary preparations for you and yours. You are gold that has been tested by fire. Your dross is negligible. Keep your eyes on Me; forget not my sayings and standards. Keep them in your mouth and on your lips.

A judge in court:

> The time of judgment is at hand. The Lord is about to release several tribulations on the world. AIDS is only the beginning. His judgment is pure. Those who seek the Lord and walk in His ways will be secured by His angels and protected through the trials. Stand firm in your faith.

Vision of a red tail and a black tail of scorpions:

> The Lord has two inflictions for the world. One is already on us like the sting of a scorpion. We call it "AIDS"! The second, worse than the first, is yet to come. Stay in God's way and you will not be stung.

Vision of planes, a crucifix and Egyptian or Hebrew type writings in the sky:

> The Lord is passing judgment on the U.S.A. This is the

first country in history to be founded on His precepts, and He is about to reclaim it. Mene, Tekel, Parsim.* He will overthrow the powers of evil and will restore His precepts for He has heard the cry of His people. It will be a time of difficulty, but His judgment has been passed, and it will be.

There was writing on the wall during the rein of King Belshazzer. The writing in the sky is the same as the writing on the wall, which meant the end of the kingdom of Babylon. King Belshazzer died that night

Vision of someone talking to me: The only thing I remembered was the word "AIDS":

I have allowed "HIV" and "AIDS" to come upon this country because of its immorality. This will not be the only curse that will come upon this nation, if the people do not turn from their wicked ways. I will consume their flesh if they continue in their immorality.

Vision of a skinny boy, 18 to 20 years of age, sitting on the floor of a porch. He got up and spoke to me. He had gaps or space between his teeth:

Future days, food storage and money problems will result in poor living conditions with children losing teeth and other things.

A long dream – my brother, Pete, and I stole a bulldozer from a large building under the control of the Antichrist's people. They came running after us, but did not shoot at us. The next thing I knew, I was digging a 20 feet deep pit out at the land. I could see the white chalk rock. Then I saw a gallon plastic jug of water, a two

gallon jug of milk and a two gallon jug of coke:

> My prayer partner saw 20 foot deep trenches going in every direction. Then he saw concrete being poured on top, then soil and grass planted. The people were in small areas off the trench. When they came together to pray they had to stand in the trenches as there was not a room big enough to hold them. The water was for the old people. Milk was for the babies, and coke was for the young people. The people had learned how to live by eating less.

Vision of a man sitting on the floor with a long tongue hanging out of his mouth full of red sores:

> Beware of the tongue. They will come back to haunt you. Beware how you talk about anyone; politician, professional, enemy, lost soul or friend. If you speak ill of anyone, your words are like daggers. They damage those, who hear them and those, about whom you speak. My people must speak a positive message or they will become sick from their words. Make it your special work not to speak ill of anyone.

Vision of a gas burner with many individual flames. Each flame was yellow in the middle with blue on one side and green on the other side:

> When the Lord comes with fire, He will burn everything that is not of Him. There will be no escape.

Vision of a green corrugated background with an address in the middle. The picture was so fast that I only able to read the word - "New York":

> I tell you My son, that it will be destroyed, as well as other

279

cities. What you see are the after tremors of great destruction. From what you see, very few have lived. Many sins have bought this down as in the days of Sodom.

Vision of an upright stick, 12 to 15 inches long, on fire, with a flame blowing 4 to 5 inches to the right of the stick:

This is the purifying fire of My Spirit that is to come upon the earth to judge the earth. My Spirit comes as a mighty wind.

Vision of a group of 10 to 12 men and women posing for a picture:

What you see is a picture of a family that will be destroyed. Many families will be destroyed because the door has been open to the enemy, and it has not been closed.

Vision of purple and green then an image of a scorpion:

I have given you the sacrament of reconciliation to protect you from the sting of sin to bring you within My new life.

Visions and messages to my wife, Ann, and me

Vision in which I walk through a heavy curtain veil with my crucifix in my hand:

It is I Who send you. It is I Who cause you to pray with whom I bring to you. It is I Who am there to lead you through the darkness of the world. It is I Who guides you through the curtains. It is I Whom you trust. Those that I bring to you are those that I have given to you to guide and care for as My shepherd on earth. They bring you their problems and their grief. They do not have what you have, and as such, will not receive what I have for you. Listen more to what I will tell you and show you before you give them what you have received. I am a jealous God. I want to be with you. Do not be impatient. Enjoy My presence. Enjoy My time with you. Enjoy what I show you. Discern before you share with others. Let My time with you be pleasant and fun. Come to have fun with Me. Show Me what you are doing. Tell Me about your own needs. Come to Me to be built up and made stronger in all ways. Talk to Me as your friend and confidant. Leave Me filled and happy. Start soon!

Vision of a very beautiful silver ring ½ inch wide with a narrow border of gold on both sides: There were two V inlays of gold on the silver. The bottom part of each V was on the opposite side pointing towards each other. I could not see the top of the V's as it was on the underside of the ring. The gold and silver area was covered with small diamonds. This was the most beautiful ring I had ever seen:

The Spirit says, My son, this ring is a token of My love and appreciation for your loyalty, fidelity and commitment to follow Me. My love for you is the same as the love I had for the betrothed couple at the marriage feast at Cana. With the exchange of the wedding ring at Cana two became one, just as I became one with you with the exchange of the visionary ring. My love for you is as pure as the refined gold and silver in this ring. My covenant of grace with you is as indestructible as the hardness of the diamonds on this ring. This ring is a ring of appreciation. Treasure it as much as the crown that was (previously) given to you. You are part of Me which makes you part of royalty. This ring which I have given you makes you heir to My kingdom. It is the Lord God Yahweh who speaks.

Vision of newly planted shrubs in my mother and dad's yard:

My son, I am about to show you My glory. I am about to wake the dead and the dying. I am going to shine over this spot. Walk out the door - pass through the bushes to the road of life. Minister and be ministered to. Do not hold back. You came from these roots. I came from a cave in the hill. It is not where you came from, but what road you are on and which direction you choose to follow Me. Know that I am God, and I will love you no matter which way you choose. Come close, draw near and hear Me speak to you. Know that My joy for you is complete. I will keep using you.

Vision of several small children was playing at my feet. One little girl rolled her head back and looked into my eyes with her blue eyes:

This child represents all of your grandchildren to come. The blue in her eyes is my gift of holiness. There is much evil in the world, but by your act of prayer and intercessions, you are laying a foundation for your future generation. God will maintain a purity and innocence about them. He urges us to maintain our works of intercession and prayer.

Vision of Ann, my wife, smiling and calling me to her with her finger:

Michael, My son, she calls you as a young love calls to her beau. Refresh her with a new found love of a young man. Shower her with those things that she would not do for herself. Give her the love of a passionate lover. Let her know that there is no part of her that is not loved with the love of a new groom. Inoculate her with an intense love. Make her feel the love of your first love. Tell her that I have blessed her and that you have been blessed because of her love for Me. She is Mine. I would have her know one one-millionth of the joy she is going to have with Me. Bring her to this joy with patience. Be alone and away. Let her experience this often. Be gentle and strong. I will give you renewed strength that you have not known. Do not be afraid. The heavens will rejoice with you.

Vision of an older man sitting in a chair, shaking his head, as he looks at me:

The man represents Christian people of your past that came to know you as they were going through their time of interest in their faith. They see you as having moved on and on in disbelief of their own state as to yours. This is symbolic of many of us in the world, who do not want to change our lives. We have become comfortable with our sins. We are not willing to let go of our lifestyle. Our stubbornness is bringing about the calamities, which we have begun to see. There will be many more calamities, worse than this flooding (1993), if we, as a nation and as individuals, do not surrender to God immediately.

Vision of my wife kissing me on my right cheek:

I have given you your wife as a helpmate unto you. She is to always be a part of your decision-making. Her discernment is to be relied upon. The two of you are to be as one with Me.

Dream that my workshop was robbed and completely empty:

Are you prepared to lose even the things that give you real pleasure? Can you give them up? I am preparing you for a deeper relationship with Me.

Vision of a car parked across one of my driveways blocking the driveway:

> Be careful of the efforts which the enemy will make to stop others from coming to you for prayer.

Vision - I was sitting in a large new yellow pickup in the driver seat.

> Yellow pickup is God's color. You are God's workman. God is encouraging you to continue working.

Lord speaks about prayer:

> There is no prayer that leaves your heart and your mouth that does not come back to you ten fold. Your prayers are heard. They protect, enlighten, and lift up those for whom you pray. They give Me great pleasure.

Dream concerning problems at work:

> Do not be anxious about your work. I am with you. The difficulties you face are temporary. Bear with them. I will change the situation soon. But you must take each day, one at a time. Do not let others pressure you into feeling insecure. I am He Who gives and He Who takes away. You are in My hands. Do not be anxious.

Vision of a large crowd of people and a word was spoken about my ears being healed but nothing happened:

> People will come from all over the world with advice on how to be healed. Do not pay any attention to them. I have healed you. It will be manifested in My time.

Vision of myself, unshaven with a dark beard. (My beard is now gray):

> The black beard is a symbol of youthful vigor and power. Your spirit is young and powerful; your prayers carry great weight.

Vision which I was walking to my mother and dad's house with three or four white children: They turned and walked across a yard to where a black neighbor lives:

> Do not be thoughtless as children. Be sensitive to each other's fears, beliefs and needs. Respect each other, and build up relationships. Carelessness of thought and action can cause great harm.

Vision of a Holstein cow with bulging milk veins, heavy producer:

> There will come a time when the people will not be fed. I tell you that you are the milk sack of that cow. They will come to you to be fed My Word. They shall have their fill. Each udder will give a different knowledge of Me. You are ready. I am about ready for you to feed them.

Vision of a Collie dog:

> A Collie dog herds sheep. You are the Collie dog. You will herd God's sheep.

Vision, I was making very large holes on a sloping hillside so another person could walk more easily up the hill. The holes were too far apart for a person to step from one to another:

> The holes far apart on the hillside are a quick guide for Christians to follow to Christ. But it takes large,

determined steps to follow Him and it is an upward climb.
God has called you to pray for others. They have to be
prepared to take large difficult steps up to Him.

Vision of a man planting seeds with a grubbing hoe:

The man is you and the seeds are your prayers.

I received words of knowledge about not having enough money:

Do not worry about tomorrow or your finances. I give.
I take away. I will always care for you. I will meet your
needs. Reject Satan and his attempts to alarm you.

Vision of Ann and I walking to the guest bedroom with a man.

The man is Jesus. Jesus is a constant guest in your home.

Vision of a large 9X12 envelope that was completely covered with many different kinds of stamps:

The Lord said the stamps represent many people from all
over the world thanking me for my prayers.

Words spoken to me, "With all my strength I will teach abundant life":

My call to you is very clear. Despite the easy ways the
world gives, which many choose to follow, there are many
who are listening to Me and trying to do My will. There
will be new life in My Church; a source of strength and
growth, and I will never turn away from them. Follow
through on your desire to follow Me. The reward is very
great.

Vision of myself right in front of me looking at me. This was in details and color. I could see the details of the shirt I wore:

> It is the beginning of a new gift for which you will be used. You will see yourself in other places as the Spirit sends you! (Bilocation)

Dream - I was in my home and then I was suddenly in a friend's living room about 2 a.m. This was embarrassing, to be suddenly in someone's home, when he does not know you are there. I went to the front door, which was locked, to be sure I did not drive over. There was no car in front of the house. I knocked on the front door to awaken my friend. We visited a while:

> My prayer partner said this was from the Lord; Mike being in two places at the same time. I'm moving Mike around. He is to pray for My will and not wonder. He is going to see things that I will show him. Some things will be told to others. Some things are not to be revealed. I am protecting others through him, as I send him. He is to pray prayers of protection. Some will receive salvations; others will be healed; yet others will grow. Prepare to travel! (Bilocation)

Vision of myself when I was two or three years of age:

> Remember when you were young? You had much growing to do. You have come a long way but you are still young. You will grow much more. Trust me.

I asked the Lord about my parents, and why he has not manifested the healing of my ears and speech:

> Be patient, Mike. I have heard your prayers, and I have answered them. You are a special instrument I have raised

up. I choose to use you in My way for the greatest good of those who meet you. Your parents are in My hands. I am healing them now through their sufferings. I am with you. Do not fret about delays in seeing My healing on you or them. Be patient and trust Me, especially when you do not see the results you want. For eternity you will see the results of your prayers. Wait on Me.

Vision – my wife and I had given one of our sons a plate with a picture of Christ on it. There is something about the Lord blessing the homes with His picture.

Urge the children to consecrate their homes to the Sacred Heart.

Vision of a man directing me to where a meeting was:

Whenever you need direction, I will send My messenger to you. Do not worry about where to go or whom to call. I will not let you go undirected.

Dream – I was in church at the back. I started shaking and trembling and fell to the floor. Then I was standing next to a large pillar praying in a very unusual tongue with distinct sounds. My lips were round and my tongue was sticking out moving up and down against my lips. There was a man standing in front of me listening to what I was saying:

My son, My words are deep. They will carry several meanings. Be open to the Spirit speaking. My son, Michael, will have the power of the Most High to fall upon him. He will be brought to his knees but not of the stone-heartedness of My Church. They will see and they will hear through stammering lips. They will not know or understand. They hear My message and their hearts become

288

hardened. They rely on themselves for their needs. They do not understand the anointing that is on Mike. They will reject him and Me as they do. This will happen in the final moments. The supports or pillars of the Church are where their hearts and souls lay. They are a lost generation. My prophet, Michael is their last chance before My great destruction.

Vision of a man who resembled my dad:

Beware of false prophets. If you can be fooled into believing someone looks like your dad, you can be fooled into believing false messages about Me.

Vision of a fire in a bowl on a white stone altar, then a spotlight on my empty bed. The spot light continued on my bed:

These are the sins covered with My blood that are on fire. They burn to ashes, never to be seen or heard of again. This fire will never go out. All sins are covered with My blood when repentance occurs. In this case, they are the repented sins of My son, Michael. They are as they never happened. The fire burns with blood fueling it. His bed is empty. He does not rest. He does not get the needed sleep to replenish his body. He is to change his schedule that he may enjoy his rest. He is not to use these things of the bed post to wake himself up or to keep himself awake. I want him full of rested energy, not just standing on one leg as he does his work or comes to Me. He is to enjoy his rest. I am important but he is very important to Me.

I have called you to a special role of intercessor. Your prayers are powerful. They rise like perfume to Me. When you pray, I listen and I answer. But I have this one thing against you. You are too concerned with little things in life, which now serve to distract you. Put aside your worries about if you should fast or how long. Whenever you fast, it is good. I will bless you for it. Your prayers are always answered, but not always in the way you want to see them answered. Keep constant in prayer at whatever time I wake you to pray, but do not become legalistic about how and what you do. Not everyone can intercede. I have chosen you to help those who cannot. Be certain that I am blessing you. Put aside your doubts.

Vision of a long stem rose in which the bud has not opened. I had knowledge that the rose was gold in color:

As a suitor seeks to woo his beloved I come to you with the "Rose of Glory." I bring it to you for your joy. Because I love you, I want you to have it. As a loved one rejoices in the gifts from the lover, and treasures the gifts, so must you receive My gift. Put My glory, given to you, in the pages of your heart.

I heard a voice which said, "Your accomplishments":

Your accomplishments are not from you but from Me. Ask Me what you want to know and do. But ask Me first, if this is what I want you to accomplish or pursue in the laboratory. Ask Me first.

Vision of a horse in a stall with an abundance of straw, fed with all its need taken care. I saw a brass lamp with three light bulbs and a camera:

My son, make your eyes My eyes. Allow them to focus on how the light of Jesus illuminates the projects of your life. I am taking care of all your needs by supplying you with the best quality that can be given. Relax; concern yourself with no more activity than I bring forth for you each day. The past is for building upon. The future is for hope. The present is for serving now. Be sensitive to your family. Be cooperative with your community. Be faithful to your business. Know that I am with you always for I am the Lord God Yahweh who speaks.

Long dream – I do not know at whose house I was. I was on the back porch. The back yard had a tall wooden fence around it. A man was standing guard under the porch with rifle. Later we were in the house when the doorbell rang. I went to the front door. The man with the rifle was standing behind me 8 to 10 feet away. As I opened the front door, there were five men, one was black. The black man was the one who rang the doorbell. When I opened the door, he pulled a pistol on me. I tried to get a pistol out of my pocket to shoot:

> The man with the rifle is God. He is your protector and your help. The "gun" in your pocket is God's Word. You will be attacked because you stand by God's Word. You will use it to defend yourself, and God will be behind you, protecting and helping you. Stand firm!

Be Patient:

> Be patient. Know at this very moment your prayers are answered. Be patient, as Jesus is patient, in waiting for Me to instruct Him to come back again. Have perseverance, endurance and hope that all things will come to good. I am pleased with your faithfulness in prayer and commitment to come before Me daily. Your rewards will be many. Remain virtuous and humble. I love you. You are My children.

Vision of my wife, Ann, in a very attractive red dress with a white collar. The dress had pictures of different things, like a person swinging a golf club or someone walking a dog, etc. scattered over the dress:

> My heart sings for joy for My daughter. She is a light to My eye and a joy to My heart. As I see her, she has a heart full of joy. Her dress expresses her excitement. She is as a young woman.

Vision – a tiny red light was seen on the right side inside my right eye next to the pupil.

> This red light represents the continuous presence of the Blessed Sacrament within you until you receive communion again.

Dream - I was standing on two poles that were being carried on the shoulders of two men. I was being carried throughout the country side proclaiming to everyone "Israel is set free! Israel is set free!" Then I started praying in tongues. The power of God came all over me. Then I proclaimed again "Israel is set free!" I did not sleep the rest of the night as I could feel the excitement of being carried on the poles on the shoulders of the two men proclaiming "Israel is set free!" and the feeling of the power and the anointing of Lord on me:

> You have led the charge in the spiritual battle, and you will be given the privilege of being one of those who will announce the final victory over Satan. Israel, the Body of Christ, will indeed be set free. You will announce that victory to the acclamation of the people raising their voices in a hymn of victory. It is a hymn similar to the ones the Israelites sang, when David was victorious over the Philistines. The dream is intended as a vision of what your efforts in prayer, fasting and intercessions will result in.

Vision of my wife, Ann, saying to someone, "No, I don't want to hear that":

> Ann was protecting her spirit. Our spirit is attacked and weakened by impure words spoken, thoughts or things we see or hear or to which we listen.

Vision of my wife, Ann, in a white dress with numerous small red tulips with green stems and blades scattered all over as a polka dotted dress. Ann had a very loving, pleasing, desirable countenance or look about her:

> This is what I want from all of My children. The radiance you saw was My presence within Ann. This radiance will cause all to come to Me.

Vision - a close view of my wife's Ann's beautiful eyes, looking to my right:

> My prayer partner said he saw Ann, as she is now, standing in the wind with a long print skirt on and her hair blowing in the wind. I asked the Lord what this meant. He said, "The wind is the wind of My Spirit. I am not through with her yet. When I get through with her, she will look like this." I then saw Ann as a young bride in a pure white wedding gown.

I was concerned that some prayer partners would say something was not from the Lord and yet, others would get a powerful message. I asked the Lord why?

> When you pray for discernment and hear from one prayer partner that message is not from God and another says plainly and powerfully it is, you are to realize that you are under constant spiritual attack. God has given you many

ears, prayer partners because all men are imperfect, and Satan can get through in some way in each of them. That is, each man has some weakness in his spiritual defenses. Do not worry about this situation. God's Word to you is so powerful, that it will get through. Each prayer partner is called to feel God's anointing in some area because he wants to minister to them. That area is usually where they are strong.

I had turned the light off to go to bed. When I shut my eyes, it was as if there was a light in my face. When I opened my eyes, it was pitch dark. When I closed my eyes, there was a light in my face. I did this several times. It was pitch dark, when my eyes were open, and a light in my face, when my eyes were closed:

> When the eyes are closed, we walk by faith, lighted by the power of the Spirit. When the eyes are open, they see as the world sees, and they are clouded by the flesh. This light is the power of the Holy Spirit seeing through the darkness by faith.

Dream – there were three different eagle nests on the block where I lived. Two of the nests were on opposite corners and the third was in the middle of the side of the block. The nests were on very tall aluminum light poles:

> They (eagles) have been placed near, so that you will know that I and Mine are very near. The eagles see and take to wing, scouring for the enemy, whether they fly or are on the ground. They will attack, protect, and warn of danger. You will be taken up by them. Be happy about what I am doing for you.

Vision of a pocket knife, similar to a Boy Scout knife, with a ring on the end. Words came to me that I should have brought Ann a pocket knife for survival:

> The knife represents the Word of God. It is God's Word that will help us to survive.

I woke up with a crick in my neck. I asked a prayer partner to command the spirit that was attacking me to identify itself. My prayer partner received the following words:

> My Word has been purified and is more precious than gold. I bring you to My Father. I bring you into His throne room. I ask you now to mentally prostrate yourself before Him. There you will hear His voice speak to you. There He will give you word of your affliction. Know that I am your Lord. I will not forsake My servant, Michael.

Words to my prayer partner and me:

> Men of God, bones and flesh of Adam, be prepared to receive the riches I have in store for you. Your walk with Me depends on your faithfulness to come before Me daily. Spend 15 minutes a day with Me in silent prayer in order that at this time, I may reveal to you the true purpose for your existence on this planet. I will multiply your finances, according to the attitude in which you give. It is not the amount that is so important as it is the regularity and joyful attitude. Be faithful to your pledges, in order that I may multiply your riches. All that you have, materially and spiritually, first belongs to Me. I give it to you with love. Always remember that I am your source for all you need, spiritually and materially. Ask and you shall receive. Seek and you shall find. Knock and it will be opened. I love you beyond all that you can imagine. I am

ready to bless you beyond all imagination. Come to Me in love and submission. Fear and trembling are not of My nature. I am your Father, Yahweh Sabbath who speaks.

(Note- **Silent prayer is not verbal prayer.** The Lord is asking us to be silent for at least 15 minutes so that we can hear Him speak to us.)

While taking a shower, I had a vision as I glanced up into the heavens; I saw two specks of silver light:

These are My two sons of righteousness, Elijah and Moses. Their light will become brighter and brighter as the days go on.

Vision of a large bonfire by the fence and close to the front gate inside my yard:

This is a spiritual fire that cannot be seen by others. It is a purifying fire. It is for your protection and the protection of others. It keeps the power of darkness away.

Bill Alexander, my prayer partner, standing outside a room with plate glass windows, but it did not look like him. Bill said this was a description of the ground floor of DFW airport, where he works:

As you continue to pray together, your old nature will be transformed to the very point that you will not be able to recognize the old man. You will be transformed into the likeness of My Son.

As Bill, my prayer partner, was driving home, he saw the end of a rainbow on my house, when he turned from Loop 12 onto Highway 183. The Lord then gave Bill the following words. "I am calling you to continue to meet together, for there is much I intend to do with both of you. I will and I intend to transform you and your families and any and all that come in contact with each of you. They will see Me when they see you. My intent is to make you closer than blood brothers for the spirit is stronger than the physical."

Vision of two eyes of a man:

These are the eyes of My protection that search over all the earth. They land on My children, who walk in My way, to guide and see them through whatever comes their way. These eyes have fallen upon you and your family to watch over you and yours forever. These are the eyes of My Spirit resting upon you.

Someone poked me in the ribs in the middle of the night. I jumped. Ann was on the other side of the bed:

The Lord says, "I cannot get people to pray. I have to go to those who will!"

Vision in bright color – I was fixing a peanut butter and banana sandwich. I mixed the peanut butter and banana, then put it on some bread to make a sandwich:

Just as peanut butter and banana are easy to make, so shall your words be to My people!

Vision - while lying in bed with my eyes closed, I saw a red rose fall on the pillow by my nose and mouth:

Jesus said, "My rose to Michael is My thank you for his service. His breath is of the Holy Spirit. His words are My words, and they are anointed of My Father. He has been given a special anointing, and so have you.

Dream - I had a deep experience with the Lord, but did not remember anything when I woke up. Before I went to sleep, I told the Lord that I had been praying for a lot of things for a long time, but nothing was happening:

The Lord said, "Keep running the good race."

My wife, Ann, had a vision of Jesus looking at her at the prayer meeting with the look – "Didn't I take care everything?"

Her sons are cared for and will be warriors in His house.

Vision of a black rock, then a man appeared in the middle of the rock wearing a white garment with a white rope around his waist. I assumed this man was the Lord:

> Out of the ashes you will move mountains and experience new life as you do not know. Yet, I tell you, what you saw in the rock was nothing. Soon, you will know more of what and Who I am, that has been hidden from you and others. Do not try to interpret, so do not go to great lengths to understand. Take Me as Who I am to you and that of what you know and have learned about Me. Stay on those things that I show you, and be prepared not to lean on anyone else. My time is now. Prepare yourself for My return and what I am about to do. Do not look past the end of your nose for any answer to Me. Listen to what I say - not others. Listen.

Vision of strange-looking cattle with long horns going straight up. Then I heard a voice – "Sorry, I cannot permit you to live in Mexico":

> It is time. It is time. You shall not go hither and fro. I would have you go to the paths that I have made for other saints that I am calling. You hear My voice, and you

respond. I will speak to you, and you will hear, and you will then go to where I send you. Make yourself ready in all things.

Vision of a cow's udder:

A calf comes to its mother to be nursed. It pushes on each udder to empty the sack. So shall you nurse those who come to you spiritually. You shall be in charge of distribution of all things assigned to you. Strict discipline will be necessary. Be ready to serve!

Vision - a friend walked up behind me with big smile, touching me on my left shoulder with his right hand:

Do not give your own interpretation; give Scripture and the Church's teaching.

A man called my name, "Mike" three times. I did not recognize the voice. Then purple flashed before me three times:

The man is the Lord. He wants you to continue to repent for the sins of this nation.

St. Vincent Ferrier's name came to me in the middle of the night

Ask him to intercede for you.

Vision of Ann with a white, rope-like ring, with a large diamond on top. Ann was very excited. She said this was her wedding ring:

Can it be that you should know of My bond for each of you? Yours is somewhat the same. Yet, yours is larger with diamonds and bright red sapphires and studded with flakes of gold and diamonds. It is My gift to each of you. You shall wear it in My kingdom and all that see will know you are Mine.

As I finished reading the book on the Bible Code, I started to doze and heard my nickname, "Mickey":

Just as Samuel was called by name, so you are called by name by the Lord. Just as Enoch walked with God, you are called to walk with God. The Lord walks before you and beside you and calls you by name. Open your heart to Him for He desires to reveal His friendship for you. Strive to know His voice when He calls.

As I was thinking about or looking at a sunflower, suddenly there was a bright light like the sun in my face:

Do not forget, My son, that all around you, the Lord's creative hand is still at work. Even Solomon, in his glory, was not as beautiful as the flowers of the field. He gives you His light that you may see His creation and His hand at work.

While at Mass, after receiving Communion, I had a vision of a wall of reddish fire, with flames moving in every direction. In the center was a reddish area with no flame. This picture was shown to me again two days later:

The flame is the Holy Spirit. The reddish center is the blood of Jesus. The Lord said that no matter what trial, tribulation or fire we go through, we will be protected. My Word goes forth, and it cleanses. My blood is little, yet it purifies much. Your sins are forgiven through this fire, which heals our relationship. Though this is for all, few will know and experience this love I have for them.

Vision of a teenage girl walking down the step from the upstairs

bedroom:

> This is your unborn daughter that is in the kingdom. She
> wants you to ask her to intercede for the family each day.
> I named her Michele.

**Dream – I was sitting in a chair with a two year old girl in my lap
hugging my neck really tight.**

> I had knowledge this child was my unborn daughter. My
> prayer partner had understanding that this is a different
> daughter. My wife chose the name Angelia.

**Knowledge came to me that there would be a Roman Catholic
Church in my neighborhood:**

> Prayer partner received understanding that this church
> was my house. He saw people all over my front yard. This
> church shall be that which was as Priscilla and Aquilla. It is
> a church that meets at your house. It shall be as it was then
> with many signs and wonders bound together with love.

> 1 Corinthians 16:19: The church of Asia salute you,
> Aquilla and Priscilla salute you much in the Lord with
> the church that is in their house.

**Vision of a white bearded man standing next to me looking sideway
toward the ground:**

> This man is Moses. He was standing beside you explain-
> ing what is going to happen to the earth. Moses said I had
> written of it and will understand. Prayer partner asked,
> "Why Mike?" Moses responded, "He will be part of what
> was, what is and what is to come!"

Dream, Ann and I were in a restaurant sitting across a table from a black man and his young son (5 or 6). The man was tired and was catnapping. I told him I was tired and sleepy too:

> The black man catnapping, with his young son, are symbolic of "other" people who have to face great difficulties. Your feeling of tiredness is real, but not as bone deep as his. The Lord is reminding you to pray for those less fortunate who have to struggle very hard.

Words spoken while in prayer:

> I have a lesson for you – a lesson for you. My lesson is strong to you. I have come to warn you and give you praise. The world chooses not to tell you the truth. My son, you have always been faithful and trusting. You are at a time when you should not trust anyone, except Me. Your coming and going should always be by My Spirit. The tongue of the adder is ever about you. Challenge everything in the Spirit with My blood covering you.

Visions and messages of my mother, dad, relatives and friends

When my dad had a light stroke, I asked the Lord why He allowed this?

> It is with My permission your father has had this stroke. I will use this and other afflictions to bring him back to Me and make him ready to come home. Do not be concerned. I have heard your prayers. I will not abandon My people. Keep your father always before Me in prayer, for Satan wants him. Remember Abraham and his raised arms. Do not stop your prayers. The battle is won when you pray.

Vision of my mother and dad, when they were young, in a café:

> As it used to be, it will be again. The time is coming when your parents will leave you. Do not be afraid for them. Your prayers have been answered. They will rejoice together with Me at My table in heaven.

Vision of my dad walking into the Catholic Church in Clarksville: He looked like he was 50 years of age with dark hair, and with no trouble walking:

> This was a time in his life when he was talking with Me. Now he is not capable of doing so. It is important that we do this when we are capable because there will be a time when we will not be able to. He is now 95 years old (1995).

I am going to share something that I do not fully understand. I received knowledge that my aunt and uncle were in heaven, but were still in bondage. I prayed for an understanding of the bondage:

> Their bondage is that of the doctrine of the Church that is not Mine. They are holding fast to what was taught them that does not exist here. (I prayed for the bondage to be broken.) My prayer partner saw a picture of an angel distributing Communion to my uncle. As soon as the angel placed the Host in his hand, Jesus appeared in his hand. My uncle embraced Jesus and was set free. My aunt did the same. Their faith in the bread and the wine of the chalice was the key to accepting the existence in heaven.

I asked the Lord how they could be in heaven and be in bondage?

> There are those that allow themselves to be deceived

without knowing it.

Vision of my dad and one of his close friends. Both are with the Lord:

> My prayer partner discerned that my dad's friend was in a lower level of heaven. My dad had been praying for his friend to be able to come up to his level. As we prayed, my prayer partner saw my dad and his friend together.

Dream – my brother Pete went to my grandmother's house to get a saw to cut down a tree. Next my Uncle Maurice (who is in the kingdom) and Pete were using a crosscut saw to cut a large tree laying in the front yard into small sections:

> Your grandmother, uncle and all your relatives in heaven are there to support and help you and all of your loved ones here on earth. Your dream of your uncle and brother working together is symbolic of their willingness to help. Tell your brother and your sons to talk to their ancestors and seek their prayers. God will honor the love being shared.

I dreamed of my grandmother, who died in 1944:

> My prayer partner asked me if I had asked my grandmother to pray for me. I said, "No." He said, "She wants you to ask her to pray for you."

Dream – I was sitting at the table with my mother and dad. My mother had prepared a good meal. I had a box with 12 small compartments with 12 different spices and herbs:

> I have given many gifts to the earth. Among them are some of the simplest. These are some of those. I would

have you know the origins are from Me as gifts to your
life. It is these that help offer good health to those who
know how to use them. These will help you live in better
health.

Vision of a blue dot, then my Aunt Julia in a blue dress sitting on a couch. Julia is in the kingdom with the Lord:

Your aunt is ready to intercede before the throne for you,
but there is more. The color blue is Mary's color. She is
with any prayer your aunt makes for you because they
pray together to glorify Jesus. We need to be continuously
asking for prayers from our loved ones in heaven. It is a
great and powerful gift of support we have.

My dad's eyes really popped out as he was seeing something:

Because of your prayer, the Lord will show your dad
some things that are and some things that are to come.
(My dad spoke excitedly of a vision of heaven.)

Vision of Miss Lillie Branson, my high school English teacher in the 9th and 10th grade. She is with the Lord:

The Lord wants me to ask her to intercede for me each
day when I pray.

Vision of my high school principal, O. R. Caldwell, with a grin and a pleasant look on his face:

Mr. Caldwell wanted me to know that he was in heaven
interceding before the throne for me and all of his students. (Mr. Caldwell belongs to a Protestant denomina-
tion, but I do not know his faith.)

Vision of a woman, who I had knowledge was a relative.

> This woman is an intercessor from your dad's side of the family. She lived in a log cabin in this country.

My dad passed away on February 21, 1996 at the age of 95. He and my brother, Pete, had just finished eating supper. Pete helped him back to the bedroom where they said the Lord's Prayer. Then he stood up for Pete to pull his pajama up and died in my brother's arms. He told my brother earlier that he would be leaving that day. As I was praying, asking the Lord to have mercy on my dad, I had a vision of a flashing yellowish green light, on and off. Then I had a glimpse of a blinding white light that I knew was the Lord; followed by a vision of a blue statue of the Blessed Mother. I knew that yellow meant the presence of Lord, and green meant new life. I assume yellowish green meant the same:

> Your father received the power of the Holy Spirit in his last days. He has entered into My Father's kingdom and is rejoicing not only with his Alma, but with the Blessed Mother, whom they besought for help so often as a couple. Be assured that there is much rejoicing at his entering into the kingdom. Your family will see many blessings from Donovan and Alma's faithfulness.

> Note - Toni, my dad's nurse, said she had a vision of my dad, after the funeral, with a big smile on his face. He was wearing black pants and a white shirt with a crown on his head. He walked up to Toni, put his hand on her shoulder and said, "Toni, I made it home. Continue to pray and your reward will be great in the kingdom." I had been praying and asking the Lord since 1970 to baptize my dad with the baptism of the Holy Spirit. He experienced it about four months before he died. Toni said he prayed all the time in tongues. He had many visions and heavenly

experiences, and was greatly disappointed when he had to come back to the earth from those experiences.

Vision of one my cousins:

The Lord says, "I am going to reveal the truth to him. Pray that he will receive the truth."

Vision of Dr. Ernest Laake who has gone to be with the Lord:

Dr. Laake wanted to thank me for my prayer. This is the second time I had a vision of Dr. Laake wanting to thank me for the prayers I said for him while he was on earth.

Vision of my Aunt Julia, who has gone to be with the Lord:

The Lord wants you to ask her to intercede for your son, Paul.

Vision of a relative:

As we began to pray, my prayer partner saw the word "PRAY". He said, "Don't you pray for this person every-day?" I said, "Yes!" Let's continue to pray.

Each time Mike prays, it is like two plates of the earth pushing together until it breaks into an earthquake, and a volcano erupts, which is her faith. She comes a little closer to Me every time Mike prays for her.

Vision of my sister behind some furniture. I could see a part of her face and head:

There is a lot about your sister that you do not know. Pray for God to heal those unseen things.

Dream involving my wife's dad:

> This does not represent Ann's dad, per se, but it is an-
> other call for the healing of the generations. The prayer
> for healing of the generations will cover transferred sins,
> such as drinking or eating too much, lewdness, anger,
> frustration, self-hatred, etc. Pray that these be removed
> from interfering with your family lives.

The Lord speaks about prayer:

> It is not you who received the glory. It is I that received
> the glory. I would have you come to Me alone, with joy
> and all isolation. There is an anointing on your prayer
> life. I would have you come to Me alone. Open yourself
> and dance, shout and sing before Me. You are My chosen
> to help liberate the lost souls.
>
> Your prayers are anointed and are as incense before My
> throne. What I want from you is not sacrifice, it is your
> heart. Be comfortable when you pray to Me. First sur-
> render without condition. Then relax in My love and I
> will lead you in prayer. Do not allow yourself to become
> burdened by the sameness of every-day habit. Let go of
> your human need to detail all names and all things you
> pray for, and bask in My loving care. For I know these
> things already. Yet, it is good to mention them occasional-
> ly. Your heart, warmed and given to Me in total surrender,
> is your strongest and deepest prayer. Where your heart is,
> My answers are, and I will not deny your love of Me by
> holding back My love of you. In all things, trust what you
> believe of Me, for My promise does not fail.

Words received in prayer:

> My son, I see your heart. I know the sincerity of your

intentions. I want to encourage you in your prayer life, for many are helped by your efforts. Do not be afraid for those whom you love. Do not be concerned for the future. My hand is on you, and My protection is around those for whom you pray.

My son, I have chosen you as My leader for My people. Not as a leader in front of men but one who is observed. You see My children idle and not knowing what to do. You have caused My sheep to grow into rams, those that choose to be spotless that follow My son wherever He goes. I have given you this satchel to take My sacrament wherever I send you. Those I have given to you: you have caused them to grow. You see the string made of fiber of My bounty because you have touched it in this way I have made it to grow before My children so that they may follow your steps.

Visions and messages of Popes and Clerics

While praying before the Blessed Sacrament, I had a vision of four sheets of paper that were stapled at the upper left corner. The papers were turned over, one by one, without hands before my eyes. The fourth page contained the names of all the Popes from St. Peter to Pope John Paul II. I had this vision before Pope Benedict XVI was elected pope. The Lord says:

These are My servants of servants. They have shown forth My power throughout the centuries, even when they were not faithful. My power has been made manifest through them. They are evidence that My Church is the true Church. Even the power of darkness cannot and will not prevail. My power is still at work through them.

Vision of Pope Pius XII

Pope Pius XII has been given a special assignment by the Lord to pray and intercede for one of my sons.

Vision of a priest walking off the altar, who sat down in the pew, because it was not his time to say Mass. An older nun came over to the priest and was told to go up in the choir to sing:

Many priests have become ritualistic about their status. The participation has to become more heart-given. They must see themselves as servants rather than directors, givers instead of receivers.

Vision of a priest walking along the fence line around our property.

My prayer partner received understanding that this priest is in heaven. He was walking the boundary of our property, putting a blessing and hedge of protection on our property. Then he saw this priest saying Mass on a white stone altar on the lot south of our house. As we continued to pray he saw the priest saying Mass on an altar in the air above the property. Then he saw this priest assisting Jesus Who was celebrating the Mass in heaven surrounded with hundreds of priests. We did not received understanding who this priest is.

Vision of Bishop Thomas K. Gorman (deceased- Dallas), sitting in a chair, in the aisle of a large church, with two slim young men talking to him:

This is my servant, in whom I am well pleased.

Vision of a priest with a red cap on his head:

> Very few priests preach the Word of God. The red cap on the priest represents the authority of the Church. When the priests start preaching the Word of God, the people will start coming back to the church.

Vision of Father Greg Kelly in a white alb:

> He is one of My anointed, set apart for Me, but I am not finished with him yet.

Vision of Father Greg Kelly standing at the altar. My crucifix was on the altar. Father Kelly said to me, "You need to put Jesus on the cross". Jesus was in my hand. I put Jesus back on the cross. Then Father Kelly said we will go ahead and do it. He started doing something on the altar:

> The Levities were once My priests before the ending of the sacrifice. I am now a part of the Holy Unbloody Sacrifice that has taken place on all altars. My image had been scorned and defaced by others. My son, Michael, was protecting My image in love. When he was asked for My Body, it was Michael in whose care I was given. Know that the Holy Sacrifice, as you know it, will be watered down and diluted to make it more acceptable to all. Know My Holy Sacrifice, the steps, the words, the actions. Know every move and why. Teach those who prepare themselves. Your numbers will be fewer, until I return. Peace will come only when I come to set up My kingdom.

Vision of an old priest, in his 80's or 90's, with long white hair halfway down his back. He was lying in a hospital bed, being rolled into a church without anyone pushing it. He was dying, and he

wanted to hear Mass one more time before he died:

> Jesus said, "I would say to this good and faithful servant, well done. To be at the Holy Mass one more time before death is good and right. I would put him before you as an example."

Dream – a head of a lion, with an open mouth, was tied to a trunk of a peach tree, a couple feet off the ground. The lion's head was a trap to poison wolves. A wolf was wandering by and was lured into sticking his snout into the mouth of the lion. As the wolf stuck his head into the mouth, a poison was sprayed onto his face. The wolf immediately went down. While on the ground dying, the wolf stuck his snout into the mouth of the lion again and was sprayed a second time:

> The wolf represents the clergy that have strayed and are lost. The wolf, when he stuck his face into the mouth of the lion, was sprayed with poison and immediately slumped to the ground. The wolf could not believe what was happening. As he lay on the ground dying, he lifted his head and stuck his face a second time into the mouth of the lion and was sprayed again.

> I have been deceived, and so will others be. Yet, you cannot tell us what I believe we already know. We have bought the lie. We succumbed to the pleasantness of the peach tree and the carcass of fresh blood and meat to devour. The words of the trapper have placed us at his mercy. We dropped our guard a long time ago. The sweetness of the blood and not being on guard will, and has already begun to destroy us. My overconfident brother priests will soon follow and fall to the trapper.

Vision – I was up in the air looking down at a 45 degree angle, at a very large cathedral. There was a large crucifix suspended in the air, close to my face. I could see people standing and walking by on the sidewalk in front of the cathedral. Then I had a side view picture of a man, dressed in white, wearing a white skullcap, sitting in a chair inside the cathedral. I assumed this man was the pope, but I did not recognize him:

> This is the sign of the time. Many people are lingering outside the church because of their lack of faith in the death and resurrection of the Lord. The pope is baffled as to what to do about people not coming to church. There is a wave of unbelief in the crucifixion and rising of the Lord from the dead.

Vision of a person wearing a black cassock with buttons all the way down in front but no head. This is the second time I have seen this picture as I forgot to write it down the first time I saw it:

> My prayer partner saw the faces of different priests that are involved in the Community of God's Delight. The Lord says, "These are My servants, pray for them."

Vision of a priest with a red cross on a white vestment sitting on something, about six inches off the floor in my kitchen. He extended his arm for me to help him up:

> The priest is symbolic of the righteous priests. The red cross is symbolic of the persecution they are facing because they refuse to live superficial lives. They need prayer and support. They need to know that they are appreciated.

Dream – a priest, whom I did not consider to be a good speaker, was loved by everyone:

> Popular speakers are those who say what the people want to hear. God's words are not always easy to accept. A popular priest may be saying nice things but avoiding God's words. God is warning us to listen carefully, and not to be deceived by clever speech.

Dream – I was being shown pictures of priests, one priest at a time on a page of a book. There were 9 or 12 priests on each page:

> God's Church is under attack. He is asking for special prayers of protection and help for His priests, for many will try to deceive them. Pray for them daily.

Vision of a tall black man: I knew him in the picture but when the vision was over I did not know who he was:

> The black man was Bishop Gabriel Consum Ganaka of Africa. Pray for him.

Vision of a priest, standing next to me, wearing a black garment with red seams on the end of his sleeves and down his garment in front next to the buttons. I could not see his face:

> He speaks to you in whisper. He is telling you what is to come. How you are to know those being sent to you. He is speaking of the time of travail, the time before the Man-child comes into the world before the dragon. He is telling you of the serpent, and what you can do to keep him under control. He speaks, but he does not know you cannot hear yet. You will hear.

In a prayer session in our home, I had a vision of a handwritten note posted on the wrought-iron post near the front gate of our property which said, "We have a flag."

Two of the people praying had a vision of the Pope's yellow and white flag flying high in our yard.

Vision of a number of people, including several priests, standing around on a lawn visiting in groups of two and three: One priest, with a pen and a note pad, was taking notes. I had knowledge all of these people were asking questions about the Holy Spirit and the manifestation of the Holy Spirit. I knew one of the priests:

The people of God, the people in My Church, have a hunger. I have put a hunger in their hearts. I have put a curiosity in their hearts to know more about Me. This is going to happen more and more. I indeed mean to fill them.

Vision of a priest standing in front of me, lifting a small wafer up to his waist, consecrating the hosts, one at a time and handing the hosts to me. He instructed me to open a button on my shirt and place each host within my shirt after each consecration. Then he held a small crucifix, 6 to 8 inches, before me:

You will be My carrier to those that are shut in or who are in hiding. These are dangerous times that are coming. Purchase a pix, and be ready to serve.

Vision of a man in church, telling me to go out and get someone who can preach, then a vision of a priest on the altar with words of knowledge, "He will preach and teach, what he has heard and seen":

I am telling you that all of those that are not preaching Me and Me as the Lord, Who was slain and Who has risen, I am going to do away with. I am now of My Spirit and what I am doing in My Church today. All of those that do not preach this will be thrown into the Lake of Fire. I will give them a chance to repent, but if they do not, woe to them. The age of salvation is about to come to an end. I am about to pour out My Spirit on the U.S. Church, in one more powerful outpouring. This will be even greater than the latter outpouring was.

Vision of a priest with his vestment on, turned his head, looked at me and started snickering and giggling. I had this vision while at Mass:

Many priests would consider our prayer life strange or even a joke. They have no inner depth in their own prayer lives, and they should not be allowed to bother you or me or any lay person who prays.

Vision of a priest wearing vestment turned to me and said, "Just the family":

Can you see? I am about a new and final work. I will restore the family. I will bring about much change to cause this to happen to those who are not willing and not trying. I am bringing about the restoration of the lost. This is the last of my assignments before what is to come upon the whole earth. My light will penetrate everywhere. All will come to know what is happening and will happen. It is I that will make those changes. With Me are the angels who will carry out My Father's Word. The earth will be shaken, days and nights will change but the family will remain.

Vision of a man with knowledge that he was a priest. As he was walking across the room 15 feet in front of me, he turned around and extended his hands toward me. The next day I had a vision of three priests in Mass vestments getting ready to put a stain glass window into a top half of a door.

> The window was a picture of a gold chalice with a host above it. My prayer partner saw one of the priests turn around and extend his hand toward me and said, "I am well pleased with you." My prayer partner said the priest that extended his hand was the Lord. The Lord said, "I am well pleased with you."

Visions of Crucifixes and Crosses

Vision of a large golden cross:

> Compassion, mercy and healing are poured out on the world from My cross. There has never been anything more precious to man. The value of My gift to you is so little recognized, yet, My mercy is poured out even to the most awful sinner, if he would turn to Me. Receive My gift from Me. Time is short.

Vision of a small village on a hillside with a very tall pointed church steeple rising high above the homes: There were two golden crucifixes, just like the one which I pray with in the night, extending high above the village. One crucifix was higher than the other.

> The little village represents all the small and big towns of America. The cross above the town means that as long as my people will seek Me and My cross, I will hear them, and visit their land and bring them back to Me. I will heal their land.

Vision of the large crucifix that I hold in my hand, when I pray in the night, was corroded, melted and disfigured:

> This is what the world is going to do to My cross in the coming days. There is going to be a total lack of reverence for Me and My cross. That is why it is disfigured. My church no longer teaches My death and resurrection, without watering it down. Today it is hard for My people to believe that My shed blood washes away their sins. The Church is in decay and rot. It is corroding. My cross has been abandoned. I have been and am being left out of their daily lives. So few choose Me over the world and pleasures. Do not let My cross be corroded. Keep Me in your daily life. Bring Me into your heart. Fight for Me in others. Stay firm, hold fast, walk with Me, share Me and keep Me in your heart.

Vision of a large golden crucifix with a flat round base and a round golden net behind Jesus. The net is a part of the crucifix:

> Jesus is the net. He catches all who come to Him. Jesus is the attraction. From the net they become part of the whole.

Vision of a large, beautiful, golden cross that looked like a weave of a large piece of heavy fabric being carried in the air by someone. It appeared to be very large, as I could see the horizon under it. There was a soft golden light being reflected off of it, as in the twilight light in the evening:

> Compassion, mercy and healing are poured out on the world from My cross. There has never been anything more precious to man. The value of My gift to you is so little recognized, yet, My mercy is poured out even to the most awful sinners, if they would but turn to Me. Receive My gift for you. Time is short.

318

Vision of a large crucifix glowing in the dark. Though I could not see the beads, I had knowledge this crucifix was a part of a rosary:

> All revelations through the centuries to individuals about Mary and her relationship with Jesus, have focused on Jesus, the Man, the Son of God on the cross. All of Mary points to Him. We are to judge all reported revelations about Mary on this basis. If she is not pointing to Jesus on the cross, the revelation is untrue.

Vision of a Catholic Church with a very high dome: There were two crosses on the wall, one on each side of and very high above the altar, close to the ceiling:

> My prayer partner saw the Dome of the Rock. The crosses on each side of the dome mean that the Son of Man, the Son of God, will be lifted up by all religions.

Vision - a black coral cross on a gold chain was on my neck. Ann reached up and turned the cross over. The cross was tied together with gold string. There was gold on the end of each stem of the cross. Black coral is an endangered species:

> Christians are an endangered species. Gold signifies trial by fire. The black coral is becoming extinct. It is a symbol of greed and recognizable to others, so you are a part of what is extinct in My kingdom. See yourself as a living part of that cross. Know that I love you and have chosen you.

> Black coral is precious. The black color signifies that the cross is seen by the world as unattractive and to be avoided. However, when you embrace the cross, you are holding the most precious thing of your life. The gold, holding the cross together, is like precious glue; valuable in itself,

319

but less valuable than the cross. Seek the cross My son! There is more value in its blackness, than in all the riches the world seeks first.

Vision of a white gold, crucifix, with the Lord's left hand off the cross:

It is a time when people will not know Me as the One who hung on the cross, but will know Me as a prophet. I tell you this will be a time of great calamity and great turmoil not as the world has known. You and yours will not be here to see it. But it can be told to those who believe. Do not worry, My people will prevail.

Vision of a large golden crucifix decorated with jewels of red, white, blue and green stones:

Our focus should be on Jesus, not on the jewels or the gold.

Vision of a woman wearing two crucifix ear rings with hooks in her ears:

Do not wear this cross, as this woman is, without any meaning. Wear My cross with meaning and dignity. Let My cross be more than just a symbol in your life.

Vision of an earring with a gold cross:

There are many who wear My cross as an ornament, but pay no attention to what My cross means. Woe to them! I will not let them be inattentive to My sacrifice. Come back to truth. Turn away from the superficial. Do not make light of what I have given you.

Vision of a reddish brown crucifix rising from the ground high into the air. The sky was purple:

> This is for those who sleep that are alive. Have you been sleeping knowing that I am coming? Arise, get up and move forward. Do not be caught sleeping like the maidens, whose lamps ran out of oil.

Vision of a hook throw rug on the floor with a large red cross:

> A rug's purpose is to lie on the floor. The cross is My blood shed for My people. I laid down My life for them. This is what the Christian life is, the laying down of our lives.

Vision of a small bright gold cross about six inches high with a round base.

> Soon things will be as they were. No longer will My name or what I have spoken be diluted. My Spirit will expect the best from all My people. They will worship Me again. My kingdom will reign.

> The cross is to reassure you that there is power in His cross. He has accomplished all in the cross. Your peace is in the cross.

Vision - a reflection of light off of my bronze crucifix, while I was praying in the middle of the night:

> The light of My Son will become brighter and brighter in the world, as He is lifted up.

Vision of a wreath with a cross in the middle:

> You have your life as a result of My death on the cross.

Vision of a large brown envelope with the word, "important" written across it. Then a vision of a green glass cross about five feet tall, with a light behind it. Then I saw a bright star in the sky:

> The paper in the envelope is the scroll of My Word. As it is studied, I am revealed within it, for I am the Word made flesh. As it is studied, My cross is revealed and new life is found, for I am the Light of the world, the Bright Morning Star.

While thinking about Jennifer Williams and her surgery, I had a vision of 4 or 5 inch bright silver crucifix lying on the back floorboard of a car:

> The crucifix is on the floorboard of Jennifer's car. The Lord said that He was with Jennifer before, during and after the surgery.

Vision of San Damiano's cross:

> This icon was popularized by St. Francis. Just as St. Francis contemplated the cross and the Passover of our Lord, so are you to do the same. The Lord's passion and death is the key to what the Lord wants to teach you. This particular cross is the key that opens many gates.

Vision of a crucifix on a chain, hanging on the end of a piece of furniture:

> The Lord has been set-aside carelessly from His place of honor in the homes in this country. Pray that He will be returned to a place of honor.

Vision of a woven basket with a handle across the middle and a cross on the middle of one side:

> Keep thinking about the Easter basket. The cross on it is telling us to keep Easter for what it is, the death and resurrection of Jesus.

Vision of a ring on a section of a finger. There were two crosses dangling from the top of the ring with a space in between:

> The first cross symbolizes the blood shed by Jesus for His people. The bloody sacrifice represents atonement for man's sins to unite man again with God and to satisfy a universal law for atonement of sin. The ring symbolizes that once blood is shed, a new life covenant can be made between Christ and His people. The ring is available to all people, who have accepted Jesus as Lord and Savior of the world for this time and for the time to come. The second cross symbolizes the persecution of man on this earth for their faith in Christ Jesus. This cross is carried only on earth in this era for all who wear the ring. Persecution will exist for Christians worldwide, but this cross is only a temporal one and when a person carries this cross, his reward in heaven will unfold as a beautiful gift of the Holy Spirit which man cannot experience on this earth without the advent of the Second Coming of the Son of Man.

Vision of a man sitting in front of me. He turned and lifted a large bronze crucifix in front of my face:

> This man is a traditional Catholic, who is afraid of changes. He holds onto the crucifix. If you acknowledge the crucifix, he knows you are O.K.

Vision of a purple cross:

If you want to understand repentance and forgiveness, reflect upon the cross.

Vision– I could see where a cross had been removed from the wall:

The cross that Mike saw with just the image remaining is Christianity in our country. It is not all gone, as there is still a remnant left.

Visions and messages from the Holy Spirit

Vision of a friend, who has a close walk with the Lord:

He is mine. He loves and wants Me. He comes to Me for praise and worship. Yet, he has difficulty giving Me his heart. He wants control. I can help him. Make him feel warm and wanted. Show your love and concern for him and his family. He is on guard all the time. Pray for a break in the wall he has built to protect himself. Let the trumpets blow, let the march begin, don't stop until the walls are down. Then love him, as I would love him. I want to use him in a new and much different way. Speak to the four walls, and march around them, and they will come down.

Vision of purple and green then an image of a scorpion:

I have given you the sacrament of reconciliation to protect you from the sting of sin to bring you within My new life.

Vision - poof a light purple bubble. This happened three times. I had knowledge this purple bubble represented someone's angry thoughts, then a picture of a heavy teenage girl:

> The purple bubbles indicate error in thinking. The young people see movies and television programs, which depict very godless methods of living as being "normal". Consequently, our youths are confused as to what is right or wrong. The media must change its message; and come back to the truth. We must protect our youths.

Prior to Mass, I saw a sticker on the back of a car, driven by a black man that said, "If you want peace, work for justice." While at Mass, I saw a vision of a white man, then a word of knowledge of violence:

> The self-righteous ones call for justice. What they want is revenge. A spirit of violence is loose in the world. Put on your armor. Do not be fooled by words which sound good. Beware of the self-righteous.

Vision of young baby calves that were black with white faces:

> My low animals can be many colors, yet it makes no difference to them or to you. Learn from this. Come together in peace between all races. Seek this or no peace can come about.

Vision of a baby boy with oil being put on his bottom to get something off. I could see small patches, like paint, with the edges curled up:

> The children are Mine. So many adults have turned away from Me and now My children suffer. I am the oil of healing for their hurts. Come back to Me and let Me heal My

325

children. You are not able to do this alone.

Vision of people in a fishing village. They had killed the first sperm whale of the spring, which was significant. The people were cutting the whale open and getting the blubber:

The sperm whale is symbolic of God's generosity. The whale, you saw, is symbolic of the end of an era. As the harvest has become smaller, so will God's generosity to us decrease. There will be famines and shortages. Expect them. Be grateful to God for His mercy on us, for He has given us a time to prepare.

Vision of two judges, one white and one black with their right hands raised. One was swearing in the other:

Conflict between whites and blacks will become more apparent, even in the way they pray. What I want is brotherhood between all races not conflict. Put pride aside.

The Lord says:

When you do something in obedience to My will, I am very pleased. When you do that same thing in order to appease Me or to ask forgiveness by your actions, your focus is less on My grace given to you and more on your actions, seeking a response from Me. You have My grace already. Nothing you do can earn it. I seek your humility in accepting My grace. You are not the center - I am. So when you go to Mass without seeing your own action of going to Mass, seeking only the joy of being in My presence, I am most pleased.

Vision of an envelope with the words, "Do not bend":

The envelope represents God's message to us. It is

precious. It is to be received, and accepted, as He sent it. He does not want His message bent out of shape, re-worded, or damaged in any way.

The Lord awoke me at 3:13 a.m. to pray. As I was praying, I saw a picture of purple after purple, over and over. Purple means to repent:

> The world must turn to My mercy. Repent! Repent! Repent! You fall, but you do not ask for forgiveness. Come back to Me. Your fall can be healed. Trust in My mercy. Put aside your pride. Stop your sinning.

Vision of a symbol that I recognize as a symbol of the female reproductive organs:

> The world seems preoccupied with sex. The person is not the point of focus. The sexual organs are. This is not God's plan. We must avoid exposing ourselves and our dependents to these errors, so as to avoid being made complacent to the truth.

The Lord's response to a friend's prayer request:

> I will meet your needs. I will honor your faithfulness. Rest in Me. Wait for My time. I am pleased with your warm heart and loving concern for the people I have put into your life. I ask you to stand firm in your walk with Me. I am the answer to any and all of life's difficulties. Keep your eyes on Me, for your redemption is near.

Vision of a video camera aims at a little girl sitting on a stool behind a glass window. The girl is dark because of the light behind her.

Do not be deceived by what is insinuated or suggested in

the media. When God speaks and acts, it will be clearly visible, open and understandable! There is no deceit in God.

Vision of a man in a business suit wearing glasses:

The man, in the suit with glasses, is symbolic of the world, which values money so highly that it fails to see God clearly.

Vision of an older woman wearing a wide brim hat and a smile on her face:

The lady is smiling and filled with joy, because of a spirit-filled life, a life that is centered on Me. This is what I want for My Church.

Vision of a meadow full of beautiful, yellow black-eyed flowers:

Lilies of the Field

Matthew 6:28-34: And why worry about your clothes? Look at the field lilies! They don't worry about theirs. Yet King Solomon in all his glory was not clothed as beautifully as they. And if God cares so wonderfully for flowers that are here today and gone tomorrow, won't He more surely care for you, O men of little faith? So don't worry about not having enough food and clothing. Why be like the heathen? For they take pride in all these things and are deeply concerned about them. But your heavenly Father already knows perfectly well that you need them, and He will give them to you if you give Him first place in your life and live as He wants you to. So don't be anxious about tomorrow. God will take care of your tomorrow too. Live one day at a time. (16)

Early in the morning before daylight, I had a vision of two rays of sunlight peeping over the horizon.

The rays of light represent hope in a world of darkness.

Vision - one eye, sharp and clear while another eye was like a reptile, as it had a lot of skin around the eye:

My eyes are clear. They are truth. Follow it. The eye surrounded by skin is deceitful and leads to error. Do not follow its way.

Vision of one closed eye. I have seen many visions of one eye of the Lord looking at me in the past:

The closed eye is the Lord. The eye is closed as a symbol that He is allowing us a short period of time to repent.

Vision of a man in a long white garment, as in the biblical days, with a young boy walking beside him:

My prayer partner saw a picture of a man and his son cutting grass. The man had polio from childhood and walked with a limp. The little boy had a toy lawn mower walking behind his dad doing the same thing his dad was right down to the limp. We are to do as our Father in heaven does.

The year, 1938, came to me two times:

God allowed Satan to enter the world and begin World War II to cause His people to go back to Israel.

Vision of a woman wearing a cloth type bonnet of the pioneer days and in the 30's, 40's and 50's to keep the sun off their face:

This woman remembers a relationship she had with the Lord when she was small. She is longing for this relationship again.

Vision of a large, open safety pin in the form of a blue neon light:

While we were praying for understanding, my prayer partner recalled, earlier in the day, how he had put a safety pin through the skin of his daughter, when she was about six months old. This daughter, now, has children of her own. The Lord asked my prayer partner who was this child? He replied, "My first born daughter." The Lord replied that Jesus was His first and only born Son.

Vision of several pieces of gold jewelry on the carpet. One piece was a heavy gold ring:

Your praise and worship is above any gold on earth.

Vision of a beautiful Persian rug with fancy designs with baby Jesus at the top center of the rug, then a vision of a beautiful pale green screen with Arabic writings.

The Persian rug and Arabic writing are symbols of the Muslims. The Arabic writings say, "I am Jesus Who saves." Baby Jesus in the Persian rug shows that Jesus will save the Muslims.

Vision of a man dressed in black clothes with an Arabian cloth woven head wrap, standing before the altar and serving as an altar boy. He had a rosary in his hand:

The man at the altar represents the Muslim world, which is going to turn to the Church.

Vision of a young man's lips:

> Faith comes by reading and hearing the Word of God through the mouth. Vision of a very large eye:

> This is God. He does not miss anything. He sees all.

Vision of a reddish rooster crossing a road, at an angle, at a fast pace, with someone walking beside it. The outer one-third part of the long feathers was real gold:

> The cost of food in the near future will be as expensive as gold. The rise in cost will be gradual.

Vision of a tube with a small sheet of lead at the tip:

> I offer My alabaster of healing, but My people are impervious like lead. I would cover them with My healing, but they have hardened their hearts.

The word "Apostolic Institution" was spoken to me:

> A small body of believers given to carry a message to others with the power of God working in and through them. Signs and wonders follow them.

The Lord controls the environment:

> I give you all that you need in your environment, in order that you may be comfortable: sufficient water and mild temperature. Know that I, Yahweh, your God, am in complete control of your entire environment. Whenever you wish to know that I am present, experience Me by knowing that I control the elements of your environment. I am, at this moment, supplying you with all needed life-giving elements. For without Me in control, this planet would

burn up. Someday this will occur not for any other reason other than the fact that more species have violated the physical principles of My divine order. When this happens, you will have the evidence of My wrath. I will not bless a people who will violate My divine order. Pray for mercy in order that your brothers (all humanity) have sufficient grace to accept Me as Lord and Savior, before the above time comes.

Dream about a friend, who was being threatened with a lawsuit:

Guard your heart. Do not let any bitterness and unforgiveness enter in. Forgive them, for they know not what they are doing.

June 1994 – words the Lord spoke to a person with whom we prayed:

You have sought your ways, not Mine. You have decided not to follow My Word to you. Are you moving in the rank of My people? Are you living a life of love for those around you and those I have placed with you? Are you holding on to your ways to do things? Are you taking every opportunity to meet others and build relationship? Start a ministry of love for those I have given you. If you continue to run away, or exclude yourself or hide in your home, you will not be ready when the allotted time comes. My Son walked among them, loved them, sat with, talked to, walked with, laughed with, cried with, gave aid to, ate with, and visited with My people. Your structures are not what I am about. I am about building relationships. Your world, that you have built, and chosen to live in, is too small for 99% of all My children. I want you to let go of your structure and walls; come walk with Me. Start by being a volunteer helping others. Know that you are rich with knowledge of Me. Be as I am, so when My people see you, they see Me. I say again, get out from your structure and walk. Come and love with Me. My people need people with the gifts of help. Start where you will, but just start so that you will be ready.

Vision of three separate heads of snakes: I could see the head and part of the body of each snake:

My time of coming is near. When the three evil kingdoms join the rest, My coming will be even closer. You will not be in the dark. You will know and see, just as we know and see the changing seasons. You will know the time is near.

(My prayer partner said the Lord said that I would know about this, as I wrote about it. I said I do not understand. We prayed for understanding. My prayer partner received knowledge that the three snakes represented the three nations that were to join seven other nations to form the ten-nation beast kingdom.)

Vision of a cultivator on wheels that is pulled by mules. The cultivator was red as in an image that remains in your eyes, after looking at bright light.

The red color is the color of My blood. The shape of the plow is the tool that breaks the earth, which is our flesh and makes it plowable for the seeds of the Lord to take root within us.

Vision - a double glass doors tabernacle with the hosts in a clear glass bowl within the tabernacle. Words written on the bottom of the glass doors were, "This is for you to help you go." The tabernacle was sitting on a post about four feet off the floor in the

center of the room:

> This is for you. It is for the healing of your body. It is there to minister to your organs and your blood streams. Take and eat it. Know that this host is healing you and regenerating your inner body. This host is special like no other that you have taken. Do not hesitate to consume Me.

Vision of one of my bosses looking at me:

> Fear not My son, for I will uphold you.

Vision of a head of a bright eyed baby less than a month old:

> Pray the Lord's blessing on this child to be used mightily by the Lord.

Vision – I was under a very large tree with large overhanging branches at the very top. The leaves looked like pecan. I could see the sky through the spaces between the leaves but I could not see the tree trunk. This picture remained before me longer than most pictures:

> This tree is the tree of life. As long as you stay under its large branches, you will produce much fruit. If you get out from under the branches, you will dry out and die.

Vision of green then purple, again green then purple, over and over:

> Green is new life. Purple means to repent. Even when we receive new life, we still need to repent.
>
> (Note- The scripture says Daniel repented daily for the sins of his people, the Israelites. We need to repent not

only for our sins but the sins of our nation.)

Vision of a man right in my face: The words that came to me were, "What is my name? What is his name?"

"My name is the King of kings and the Lord of lords. His name is the deceiver and thief."

Vision of a cute bunny rabbit on top of the rim of a heart-shaped (love) vase then purple, purple, purple which means repent, repent, repent:

This is what the world has done to the meaning of Easter. The bunny rabbit was made the symbol of Easter instead of the cross of My Son which is the real meaning of Easter. I will forgive the people if they will turn from this abomination.

Vision of a friend with whom I worked, sitting next to me, telling me something:

He is telling you about his needs, which he wants you to pray for. It is symbolic of people at work, who want to talk with you but do not know how.

Vision of a young baby bird, with very short feathers, on the ground under a tree. It had fallen out of its nest:

This is part of the tree of life. Even if you fall, but stay under the branches of the tree, I will protect you.

Vision of 40 to 50 cars of the 20's and 30's vintage parked in a grass field or pasture:

The cars of the 20's and 30's were the beginning of the

industrial revolution that caused man to depend on himself more than on God.

Vision of a young woman, who looked familiar, then it dawned on me this woman was someone I knew before she was married 26 years ago. Then purple over and over, which means to repent:

> I love My daughter. She is in great pain from sin. She lacks discipline and the will to do what is right. Her sins go back to her childhood. She sees herself as having been denied. Her self-will and lack of discipline, take her further away. The colors represent the volume of sins that go with her as an insatiable appetite. There are those who come to the kingdom this way because I have given them their free will. I cannot change what they will do. Put her on your general prayers.

Vision of an old woman with a long nose lying down as if she was sick:

> The woman is My Church. My Church is sick. It is sick with the disease of sin. I mean to breathe My Spirit into her and awaken her from this disease of sin.

Vision of a young woman with red hair down her back to her waist:

This woman is Joan the Arc. She is in heaven and is a powerful intercessor. We are to ask her to intercede for us.

While praying in the dark early one morning, I had a vision of a beam of light like a spotlight, a foot in diameter, coming down from heaven next to me. My prayer partner received these words.

> This is the light of the star that guided the three wise men to the new born child, Jesus. The light of this star is also guiding you to a deeper relationship with the Lord.

A beam of light on the ground moving ahead of you would be an easy to follow. It would be impossible to follow a star in the sky that does not move.

Vision - a friend was standing in a room. His features began to change to the point that I did not recognize him:

My prayer partner saw my friend standing in the outer courtyard of the temple of God. He was offering lambs on the altar of sacrifice with their smoke rising to the heavens. He heard the Lord say to my friend, "Obeying is better than sacrifice. Come into the inner courtyard; come through the curtains of the Holy of Holies into My presence." My friend did that. When he came out, he was transformed. His hair was white. His face was radiant and shone just as Moses when he came down from the mountaintop or as Jesus at the Mount of Transfiguration.

I asked the Lord about the apostasy that is coming upon the Church:

A purifying fire will fall upon My Church. Even some of the very elect will fall away. Only those strong in Me will stand. Those whose foundation is built on solid rock will stand. Those whose foundation is in sand will not.

Vision of a horse with a saddle on whose right foot was sinking and being pulled into quicksand:

My prayer partner had a picture of a star and half shaped moon, which is a Moslem symbol. This horse is the Moslem people. The more it thrashes in what looks like quicksand, the more it is throwing out a substance that is destroying the earth.

337

Dream – a lesbian, about whom I had knowledge that she had tumors on her female organs: I said something about the scriptures, on which she challenged me. I said the scriptures are the Word of God. She threatened to bash me in the face. I told her that if she did, God would punish her. She asked me how? I told her I did not know, but a lot of people get sick. I asked my prayer partner if this dream was from the Lord. He received the following words:

> You cannot pick and choose My Word to you. It is either true or it is not. You either accept all of it or none of it. Do not fear about your physical health for I am a God Who heals. Do not rebel, agree, obey and live.

> My prayer partner received knowledge I was to prophesy these words daily in my prayers for one week, and they will be brought to fruition, just as the words of the prophets.

I prayed for discernment for a family with a child that had had several operations for tumors:

> These sicknesses are each a monument to your remembrance so that you will not forget Me. You have gone on your own. You are not pursuing Me. You have almost taken Me out of your life. Yes, there is hope for you. Yes, but you must pursue Me and pursue Me. Put Me in your heart and on your lips and in your prayer time.

Vision of sunflowers as far as you can see:

> Solomon in all of his glory was not arrayed as these. I am carrying you upon eagle's wings. I have always carried you upon eagle's wings.

Vision of a Russian girl with a big red rash around the area of her left eye working in a chemistry laboratory:

> Many will die from this sickness, those who believe and those who do not care. This is nuclear foolishness, and from greed to be on top and in power. I cannot hold back their foolishness. Many are fools in the understanding of scripture.

Vision of a tall, flat, fan-shaped shrub covered with pinkish white flowers and long narrow dark green leaves:

> My prayer partner sees a bride and groom, wearing a white wedding gown and a tuxedo, waiting for someone to marry them. Jesus steps out to marry them. As the bride and groom kneel-down, Jesus lays His hand on their heads and marries them. I am calling My bride to Myself. My bride is those who believe in Me. (Father speaking) My people, Israel, I will call one by one, as they believe in My Son, or I will call them as a nation.

While at Mass I had a vision of a map of Alaska. I felt like I was high in the air over the sea. The word "port" came to me with understanding it was referring to a port along the western shore of Alaska:

> My prayer partner saw the oil in the Middle East drying up. Alaska is an oil-rich state. Our oil reserves will come from Alaska, when oil is hard to get elsewhere.

Words came to me, "Tell him (a friend) I would rather whole lot more than to suffer:

> My prayer partner said the complete sentence is "Tell him I would rather stand up for what is right (cause division) a

339

whole lot more than to suffer. Surely, obedience is better
(to do what is right) than to have sacrifice."

Vision of a man and a woman in a hospital room with a newborn baby. I had knowledge that the baby's clothes were taken off and the baby was placed on the mother's breast to be fed:

> As a baby comes naked and defenseless to its mother
> to be nourished, so too must we come to our God. The
> woman represents the Church. The baby represents us,
> the members of the Church. The man represents God.

While we were in Mexico, I had a vision of a tall, slim, nice-looking, young Mexican woman in a poor village:

> This woman is My heart and soul in this village. The Lord
> is using her to reach these people.

Dream – I was at a prayer meeting after a Mass. Later I saw the leader in priest's vestment and members of the community weeping and crying; some were prostrate on the floor. They motioned for me to come in. I sat down on the steps and started weeping and crying. I immediately woke up from the dream and had a picture of a burnished gold crucifix dangling in my hand. This crucifix may have been part of a rosary:

> My intent is to bring all members of the Community
> of God's Delight into a deeper understanding of
> My life, My passion, My death, and My resurrec-
> tion. The leader was in priest's vestments because we
> are all a royal priesthood and a holy nation. My in-
> tent is to burn the cross of My Son into your mind,
> soul, and spirit and to burn My image into your heart.

Vision of a piece of iron covered with rust and dirt. Someone started scraping and sanding.

> The heart of My Church is strong, but on the surface there is much, which seeks to hide this truth. I am cleaning the surface of all rust which are the lies and confusion. I mean to expose the pure iron underneath so that the liars of the world will see the heart of My Church. Behold, I am removing the rust. Look and see the iron below.

Vision of someone swimming in deep blue water, swimming to stay afloat in the turbulent water:

> Our life on earth, when we have the Spirit of God operating in our lives, is like swimming a deep sea, always staying afloat so that we may breathe and not drown amidst life-threatening turbulent waters. Such is life on earth, with demons all about you that play the role of the deep sea, waiting their chance to bring you down from the surface so that you may not breathe for evermore and claim your life for eternity. So breathe the Holy Spirit of God at all times and know what waits below in the wicked sea.

Vision of a steel animal trap hanging in a tree. It was not set:

> This trap is the trap of Satan and sin. But the trap has been sprung and its jaws have no power in the life of My people, as long as they walk with Me. The enemy will try, but his power is sprung.

Vision of a group of adults and children sitting side by side: I was giving each one a coin, a penny or a dime. A small coin was all they needed. It filled the cracks:

> The coins you saw symbolize your prayers. Each prayer

may seem small, but they filled the cracks in other lives and prevented greater evils from getting through.

Vision of thousands and thousands of fish eggs suspended individually throughout the water:

Fish eggs are men that are to be harvested. Many will not make it to maturity unless you pray for them.

Vision of a small tube of light around the edge of a stained glass window with birds on the left side:

Just as a wake follows behind a ship so are your prayers that follow behind you. Like the wake hitting the shores so are your prayers touching people you do not know. Your prayers build up and cleanse those you do not see. The light is seen as "tubes" because it must cut through much darkness (doubt, sin, error, etc.) Where faith is pure and lives are given truly to God, the light shines brightly, like the sun on clear glass.

Words spoken to me, "Be a warrior for the kingdom":

The Word of God is a mighty weapon to be used to accomplish God's will. Pray for more men to become prayer warriors. For if more men will fight the good fight of faith, He will hold back His hand of wrath.

Vision of an ear:

If you have ears to hear, listen then to what My Spirit is saying to the churches. Time is short. You will not know the day nor the hour, but you will know the season. The season is now beginning.

Vision of a Monarch butterfly, a wonder of God's creation

I had a picture of a Monarch butterfly during my prayer time. My friend received the following words while we were in prayer:

> The butterfly is a delicate and beautiful creation. So easily could you crush it, yet it has the power to rise up and fly hundreds of miles. It is indeed a wonder of my creation. Yet, you are so much more than a butterfly. You have the strength to endure far more than you can ever know. Endurance begins with your determination to end the race at the finish line. Keep the frail butterfly in your sight. When you feel to fall aside, remember its endurance and pick yourself up and continue your journey.

The Monarch butterflies fly up to 2000 miles from Canada and the northern states to Angangueo, a mountainous area in central Mexico to spend the winter. El Rosario is a mountainous preserve that shelters some 300 million butterflies after their fall migration. In the spring these delicate creatures begin their trek northward eventually reaching the northern states and Canada. (52)

Vision of standing next to a mulberry tree loaded with black mulberries. Someone, who was with me, picked a few of the berries and gave them to me to eat. The tree had no leaves:

> Jesus was called "Master" by His twelve disciples. Jesus asked them, "Why do you call Me Master? A master can only be as great as his followers that he serves." This statement represents the parable of the black mulberry tree. You eat the fruits of the great harvest. As you serve mankind with love, fellowship, and as a witness for the Lord, you play the role of a servant. Always remember, a great servant will make a great master for the Lord.

Total surrender:

What I am asking of you, My son, is total surrender. Are you willing to give Me your every thought, breath, every feeling, all that you are? This is the price I am asking of you, is total surrender. Will you give Me this when I show you what I want you to do? Will you follow My way and not yours?

The Lord speaks to me about prayer:

Mike, how you pray does more for you than for Me. I see your heart. I already know your needs. I do not need them explained to Me. When you pray, do not be concerned with details. Do not become dependent on rituals or time limits. I see the surrender of your heart. I know your sincerity in seeking Me. I enjoy you coming and spending time with Me. This indeed should not stop. But remember, I am He who is all-powerful. If you use many words, expressions and methods of prayer, you affect only yourself. I do not need details and great descriptions. I know before you think of them, all the things you want to say. Come to me to praise! Come to enjoy being in My company. Bring the names and needs of all for whom you love and pray. Write them down. Mention perhaps those most on your mind. But you do not need to tire yourself with details. Sit quietly with Me. Let Me hold you. Let Me minister to you. Your prayers are already in My hands. I enjoy the surrender of your heart, mind, soul, and time.

Do not judge

My daughter - it is not for you to judge My son. Just as you have taken a vow of love unto death through whatever, now is the time of sickness that you do not see but that you are experiencing through someone whom you have come to love. Your calling is greater at this hour. You should know all the wonderful things that you have done and are about to do. It has been and will be written in the Lamb's Book of Life. I will give you the grace through each trial as your husband is attacked by this sickness. Turn aside from those thoughts that will bring you great hurt and despair. Continue to pray for a peaceful death for My son. Ask for forgiveness for the things that he is doing when he is not in control. This is what you have been called to do.

Vision of a man hiking in the mountains like the Swiss Alps:

This is the voice crying out from the past. They cry out for food and things of comfort. You will try to feed them but the world does not produce enough to feed them. They can only be fed by Me. Only I can give them enough of what they want. The world will collapse trying to supply the need. No organization of the world will be able get them under control. All will be lost and destroyed. Your nation will no longer feed the world. The words from the mouth of this man will destroy many. Do not go to any world trade organization. Time is short for My arrival and My Father's destruction. It is only the Holy Spirit that protects this earth. Do not be fooled by the world's ways. Be ready! Be strong! Be prepared! Be holy! Be separate! Be Mine only!

A friend came to me and said he paid his rent and gave what he had left which was 10% to the Lord. He did not have money for food or gas. I told him he was not to do that. He may have to tithe 1% instead of 10%. I asked the Lord for confirmation on what I said:

All the cattle in the fields are Mine. All the goods of the earth belong to Me. What can you give Me that I do not have already? It is not sacrifices that I want. I want your hearts. Give Me first your surrender, all else will follow. You have responsibilities and duties you must meet. Do not deny those commitments. You should tithe, yes, but do so with My direction, according to your means.

I asked a prayer partner to pray with me for a friend who had some malignant sores removed from his skin. The Lord spoke these words:

You are out on the fringes of your life with Me. Your commitment to Me is not as genuine as you would have others think. It is times as these that you attempt to be more serious. I still love you and have you in the palm of My hand. This does not mean a great miracle will happen. Quite the contrary. I am waiting on you for a true, sincere, long term, daily relationship. Do not look to those around you. Get alone with Me and My Word and My Holy Spirit. I am waiting.

Vision of a group of pink and yellow flowers:

These are some of My innocents - some of My chosen ones, their life stems from hope. I am about to pick them and take them. They are wondrous in prayer. Their lives are full of color. I am going to take them out of the world with Me so their prayers can no longer sustain this earth as you know it. Their prayer requests are answered. They know Me and My Father and My Father's will. They will be some of the first.

A small flower is beauty, which calls attention to Me. Without My hand, this beauty does not exist. It serves to please the eye and calm the spirit. Flowers are symbols of My love and care poured out on the world. Yet the world will not see Me in My creation. Instead men in their arrogance see themselves at the center of this beauty and ignore Me, the creator of it all. Beauty will fade away. When men turn from Me, sin comes in and kills the beauty I have created, and the world becomes a dull and dreary place. Come back to My beauty, My children. I want to fill you with peace and joy.

I heard a voice which said, "Let's add to the covenant, be a people of My delight":

Know you are "My delight!" Live all day knowing you are "My delight". Like waking up in the army, you know you are in the army, so wake up knowing you are "My delight". Rejoice and live this delight.

Vision of a ripe yellow ear of corn on a corn stalk:

There is a great harvest coming upon earth. This corn is evidence of that harvest. I tell you the truth, the harvesters are few, but there are enough. The time is short for this harvest to begin. My barns will be filled to over flowing.

The words, "Dun nun na" came to me. I had understanding that they mean "You are not sick".

You are not sick. I am telling you. You have followed My leading for yourself. You are caring for your physical person more than before. You are not sick but you must care for your body and your mind; rest and supplements will help. Do not deny yourself these. Give care to what you eat. Eat what will build your body and mind; do not trash it! Be regular in these as you are in your prayer and devotional life.

Vision - someone mentioned something about a comic strip and Jerusalem:

> The world sees Jerusalem as folly and foolishness. God sees Jerusalem as His city and a holy place.

Vision of houses in which the outside sidings of some look like woven basket; all were different. These homes were white, with bright-colored trim and shingles. The trim on one house was green, another was purple, others different colors. The houses were very attractive and brightly colored:

> In My kingdom there are many houses like you have never seen before. The colors are of great joy, the designs, unlike any you have seen. I have a home prepared for you. Be steadfast in your trials. The future is yours with Me in joy.

Vision of a woman crying about her child:

> Weep, you mothers of sons, mourn, for your sons are lost. I have called them, but they chose the world instead. Great sorrow comes to you because your sons are stubborn. Yet, still, I will save them. Let them turn back to Me. I will turn your sorrow to rejoicing.

Vision of a new born baby:

> I want you to be as a new-born baby is innocent. I want you to be as needy of Me as the baby is of its mother. I want to care for you as a mother cares for her baby. Surrender now. I will cleanse you. My blood will wash you clean. My Spirit will fill you. Come now, before it is too late.

Vision of a wooden barrel with a bright, colorful Mexican painting and decoration on the inside, not on the outside:

> Inside of some very unassuming, dull people, there is great beauty and life. Do not judge from outside appearance.

Words came to me about our prayer community being the largest in the world: (Community of God Delight)

> Our community has affected more people all over the world than any other community. In that sense, we are the largest community in the world.

Vision of a black leopard:

> Be careful with your time, for the enemy is as a beast of prey, cunningly awaiting for the opportunity to devour it. Be on the alert. Pray constantly to be in union with Me. Know that My presence is with you at all times. Also be aware that there is an added message, the same leopard stalks your family at this time. As the head of your family, pray in order to keep the spirit of cunningness from attacking them and their time spent with Me. Your prayers keep this spirit in check. Know that this is a powerful spirit, one that would devour you, were you not on the alert for it. Your prayers of intercession for yourself and for your family bind this strong enemy. Know that I am with you and assist you in your effort. For this is the Lord God Yahweh Who speaks.

Vision of a dead bird with some of the bones in the skull visible:

> The bird was graceful and beautiful in life. Now in death, its beauty and grace exist no longer. The souls of those who do not seek Me are like this.

Vision of a prayer book with ribbons for dividers:

> The common prayer of the Church is a good guide for daily prayer. God wants us to pray as a people daily.

Vision of a TV weather map showing the temperature in the midwest: The temperature in Chicago was 70 degrees in December:

> There will be many unusual signs and circumstances happening to show people that I am God. Unusual natural phenomena will become commonplace, until the people turn back to Me.

Vision of a woman, who said, "The further north she goes, the thinner she gets":

> The woman going further north is actually moving away from God. The further away she moves, the less she is nourished, the thinner her faith becomes.

Vision of a heart-shape, single-lens eye glass in a frame for use by both eyes:

> Everything you see, you should look at through My heart. Be compassionate and patient as I am compassionate and patient, no matter how difficult the trials you face.

While seeking for an understanding on how to pray for a young lady, the following words were spoken to us:

> The lamps of her life have been darkened. They smolder from the sins in her life. She fights Me out of hurt and resentment. She is strong-willed and will not let the prayers for her penetrate. She sees Me as the last hope at the last moment. Fasting will not help at this time. She is

Mine because of her commitment to Me as a child. She wants to be set free, but cannot let go of her preconceived thoughts of Me. She suffers from rejection and idolatry. She is but at the door of My kingdom. She wrestles daily with her hurts. She tries to cover them up. Pray that her heart of stone be broken and that those who are with her will shine as an example of My love. I have brought her to this place so that she will choose Me and let go the things of the world. See her healed from the inside out. The victory is ours.

Vision of a man in a backpack, smiling and talking to me.

This man is a symbol of a Christian, a symbol of a true Christian, willing to get up and go, when God calls him.

Vision of a black child with one blue eye:

All races belong to Me. Love one another without thought for color. I am the painter. I give life. All are My children. Love one another.

Dream, someone said, "Most members of the community do good to make it to Mass two times a week".

Pray that the members of the community will try to go to Mass more often.

While at Mass, I had a vision of a box of wooden two-colored strike matches. There were at least three different two colored matches in the box including orange and white tip matches. I had knowledge that some of the matches would not light when struck:

Matches represent people in the Church. When struck, some will not light, others will. All are in the Church but some will not light. Some will be saved - they carry the light. I wish that you be hot or cold but you are lukewarm (will not light). I will spew you out of My mouth. All are called by Me and given the power to give My light to the world. There is no race of people that I have not called. I call you as My brothers, My sisters, My friends; I want you to work together for the common good of My Church, My family. Many are being counted in My fold, but not all are carrying the light. Yet, even those are connected to others, who will light them up. Do not despair. When one is lighted, this light will spread to the others, who have allowed themselves to be counted in the fold, even if they themselves do not carry the light as yet.

Three days fast, water only, for a family on a verge of a divorce:

Love is never lost nor wasted. I am love, and through Me, you can love. The prayer of your heart, the fasting and the pain you accepted are signs of My love in you being poured out on them. You have prevented a permanent evil from being poured out on this family. They will come to know Me, and their children will not be lost. I will lead them to truth and peace. You will see My love work in the midst of this disaster.

A friend asked me to ask the Lord a question. The Lord did not answer his question but the friend received the following message:

Pray with faith. Surrender your prayers to God. You cannot reserve the right to worry about what you have given God to take care of. Trust him, even if what He does is not what you want. He sees all and acts in your best interest and in those of your family. The final state of each one will be better than it is now.

Dream in which I was among my wife's American Indian relatives. I prayed for an Indian boy that was healed:

> The Indian boy does not represent one person, but a healing of the generations. The sins and curses of the fathers are passed down to the 3rd and 4th generations. Pray for the healing of the generation. Plead the blood of Jesus as a filter between all communications between generations. (When the fathers do not obey our Father, God, it can affect their children and their descendants for 150 years or more.)

Vision of one gallon of milk with four percent cream on top:

> Milk is God's word to us - spiritual food. The four percent means it is "full cream". Do not accept the diluted word of God - only the "full cream."

Vision of a beautiful white stone building with a reddish stone alternating every two or three white stones: On the corner of the building, a few feet off the ground was a reddish rock, shaped like the head of a cat:

> The white building is the Body of Christ, the Church. The red stone with the cat's face is symbolic of Egypt. The red stones in the building represent the members, leadership included, who are more focused on the world (Egypt) than on Christ.

Vision of a fine detailed pencil-drawing of a little girl:

> The drawing of the little girl is significant. God has seen the lies which the world is promoting, especially about the role and sexual freedom of women. The little girls of this world are in tremendous danger! See a spirit of lust

seeking to take them over! I see selfishness, vanity and betrayal to be their constant companions. I see great pain for them in the future. We must pray for our children but especially our young girls, that they not be led astray. The drawing you saw signifies innocence. The world will try to remove that innocence and place "self awareness" in its place. God does not want his flowers defiled. He wants them to be fully female, fully women, pure in heart and spirit and loyal in love. He does not want the life style the world will try to force on them.

Vision of a short, bearded judge, sitting high on his bench:

There are many judges sitting on benches who have no place as judges before Me. I have condemned them. They fool no one. The lies of the world come through them. I mean to show them up for their lies.

Vision of a square glass plate with a mother and her two children carved into the glass. The glass was suspended by two chains attached to holes on the upper corners:

The picture of motherhood in the world today is a lie. It is beautiful in concept, but as fragile as glass, when lived by the world's standards. Without God at the center, the beautiful picture shatters.

A friend expressed concern about not being able to have sex and asked me to pray with my prayer partner about it. The Lord said:

Put sex in its proper place. The world is obsessed with sex and performance and all the other attributes it calls "manhood". Sex is a beautiful gift from God to be used as a sign of surrender and oneness between two people, a man and a woman, united in God. It is not a performance, or a duty, or any of the circus nonsense the world says it is. As we grow older and our appreciation of God becomes deeper sometimes our responsibilities become more pressing than the youthful urging of our bodies. God has given us the blessing of change to grow in the spirit and die to the flesh. Be patient and put aside fear. Focus on Christ. Trust in God. Relax with your wife. You have nothing to prove. Your ability is only temporarily delayed. You do not need a doctor.

Vision of a mad dog:

Many people will be like the dog, out of control and full of fear of death at the end. They will have lost their good senses. Some of those you know will turn and be like this.

While at Mass, I was thinking of St. Peter. Then I had a vision of a woman dressed as in biblical times with a brownish net-like covering over her dress and upper part of her body. Suddenly, there was a picture of a large bearded man in my face.

You were at Mass. Your spirit was turned to St. Peter. His mother decided to show him to you. Mothers are proud of their sons.

Vision of a large open book with sentences printed in blue:

Lamb's Book of Life - not only has names, but positive paragraphs about each attribute, the glorious notes of our life - those notes which God recognized as values.

I prayed for a woman in intense pain:

I do not wish her to be in pain. I want her to be free. This is a result of her decision for her life. She needs to make herself clean before Me. I don't want her to be whole, without her coming before Me.

Upon talking to this woman, she said, "I told my husband before I married him to never mistreat me, because I cannot forgive those who mistreat me." I knew this was "the decision" she had made. The Lord said if we cannot forgive, how can He forgive?

Dream - a tubular root, about the size of a carrot with two small white roots shooting out like a fork. The white roots were five or six feet long:

> The two roots are the two sons of Abraham, Isaac and Ishmael. The roots represent the great division between the Judo-Christians and the Muslims.

A friend was concerned whether he was hearing the Lord correctly:

> Unless you learn to trust Me absolutely, you will not survive the trials to come. Learn now. Let go, and let Me take care of your needs.

Vision of a man dressed as a pilgrim:

> My prayer partner had a picture of Abraham Lincoln. He received these words: I want men, as in his day, the way he was. Men with integrity, men of substance, men of character will be the kind of men to whom the world will look.

Words spoken to us:

> My people have forgotten how to pray. My people have forgotten how to stand firm. Beware of your lukewarm nature. If you do not stand firm, you are open to all diseases: all attacks of the enemy. If My people will pray

daily: If they will surrender unconditionally to Me, I will protect them from all harm, even if it is the worst plague known. What I want, are hearts given to Me in truth. This world has forgotten Me. Words will not be enough. I want your hearts. You are forewarned so that you can be prepared. You must examine every stage of your life. Is it all surrendered to Me? You will have to make hard choices very soon. If you are not totally surrendered, you will be subject to deceit and will be deceived. My people must stand firm and trust Me. The world must see your dedication. Surrender and pray for perseverance. Prepare yourself and your families for difficulties. Store up food and fuel for soon you may be denied them. Cherish your freedom while you have it. Pray for the world and trust Me.

Vision, I was walking out into a yard with a teacher who wanted to talk about dead limbs on the trees. Immediately, I said there is a dead limb. Then in the sky, there was a small trail of pitch black smoke of which at the end was a small ball of fire:

Teachers need to be taught. There is deadwood in the branches of the Church. The deadwood, by its stubbornness, will bring fire and brimstone into the body. This is far off at this moment (Feb. 19, 1991), but its effects are already becoming visible. We, who are seeking truth, need to speak out in word and action, when the chance is given. "Teach the Teachers."

Vision of a bar of soap with an outer layer of a different color from the inner bar: The bar was broken so I could see the cross section. There was a jagged piece of glass in the outer layer. Though I washed my hands with this soap, it did not cut my hand:

The bar of soap represents the cleansing of confession (reconciliation). Today people no longer are properly taught about this sacrament. The glass in the soap is symbolic of the danger of bad confessions. The different colors of soap show that some confessions are better than others. Not all are acceptable. The outer layer of the soap is God's blocking grace from a bad confession. You washed, and you came clean. Now God wants more (all) of us to be washed clean in truth.

Vision of a baby being fed some type of food:

The baby represents us, Catholic and other Christians truly trying to come to God as children to be fed by Him. But the food the baby is eating represents a warning. The Lord wants us to be very careful of any new teachings. We are not to swallow, as babies do without chewing well on the new messages. In fact, if there is doubt, spit out the message (food) as a baby spits out what it does not like. Be innocent for God but not stupid.

Vision, I was standing next to a friend who was holding an automatic pistol:

The gun belongs to my friend. He said the gun was for his protection. My prayer partner said I told him that the Lord was my shield and protector.

Vision of a cow and three baby calves in a small room in a lumber yard: Several men were in and out of the room. There was no room to move around:

The cow is symbolic of the "new age" religion and other "fad" beliefs, which spring up and produce offspring of other "beliefs" (calves). The crowded room, with no room to turn around, is symbolic of the confusion these religions bring to people of small faith. Avoid these fads.

Vision of a stone bust of a man:

We spend a lot of time honoring dead men that should not be honored.

Vision of a black child in grassland with a few trees. I had knowledge that this was Africa:

> The black child is a symbol of the beginning of awareness in the world of Africa. Very quickly, this child will come to maturity. Africa is about to become a major element in the way the world is affected. The black race is going to affect much of what you do in the future. The world must deal with emerging nations. There will be horrific upheavals and changes, but My hand is on them too. Use love and patience, and remember that they too, are My children, even if they have not matured as yet.

Vision of a card on the floor. My attention was on the stamp which was a picture of a tall cathedral as seen in Europe:

> The card has a stamp with a picture of a church. The church is where Jesus is. He is the One Who gives the living water. It is there we find Him. We need to pray for the Church in Europe as Christianity is under heavy attack there.

Dream, my son, Mark, said three of his best friends with whom he went to school were minorities. They came to Houston within one day of the (market) crash:

> This dream is symbolic. The world is shrinking more and more. The races are beginning to cooperate better. It is not going to be easy. It will take bloodshed and more (the crash) but the races will come together. My Church will be one.

Vision of a black horse galloping along the edge of a deep cliff:

Satan is running wild. He seems strong and invincible, but he will fall off the cliff soon.

Vision of a very bright electric light bulb in an aluminum shield:

Use the discernment I have given you for Satan can and will disguise himself as an angel of light.

Vision of a table with many cut, long stem, deep-red roses laying on it:

These roses are for those who have shed their blood for Me.

Vision of people walking and doing things. Then picture of a traffic light that was green:

The green light is God's permission to us to choose. The time of accounting is coming. The light will turn red, and we will no longer be free to choose. We will then have to answer for our choices.

Vision of a door with a cutout section below the door knob and plate: Pull the block of wood out and there is a key hidden within:

The time for evangelization is almost over. The time of purification is now beginning. The key to the door is for those who have chosen without being evangelized. The key opens the door to Me. They will come and use the key to open the door to Me and put the key back for the next to enter. You saw this, to be advised that My time of purification has already begun. It is too late to attain sainthood with the time left. (Sainthood is like the lives of canonized saints.) On one side of the door is the throne of grace. On the other side of the door is an anteroom. Many are called to the anteroom but only a few are allowed into the throne room. God chooses those whom He invites into the throne room. The key is available only at His choosing and is hidden from those who remain in the anteroom.

Vision of isolated tall blue flowers scattered among many different kinds of flowers in a landscaped area:

You see before you My flower garden. In it are My people. The flowers you see that are tall and blue, are those who are close to My mother. They have been raised up by their devotion.

A man on his death bed asked his daughter-in-law to promise to take her children to a certain church where they could get good teaching and not to a spirit-filled church:

The Lord says, "No promise is binding that keeps children or anyone away from God."

Vision of purple and green, then purple with a dark cloud in the center. Light was coming through the purple but not through the dark cloud in the center. This picture flashed on and off several times:

We asked the Lord for the meaning of this vision. He said, the cloud was the leadership throughout the country that preaches not to worry, that we do not need to repent, everything is O.K. It is this lie that is the deceit, which supports abortion and the killing of the young. The cloud signifies the blocking of the truth. The purple shows the need for repentance. The flashing on and off is God's insistent love, telling us to pay attention to the truth, to repent. We need to pray for our priests and other leaders who are not giving us proper leadership.

Vision of a Korean or Asian man in a business suit standing before me:

Pagan nations will be given influence and power by Satan to infiltrate our society. We Christians cannot compromise our faith for money. No pagan leader, no matter how powerful, must buy our allegiance away from God's truth.

Vision of a young girl with her breast exposed:

This young woman represents sin in our nation. We men have allowed our women to become immodest.

The word "reactor" was spoken to me. Then a vision of someone handing me three labels with red letters written on them. I could not read them:

Is not My Word written in your heart? I tell you, it is written with My blood. I am speaking to you that you will know that you will see and hear of great things that My blood will bring to the forefront of man's mind. It will be written in their hearts. Those who will know will be few. Be glad to see these people. Open your heart and your homes to them that know and accept the blood written in their hearts. Their feet shall surely be under your table. Be prepared!

Vision of a woman that I thought might be the Blessed Mother. My prayer partner discerned that this woman was Elizabeth:

It is in this age that you will experience the way, the truth and the true life. My Lord and my King is coming with great power and glory. His kingdom on earth is not yet set, but soon all will be in place. Know that I bring great joy. Prepare yourselves for Him and His coming. This age will see the King, as I was full of joy of life that was in me so shall you be. Go and prepare. Do not be afraid.

Vision of two and three-years-old boy and girl dressed in their Sunday best:

Come to Me as these little children, for I will dress you in the very best that I have. This dress will be the new life I have for each of My kids, dressed in the fruit of My Spirit. For at My coming, I want to see My Church in their Sunday best.

Vision – I could see a room with a number of shelves being dusted with a dust broom. Suddenly, I saw a small statue of Buddha, then purple, purple, purple (Repent, repent, repent):

These false gods and idols are in the living rooms of America. Repent for these idols and come against all false gods so My Spirit can reign in freedom.

Vision of a Milo seed head:

The Lord provides for the birds of the air, and He will provide for all of your needs as well.

Vision of older lady – 70 to 80 year old. She thought she lost some of her money. I told her, "No!"

Store up your riches in heaven and not in this world.

Vision of an envelope address to my wife and I from Mr. and Mrs. John McCallie. I was not able to read where they were from. I asked my prayer partner if this was from the Lord.

> He said, "Yes! They need your prayers. You will learn what the prayer was for when you meet them in the kingdom."

Vision of a circle rainbow in which the inside color was orange:

> A rainbow is the sign of My promises. The one color, orange, is the fire of My heart. I intend to burn My promises that are found in My Word, onto the hearts of My people.

Vision of a woman in her 40s who was standing before me looking down with a spotlight around her head and chest. I did not know the woman.

> Ann is her name. She has been deeply hurt and the Lord wants to minister to her and heal her. Pray for the forgiveness of her sins and that the Holy Spirit be stirred up within her into a mighty flame.

Vision - looking down at a small reflection of light that suddenly becomes a large blinding light:

> Always put things to the test of My Word. This light is the enemy. Does not My Word say "Satan can be disguised as an angel of light?" Put things through the test of My Word.

Vision of a barbed wire fence in which the wires between two posts were cut:

> The barbed wire fence is representative of the boundaries

we place on ourselves and our abilities. God has no bound-
aries. He said, "The things I do, you also will do." He has
cut the fence. We must dare to reach beyond the imagined
limits.

Vision of a very beautiful child under one year of age:

I want My people not to stay as beautiful babies. My plan
and My will is for them to grow up into mature brothers
and sisters, for the battles yet to come. It will be mature
people that will have the victory. It is mature people, not
babies, that know how to obey their leader.

**Vision - a man reached through the window of my car and picked
up a quarter. I demanded that he give it back to me. He refused.
We got into a scuffle:**

They will steal and rob you. Do not be afraid. Put out
monies and things to be taken, lest they tear your wall
down, where your treasures are hidden. They are bold.
They are in need. Prepare and make those with you understand. Show love. Be prepared.

Vision of metallic purple – a very attractive purple:

Metallic purple – sins of the world made to look appeal-
ing and attractive to go after.

**Vision - while at Mass, a man standing in front of me, moved his
finger and arm down implying "right now." Later a vision of a
different man, indicating "not yet":**

Although the discernment on what I, the Lord, show you
will sometimes be contradictory, I will clarify all things,
for I am the One who am revealing these things to you.

Vision of two large white books with green letters A to M on the first book and N to Z on the second book:

> These books list those who have been washed with the blood of My Son. These are those whose names will be called first. They are without stain or blemish. These are My earthly warriors. They pray and work every quadrant of the Spirit. They do not stop. They have given up all for Me. They come to Me exhausted from their race - each has won. Each has Me as their center. They lived in this world but are not of it. They are Mine.

Since my understanding is that the number winning the race for the prize of the high-calling is limited, I said, "Lord, these two large books certainly contain far more than 144,000 names?" My prayer partner then received knowledge that these two books contained the life history of each person that had won the race for the prize of the high-calling. The words flow with beauty.

Vision of a small child 1 ½ years old, still on the bottle. He had been wandering around and came back to his grandmother, who sent him to his mother. She gave him a bottle of milk, which he raised up to his mouth to drink:

> This is a semblance of those that I have sent to you. They have just left their mother's breast. This woman is the world. She does not wish to care for her child, My people. They will come for nourishment but it is only milk that you can give them at first. Their knowledge of Me is little. Speak of Me in stories and in blessings. They are very weak. Some of these will be lost. Do not fear, for My angels will pursue them again and again!

While praying early in the morning, I had a vision of myself sitting in a Church pew. Sister Mary Virginia, a nun and a friend, was sitting in a pew about fifteen pews in front of me. She turned around and pointed her whole arm at me with a stern look on her face and said:

"Pray, pray, pray.

Dream – though I had knowledge the wife of a college classmate was not sick or anything of that nature, she had written her own obituary. I asked my prayer partner if this was from the Lord? He said, "Yes!"

> This is not an obituary of her physical death, but an obituary of her dying to self, turning from sin and worldly desires, and turning wholeheartedly to the Lord.

While at Mass, I had a vision of a belt buckle, not fastened and poorly attached. Then a woman who walked up to me and placed one finger close to my ear and the other finger on my lips:

> I am the belt buckle. I bring and hold all things together. The belt is the belt of truth. The woman touching my ear and mouth meant "Hearing and speaking the Word of My truth will set you free."

Vision of a middle age woman

> It is time. I must wish you had warned me. They do not know. It must be done quickly. I believed otherwise but now I understand. So many have been misinformed. Why did it take me so long? I don't know if I should tell others. Give me your advice.

My son, Mark had a dream in which he was half awake. He and his wife and three children were at Mass. At the consecration of the bread, the priest did not say the words "This is My Body." Mark said in the dream, "He immediately told his family to get up, we are leaving."

If the priest does not say the words, "This is My body." We are to leave.

While I was praying the rosary at 5 am, in a vision a woman sat down next to me. I put my arm around her. I did not recognize her. I asked my prayer partner to pray with me for understanding.

He immediately received understanding that this woman was St. Catherine of Sienna. She is a spiritual adviser and will be helping me to receive a deeper understanding of God's Word. I will be receiving clearer messages from the Lord. I am to ask her to intercede for me.

While at Mass, I had a vision of a round faced woman with a black cloth wrap around her head and sides of her face. The image was not real clear as she was within a darkened area. I had the understanding that she was a Nun.

When my prayer partner, Bill, prayed with me, he understood immediately that this woman was Sister Lucy of Fatima. She said, "Tell Mike I have him covered."

Vision of St. Peter being crucified upside down. His feet were nailed at the top of the pole while his hands were nailed to the crossbeam below.

The Lord said: A high cost but greater reward.

Vision - I walked into a round room about 25 feet in diameter with a high round dome. There was a bishop standing in the room dressed in golden vestments with a miter on his head and a staff in his hand. Next to the wall was a woman dressed in white lying on top of white sheets on a bed. I had knowledge this woman was Luisa Piccarreta. I could not tell if she was alive or dead.

I asked my prayer partner if this vision was from the Lord. He said, "Yes! The bishop was Pope Benedict who was in the process of declaring Luisa Piccarreta a saint."

Vision of Deacon Bob Scroggins a good friend of mine who is with the Lord. During my prayer time early in the morning Deacon Bob walked up and anointed me, and said, "Continue to pray and do what you are doing."

Vision – a number of young men (12 or so) coming out of a downtown store. They were wearing short pants or bathing suits. No shirt.

The Lord has called men to lead His Church. The young men, partially clothed, are not properly dressed to lead His Church. They need to be clothed in the Holy Spirit.

While at Mass, I saw a vision of a cotton field loaded with white cotton. The cotton was bright with the sunlight reflecting off the cotton. There was a wagon in the field but no workers to gather the cotton. Some cotton was hanging on to the bolls and stalks while some had fallen to the ground. The cotton was being ruined and lost because there was no one to gather the harvest:

The Lord is saying the harvest is great and ripe but the laborers are few to gather it.

Vision – I was walking to the altar to receive the Communion. Something distracted me. This priest could read soul. He knew I was not focusing on Jesus. He refused to give me communion. We must avoid distraction and keep our focus on Jesus when receiving His body and blood.

Just before I woke up at 5 am to pray, I heard a loud inaudible gun shot.

This shot is the revolution of My Son, Jesus that will be heard around the world.

Comment

These are only a few of innumerable pictures, visions, understandings and discernments that have been received. The Lord is bountiful in His gifts, to those, who dare open to receive His treasures.

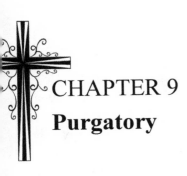

CHAPTER 9
Purgatory

While praying before the Blessed Sacrament after Mass the Lord said: I want you to show My people My mercy throughout the two books I gave you. This paper on purgatory truly shows the depth of His mercy in the forgiveness of sin, especially after death.

A vision of millions of stars in the sky: This picture remained before me longer than most pictures before it faded. A prayer partner spoke the following words to me:

> These are the stars that I showed Abraham saying that his descendants would be as numerous as the stars in the sky. These stars for you represent the people in purgatory who are in need of your prayers. Be diligent during this time of Lent in your prayers for the forgiveness of their sins. Know that your prayers are heard and are of great value.

I was very reluctant to write about purgatory. Thoughts on purgatory came to me for several weeks and then all through one night. I had a sense that the Lord wanted me to write about purgatory. Two different prayer partners received knowledge, "Yes!"

Purgatory is a controversial subject, as many people do not believe in purgatory. Pastor Roland Buck, a Pentecostal minister, had 16 visitations with angels. As a consequence, he wrote a best seller called *Angels Among Us.* It is interesting that the angel told Pastor Buck that there are people who have died and are on their way to heaven but have not gotten there yet. Pastor Buck told the angel that this was completely against his theology. The angel told Pastor Buck that he was not interested in his theology; he was telling him what was a fact. (53)

Sin is like a vat of dark colored dye

A friend was suffering from intense pain. Upon talking with this person, I learned that he had some deep resentments and hurts. I told him that he had to forgive those who had hurt him. Later the Lord revealed to me that this person had repented for his sins. The scriptures say that if you confess your sins, the Lord is faithful and just to forgive those sins and he will cast those sins into the depths of the sea, never to be remembered anymore. I said, "Lord, why is this person still suffering if his sins have been forgiven? It seems, if he is still suffering, that you are remembering his sins?" A prayer partner received the following words:

> Sin is like a vat of dark-colored dye. When you fall into sin, your pure, white, unblemished spirit takes on the color of the dye. The longer you stay in the dye the deeper the stain gets in your spirit. Repentance from sin makes the spirit be lifted out of the dye by God's mercy. He rejoices to have saved you from death by drowning in the vat. There is great happiness that you are restored to the living, but your spirit still has the color dyed from sin. Living outside of sin, suffering is the reparation of the spirit. Before the soul can be completely pure white again, the stain has to be removed. Suffering on earth cleans the soul faster than suffering in purgatory. Suffering is caused by the stain still remaining on the spirit.

Purgatory

My intentions are not to scripturally prove purgatory other than to quote a few scriptures, which for me support the existence of purgatory. My intentions are to share dreams, visions or pictures and words or messages I have received pertaining to purgatory. I was concerned about naming the people for whom I received knowledge to pray. I asked my prayer partner to pray with me for an understanding on what I was to do. We received the following words:

My truth will speak for itself. Report it as it was told to you. My truth will stand on its own.

A second prayer partner also received, "Yes!"

> I have given these for you to know because you are willing to intercede. You have completed what many others started, and with others, you were there from death through the judgment.

Dick Dowling

In the early 80's, I had a dream in which a Baptist friend spoke to me and said to pray for Dick Dowling. I did not know anyone by this name, other than the Dick Dowling who was in command of the Confederate troops at the Sabine Pass in the War between the States in the 1860's. Another Baptist friend was my prayer partner at that time. I asked my friend to pray with me, "Is this dream from the Lord?" He said, "Mike, I am positive this is from the Lord." Then I said, "Hold my hand." I quoted 1 John 5:16. "If you see a brother (or sister) commit a sin, which is not unto death, you shall pray and it shall be forgiven him." My friend got real excited and said, "He is set free. He is set free!" My friend did not know anything about purgatory and did not know that we were praying for someone to be set free from purgatory. All he knew was that someone had been set free.

President John F. Kennedy

A month later, I had an impressive vision of President John F. Kennedy. I called my Baptist friend on the phone and asked him to pray with me, "Is this vision or picture from the Lord?" As we started praying, he said, "I am positive this is from the Lord". For some reason, I said, "Let's pray." As we began to pray, my friend started receiving knowledge of President Kennedy's unrepented sins. As each sin came up, I quoted 1 John 5:16. This went on for thirty minutes. Then my friend said, "He is set free!"

Ten years later, I had a picture of John Kennedy. My Catholic prayer partner discerned that John had just been released from purgatory. I said I thought he was set free when we prayed for him ten years ago. My prayer partner said he was set free, as his sins were forgiven, but he had to make reparation for his sins.

Vision of my aunt

Another month later, I had a picture of an aunt that had passed away some 15 years before. She had three sins for which I repented. My prayer partner received knowledge that she went right into the kingdom of heaven.

Vision of a friend

A week later I had a picture of a friend that had passed on. He had three unrepented sins. Knowledge of the first two sins came quickly. There was a long delay in the third sin. It was as if he did not want me to know what the third sin was. When the third sin came up, I knew he did not want me to know the sin, but he wanted to be set free. This indicated that a person must be willing to reveal their sins to be set free. The scriptures say to confess your sins to one another that you may be healed.

Robert Kennedy

Sometime later, I had a vision of Robert Kennedy. After praying, my friend received knowledge that he was set free. At another time, I had a picture of John and Robert Kennedy and another person, when they were young. I asked my Baptist prayer partner who this third person was. He received the name "Joe Kennedy." He said it must be their father. I said, "No!" He was the same age as John and Robert. I knew this was their brother, who was killed in World War II. The Lord revealed to my prayer partner that, when a person's life is taken quickly and unexpectedly, he will be given an opportunity to repent at another time.

Scriptures for purgatory

The scripture below says that a sin against the Holy Spirit will not be forgiven in this world or in the world to come. This implies that a sin against Jesus can be forgiven in the next world or age to come. If this was not the case then practically no one could be saved. All of us have sins of commission and omission that we are not aware.

> Matthew 12:32: And whoever shall speak a word against the Son of Man, it shall be forgiven him; but whoever speaks a word against the Holy Spirit, it shall not be forgiven him, either in this age or in the age to come. (1)

In Matthew 5, the Lord is talking about sin, judgment, punishment and hell. The following scripture says that, if you are before the altar of the Lord and remember that someone has been offended by something you said or did, you must leave the altar, go and apologize and be reconciled even if it is a member of your family. Otherwise you are in danger of judgment and will be cast into prison and will not come out until you have paid the very last penny. This is one of the strongest scriptures in support of purgatory, as it pertains to the purity of your soul before the altar of the Lord.

> Matthew 5:20-26: But I warn you - unless your goodness is greater than that of the Pharisees and other Jewish leaders, you can't get into the kingdom of heaven at all! Under the laws of Moses the rule was, "If you kill, you must die." But I have added to that rule, and tell you that if you are only angry, even in your home, you are in danger of judgment! If you call your friend an idiot, you are in danger of being brought before the court. If you curse him, you are in danger of the fires of hell. So if you are standing before the altar in the temple, offering a sacrifice to God, and suddenly remember that a friend has something against you, leave the sacrifice there beside the altar and go and apologize and be reconciled to him, and then come and offer your sacrifice to God. Come to terms quickly with your enemy before it is too late and he drags you into court and you are thrown into a debtor's cell, for you will stay there until you have paid the last penny. (16)

> Matthew 18:30-35: But his creditor wouldn't wait. He

had the man arrested and jailed until the debt would be paid in full. Then the man's friends went to the king and told him what had happened. And the king called before him the man he had forgiven and said, "You evil-hearted wretch! Here I forgive you all that tremendous debt, just because you asked me to - shouldn't you have mercy on others, just as I had mercy on you?" Then the angry king sent the man to the torture chamber until he paid every last penny due. So shall My heavenly Father do to you if you refuse to truly forgive your brothers. (16)

When the man paid the last penny, the king set him free from the torture chamber. God the Father will also set us free when we have made reparation for our sins.

1 Corinthians 3:11-15 speaks of every man work being tested by fire. If his work burns up, he will lose his reward but he, himself, will be saved by fire. This could be the purifying fire of purgatory.

There are other scriptures, which imply the existence of purgatory. Revelation 5 speaks of creatures in Hades praising God. These creatures certainly are not demons or people who are damned for all eternity. These creatures are people waiting for their release from prison to be with the Lord.

Revelation 5: 3, 13: And no one in heaven or on earth or under the earth (in the realm of the dead, Hades) was able to open the scroll or take a look at its contents....And I heard every created thing in heaven and on earth and under earth (in Hades, the place of departed spirits) and on the sea and all that is in it, crying out together, to Him Who is seated on the throne and to the Lamb be ascribed the blessing and the honor and the majesty and power forever and ever - through the eternities of the eternities! (5)

A scripture I used in praying for people in purgatory is 1 John 5:16 - If you see a brother or a sister commit a sin which is not unto death, you shall pray and it shall be forgiven him (paraphrase).

Is not My Word like a mighty hammer that crushes the rock to pieces? Send forth My Word and crush the rock of his heart.

Someone asked me to pray for an understanding for someone who had passed on. I had assumed that this person, who was a personal friend, was in heaven. My prayer partner received knowledge that she was in purgatory. I asked the Lord if she wanted me to pray for her. He said, "No!" I said, "Lord, why? Is it that this person does not want me to know what her sins are or what?" The Lord revealed that this person not only did not want her sins revealed but she did not feel worthy to leave purgatory. A week later, I had a picture of a man outlined in purple. Then I saw two hands, outlined in purple, come together as to pray. I knew purple means to repent, but I did not know who this man was. Through a prayer partner, I said, "Lord, do I know this man? The answer was "No!" Then I said, "Lord is this man in purgatory?" He said, "Yes!" We prayed and repented for three unrepented sins, but the man was not set free. I said, "Lord, are you asking me to pray for this person every day?" He said, "No! I want you to pray now." "Is not My Word like a mighty hammer that crushes a rock to pieces? Send forth My Word and crush the rock of his heart" (pride).

> Jeremiah 23:29: Is not My word like fire (that consumes all that cannot endure the test)? says the Lord, and like a hammer that breaks in pieces the rock (of most stubborn resistance)? (5)

We received knowledge that he was set free. Then I said, "Lord do you want me to pray this way for my friend?" He said, "Yes!" My prayer partner received knowledge that she was set free. The Lord did not require her to reveal her sins. Now when I pray for people in purgatory, the Lord does not always require that their sins be revealed.

A friend felt that, when I quote these words, I am forcing someone to repent against his free will. The Lord said He does not force anyone to repent against his free will. I am simply quoting the words the Lord gave me. When I pray this prayer, God sends forth His Words that are like fire. The Lord can make His Word say whatever He wants to convict the person. It is God's Words that convict the person, causing him to repent on his own. This does not violate a person's free will. One can always choose not to repent. A person does not always repent the first time I quote these words. I may have to pray for this person over a period of time before he chooses to repent (Jeremiah 23:29).

My prayer partner, Bill Alexander, received the following message from the Lord.

> Words, Words, Words: Hear My Words. I am the Word. I have existed from the beginning. All things were made through Me, the Word. Words are important, pay heed to My Words for I am present in My Word. May it be done unto you according to My Word. My Words bring life. My Words brings truth. Listen to My Words that would come forth from your brothers and sisters. My Words bring faith. My Words bring power. My Words bring comfort. My Words brings conviction. My Words are the source of life. They bring light to you My people. The light of My Word shines in darkness. Let My Word shine in you. The words of the world bring darkness and fear. My Words, the Words of the Spirit bring the fruit of love.

George Washington

I had a vision of an old man with many wrinkles in his face. I had knowledge that this man was George Washington, though he did not look like George Washington. My prayer partner received knowledge that this was George Washington and that he was in purgatory. One of his sins was resentment for being in purgatory for so long. This is a sin that was committed after death. After repenting for his sins, he was set free.

Deep in purgatory

I prayed for two presidents that were so deep in purgatory that two different prayer partners thought they were in hell. After praying for these two men for one and two years, respectively, they were set free. I had a vision of a beautiful green Luna moth flying in the room front of me. My prayer partner said someone, for whom you have been praying, has been set free. I asked my friend if this person was President Truman? My friend had a vision of President Truman, who said, "Tell Mike, I have been set free."

Stealing a banana

We were praying for an old friend who was in purgatory. We repented for each sin as we received it. Then my prayer partner saw a picture of him stealing a banana and put it in his pocket. We thought it was funny that the Lord showed us this picture. Nevertheless, we repented for his sins. Jesus laid His hands on the man's head and there was a light around his head.

A Muslim Friend

A Muslim friend's brother passed away. He asked me to pray for his brother. This request sent chills up my spine. I did not know what to expect. We received knowledge that that he was in purgatory and that I was to pray that he would accept Christ as his Savior. I had great concern about this discernment, so I asked four other prayer partners to pray for confirmation. A prayer partner saw him sitting on a fence. He liked what he saw about the Christians but was reluctant to step over. He wanted to hold on to his own tradition. It took two years of praying before we received knowledge that he stepped over and accepted Christ.

Vision of a Hindu Woman

I had a picture of a dark skinned woman in front of me who said, "Damn." My prayer partner received knowledge that this was a Hindu woman from India who was in purgatory. She said, "Damn" because she had been witnessed to and had a chance to accept Christ as her Savior but chose not. The Lord allowed me to repent for her sins and allowed her to come into the kingdom.

Prayer partner received knowledge that in three months the Lord was going to use me in a powerful way to set many people free from purgatory.

When the three months were up, I was given a prayer that the Lord told St. Gertrude that a thousand people would be set free each and every time she said this prayer. I asked five different prayer partners to pray for confirmation. All said, "Yes." The prayer is

> "Eternal Father, I offer Thee the most precious Blood of Thy divine Son, Jesus, in union with the Most Holy Sacrifice of the Masses throughout the world, for the holy souls in purgatory that they will be set free."

We received understanding that anyone who is in the Lord and living a righteous life can say this prayer (54).

Friends in a state of shock

On several occasions, while praying for friends who had died, my prayer partner received knowledge that all were in a state of complete shock, as they did not believe in purgatory.

A few hours after my aunt passed away, I asked the Lord if she was in heaven or purgatory?

The Lord said she had not yet been judged. Later, I learned that she was in purgatory. I have found that very few people escape purgatory. Even the religious, who supposedly lead very saintly lives, spend time in purgatory.

Relative in purgatory

I had a picture of an uncle that had passed on and was with the Lord. My prayer partner discerned that my uncle wanted me to pray for a relative that was in purgatory. It turned out that one of his uncles, who had died at the turn of the century and had been dead for almost 85 years, was still in purgatory. I had to pray for this person for almost six months to get him set free, even though I had repented for all of his sins, when I first started praying. This puzzled me. Is it that reparation can only begin after repentance? I do not know.

A list of people I pray for.

I made a large list of forty to fifty people for whom I knew to pray. There were many people for whom the Lord asked me to pray, some that I knew but most I did not know. For those I did not know, the Lord would usually give me the person's names and when and where they lived.

I have prayed for the people that I have known that have passed away. I have listed those that I do not know such as presidents, leaders, pioneers, movie stars, even those that lived long ago. Each week as my prayer partner and I prayed, we would go over the list and ask the Lord if He was ready to release any of these people from purgatory. Sometimes no one was released, other times there would be two or three released each week. It is interesting that on a feast day of the Blessed Mother, that as many as twenty or more people on my list were released. I added other people to the list as the people on the list were set free.

Vision of the Blessed Mother:

Jesus has given Mary all authority for each intercession for every person here on earth and in purgatory. We are to give each request to her. She will bring each request to the throne room of God.

A vision of Mark Twain

He was in purgatory and needed prayers. He was set free two weeks later.

A month later, I had a vision in which I was looking at a man in a cellar that looked like Mark Twain. His hair was all messed up. He was looking up to me.

This man was Mark Twain. He was concerned about his wife, his brother and a friend, who were still in purgatory. We prayed for them and they were all set free.

Vision – at the foot of a large steep hill was a small bowl-like pit reddish-orange in color. The rest of the hill and top soil were grayish color.

The pit of redemption: This is symbolic of purgatory. I believe that God is indicating that many of us believe we are living "good lives", but in reality we are off-base. This should not be the case. We need not be heading to purgatory. We need to get right with God and change our ways.

Vision of a card with Richard Burton's name engraved on it. A few minutes later, I had a vision of a card with the name R. T. Learn engraved on it.

Richard Burton and R. T. Learn were in purgatory and needing prayers. My prayer partner believed that R. T. Learn was a teacher from the Dallas area and that he had been dead about five years. R. T. Learn was set free five weeks later. Richard Burton was set free at a later time.

Vision of an old woman:

I had a picture of an old woman wearing a bonnet with a big smile on her face. Some of her teeth were missing. She looked to be in her eighties or nineties. The discernment was that she died at the turn of the century and that she had just been set free from purgatory. She came to thank me for getting her released from purgatory.

I have many visions of people I do not know. My prayer partners discerned that many of these people are people thanking me for help in being set free from purgatory.

Vision of an old boss, who has gone to be with the Lord

I had prayed for him earlier to be set free from purgatory. He wanted me to pray for his brother, who is alive.

A childhood friend died. Her family were Jehovah Witnesses

We received knowledge that she was in purgatory. As we began to pray, we began repenting for her sins, as we received knowledge of them. She had been badly mistreated by her husband and did not want to forgive him. I quoted the words the Lord had given me to set another person free from purgatory. "Is not My Word like a mighty hammer that crushes the rock to pieces? Send forth My Word and crush the rock of her heart (pride)." She immediately started weeping and forgave him. Then she could not forgive those that had deceived her about Jehovah. I repeated the words again. Suddenly she was before the Lord but she did not know Him. (It was as if I were expecting to see my brother but saw someone else.) Jesus began telling her Who He was. She accepted Him and went into the Kingdom.

Vision of a checker board: My prayer partner asked me if I had been praying for some old men with whom I used to play checkers. I told him, "Yes, most of them have been set free from purgatory.

The checker board signified the old men with whom I used to play checker. They wanted to thank me for my help in setting them free.

Someone called my name in a loud voice waking me up from a deep sleep.

The people in purgatory are waking you up to pray because they want to be set free.

Heard someone call my name.

This is someone in purgatory asking for help, someone for whom you are praying.

Christmas night I was dumping some cooking waste in my backyard. I heard someone call my name "Mike." I looked around but I did not see anyone. As I continued back to the house, I heard someone call my name again. I turned around. There was no one there.

> My son, you will have many of these calls. I have chosen you among many. The voices you have heard will be different as time goes on. These voices are calling for help. They are in distress and see the light as you move about. They are calling for freedom of their sins and have lost their (spiritual) sight. Pray for their conversion.

Vision of my Uncle John: Words received from the Lord

> Here I am, and here you shall know, I have come to you so you will know. There are many in need of your great deeds (prayers). To those who know, they wait to go. There are others to be set free. Give me your ears, so you will hear. Draw close for those, whose names (in purgatory) you shall know. The oil of gladness has been poured upon you. It is known to all those, who hear the prayers of My saints. Your effort to free My people is well known. My angels rejoice at your ever-prayerful word. Do not cease in your efforts to break the chains of bondage of sin.

Vision of someone talking to me: The only thing I remember is the name Bobby Gifford. I do not know anyone by this name.

The Lord revealed that Bobby Gifford is in purgatory and needs prayers, because there is no one to pray for him. He was eventually set free.

Vision of Johnny Jayroe, a friend with whom I had worked, with a big smile on his face.

> Johnny died and was in purgatory. He wanted to thank me
> for praying for him. He had been set free.

Vision of a friend who is with the Lord, sitting in a chair asking me to do something, then his face changed to an image of his brother or brothers. I believed he was asking me to pray for his three berothers, who had passed on.

> My prayer partner received knowledge that his brothers
> were in purgatory. We prayed for their release.

Vision of an old friend I knew when I was young boy. He died long ago.

> He was in purgatory and needed prayers. He was eventu-
> ally set free.

Vision of a friend in purgatory who was in deep agony: His eyes were glassy with thick tears; his face showed intense pain. He was pleading and begging me for help. In life, he was very critical of the Catholic Church. He played around on his wife, and seldom went to church. When he did go, he received communion. From then intense pain on his face and thick tears in his eyes, he suffered terribly.

> This friend was eventually set free.

Vision of someone I knew. He was killed in an automobile accident. He had been dead close to 30 years.

He was in purgatory. We received understanding that he had violated a girl and lied about it. He was set free.

Vision – I was on the stage with John Wilkes Booth before the assassination of Abraham Lincoln. I saw several images of Abraham Lincoln.

It was discerned that John Wilkes Booth was in purgatory. We repented for a number of his sins that were revealed. He was set free later. We prayed for Lincoln's wife and their three sons. They were all set free from purgatory.

Vision– two wine chalices with the Blood of Christ sitting on a shelf behind the altar after Mass. In my mind, I picked up the two chalices and drank the Blood of Christ for the poor souls in purgatory.

> My Blood is given for you. It pleases Me to have you drink of it. Your intentions are pure and the souls rejoice. I honor your prayer.

Vision – a lady walked into a room, in front of me, with her husband and two small children between ages of 3 and 5. The woman was wearing a very attractive red dress.

The woman had died and she wanted me to pray for her family. First I asked the Lord for her name and if she was in heaven or in purgatory? Her name was Susan Elizabeth and she was in purgatory. We repented for her sins but she still had to spend time in purgatory. We asked the Lord to protect her family and to lead them to Himself.

Long dream with General Douglas MacArthur. He was tall and had black hair. He looked older with more wrinkles on his face. He had a deep cut from his forehead down the right side of his face. General MacArthur and I were walking, talking and visiting. He was not wearing his military uniform.

My prayer partner discerned that General MacArthur was in purgatory and needed some prayers. He was eventually set free.

Vision of an eight or nine year old boy.

This boy was in purgatory. He was set free.

Picture of a young man with glasses (we understood that he had died but had not left the earth).

I asked the Lord if this picture was from him. If the answer is yes, who is this person? My prayer partner discerned that this man, who was about thirty years of age, had passed away. I asked the Lord if this person was in heaven or purgatory. He said, "Neither, he had not left the earth." I said, "I do not understand." My prayer partner said he had deep fear and concern for his two boys. He knew if he left the earth, he would never come back. I repented for the sin of fear, quoting the scripture, "For God hath not given a spirit of fear but of power, and of love, and of a sound mind." Then I told him not to be concerned for his two boys as the Lord would take care of them. My prayer partner received knowledge that he did not believe. Then I prayed the prayer the Lord gave me, "Is not My Word like a mighty hammer that crushes a rock to pieces? Send forth My Word and crush the rock of his heart." My prayer partner saw him in the tunnel weeping. When he passed through the tunnel, Jesus met him and embraced him. I asked the Lord "Whose prayers enabled this man to get my attention?" The Lord said it was his own prayers, for as a child, he gave his life to Him.

On a number of occasions, my prayer partners received understanding that the person for whom we were praying had not left the earth. St. Anne Catherine Emmerich was a nun and visionary with the stigmata, the wounds of Christ, who lived in the late 1700's and early 1800's. Sister Emmerich had many visions and encounters with the poor souls in purgatory. Her diary documented numerous souls that were neither in heaven, purgatory nor hell but were wandering the earth in troubled anguish, haunting deserted places, ruins, tombs and scenes of their past misdeeds.

She also wrote about one particular woman who had been dead some 20 to 30 years. The woman was raped and had an abortion. The woman had gone to confession in tears to a man passing through town posing as a priest. Anne Catherine Emmerich saw the woman in inexplicable pain and afflictions holding a dark skinned child. The Lord said her confession was not sacramental and that she would have to wash the child white with her tears. (56) This example clearly shows the magnitude of sin and the importance of a proper sacramental confession. Sins that are improperly confessed must be repaid to the last farthing.

Dr. Kenneth McAll in his book, *Healing the Haunted*, discusses many cases of souls roaming the earth after death. Most cases involved people who were murdered. An example is the Bermuda Triangle, where slaves were thrown off the boat to lighten the boat during a storm, or prison camp where prisoners were inhumanely treated and died. The haunting stopped when a Mass was offered or prayers were said. (56)

Vision of a Mexican man about 30 years of age with a neatly trimmed mustache and wearing a hat .

Luis Cortinas was a friend. This man is Luis Cortinas' father, who is in purgatory. We repented for a sin. My prayer partner saw Luis coming to meet his father to take him into the kingdom. Luis and his father both had halos on their heads. My prayer partner said this was the first time he had seen a halo.

My Grandfather

My grandfather did not go to church. We were greatly concerned about his salvation. Approximately 33 years after his death, one of my prayer partners received knowledge that my grandfather was in purgatory and that he would be there a while. I asked the Lord if I could get him set free through prayer and fasting. My prayer partner received knowledge, "Yes, with three days of prayer and fasting." I went on a three day fast with nothing but water. My prayer partner received knowledge that my grandfather was set free. Because of the life he led, I asked two more prayer partners to pray because I wanted to be sure. They both said, "Yes!"

Dream – children were going to pray for their dad, who was my friend. I thought their dad had already been set free from purgatory six months earlier. I was puzzled. Were they praying for their dad or their dad's father?

My prayer partner saw my friend in a purple robe, kneeling before the Lord indicating that he was in heaven. Purple means to repent. It was discerned that my friend wanted me to pray for his dad, who was in purgatory. Two sins came up for which we repented. My prayer partner received knowledge that my friend's father had never been baptized. I asked the father if he was ready to accept Jesus as his Lord and Savior. The father lifted his arms, indicating, "yes." I (in my mind) poured water upon the father's head, baptizing him in the name of the Father, of the Son and of the Holy Spirit. Then two angels lifted the father by both arms and took him to Jesus, who was waiting in the distance.

When the Lord informed me that a person has not been baptized, I had understanding that the Lord wanted me to baptize this person. I visualized myself pouring water on this person's head, baptizing him in the name of the Father, of the Son and of the Holy Spirit. I asked my prayer partner to pray with me for an understanding as to who was actually pouring water on this person's head as I said the words. My prayer partner had a vision of Michael the Archangel dressed in full armor with a whole court of angels also dressed in full armor with him. Michael had a pitcher of water, which he poured on the person's head as I said the words, "in the name of the Father, of the Son and of the Holy Spirit."

I do not understand this scripture below, but the Lord has asked me to baptize people in purgatory who had never been baptized.

> 1 Corinthians 15:29: Otherwise, what will people accomplish by having themselves baptized for the dead? If the dead are not raised at all, then why are they having themselves baptized for them? (3A)

Vision of a man whose eyes were dark.

The eye is the light of the body. When the eye is dark, the body is

389

in darkness. My prayer partner discerned that this man was Mohandas Gandhi of India. I asked the Lord if Mr. Gandhi had any sins for which he wanted us to repent. The only sin that was revealed to us was unbelief. After repenting for the sin, I asked Mr. Gandhi if he was ready to accept Jesus as his Lord and Savior. We did not get any response. I prayed the prayer the Lord gave me, "Is not my Word like a mighty hammer that crushes a rock to pieces, send forth My Word and crush the rock of his heart." Then my prayer partner had a picture of Mr. Gandhi standing before a multitude of followers. He is interested but he is not ready at this time. My prayer partner had knowledge that if Gandhi accepted Jesus that a multitude would follow him into the kingdom. I continue to pray for him.

Vision of a face of a woman in unusual colors. It was like an orange-colored spotlight across her face, just above her eyes and beneath her nose.

This woman is Mr. Mohandas Gandhi's wife who is in purgatory. We repented for her sin of unbelief. I asked her if she was ready to come into the kingdom. My prayer partner immediately had a picture of Jesus laying His hands upon her head. I said, "Lord, do you want me to baptize her?" My prayer partner suddenly had a picture of Jesus holding a vase with two round handles pouring water over the top of her head. Afterward, I asked Mr. Gandhi, her husband, if he was ready to come into the kingdom. My prayer partner had a picture of Mr. Gandhi standing behind a smoky glass shield, indicating that he was not ready. (I had this vision his wife eight days after I had the vision of Mohandas Gandhi)

Vision of a group of people in an old picture. Then picture of a young girl that I assumed was in the group picture.

This young girl was in purgatory. We prayed for her and she was set free.

Vision of a blond girl about three years of age standing before me

looking at me. Her hair was cut bowl-shaped around her ears.

This young girl is Helen Keller. When we repented for her sin, she started singing, dancing and was very happy. She was set free.

About a month later, I asked Mohandas Gandhi if he was ready to accept Jesus as his Lord and Savior?

He did not respond. I quoted the words the Lord gave me, "Is not My Word like a mighty hammer that crushes the rock to pieces - send forth My Word and crush the rock of his heart." My prayer partner said Mr. Gandhi is ready to listen. Mr. Gandhi said, "You will have to prove to me that Jesus is the Son of God". I quoted the 1st chapter of the Gospel of John: "In the beginning was the Word, the Word was with God, the Word was God. The Word became flesh and dwelt among men." Mr. Gandhi said that was not enough proof for him to come into the kingdom." My prayer partner said we will have to continue to pray. I had two Masses said for Mr. Gandhi.

Mohandas Gandhi – a week later

I repented for the sin of unbelief and quoted part of the 1st chapter of the Gospel of John. I told Mr. Gandhi to ask his wife about the Kingdom of Heaven. Mr. Gandhi immediately threw up his hands and said, "I believe, I believe." Then he turned around and said, "I am going to talk to my people." He talked for a long time. Behind Mr. Gandhi was the Jordan River. Jesus and Mrs. Gandhi were on the other side. Later Mr. Gandhi motioned for Jesus to come over and talk to his people. Jesus came over and talked a while, then they all started walking across the Jordan River, which was a little less than knee deep. Multitudes after multitude after multitude were walking across the Jordan River into the kingdom. After we had prayed for a while and the multitude kept coming, I asked the Lord if we could pray about the other things for which I needed discernment. He said, "Yes!" After we finished praying about 30 minutes later, my prayer partner saw multitude after multitude as far as he could see, still coming. **I asked the Lord if he wanted me to include Mohandas Gandhi in the chapter about purgatory. He** said, **"My love and forgiveness is for the multitudes."** Roger Boos was my prayer partner when we first prayed for Mohandas Grandhi. Roger received understanding that if Mohandas Grandhi accepted Jesus as his Lord and Savior, he would bring a multitude of his people into the kingdom. Bill Alexander was my prayer partner when he accepted Jesus as his Lord and Savior. Bill saw multitude after multitudes walking across the Jordan River into the kingdom.

Picture of three young boys dressed like in the Colonial days. The oldest was about 14; the other two boys were about 5 and 8 years of age.

The discernment was that this was Quincy Adams and his brothers. Quincy was in purgatory. We repented for his sins, but he had to spend more time in purgatory. One of the brothers was in heaven. The other one was in purgatory and had never accepted Jesus as his Lord and Savior. Not knowing his name, I said, "Mr. Adam are you ready to accept Jesus as your Lord and Savior?" My prayer partner saw Mr. Adam leap up and take off running, saying over and over: "I am tired of burning! I am tired of burning! I am tired of burning!" In my mind, I poured water on him baptizing him in the name of the Father and of the Son and of the Holy Spirit. I don't know what really happened but my prayer partner said he saw a glow of light around him.

Vision of a woman's orange pajama top laying on the floor. The collar between the neck and the buttons was decorated with several long, narrow, orange, plastic decorative items.

This pajama top belonged to a woman who was raped. She committed suicide and was in purgatory. We repented for her sins and she was set free and was taken into heaven. Her name was Helen.

Vision of a person who had experienced the Baptism of the Holy Spirit but chose to retain certain sins in his life.

My prayer partner received knowledge that this person had committed some sins, the most serious being fornication. His life was taken from him unexpectedly and he had been dead and deep in purgatory for 10 years or more. We repented for his sins. The Lord wiped the man's face and took him into the kingdom.

I have prayed for many people that have not gone to church and lived a somewhat sinful life. They were neither deep in purgatory nor appeared to be suffering. They have been set free after a week or so in purgatory. This picture was a revelation and an understanding for me that people who have tasted the power of God and the power of the world to come, are judged more severely than those who have not experienced the Baptism of the Holy Spirit.

> Hebrew 6:4-6: It is impossible for those who have once been enlightened, who have tasted the heavenly gift, who have shared in the Holy Spirit, who have tasted the goodness of the Word of God and the powers of the coming age, if they fall away, to be brought back to repentance, because to their loss they are crucifying the Son of God all over again and subjecting him to public disgrace. (2)

While praying for people in purgatory, I had a vision of two women, one kissing the other on the forehead.

The kiss on the forehead is a sign that the old lady finally has received her daughter into heaven. The prayer you said released her.

The "National Geographic" had a picture of a skull of a Neanderthal man. I asked my prayer partner to pray with me for understanding – was this man in heaven, purgatory or what?

This man was not in heaven or purgatory. He was not human as his existence ended at death. Another prayer partner confirmed this.

Vision of a tall beautiful woman with pretty white teeth and a beautiful smile on her face.

My prayer partner received understanding that this woman was Marie Antoinette and that she was in purgatory. Neither my prayer partner nor

I knew who this woman was. Later we found out that she was married to King Louis XVI and she was the Queen of France. We repented for two sins but she had to do more time in purgatory.

The name Sitting Bull came to me.

I asked the Lord if he was in heaven or purgatory. My prayer partner received words that Sitting Bull had never been baptized. I baptized him in the name of the Father and of the Son and of the Holy Spirit by closing my eyes and pouring water on his head. He went right into the kingdom. Then I said to Sitting Bull, "Aren't you going to invite your people to come into the kingdom?" My prayer partner suddenly saw Sitting Bull on a stage talking to his people (a great multitude) who were kneeling on the ground sitting on their heels. As Sitting Bull was talking to his people, Jesus walked up and baptized all of them and took them into the kingdom.

Vision of an American Indian chief wearing a bonnet. He had no eyes, just white blanks where the eyes were supposed to be.

You do not see with your natural eyes, you see with your spiritual eyes. As we continued to pray, my prayer partner saw an Indian chief on a horse facing the other direction. Someone called the name, "Cochise," and the Indian chief immediately turned around. Cochise was a famous Indian chief. We prayed for Cochise and baptized him. He led all of his people, which included Geronimo's people, into the kingdom. I asked the Lord if He wanted me to include the Indians in this chapter on purgatory. The Lord said, "The sacrifice of My Blood is for all men, if they accept it."

Vision of a man and a woman, both had grins on their faces as they looked at me. They looked almost alike. I had a sense they were man and wife.

A couple was set free from purgatory by my prayers. The Lord said I did not know them.

The name Mrs. Vaughn Richardson came to me. She was the wife of my old barber when I was in high school.

My prayer partner saw her being called to come into the kingdom. Though I wasn't praying for her, my prayers for the people in purgatory set her free. My prayer partner received the following words: "The prayers of a righteous man avail much."

We prayed for a friend who died and was in purgatory.

The Lord said he had this against him: He used My name in vain all his life. When I repented for the sin of profanity, the Lord embraced him and said that otherwise, he was a good man and took him into the kingdom.

Dream of one of my college professors who passed away a year and half earlier. We prayed for him to be released from purgatory and he was set free.

My prayer partner received knowledge that his brother was deep in purgatory and he wanted us to pray for his brother. After repenting for a number of sins, the brother was set free from purgatory.

A friend asked me to pray for a homosexual that he knew who had died of AIDS. I asked the Lord if this person was in purgatory.

My prayer partner saw a black, disfigured human standing next to a black charred tree. When I asked him if he was ready to repent, he immediately took off running into the pitch darkness. The following week, I asked him if he was ready to repent? He took off running again. I spoke the words, "Is not My Word like a mighty hammer that crushes the rock to pieces. Send forth My Word and crush the rock of his heart." The Lord called his name. He immediately stopped and fell to his knees. The Lord said, "You cannot run or hide from Me. If you go to the center of the earth, I am there. If you run to the depth of the sea, I am there. If you go to the highest heaven, I am there. You cannot run or hide from Me. Surrender to Me." He started really weeping and crying before the Lord. We repented for a number of sins, but homosexuality was not one of them. Apparently he repented of this sin before he died. The Lord then lifted him up and took him into the kingdom.

A vision in which I was standing on one side of a street by some buildings. On the other side of the street was a blank space. A voice said, "His first wife is buried there" referring to the blank space.

As we began to pray, my prayer partner saw a building on fire. He had knowledge that the wife had died in the fire. This occurred in the late 1800's. I asked the Lord if she was in heaven or purgatory? My prayer partner was puzzled as he had knowledge that she had not, yet, left the earth. He asked me if this was possible. I told him, "yes!", that another prayer partner had received this understanding on several occasions. As we continued to pray, this woman was seen playing the piano. She was very attached to the piano. Not knowing how to pray, I asked the Lord if there were any sins for which she needed to repent. The sin of covetousness came up. After repenting for the sin of covetousness, my prayer partner saw her holding on to an approximately 6 inch by 6 inch square gold box, which was the sin of idolatry. After repenting for the sin of idolatry, I asked the Lord if He was ready to take her into the kingdom. The Lord said, "She needs to be baptized!" I immediately pictured myself pouring water on her head, baptizing her in the name of the Father, and of the Son and the Holy Spirit. Then the Lord reached down and took her by hand, and lifted her into the kingdom. I said, "Lord, whose prayers enabled me to pray for this woman?" My prayer partner immediately saw a distinguished looking man dressed in white with a stove pipe hat, a monocle in his eye riding a beautiful white horse. The Lord said it was the prayers of the man dressed in white, who was her husband.

Vision of one-half page of typewritten prophesy with the word purgatory in the prophecy.

The Lord said, "There are those who do not believe in purgatory, but they will believe in purgatory."

Someone I knew passed away the week before. While praying for him, we received knowledge that he was in purgatory. When he was a youth, he set some beehives on fire and burned up the bees. He had an extremely guilty conscience.

I had to talk to him to get him set free. I told him that there was no condemnation for those who are in Christ Jesus. Jesus said if we confess our sins that He, Who is faithful and just, will forgive us our sins and that He would throw our sins into the depth of the sea, never to be remembered anymore. My acquaintance repented and went into the kingdom.

We prayed for a friend's father who died in 1973.

He was in purgatory. He had committed blasphemy and was angry with God. I repented for the sin of blasphemy. He immediately responded. I told him to repent for his anger. He did not know what to say or how to repent. As I said the words repenting for anger, bitterness, resentment, unforgiveness, he repeated the words exactly as I said them. He was taken into the kingdom.

A monsignor had told me that he did not believe Jesus was crucified. If he had been crucified, it would not have been on Good Friday as there were too many people in town. After the monsignor died, I asked the Lord if he was in heaven or purgatory.

My prayer partner kept seeing an empty hospital bed and a vast empty space. Finally we received understanding that the monsignor had not left the earth. He was the head of a deanery and he was holding on to it. When I asked him if he was ready to repent, he would not respond. I came against the sin of pride and told him to turn loose of being the head of a deanery. He immediately responded. I repented for the sin of unbelief. Jesus then took him into the kingdom.

Prayed for a medical doctor that was accused of having sexual relationship with a 15 year-old girl. He committed suicide before he could be arrested.

When I asked him if he was ready to repent, he hollered, "No! I am not going to repent. I claim, 'there is no God'."

Prayed for a friend who had passed away

This friend was in purgatory holding a small baby. She had had an abortion as a young girl before she got married. After repenting for each of her sins, I asked the Lord if there were any more sins. He said, "No!" When I asked her if she was ready to leave purgatory, she would not move. After asking a number of times if she was ready to leave and she would not leave, my prayer partner received an understanding that she was not going to leave without the baby. The baby had not been baptized. In my mind I poured water on the baby's head "in the name of the Father, and of the Son and of the Holy Spirit." My friend and the baby went right into the kingdom.

While praying before the Blessed Sacrament, I had a vision of a clean-looking young man with a crew-cut, dressed with a shirt and a tie, standing in front of me looking down at the floor. He would not look at me.

My prayer partner received understanding that this young man was one of the twelve Texas A&M students killed when the bonfire fell on them. He was in purgatory and wanted to be set free. This young man's service was held in a Baptist Church. We prayed for all of the students. Some of the students were already in heaven. Some of the students were set free when we prayed for them. Others had to spend a little time in purgatory before being set free. What was interesting was that the Lord revealed that one of the Catholic students had never received the sacrament of confirmation, a sacrament whereby a Catholic accepts Jesus and receives the Holy Spirit. The scripture says that one must be born of the water and the Spirit to enter the kingdom of heaven. My prayer partner and I simply asked Jesus to baptize the student with His Holy Spirit. Afterward, Jesus took him into the kingdom.

In the middle of the night, I heard a woman say, "Did you tell him my name was Alexandria"

I asked my prayer partner if this was from the Lord? He said, "Yes, this woman was an Egyptian princess, who was in purgatory." We prayed for her and she was set free. I asked the Lord with whom was she talking. The Lord said she was talking to Padre Pio. She wanted Padre Pio to tell me her name and ask me to pray for her. The Lord allowed me to hear her talking to Padre Pio.

Vision of two photographs, side by side. On the right was a picture of my dad, who has gone to be with the Lord. On the left was a black man.

My prayer partner said the black man was a friend of my dad. He is in purgatory and your dad wants you to pray for him. We prayed for him and he was set free.

Prayed for the first wife of a friend who died almost 50 years ago.

My prayer partner received knowledge that she had not left the earth, because she did not want to leave her husband. We received knowledge she had not been baptized. After we baptized her, the Lord took her into the kingdom.

Prayed for my wife's classmate who committed suicide because his girl friend left him for someone else.

We received knowledge to repent for the following sins: suicide, jealously and bitterness. My prayer partner saw him running and hollering, "Lord save me!" After repenting for the sin of fear and stealing, he was set free and taken into the kingdom.

Vision of my Aggie ring, which I left in my lab jacket in 1962 and lost.

I was told," Mike, your ring was not lost. It was stolen by another Aggie who had lost his own ring." This person was in purgatory. I asked him if he was ready to repent for his sins. There was no response. Then I said, "I forgive you for taking my Aggie ring." He then broke down crying and the Lord set him free.

Heard the last name of a family from my home town. (Woman had been raped by her two brothers)

The last name of a family from my hometown came to me. I knew one of the children in this family. I asked my prayer partner to pray with me for discernment. Is this name from the Lord? My prayer partner said, "Yes!" The mother of this family was in purgatory. Her two brothers had raped her as a young girl. She could not forgive them for what they did. I repented for the sins of her brothers by quoting 1st John 5:16. After I repented for her sin of unforgivenesss, she was taken into the kingdom.

Prayed for a Jewish man and wife who had died.

After repenting for some of the man's sins, we asked the man if he was ready to accept Jesus as his Lord and Savior, he replied, "Yes, I have been absent from my Lord for too long." My prayer partner saw an angel pour water on him to baptize him. When we prayed for the wife, she said, "Lord, why would you have anything to do with me? My sins are many." The Lord replied, "Yes, I know. What about the woman at the well, her sins were many?" The wife repented and went on into the kingdom.

A dream of a young blond-headed woman several times during the night. I had understanding that this woman was my father-in-law's sister. Her husband often beat her. She died from a brain tumor when she was in her twenties.

My prayer partner said she was in purgatory. I repented for the sin of anger and resentment. The woman went into the kingdom.

I ask the Lord about an aunt and two great aunts that were nuns.

One nun was in the kingdom. Two nuns were in purgatory. One nun repented of her sins and went into the kingdom. The other nun did not want me to pray for her as she did not want to reveal her sins. It is interesting that this nun asked me very personal questions when I was in college. Do you go to Mass and receive communion every Sunday? How often do you go to confession? Do you say your prayer every night and etc? Two weeks later, she repented as she wanted to go into kingdom.

A friend had passed away. He was a poor country boy, who through hard work became a millionaire. My prayer partner saw this friend sitting in an expensive leather chair behind a desk. We had understanding that he was in purgatory because of his love of money.

When I repented for the sin of greed, he stood up and said, "So that's what it is." Satan, as a roaring lion, immediately took a swipe at my friend with his paw. My friend said, "Oh no, I belong to the Lion of the Tribe of Judah," and ascended right into the kingdom.

Vision of a Catholic bishop who died 25 years ago.

My prayer partner said the bishop was in purgatory. We repented for four sins: pride, anger, disobedience and rebelling. The bishop was released from purgatory.

A brother of a Dominican priest, who was a soldier, committed suicide with a rifle about 15 years ago. The priest asked me to pray for his brother.

The brother was in purgatory. He was set free when my prayer partner and I prayed for him. He said to tell his brother, the priest and the family that he is truly sorry for taking his life.

Nephew borrowed money from my grandmother

In 1916, my grandmother received some money from an insurance policy after my grandfather died. A nephew borrowed this money with a promise to pay it back. The nephew paid the money back in junk merchandise instead of money. This deprived my grandmother of money she needed for eight young children. This nephew, after being dead for approximately thirty years, appeared in a vision to my aunt, the only surviving child, who was within a few weeks of her 97th birthday and said, "Will you forgive me for what I did?" My aunt replied, "Yes, I forgive you for what you did." He was in purgatory all this time making reparation for his sins. The Lord allowed him to ask the living child for forgiveness. My prayer partner received understanding that he had just been released from purgatory. My aunt told the family about the nephew asking her for forgiveness.

A Protestant friend had a vision of a small child on the palm of a hand before his face. He asked me to pray about this.

My prayer partner saw the face of a small child in tremendous pain. We received understanding that this child had been aborted. I said, "Lord, what do you want me to do?" The Lord replied, "I want you to baptize this child." The child went on into the kingdom. When I shared this information with my friend and his wife, they admitted that there was an abortion in the family.

A small little girl appeared in the room at night.

A woman said a small girl began appearing in her room at night while she was in bed. The little girl eventually began sitting on the edge of the bed. A niece of the woman asked my prayer partner and me to pray for an understanding of who this little girl may be. As we began to pray we received knowledge that this little girl had been aborted. When the woman was asked if there had been an abortion in the family, she said, "Yes!" She had helped her daughter get an abortion. We told her that she and her daughter needed to repent for the abortion. We asked the Lord to baptize the child and to take her into the kingdom. After we prayed the child no longer appeared in the room.

A professor at Texas A&M gave me a C where my grades showed I should have had a B.

After he passed away, I asked if he was in heaven or purgatory. He was in purgatory and was in shock as he did not believe in purgatory.

When I asked him if he was ready to repent, he did not respond. When I quoted the words, "Is not My Word like a mighty hammer that crush the rock to pieces, send forth My Word and crush the rock of his heart," the professor repented and went into the kingdom.

Vision - a stocky, bald headed man standing next to me with a big smile on his face.

A prayer partner received understanding that this man had just been released from purgatory through my prayers.

We prayed for a young lady around 20 year of age who was killed in an automobile accident. She was a topless dancer and lived a wild life. She had been baptized by her mother but did not go to church.

We received understanding that she was in purgatory. When we asked her if she was ready to repent, she was unable to respond. There were many, many serpents crawling all over her, tormenting and smothering her. I commanded the serpents to get off of her. The serpents did not respond. I asked St. Michael the Archangel to pour holy water on the serpents. The serpents left immediately. The young woman said, "Please help me." After we repented for sins of rebellion, lust and fornication, she went right into the kingdom.

A Catholic priest in purgatory who was severely beaten to death beyond recognition.

We had prayed for this specific priest for 8 years with no luck in getting him released from purgatory. After receiving communion for this priest everyday for two weeks, my prayer partner saw someone thrust a purple spear into his heart. Purple means to repent. The purple spear was thrown into him because he had refused to repent. He had to do more time in purgatory. After receiving communion for the priest everyday for another week, we received understanding that he could not forgive the person who had beaten him to death until now. My prayer partner saw him kneeling before the Sacred Heart of Jesus with a glow of light all around him. He went right into the kingdom.

Bill Alexander's mother is in the kingdom. On several occasions, Bill heard an audible voice of his mother calling his name, "Billy." Once in a grocery store he thought his wife, Deanna had called him. Deanna said I do not call you Billy. I call you Bill.

I told Bill that his mother was trying to get his attention. I personally believe that there was someone in purgatory for whom his mother wanted him to pray. As we began to pray, Bill saw his mother's two brothers and a sister in purgatory. I quoted the scripture 1 John 5:16, "if you see a brother or a sister commit a sin which is not into death, you shall pray and their sins shall be forgiven them." Bill saw the two brothers and sister holding hands as they left purgatory entering into the kingdom.

Suicide

A friend's wife was an invalid and had suffered greatly for 20 years or more. They had run out of money and were desperate. Instead of asking for help, they committed suicide. I did not learn of this until almost a year later. When I prayed for them, the wife was in the kingdom. My friend was in purgatory. I prayed and received communion for him daily for about six weeks. Every times I asked the Lord if he was ready to be release from purgatory, I received a "No!" Finally the Lord said, "He does not feel worthy to enter heaven". My prayer partner then turned to the Blessed Mother and said, "What can you do?" The Blessed Mother just let out a deep sigh and my friend went into the kingdom.

Suicide

A Catholic priest had suffered with severe neck pain for years. After numerous surgeries with no relief, he committed suicide. The Lord revealed that he was in purgatory. I prayed and received communion for him daily. After a month the Lord said to the priest, "You have been absolved of your sins" and took him into the kingdom.

Occult

A friend's mother passed away. We received knowledge that she had been involved in the occult. I prayed and received communion for her daily for over two months. While praying, my prayer partner had a vision of the daughter speaking to her mother. She said, "Oh mother you look so beautiful!" This was the Lord's way of telling us that the mother had been released from purgatory.

At the beginning of Lent, I asked the Lord about a great, great uncle and his family. The great, great uncle and three of his children were in purgatory. One son was set free when we prayed for him. A son and a daughter had each been married five different times. One son was very deep in purgatory. He said please help me. After praying and receiving communion for them daily for six months, my prayer partner saw them both in a dark tunnel holding hands walking toward the light. The Lord said to keep praying. They were later set free.

A 92 year old friend passed away. I do not know if he had ever been baptized. My prayer partner received understanding we should baptized him. I pictured St. Michael, the Archangel, pouring water on his head as I said the words: I baptized thee in the name of the Father, and in the name of the Son and in the name of the Holy Spirit. My prayer partner received understanding that he was in Purgatory and said you need to receive Communion three times for him to be release from Purgatory. I said I am going to receive Spiritual Communion. In less than a minute I open my mouth three times to receive Spiritual Communion. My prayer partner said, "Wow!" He saw my friend in an Egyptian mummy-type casket. Jesus walked over tilted the casket upright. The lid open my friend walked out and went right into the kingdom. This shows the power of spiritual communion.

Vision of a nun. I did not know her.

The Lord revealed that this nun was Sister Joseph. She died recently and was in purgatory. She was released from purgatory.

I was asked to pray for a person with cancer. I was told that both of his parents had died of cancer. I had a sense that this was a hereditary curse that had been passed down. While praying with my prayer partner, I commanded the spirit of cancer to identify itself. It was a spirit of infidelity. The sin was committed by an ancestor. The person's father and grandfather were both in Purgatory. When I repented for the sin of infidelity, both father and grandfather were released from Purgatory. The Lord said, "I have been waiting a long time for the repenting of this sin."

Vision of a bald-headed man turning his head sideway so it could be cut off with a sword

In the daily missal there was a story about priest named Father Paul and five women that prayed together in the 4th century in Persia, now Iran. They were arrested. Father Paul was a wealthy man and all his wealth was taken from him. The king told Father Paul if he would make a sacrifice to an idol he could have his freedom and wealth. Father Paul did a sacrifice to an idol. The king told Father Paul to convince the women to do the same. The women told Father Paul that he was another Judas. When the women would not worship an idol, the king told Father Paul to behead them which he did. After reading this, I had a vision of a bald-headed man turning his head sideway so it could be cut off with a sword. My prayer partner, Bill, said this man is Father Paul and I am to pray for him. I have been lifting Father Paul up every morning in my prayer time and when I received communion. Bill prayed with me this past Tuesday. Bill said Father Paul kept saying over and over how truly sorry he was for what he did. Bill saw him go into the kingdom.

Jim Dick Lovett

Whenever any one I know passes away, I asked the Lord if they are in heaven, purgatory or where. Jim Dick Lovett was one of my high school classmates who passed away one day before our 60th high school class reunion. Jim Dick was a district judge in Northeast Texas. My prayer partner saw the Lord take off the black robe that he wore as a judge and put on a white robe of righteousness and took him into the kingdom.

Ex-husband of a good friend

The ex-husband, a Catholic, played around on his wife for years before she found out. After a divorce, the ex-husband married outside the Church. He died from Alzheimer without coming back to Church.

He had been dead a number of years before we began to pray for him. My prayer partner saw him lying down with chains on his hands and feet. I received communion for him daily for two weeks. Afterward, my prayer partner saw him sitting on a table with chains off his hands but he still had chains on his feet. I received communion daily for another two weeks. The chains fell off and he went into the kingdom.

Mother of a friend was a lesbian, pro-abortion and apparently an atheist.

She was killed in an automobile accident. We repented for the sins of homosexuality and unbelief. We asked her if she had any comments for her children. She said, "Stay close to the Lord for He is real." It took four months to get her set free from Purgatory.

A friend's mother passed away. She was in the upper levels of Purgatory. The Lord revealed that she was holding on to things on earth. After quoting 1 John 5:16, she went immediately into the kingdom. She said, "Oh Lord, the things in heaven are so much more beautiful than the things on earth."

Father J.D. Logan, a Dominican priest passed away.

I asked the Lord if Father Logan was in heaven or Purgatory. There was a vision of Father Logan standing before the Lord, handing the Lord his book on the "Liturgy of the Hours" and said, "Thank you Lord for your Word."

A nephew of a friend was severely beaten in a home invasion and died. After praying and receiving communion for him for several weeks my prayer partner and I asked the Lord if he was in the kingdom. There was an understanding that he was a prodigal son. God the Father walked toward him, embraced him and took him into the kingdom.

Vision – an address on an envelope with fancy artistic hand writing.

I recognize the writing as that of a lady who was a friend of the family. She sent us Christmas and birthday cards when we were small children. She had been dead for years. She was in purgatory. As we began to pray, the Blessed Mother released her from purgatory and took her to heaven.

Vision – I had knowledge Jesus had died. I was looking downward, and I could see Jesus dressed in white, ascending upward in what looked like a shaft.

Jesus was ascending upward from Hades. My prayer partner received the following message, "You, like Jesus, have a heart for the souls of the dead, who are prevented by their sins from entering His Father's presence. Know there is much rejoicing in My Father's court over the many souls freed by your prayers and intercession. Persevere!"

For a number of years, I had a priest say one Mass a week for the poor souls in purgatory. The Lord revealed to me that every time I said a special prayer, a thousand people would be set free. I try to say at least 50 of these prayers a day. I asked the Lord if the Mass was more effective than the 50 prayers I said everyday? My prayer partner received the following words:

Three times as many people are set free through the Mass offered for the souls in purgatory because there is no higher sacrifice than the sacrifice of My Son for them.

Note – This prayer was given to me in the early 1990's. I have been saying this prayer at least 150 times each day since the year 2000.

My understanding of purgatory

I am fully aware of the Church's teaching on purgatory, i.e. if you die with a mortal sin on your soul, you are lost for all eternity. Yet, my prayer partners and I have prayed for hundreds of people. We have repented for almost every known sin as the sin was revealed to us, and the sinner was set free to enter into the kingdom of heaven. I am also aware of the teaching of the scriptures that there is no salvation except through Jesus Christ and the belief that that decision has to be made before death. This was the reason I had a chill go up my spine, when my Muslim's friend asked me to pray for his brother. When we received knowledge that he was in purgatory and I was to continue to pray for him to accept Christ as his Savior, I asked four different prayer partners to pray with me for confirmation, because I did want to be deceived. I have no reason to believe that we were deceived.

There are many different levels and degrees of suffering in purgatory. The deeper a person is in purgatory, the more intense is the suffering and the darker is the picture. When we repent for a person's sins, one of my prayer partners sometimes sees a person rise from one level to the next or closer to the Light. My prayer partners usually can tell how deep a person is in purgatory and whether they will be released soon or have a considerable amount of time to go. This knowledge comes through the gift of discernment. There are areas in purgatory, where there is no indication of physical suffering or pain. One picture was of a green field of young wheat blowing in the wind. There is certainly no physical suffering here, except for being cut off from the presence of God. My prayer partners have seen pictures of individual alone in isolation. One person was seen sitting alone in a chair in a room. Another person was seen alone in the woods with little light. When the person in the woods was set free, he walked out of the woods into the bright sunlight, where he met the Lord. When someone is released from purgatory, my prayer partners will have an understanding, such as a picture of Jesus embracing the person, or Jesus laying His hands on the person, or many relatives welcoming the person home, or they see the presence of a bright or golden light. Sometimes persons freed from purgatory are seen walking into a beautiful garden or walking through the door into the kingdom. My understanding in praying for people in purgatory is that, no matter how rotten a life they may have lived or regardless of what faith they may be, they can be helped through prayer. The Lord's mercy is beyond human understanding.

> Ephesians 2:4: But God! So rich is He in His mercy!
> Because of and in order to satisfy the great and wonderful
> and intense love with which He loved us (5).

I believe that more people can be helped and relieved of their prison in purgatory if we will pray for them. Because of the many voices I have heard in the night from people begging for prayer, I know the people in purgatory are crying out for help. Most of these people do not have anyone to pray for them, as most people do not believe in purgatory.

Some people I pray for are imbedded in a cake of ice. The ice melts slowly as I pray and received communion for them.

It is interesting that priests, nuns and those who have lived a religious life and end up in purgatory, are the most difficult to get out of purgatory, while those who did not have a close walk with the Lord and lived a somewhat sinful life usually are easier to set free. People involved with the occult are difficult to get out of purgatory. I prayed for one person for two years before she was set free.

A brother of a friend of my son was killed in automobile accident five years previously, when he was 18 year of age. I asked the Lord if the boy was in heaven or purgatory. The Lord revealed that he was in purgatory but he would not let me pray to set him free as he wanted his family to pray for him. I do not know if the family knew if their son was in purgatory. We need to pray for our deceased relatives.

When anyone I know passed away, I asked the Lord if the person is in heaven or purgatory. If they are in purgatory, the Lord usually asks me to offer up some Masses and Communion to set them free.

I asked the Lord for a closing comment on purgatory.

> I came that all might have eternal life. For some the only way to eternal life is through purgatory. Through My mercy I have made eternal life possible even after death. My people are many; My body is one. Any member of My body can help the whole body through prayer. Pray for the dead. Many will only be healed through the love of all My members. Purgatory is a healing place for many who must wait on your love to help them through to the saving grace My death made possible for them. Pray for the dead so your prayers for yourself might be better heard.

Jesus emphasizes reparation for sin before entering heaven.

John Leary had a vision of people suffering in flames and they had a cloth over their nose and mouth because of the stench. Jesus said,

> "These are the souls who were not purified enough on earth. They suffer like those in hell except that they have been promised heaven one day. You can make sufferings on earth to help alleviate this torture later. Also, you can pray with the saints to diminish the souls' stay in purgatory. Many souls cry out for help to their relatives on earth but those on earth do not think of them." - - - 11/2/93 (57)

Some of the other numerous prophecies received by Mr. Leary are:

> I tell you many souls have come to this place you call purgatory. Let Me assure you, it does exist and indeed it is a part of My justice. It is a place where souls who had died and had not yet reached a state of spiritual perfection worthy of heaven. It is rare that souls avoid this without some major suffering or great spiritual awakening....11/2/94 (58)

> My people, many ask why there is a need for purification. You know that I am all merciful, yet I must abide by My Father's justice as well. When sin becomes so hideous, it calls for My purification. In order to free someone of their sins, they must seek My forgiveness, and there must be some payment for that sin. My death on the cross has enabled you to reach heaven, but still there must be some recompense for My justice to be satisfied. This is why some must suffer the fire of purgatory to rid all guilt and justify their actions. This also occurs for nations as well as individuals. Your sins of abortion in your country are so vile in My eyes, that you will face great chastisement by fire to cleanse this evil from your land. Pray My people, and turn from your evil ways if you expect to be received

in My arms. 2/4/96 (59)

The burning fire for the spirit soul you will see, if you experience them, are much more painful than that of the body. You would rather spend a short time in pain on earth than an unknown length of time in purgatory. 5/7/96 (59)

You should make an effort in prayer and fasting to make reparation for the punishment due for your sins. Your sins are forgiven, but My justice still demands some payment either in suffering on earth or in purgatory in the afterlife. Give up to Me all of your sufferings on earth to lessen your pain in the afterlife. Bring yourself by this work, closer to Me in heaven. 6/27/96 (59)

Give all of your pain up to Me as a prayer that I will store in heaven as payment for the reparation of your sins. 7/6/96 (58)

John Leary had a vision of souls suffering in a dark dingy place calling out for help. Jesus said:

"My son, you are seeing in this vision how many are still suffering for their sins. I have made this real for you, so you can witness to everyone that truly this place you call purgatory, does exist. It is truly a place of reparation for the temporal punishment due to your sins. Those, who do not have their suffering on earth for their sins, will have to be purified in this place of torment. In the upper levels of purgatory as you see, the worst suffering is to be without My presence. There is open to you an option to suffer for your sins on earth. Some of those, who suffer much before death, have gained heaven in this way. Pray for these poor souls regularly to alleviate their suffering. Especially, remember to pray for your own relatives and friends." 11/2/96 (60)

My people, I come to add My blessing over the people for their intentions. You are to know that those souls in heaven and purgatory are all a part of My One Body of faithful. Those souls, who are condemned to hell, are no longer accepted members, since they have rejected My call. As you make a remembrance of these souls, never forget them and pray for them continually through the years. Many are suffering in purgatory longer since their relatives have forgotten them. Pray also for those souls who have no one to pray for them. I want to remind all of you to be ever watchful over your own souls, so you may be ready for your own death....11/3/96 (60)

Those who have not been purged or purified of their sins will not go up in the Harvest Rapture. If they survive the Great Tribulation and Wrath of God, they will continue their life in the Millennium.

Sister Mother Eugenia Elisabetta Ravasio of Bergamo, Italy received messages from God the Father that are recognized as valid by the Church.

God the Father said, "Men believe Me to be a terrifying God Who is going to cast all mankind into hell. What a great surprise it will be when, at the end of time, they see so many souls they believed lost enjoying eternal bliss among the elect!" (61)

John Leary received the following message that the Lord gives special gifts to various people. My prayer partners and I have been given a gift of praying for people in purgatory.

Jesus said: "My people, you have seen various people who have been given special gifts. Some can speak to the souls in purgatory; some converse with angels; some have inner locutions or apparitions; and some have gifts to talk with the deceased. You have read books about messages from the souls in purgatory, and these souls have no evil, nor can they be influenced any longer by demons. Pray for people who have such gifts that they can discern any demons trying to pose as souls in purgatory. In this same book the old lady could tell the difference in one account when demons came to her. You also know of people with locutions and apparitions. Again My Church is cautious in testing all visionaries and the authenticity of their messages. Every time that you receive a message, you need to test the spirit for the truth. Gifts to receive messages from the deceased at their funeral are another openness to receive the last words of that soul to their family. At times you also receive a knowledge of where they are being judged. All of these gifts are a help to understand My judgments, and how souls do go to heaven, purgatory, or hell when their body dies. Your soul lives on forever because it is immortal, but your body only lives here a short time and dies. Follow My Commandments and give yourself over to My Will, and you will find your reward in heaven." (62)

My experience with Spiritual Communion

Communion and Spiritual Communion are very effective in praying for people in purgatory. I open my mouth and ask St. Michael, the Archangel to put a host on my tongue. Though I do not see or feel a host on my tongue, I accept it on faith. A person in purgatory who refuses to repent or forgive someone who has deeply hurt them, Communion or Spiritual Communion will bring them to their knees in repentance. I have found that Spiritual Communion is also very effective in exorcisms against evil spirits.

Spiritual Communion

Our Lord to Sr. Benigna Consolata: "Make as many Spiritual Communions as possible, to supply for the many Sacramental Communions which are not made. One every quarter of an hour is not enough. Make them shorter, but more numerous." (63)

Daily Spiritual Communion Prayer My Jesus, I believe that You are present in the Most Holy Sacrament. I love You above all things, and I desire to receive You into my soul.

Since I cannot at this moment receive You sacramentally, come at least spiritually into my heart. I embrace You as if You were already there and unite myself wholly to You. Never permit me to be separated from You. (63)

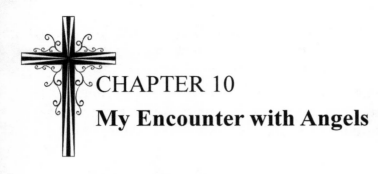

CHAPTER 10
My Encounter with Angels

Angels are messengers of the Lord, who guide and protect us. In Revelation 14 the angels fly through the air, preaching the gospel. The Lord has given each one of us a guardian angel to watch over us and to help protect us.

> Exodus 23:20 Behold, I send an angel before you, to guard you on the way and to bring you to the place which I have prepared. Give heed to him and hearken to his voice (31).

For thirty-something years, out of habit, I have asked the Lord each day to send out his angels to minister to and to protect my family and the people for whom I pray: to minister to the priests and clergy so that they would preach truths and righteousness to the people; to send his angels into the fields to help the laborers to gather the harvest; to minister to those, who are lost, so they would turn to the Lord in prayer and repentance. My prayer was for the Lord to send forth a spiritual revival throughout this nation and the nations of the world, to draw all people to himself. I asked the Blessed Mother, St. Joseph, the angels and saints to join with me in prayer and for the Heavenly Father to multiply the effectiveness of our prayers.

Less than a year ago, I had vision of thousands and thousands of angels forming a very high and wide dome. There was a row of angels standing side by side forming a tight circle. There were many, many rows of angels on top of other angels all the way to the top of the dome. I asked my prayer partner if this was from the Lord. The Lord said:

> Michael, these are My angels that I have chosen for you. They are protection for you and for those you pray and

intercede for. This dome has been built by your prayers and intercessions. The angels come and go as you pray. They each have names but I have given them to you in your name as a gift in these hours. I want you to know that I love you. I call you my love for you are doing as I have instructed you to do. You are about to go on a new journey in prayer. Open yourself to know what I am about to teach you. Listen to the words you will read and study. Make them yours that you may teach others that I will send. This dome of angels moves with you, so go freely as I send or direct you. Your face is becoming that of My Son, Jesus. I love you.

This vision and message of so many angels was overwhelming. I had, out of habit, asked the Lord to send forth His angels daily, not truly realizing what was going on. Recently, I came across a book, "Send me your Guardian Angel" by Fr. Alessio Parente, which is a story of Padre Pio and his angels (64). Padre Pio had always been harassed by the devil. One day Padre Pio was very tired, fatigued and weak. A brother padre was helping him back to his room, and said, "Let us ask your guardian angel to protect you tonight so you can get some rest. Padre Pio said, "What? No way, I have to send him out. He has work to do." Padre Pio has always told his people to send their angels to him if they needed help. Two teenage girls were talking and said, "Let's send our angels to Padre Pio. I am going to ask him to pray for my uncle, who has cancer." The next morning at Mass, Padre Pio told the two girls that their angels had kept him awake all night praying. On another occasion, a man told Padre Pio that he had sent his angel to him and he wanted to know if his angel had come to him. Padre Pio said, "Do you think angels are disobedient like you and I? No, they always do what you tell them to do."

After reading Padre Pio's book on angels, and realizing all the angels that the Lord had given me, I really started sending the angels out all through that day and night, bombarding the people for whom I was praying. The angels were sent to the priests and clergymen, to the members of the House and the Senate, to the Supreme Court Justices, to those involved in abortion, to those living immoral lifestyles, to those that are lost and in need of conviction and repentance.

The next morning, while praying the rosary, I had a vision in which I cross an underground freeway and was standing behind a concrete pillar that was three feet in diameter. Cars were traveling at excessive speed. One of the cars came across two lanes directly toward me and hit the concrete pillar I was behind, breaking the pillar loose at the base. The car, which was completely smashed inward, swirled around in front of me hitting a second pillar, throwing fine pieces of broken glass everywhere and all over me. The Lord allowed Satan to show how upset he was with me for sending these angels out. This did not frighten me. After the picture, I just continued to pray the rosary, for I knew what was going on. In the message above the Lord said:

> "You are about to go on a new journey in prayer. Open yourself to know what I am about to teach you. Listen to the words you will read and study. Make them yours that you may teach others that I will send."

Reading Padre Pio's book "On sending me your angels" taught me how to use the angels that the Lord had given me, with penetrating power and authority, to bombard those for whom I was praying. The Lord said,

> "Is not my Word like a mighty hammer that crushes the rock to pieces? Send forth my Word and crush the rock of their heart" (Pride).

> Jeremiah 23:29: Is not My word like fire (that consumes all that cannot endure the test)? says the Lord, and like a hammer that breaks in pieces the rock (of most stubborn resistance)? (5).

When we quote these words, the Lord can makes His words mean anything He wants to bring conviction on the people for whom we are praying. Obviously, this is the new journey in prayer about which Lord was speaking to me. The angels ministered with such power, authority and conviction that the Lord allowed me to see how upset Satan was for

418

sending the angels out all through the night while most of the people for whom I was praying were asleep. I asked the angels to minister with God's words to bring conviction and guilt, and especially to continuously harass the people that needed to repent and turn to the Lord.

ANGELS NEED OUR PRAYERS

A friend told me that she had a vision of a group of angels sitting on a curb. The angels were very depressed, with their elbows on their knees and their heads resting on their hands. When she started praying, the angels all came to life. Her prayers (ammunitions) went into the hands of the leading angel, who passed the ammunitions on to the other angels. These angels all went off to fight the battle for the day. The Lord was showing my friend that when we do not pray, the angels do not have ammunition to fight and to protect us against the power of darkness nor to witness, minister and protect those for whom we pray.

I had a vision of many, many neat and trim looking young men that were out of work and were looking for jobs. They looked as though they had just gotten out of the army. The Lord said:

> These young men are angels in My army. No one is pray-
> ing anymore and they do not have work.

It is essential that we spend time in prayer each day so the angels can protect us and minister to those for whom we are praying.

Daniel sought the Lord with prayer and fasting

Daniel went on a fast, seeking the Lord for an understanding. On the 21st day of Daniel's fast, an angel of the Lord appeared to Daniel and said, "God heard your prayer the first day and sent me immediately to answer your prayer. I was not able to get through because of the Prince of Persia. I had to send for Michael the Archangel and his angels. They fought for 21 days before I was able to get through." If Daniel had fasted only 20 days and gave up, the angels would not have had the ammunition to fight and defeat the power of darkness to get through to him.

Picture of a small sign in front of a small building which said: Fire and Police Department.

> The Lord revealed that the Fire and Police Department are for our protection in this life. There are two kinds of angels: the police angels and the fire angels, which are also for our protection. The Lord revealed that we are continuously under attack from fiery darts of the enemies. The police angels try to protect us from the fiery darts. When a fiery dart does hit us, it is the fire angels that come down from heaven with God's healing grace to put the fire out. Our prayers with the fire angels must be prayers of faith - a faith that is proclaimed even in our words.

When we pray for healing we can ask the Lord to send forth his healing angels. Nevertheless, we must continue to pray and sometimes fast so the angels have ammunition to get through the power of darkness.

Visions I had pertaining to angels

While praying early one morning in the den (2:00 or 2:30 AM) I heard the floor creaking upstairs like someone was walking across the floor. Ann later got up at 5:00 or 5:30. She also heard footsteps walking across the floor upstairs. She asked me to go up there and check. The door to the deck was locked. I did not see anyone up there; I even looked under the bed.

> I asked a prayer partner if this was Satanic. He said, "No!" This was an angel of the Lord. There are angels all over my house.

Vision - I saw a bright light, then there was a dark-headed woman holding a compact. She said, "Do you feel the presence of an angel?" I did not and I asked Ann if she felt the presence of an angel? She said, "No!"

The woman with the compact was an angel. She was telling you in effect that it is perfectly normal for you to have angels around you.

When I pray for understanding and discernment of a picture (vision) or words I have received, I bind Satan and all powers of darkness and cover myself and my prayer partner with the Blood of Jesus. I ask the Angel Gabriel to give me understanding and discernment whether the picture is from the Lord and if so, what is the message. I ask St. Michael and his angels to form a channel of protection so the Angel Gabriel can get through to me with the message.

Vision - a number of people were walking in the green median of a highway picking up trash. Some of the trash was not being picked up because it was too dirty – like soiled diapers.

My angels reach out to pick you up out of the garbage. Yet, some of you are too filthy. You will not be picked up. Now is the time of grace. Be cleansed! Seek to be picked up by me. Now is the time. Your life is short.

Vision of a black-haired man that was bald on top. The man appeared to be in his fifties and was smiling. The next day I had a picture of this man in a circle on the upper right side of a sheet of paper.

The man you saw represents an angel of protection sent to you by God. The piece of paper is something important you are writing. The angel is sent to protect your work. The angel's name is Aaron.

Vision of a beautiful woman standing before me smiling. There was a light-like appearance around her. I had the impression she was an angel.

Prayer partner discerned that she was an angel.

Vision - an unattractive young girl walked in front of me smiling.

The girl is an angel who carries my prayers to God.

Vision of a man with a white cloth wrapped around his head, smiling at me. He looked like a priest or a doctor.

These pictures that you get of persons looking at you or your possessions are really angels - strong guardian angels, who guard your every move, until God has caused you to reach every goal He has set for you.

Vision of a beautiful blond woman, with beautiful white teeth, smiling at me.

She was a prayer angel - when you pray, God sends prayer angels to assist you. When Jesus was in the Garden of Gethsemene, God sent angels to minister to Him. The blond woman angel's name is Anvangelica.

Vision of a picture of angels with wings

This is a picture of the past of man's lack of understanding of how My angels move about. (Note: The visions I have of people that are identified as angels do not have wings.)

Dream – I was flying high in the air. For 15 to 20 years, I have had dreams of flying in the air. Most of these were getting off the ground and flying in a room. At first I had to concentrate hard to get off the ground or go where I wanted to go. In this dream I was flying high in the sky with very little concentration. I could stop and go quickly wherever I wanted in the air.

You now have power over the prince of the air in his backyard, front yard and side yards. You have broken into his space. Now I would have you look at what you see before you. Begin to wage war and do not fear. I am already there. Michael the Archangel is already there. Enjoy yourself and penetrate the enemies' strongholds in direct prayer. Have fun with Me.

Vision - A tall young man (about age 30) instructing me to be firm. I felt this man was an angel.

Be steadfast in the Unbloody Sacrifice and to God's Word. The prayer partner replied, "He is doing that." The response was - part of the Word is going to be revealed to him. The time is coming when it will be difficult to receive the Lord's Body and Blood. The Lord wants him to be firm in receiving his Body and Blood.

Vision - A young man in his 20's or early 30's with long, uncombed hair.

This man was on death row in Florida. He had not yet accepted Jesus as his Lord and Savior. The Lord did not give us his name. As we prayed, asking the man to accept the Lord, he did not respond. I spoke the words, "Is not my Word like a mighty hammer that crushes the rock to pieces, send forth my Word and crush the rock of his heart." My prayer partner saw him on his knees weeping, as the angels ministered to him. We received knowledge that he had accepted the Lord as his Savior.

I had a picture of a boy kneeling in a pew on the other side of the church. He stood up and looked at me and said something, then he kneeled down again and faced the altar. I did not understand what he said.

This boy is an angel. He said, "Be of good cheer. Your

prayers will be answered."

A long dream in which I was on a retreat with angels. I was able to walk on water.

> You are a knight in shining armor. Your shine comes only from God Himself. You have been on a long journey through your spiritual life. You have been and are being cared for. You have chosen the higher calling of those being taken to the throne and before the altar of the Most Holy. There, the angels sing and there, they are sent forth. To be a part of this, you must be able to follow, and you must always posses, semper fidelis. Its roots are so deep that they cannot be pulled up. It has been granted to only a few. Again, you have done and are doing what is necessary to be selected. Your selection is not a result of blood or ordination but of pure love, faith and devotion to God Himself, and to His Son, Jesus, and the Holy Spirit. You are in training for what you will be selected to do. The angels are ever present, and they are with you, wherever you go. Be ready! Be prepared!

Vision of a blond-haired woman then a vision of a head of a blond child. The child's eyes were very noticeably.

> These are My angel and cherub together. They are here to bring you a message and to help protect you from harm. Do not be afraid to ask Me to send My angels to be there with you in the little things. They care for each other. Prepare yourself for a period of difficulty. You have been given a cherub to help you to praise God, when you cannot. You have been given an extra angel of protection to support you through your trial. Do not lose heart. God is with you. This trial will pass.

I heard someone say, "Look around." I looked around but I did not see anything. A few minutes later I had a vision of a real nice looking young man with auburn red hair neatly combed. He looked like he was about 25 years of age. He was dressed in a brown shirt, tie and a coat. I could see this person in front of me from the waist up.

This man was an angel named Chinini which means my glory and protector. He keep God informed about me. Prayer partner said angels are stationed at your door and are with you. Second prayer partner got the name – Zenably, red-haired leader of a cohort of angels sent to protect you. They are always around you. Fear no evil.

Vision of a man dressed in blue denim, kneeling beside me at Mass. His head was bowed.

One of several angels who are with me at all times.

While in the hospital with my dad, someone touched me on the shoulder in the middle of the night.

Your guardian angel touched you.

Vision of a beautiful blond woman with blue eyes standing in front of me, looking at me.

Prayer partner said she was an angel.

In my sleep in the night, someone tapped me three times on my ankle.

An angel waking me up to pray.

Vision of a man speaking to me as I was praying. When I did not respond, he did not complete the sentence.

It was my guardian angel.

Ann had a dream that a neighbor called on the telephone and told her that some people were going through your garbage. Do not go out there, they will attack and hurt you.

The neighbor looks at things the way the world does. The people going through the garbage are people in need. The world does not reach out to people in need. My Word says to reach out to those that are hurting and in need, because you never know when you may be entertaining angels.

The Lord awakened me about 4 AM, to pray. After praying for an hour and a half, I went back to bed. As I was lying in bed, dozing off at 7:15 AM, a loud voice said, "Whoa," I quickly jumped out of bed, as I needed to be leaving for work.

This was my guardian angel waking me up.

Vision - a woman walked up and embraced me on the street. Afterward I had a sense that this woman was an angel.

You have already met angels unaware.

Vision of a red-headed woman (30's) sort of threw her hands upward a little and lifted her eyes and eyebrows, and opened her mouth in excitement, when she saw me.

This woman was an angel.

Vision - a man was speaking at a podium. He then walked a few feet to where I was sitting on the front row. He touched my hands with his hands in a form of a gesture.

This man was my guardian angel.

Vision – my wife, Ann, was making a blouse with elbow length sleeves that were blue and green, blending together with pictures of angels.

A reminder to call on Ann's guardian angel to protect her mentally, emotionally, physically and spiritually each day.

While lying in bed, in the middle of the night, something hit the wooden bedpost, making a noise. Ann was lying beside me asleep and had not moved.

An angel of the Lord getting my attention to pray.

While thinking about the people praying the rosary in front of an abortion clinic, I had a picture of an angel in white, with one wing hanging down, as if he had been wounded. There was a light in the center of his chest.

He is the last angel. The others have gone to carry the prayers of those saying the rosary.

Vision - a man sitting at a table reaching out to shake my hand with a big smile on his face.

This man reaching out is not of God. He has come to take you away with his people. He is telling you that you are surrounded. You tell him that he is surrounded by the angels of the Lord that are standing beside each of his men. The Lord would have you to say that the living God has charge over the angels, and they will not let me be harmed.

I woke up at 4:30 AM to pray, but had trouble getting out of bed. I had a vision of a woman smiling, pointing her finger at me. I immediately jumped out of bed, went to the den and prayed until 6 AM.

The woman was a heraldic angel. My prayer partner saw a ram's horn blowing. It continued to blow. It was a call to all those, who have been chosen. It was a call to the Lord's priests, prophets, and worshippers, his intercessors. He has poured the oil over your head so that all will know; looking they will see. Only those who are condemned will not see or hear.

Vision of an old skinny man, with wrinkles on his face, dressed in a business suit carrying a briefcase.

I am here to take care of your old business - things of the past, things that are to come for you and yours. I am a business attorney for the Lord God of Israel. I am here to clear all your records of any wrongs or mistakes of the flesh or spirit. I have been sent for you and your place with the Lord God, and what you will be given to do in His kingdom on earth, when He is here. I have come to clear you of any accusers that might speak against you. I am here to clear a path. He has sent others, like myself, to do the same for others, like yourself. I am about His work for you. You shall be honored before Him. Bow down and give homage to Him, who sent me! Bow down!

While I was praying the rosary, a man dressed in a white robe walked over and said something to me with a big smile on his face. I did not understand anything he said. My prayer partner said:

> This man was an angel of the Lord telling me that the Lord is very pleased with my prayer time.

Vision of a young girl 4 or 5 years of age, sitting in a booth before me. As she turned around to look at me, I could see her face and eyes above her nose:

This young girl is an angel with the ability of looking into your soul and spirit. She represents those children that are looking for God. She is asking, "Are you the one to teach me?"

Vision of an older man, with bushy white hair and beard, standing in front of me.

> This is the angel of prophecy for your life. He watches the choices you make and sees the future your choice has created. He summons the protection and support you need when your choice is correct. He seeks the defense and protection of heaven's legions when you choose incorrectly, so that you will choose again. You do not walk alone. His job is to anticipate your next steps and lead you to God.

Angels are for our protection and for those for whom we pray. My wife, Ann, was a science teacher. She and another teacher took two vans of junior high school students on a field trip to Colorado and the Grand Canyon in Arizona. I was driving one of the vans through the mountains in Colorado. There was a road grader tractor ahead of me. When there was clearance for me to pass this road grader tractor, I proceeded to pass next to a very steep slope on the side of the mountain. The road grader tractor moved over into my lane, blocking me from passing, forcing me to brake. The left hind wheel slipped off the road onto the steep slope. There was no way to get the left hind wheel back on the road. Miraculously, we got back on the road. I knew, at that moment, that the angels of the Lord had pushed the van back onto the road.

Vision of a sign on the edge of town that gives the name and population of the town. I was not able to read it. My prayer partner had a vision of the same sign, but could not read it. As we continued to pray, we received the following message.

> Do not be concerned about the sign. Be concerned about your driving and keeping your eyes on the road. My prayer partner saw a picture of an oncoming curve on the road. Note: I had this vision just prior to leaving on a vacation into Mexico.

While we were in Villadama, Mexico, I woke up in the middle of the night with a check in the spirit and great concern about driving on to Mexico City. I got up and prayed for an hour then I received peace about going on.

> While we were driving in central Mexico the next day, two big 18-wheelers were rounding a curve toward us. A car started passing the 18-wheelers in our lane. This was a narrow, two-lane road with posts and wire guards on the roadsides. There was no room to get off the road. Our driver pulled over as far as he could. The car miraculously passed between the eighteen-wheelers and us. I know this was the Lord and his angels protecting us. Apparently this was the oncoming curve about which the Lord warned me about before we left the U.S.

We need to be sensitive to the guidance of the Spirit, because our life or lives could depend on it.

Years earlier, my son, Michael had received understanding

that he needed to be sensitive to the Lord's voice, as the day was coming when his life would depend on it. This was definitely one of those situations for his mother and dad. Before my wife and I and another couple left Texas for a vacation into Mexico, I had a word from the Lord to be sure to keep my eyes on the road when going around a curve

While leaning back in a swivel chair saying my prayers, I dozed off. As soon as I dozed off, someone touched me encouraging me to finish my prayers.

An angel touched me so I would finish my prayers. An angel touching me and getting my attention to pray has happened many, many times.

Vision - I saw an abstract picture - I was in a classroom talking to a teacher. The teacher's face and upper portions of the chest and arms suddenly became as an abstract picture. I saw several different views and colors of the picture. One view had a purple outline of the face. Then the power of God came upon me and the abstract picture became a living person in front of me, looking at me.

The Lord revealed that the full understanding and meaning of an abstract picture is only known to the artist. This is the same with the Book of Revelation. The Book of Revelation is like an abstract picture in which only the Lord knows the full meaning of all the symbols and things written therein. These meanings become clear to those to whom the Lord chooses to reveal them. I could see several different views in an abstract form, but when the power of God came upon me, I could see this person, a teacher, very clearly. I asked my prayer partner to pray with me for understanding as to who this person was. My prayer partner laughed after praying. The Lord revealed that this person was one of several angels that are around me at all times ministering to me.

431

Losing and finding my rosary

I have a rosary from Fatima with which I pray with every morning before going to Mass. A heavy silver medallion of the Blessed Mother was attached to it. My wife, Ann, told me not to take this rosary out of the house as I am always losing my rosaries when I pull my car keys and other items out of my pocket. I took this rosary to church two days in a row and lost it. I looked for it for a week and could not find it. I asked the Blessed Mother, St. Joseph and the angels and the saints to help me find it. We went to a prayer meeting then came home and sat down to watch a program on EWTN. There on the coffee table, where I had always kept my rosary, was my rosary. I asked Ann if she had put the rosary on the coffee table. She said, "No!" The only way for the rosary to get on the bare coffee table was for an angel of the Lord to put it there.

Lady asked for money and vanished.

> As I walked from the drug store, a tall, older, white woman with a few teeth missing asked me for money for gasoline. I gave her twenty dollars. When I walked about eight feet to my car and turned around to look at her, she was nowhere to be seen. I do not know how she could disappear so quick in a small parking lot. I did not see her in any of the several cars in the parking lot. My belief is that this woman was an angel who took the money to someone who needed it.

Vision of a man sitting a chair in front of me making the sign of the cross while I was praying. I immediately made the sign of the cross. I asked my prayer partner to pray with me for an understanding of the vision. My prayer partner received knowledge that this man was my guardian angel who prays with me when I pray.

Vision of a young man in a white shirt and dark pant walking up to me, taking a hold of my hands and prayed with me. My prayer partner received understanding that this was my guardian angel who was praying with me to give me encouragement.

Our dog, Darling

Our black Lab, Darling, sleeps on a rug on Ann's side of the bed, and when Darling is outside and wants to come in, she will bark. When the doors are shut, there is no way she can get in the house. Yet, somehow she has gotten in a number of times.

> The first time this happened, we had gone to bed around 8 pm. Around 10 pm, Darling wanted to go outside. She lay down on the deck indicating she did not want to come back in. I locked the door and went to bed. When we woke up the next morning, the dog was laying on a rug by the bed. Neither Ann nor I had let the dog in. We checked the back door, but it was locked. Some have said that perhaps Ann or I in our sleep let the dog in. Ann and I have not been known to walk in our sleep.

> The Lord apparently made this question mute the second time. I went to bed around 11 pm, but since I was unable to sleep, I just lay there. At 12:20 am, Darling wanted to go outside. After doing her business she wandered around sniffing. I locked the door and went to bed. Unable to sleep, I got up at 2 am to let the dog back in and found that she was already in the house sleeping by the bed. Ann did not let the dog in as she was sleeping next to me and had not moved, and I was awake from 11:00 pm to 2 am.

Another time Ann had put the dog out. She was going to let her in before going to bed and found that the dog was already in the house. Usually, when Darling wants in the house, she will bark because she cannot come in unless someone lets her in.

> The only answer to this mystery is that an angel has had to let the dog in the house. The Lord obviously has concern for our pet. The Lord is letting us know that there are angels all around us. I know we have angels in our home as I have seen them and heard them many times. In Acts

5:17-19, an angel opens the jail door during the night for Peter and the apostles to escape while the guards were asleep.

I asked my prayer partner to pray with me for an understanding on how the dog was getting into the house as this has happen nine times. . My prayer partner had a vision a small area of the bedroom's wall turning into a mist and the dog walked through the mist into the bedroom. The ninth time this happen; I had just left the house. Ann had put the dog in the front yard. Later she found the dog in the living room. There is no way for the dog to get into the living room or leave the living room with all the doors closed.

Darling passed away four days after her twelfth birthday. The above events took place the last few months of her life. She was a very devoted dog and deeply loved by her family. I had two visions of Darling laying on the floor next to me while I was praying. The last vision was six months after she passed away.

Message from St. Michael the Archangel – angels cannot help us unless we ask for their help.

At this time many, many demons have been let out hell to tempt mankind in these final hours. Heaven, at same time has sent me and thousands of warrior angels to assist and defend mankind. I, St. Michael the Archangel and thousands of Warrior Angels wish to assist you but you must ask. It is a requirement of heaven. You must ask!!! We cannot help you if you do not ask. You can ask through the prayers of the most holy rosary, or through one of the greatest gifts to mankind in this age, the Divine Mercy Chaplet or through your daily prayers. But you must ask!!! As your state your intentions before prayer let your call for our assistance be part of them. Ask for our help through the Two Hearts of Jesus and Mary and you will receive our help. Do as I recommended and you will be protected. Ask for our protection and protection will be yours. If you do not ask we cannot help you but must watch as you come under attack! Ask and you will receive the assistance of heaven through the angels who will protect you. Ask and protection will be yours. Ask and all heaven will be pleased. Ask and bring a smile to Jesus and Mary. Ask and we will defend you!!! (65)

St. Michael the Archangel said it is a requirement of heaven that man ask for help before he can receive any help from heaven. The Lord will not do anything on earth unless man asks. This is confirmed in Ezekiel. The Lord did not want to destroy Israel, but He could not find one man, who would stand in the gap to pray and intercede.

Ezekiel 22:30-31: "And I searched for a man among them who should build up the wall and stand in the gap before Me for the land, that I should not destroy it; but I found no one. Thus I have poured out my indignation on them; I have consumed them with the fire of My wrath; their ways I have brought upon their heads," declared the Lord God. (1)

My daily prayer

Lord, we ask that you put St. Michael and his angels around us to protect us from all principalities, powers and rulers of darkness. Put ministering angels around us to minister to us in spirit and truth and to protect us from sickness and harm. Take away those things within us that are not of You. Fill us with Your love, wisdom, knowledge, understanding and discernment. Direct us to the center of Your most perfect will.

Prayer to St. Michael the Archangel

St. Michael, the Archangel, defend us in battle! Be our protection against the wickedness and snares of the Devil. May God rebuke him, we humbly pray; do thou, O Prince of the heavenly host, by the power of God cast into hell Satan and all the other evil spirits, who prowl about the world seeking ruin of souls. Amen

Psalm 91:11-12

For He will give His angels charge concerning you, to guard you in all your ways. They will bear you up in their hands, lest you strike your foot against a stone (1).

CHAPTER 11
Creation

The Lord created the heavens and the earth.

> Isaiah 45:18: For thus says the Lord Who created the heavens, God Himself Who formed the earth and made it, Who established it and created it not a worthless waste; He formed it to be inhabited: I am the Lord, and there is no one else. (5)

The earth is billions of years old

The Dallas Morning News reported the find of a single-cell organism that scientists estimated to be 3.4 billions years old (66). No one knows the age of the earth. The Lord, who has existed for all eternity, created the earth. The Lord made the earth to be fruitful with plant and animal life. He created plants, reptiles, birds, and all other animals. The earth is full of fossil evidence of giant prehistoric reptiles, prehistoric animals and prehistoric men that have lived on earth for millions or possibly billions of years.

The Anger of the Lord and His Punishment

1. When Adam and Eve disobeyed God, sin and death came into the world thus affecting all men.
2. Because of the wickedness of man, God destroyed all the inhabitants of the earth by the flood except for Noah, his family and some animals.
3. God destroyed the cities of Sodom and Gomorrah for the sins of the flesh.

4. God destroyed the Egyptian army in the Red Sea. The bones of human and animals as well as numerous chariot artifacts have been found in the Red Sea. (67)
5. God threatened to destroy the Israelites in the wilderness for worshiping a golden calf. The Lord offered to make a new nation through Moses. Moses interceded asking the Lord to remember His promise to Abraham, Isaac and Jacob.
6. God divided the nation of Israel into the Northern Kingdom and the Southern Kingdom because Solomon made idols for his foreign wives. For their idolatry, the Lord allowed the Northern Kingdom to later be taken captive as slaves by the Assyrians, who never released them from captivity.
7. One hundred years later the Southern Kingdom was taken into Babylonian captivity. This was the group, from which Jesus was born, which came back to Israel seventy years later.

In the Book of Jeremiah we read that Jeremiah spoke very harshly to the Israelites prior to their being taken captive as slaves to Babylon. The Lord revealed to Jeremiah that there was a time in the past when the He destroyed the earth, man and everything in it because of His fierce anger. The Lord had a similar anger against the tribe of Judah and the Southern kingdom.

> Jeremiah 4:23-26: I looked on the earth, and behold, it was formless and void; and to the heavens, and they had no light. I looked on the mountains, and behold, they were quaking, and all the hills moved to and fro. I looked, and behold, there was no man, and all the birds of the heavens had fled. I looked, and behold, the fruitful land was a wilderness, and all its cities were pulled down before the Lord, before His fierce anger. (1)

Translation:

> Jeremiah 4:23-26: I looked at the earth, and it was waste and void; at the heavens and their light had gone out! I

looked at the mountains, and they were trembling, and all the hills were crumbling! I looked and behold there was no man; even the birds of the air had flown away! I looked and behold, the garden land was a dessert, with all its cities destroyed before the Lord, before his blazing wrath. (3)

Another translation:

I looked on the earth, and lo, it was waste and void; and to the heavens, and they had no light. I looked on the mountains, and lo, they were quaking, and all the hills moved to and fro. I looked, and lo, there was no man, and all the birds of the air had fled. I looked, and lo, the fruitful land was a desert, and all its cities were laid in ruins before the Lord, before his fierce anger. For thus says the Lord, "The whole land shall be a desolation; yet I will not make a full end. For this the earth shall mourn, and the heavens be black; for I have spoken, I have purposed; I have not relented nor will I turn back. (31)

This is a description of a severe earthquake with the mountains shaking and the hills moving to and fro. The fruitful land became formless and void. The heavens had no light. Darkness covered the earth. All life was destroyed.

This fierce anger of the Lord had to have taken place prior to the creation of Adam and Eve as there has not been a time since Adam that there has not been a man on earth. Like many Bible scholars, I believe this past anger had to do with the time Satan rebelled against God, and Satan and his angels were kicked out of heaven. (68, 69)

The prehistoric earth was a very beautiful, fruitful, peaceful place for the angels to visit and roam before the Lord destroyed it in His extreme anger. By destroying the earth, the Lord was letting all heaven, angels and fallen angels know how upset He was at the rebelling that took place.

Obviously the Scripture in Jeremiah is referring to prehistoric man, birds and animals that were destroyed by the Lord's fierce anger. The earth was made formless and void. The Lord did not create the earth to be a waste and void. The earth is old with many fossils of man, animals and reptiles living a fruitful life in the past. The Scripture in Jeremiah says the fruitful land became a wilderness. This catastrophe does not refer to Noah and the flood, as Noah and his family survived the flood. This would be twice that the Lord destroyed the earth.

Genesis speaks of the earth on day one of creation as being formless and void of life. How could this be when the earth is millions or possibly billions of years old with a very fruitful past? What evidence is there that the earth became formless and void after a long fruitful life?

The creation account described in Genesis supports a recreation.

Gordon Lindsay reported that when the Lord created something, He used the Hebrew word "bara" which means to create something from nothing. This word was only used on the fifth and sixth days when He created the fish, birds, animals and man. This word was not used on the first, second, third and fourth days. During the Genesis story of creation, the Lord did not create the earth, the water, the land or the heavenly lights as they were already in existence and had been for millions or billions of years. The word, bara, was not use for plants. Some Bible scholars believe that the plants emerged from roots and seeds that were in the frozen earth that came up after the earth warmed up and were exposed to light. We will show that the creation the Lord did in the Genesis story is obviously a recreation. (68, 69)

We will discuss the days of creation later.

The genealogy of Jesus Christ is very important in understanding the time of Adam's creation.

The Lord God made it very clear that He wants us to thoroughly understand the genealogy of His Son, Jesus Christ and that Jesus is a descendant of the descendants of Adam and Eve. It was not an accident that the Scripture recorded the age of the fathers when their first sons were born from the time of Adam on to Abraham. The Lord intended for us to be able to calculate the approximate time from Adam's creation to the present time. There would be no reason for the scripture to list the descendants of Adam and their ages unless it was intended to show that Jesus was a descendant of the descendants of Adam and allow us to determine the approximate time of Adam's creation.

If Adam was created either 20,000 or 50,000 or a million years ago, the genealogy would be meaningless. There would be no reason for names and ages of the descendants to be written and listed in the Bible. The names and ages of the descendants of Adam were listed for a reason and a purpose.

Genesis, chapter 5, gives the age of Adam when his son Seth was born and how long Adam lived; the age of Seth when his son Enosh was born and how long Seth lived; the age of Enosh when his son was born and how long he lived. This chapter gives the age of each descendant when his first son was born and how long he himself lived. This continued from Adam on to Noah and Abraham. With the genealogy listing the age of the fathers at the birth of their son, and adding the ages of the fathers, we are able to calculate that it was approximately 2000 years from Adam to Abraham.

There are 14 generations from Abraham to King David, 14 generations from King David to the Babylonian captivity and 14 generations from the Babylonian captivity to Jesus (Matthew 1:17) which is approximately 2,000 years from Abraham to Jesus. Thus, from Adam to Jesus is approximately 4,000 years. Since it has been 2,000 years since the birth of Jesus, this means Adam was created approximately 6,000 years ago. The genealogy of Jesus Christ plays a very significant role in our understanding of the time of the creation of Adam and Eve.

Gap in the genealogy

There is a gap in the genealogy of Jesus Christ between Noah and Abraham as shown below. Both Luke and 1Chronicle list the genealogy from Adam to Abraham. Cainan is not mentioned in the genealogy of 1 Chronicle, while Shelah and Eber are not mention in the genealogy of Luke. We need to remember that different names were given for some of the twelve disciples of Jesus in the different gospels. Could Shelah or Eber be another name for Cainan? We will proceed with the idea that this is not a large gap and that Adam and Eve were created close to 6,000 years ago.

Luke 3:34-38	1 Chronicles 1:1-9	Luke	1 Chronicles
Adam	Adam	Arphaxad	Arpachshad
Seth	Seth	Cainan	
Enos	Enosh	(Gaps)	
Cainan	Kenan	(Gaps)	Shelah
Mahalalel	Mahalalel		Eber
Jared	Jared	Peleg	Peleg
Enoch	Enoch	Reu	Reu
Methuselah	Methuselah	Serug	Serug
Lamech	Lamech	Nahbor	Nahbor
Noah	Noah	Terah	Terah
Shem	Shem	Abraham	Abraham

There would be no reason for the Lord to list the genealogy with the age of each descendant if there were a very large gap in the genealogy linkage.

The purpose of this is to show that the creation's account in Genesis is a recent recreation and that modern man is a recent creation with no evolutionary link to prehistoric hominids.

How many days were there in a year during the time of Adam and Noah? Are years of Adam and Noah the same as our years?

Genesis says that Noah was 600 years old, when the flood began. The flood began on the 17th day of the second month. Genesis 8:3-4 speaks of the ark coming to rest on Mount Ararat on the 17th day of the seventh month - 150 days after the flood began. From the 17th day of the second month to the 17th day of the seventh month is five months of 150 days. Five months of 150 days is 30 days per month.

$$\frac{150 \text{ days}}{5 \text{ months}} \quad = \quad 30 \text{ days per month}$$

Thirty days per month for five months shows that there were 360 days in a year during the flood. Their 360 days in a year is very close our 365 days.

Noah was 600 years old when the flood began. He got off the ark one year and seventeen days later at the age of 601 years. The Lord did not want there to be any confusion on the number of days in a year and that people did live long lives before the flood. This shows that people like Methuselah who lived to be 969 did live to be over 900 years of age before the flood. (49)

When was Adam created?

Adam was created on the sixth day of creation approximately 6,000 years ago. This is a very short and recent period of time in contrast to the age of the earth which is millions or possibly billions of years old.

If Adam was created on the sixth day, 6,000 years ago, were the first, second, third, fourth and fifth days of creation mentioned in Genesis recent?

One would assume that the days of creations mentioned in Genesis took place over a close period of time. If so, were the creations in Genesis a recreation since the earth is obviously millions or possible billions of years old with fossil evidence of many prehistoric plants, reptiles, animals and man?

Jeremiah speaks of the fruitful earth being destroyed by the Lord's fierce anger.

On the first day of creation in Genesis the earth was formless and void, water covered the earth, and darkness was over the surface of the deep. The earth being formless and void is also the description in Jeremiah after the Lord destroyed the earth. On the first day God said,

"Let there be light." He called light day and darkness night. There was morning and evening on the first day. How can there be light or morning and evening the first day if the sun did not come into existence until the fourth day? Morning and evening are caused by the earth rotating around the sun. There was light on the first day because the sun was already in existence but the sun, itself, was not visible. The Lord allowed the light to come through the clouds on the fourth day. The light was not a creation as the sun was in existence as it had been for millions or billions of years. The sun or solar system was not destroyed by the Lord's fierce anger as described in Jeremiah.

On the second day the Lord said, "Let there be an expanse in the heavens to separate water below from the water above." This is not a creation but a separation of something already in existence.

On the third day God said "Let the water below the heaven be gathered into one place, and let the dry land appear." He said "Let the earth sprout vegetation, plants yield seed, and fruit trees bear fruit after their kind, with seed in them. The Lord saw that it was good." The Hebrew word, bara, which means to create something from nothing was not used here. It appears that seeds and possibly the roots of trees and plants that survived in the frozen earth had sprouted forth. To spout forth indicate that the seeds were already in the earth and were not created.

On the fourth day the Lord brought forth the heavenly lights. The sun, the moon and the stars have existed since prehistoric times. They were not visible because of the heavy clouds that covered the earth. The Lord allowed the heavenly lights that were in existence since prehistoric times to be visible on the fourth day.

How did the plants live on the third day if the sun was not visible until the fourth day? Obviously there were enough sunrays coming through the thick clouds for the plants to produce enough photosynthesis to make food. Since the sun, the moon and the stars were already in existence and were not created, it supports the creations described in Genesis as a recreation.

The Hebrew word, bara, was used in the creation of fishes and birds on the fifth day, animals and man on the sixth day. It is interesting that

God created both man and animals on the same day. The belief is that prehistoric animals and reptiles were created long before man. God rested on the seventh day.

Genesis account of what was in existence and what was recreated.

The Hebrew word bara means to create something from nothing. Bara was not used on the first four days of creation as the earth, water, plants, sun, moon and stars were already in existence. Bara was used on day five and sixth when fishes, bird, animals, and man were created from nothing and brought into existence.

1st Day	Light	Already in existence	Made visible
2nd Day	Dome - Sky	Already in existence	Made visible
3rd Day	Sea & Land separation. Plants sprouted	Already in existence	Made visible
4th Day	Sun, Moon and Stars	Already in existence	Made visible
5th Day	Fishes and Birds	Recreated	Were destroyed - Lord's anger
6th Day	Man and Animals	Recreated	Were destroyed - Lord's anger

How long was the day in creation? Was it a 24-hours day or a 1000-years day?

The Lord can certainly do anything and everything in a 24-hour day. For the Lord to see the plants reproduce and bear fruits would mean that a day would normally be longer than a 24-hour day. Peter said, "A day with the Lord is as a thousand years." For the Lord to observe the plants reproducing and bearing fruits is obviously a 1000-years day. This would indicate that the creation days in Genesis were 1000-year days instead of 24-hours days.

2 Peter 3:8:...with the Lord one day is as a thousand years, and a thousand years as one day (1).

When did the catastrophe described in Jeremiah take place?

It must have been recent, as a well-preserved mammoth found buried and frozen in ice in Russia, was estimated to have perished 12,000 years ago. This fits into the time-frame of the 11,000 to 12,000 year catastrophe mentioned in Jeremiah.

If each day of creation was a thousand years, that would be 6,000 years for six days of creation or recreation. Scripture records show that it has been 6,000 years since Adam and Eve were created plus the 5,000 or 6,000 years for each day of recreation. This adds up to 11,000 to 12,000 years since the catastrophe and to the time of the mammoth (70), and the disappearance of the Neanderthal man and other prehistoric hominids.

The description of the earth being formless and void in both Genesis and Jeremiah, the creation of Adam 6,000 years ago as supported by the genealogy of Jesus Christ support the facts that the destruction of the earth described in Jeremiah was recent and the creations in Genesis were a recreation.

There are reports of fossil findings of Asian elephants living in prehistoric times. Question – if so, did the elephants truly survive this catastrophe mentioned in Jeremiah? Are the fossils beyond 12,000 years ago truly of the Asian elephants? Or did the Lord recreate the elephants? If the earth was truly destroyed as spoken of in Jeremiah and the earth being formless and void in both Jeremiah and Genesis on day one, no elephant or any other living creature would have survived.

All evidence points to the creation of Adam and Eve, and animals 6,000 years ago, all birds and fishes 7,000 years ago. I personally believe the elephants were recreated along with other numerous animals. There are definite evidences of evolution among the prehistoric reptiles and mammals. There are also evidences of evolution among some birds and insects today.

Nevertheless, man did not evolve as he was created 6,000 years ago after all life on earth was destroyed by the Lord's fierce anger. This was described by Jeremiah, who said there was no man left on earth.

Neanderthal man

The front page of the "National Geographic" had a picture of a skull of a Neanderthal man. I prayed and asked the Lord for an understanding – was this man in heaven, or in hell or where? I received understanding that this man was neither in heaven or hell. He was not human and his existence ended at death. Two prayer partners also received the same understanding. The Neanderthal man was an animal like other hominids and apes.

The DNA comment below shows that there is no connection of prehistoric hominids with modern man which supports the Bible account of creation.

Fazale Rana and Hugh Ross reviewed numerous laboratory and archaeological research data on modern man, the Neanderthals and other ancient hominids. It was found that the genetic makeup of the mitochondrial DNA of females and Y-chromosomal DNA of males of modern man trace their ancestors back to a single male and single female. This supports the Genesis account of the creation of Adam and Eve.

Stockholm, University of Glasgow, and the Max Planck Institute studied Neanderthal DNA and found that an excessive weight of evidence appears to decisively sever any link between Neanderthals and modern man. (71)

Summary

1. The teachings in Genesis fit a pattern of recreation instead of the creation that occurred millions or billions of years ago.
2. According to the genealogy of Jesus Christ, Adam and Eve were created approximately 6,000 years ago. This was based on adding

the ages of the fathers at the birth of their first born son from the time Adam to the time of Abraham. The Scripture details covered in this genealogy show the seriousness the Lord placed on the understanding of the time of Adam and Eve's creation, and that Jesus was a direct descendant of the descendants of Adam.

3. The creation of Adam and Eve is a recent event and not an event in prehistoric time.

4. For the sixth day of creation to be recent, day one, day two, day three, day four and day five would also probably be recent. For creation described in Genesis to be recent would mean that creation would have to be a recreation because fossil evidence shows earth to be millions or possibly billions of years old.

5. For the earth to be formless and void on day one after a long fruitful life, a great destruction would have to have occurred. Jeremiah 4:23-26 reported that the earth became formless and void by the Lord's fierce anger. Civilization was destroyed. There was no (prehistoric) man left on earth. Many Bible scholars believe this occurred when Satan rebelled against the Lord.

6. The sun, moon and the stars were not destroyed when the earth and life on earth were destroyed. They continued to function as they had for millions or billions of years.

7. The Hebrew word "bara" - to create something from nothing, was used when the Lord actually created something new such as the fish, birds, animals, and man.

8. The Hebrew word "bara" was not spoken on the first four days of creation as the earth, water, land, plants, and the sun, moon and the stars have been in existence since prehistoric time. On these days the Lord simply created a space in the heaven by separating the water above from the water below, separated the land from water on earth, allowed the seeds and roots of plants embedded in the frozen earth to spout, and the sun, moon and the stars to be visible. There was no new creation involved.

9. There was morning, evening and light the first day, and the plants were able to live the third day because the sun has been in existence since prehistoric time. The sun was not visible until the

fourth day because of the heavy clouds that covered the earth.

10. The genetic makeup of the mitochondrial DNA of females and Y-chromosomal DNA of males of modern man trace their ancestors back to a single male and single female. This support Genesis account of the creation of Adam and Eve. There is no evolutionary link between modern man, Neanderthal man and other ancient hominids. Only modern man is made in the image and likeness of God.

Modern man is classified as *Homo sapiens sapiens*

Neanderthals is classified as *Homo sapiens neanderthalensis.*

.

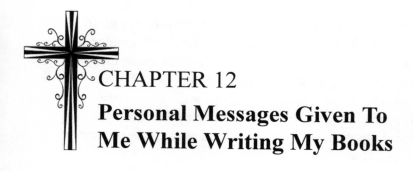

CHAPTER 12

Personal Messages Given To Me While Writing My Books

The midnight hour rapture

In 1973, I had a dream in which my wife and I woke up at the midnight hour and walked out onto the porch with our two oldest sons who were 8 and 9 years old. There was an unusual light or glow coming down from above. I could not see directly up, as we were under the porch. I had knowledge that this was the midnight hour rapture and the Lord was coming for His bride. There was a tremendous feeling of excitement. The scripture that came to me was the story of the ten virgins waiting to meet the Bridegroom. I was puzzled why our youngest son, who was two years old, was not with us. Seven years later, I received understanding that the bride is the prize of the high calling for which Paul ran a race for with all of his might. A two-year-old child is not capable of running a race for the prize of the high calling. I do not wish to imply that I or any of my family have won the race of which Paul spoke. The Lord put a strong desire in my heart to study and learn about Revelation and the end times.

Dreams - You are going to graduate school to prepare for evangelistic work.

On December 22, 1978, I had several dreams, in which three different people spoke to me and said, "You are going to graduate school." In the first dream, two of my associates at work spoke to me and said, "Graduate school requires studying." In the second dream, an elderly Christian lady said, "Mike, you are going to school." In the third dream, another Christian lady friend said, "I told you a long time ago you are going to school to prepare for evangelistic work."

I did not actually go to school; however, I spent considerable amount of time reading, studying, praying, fasting, and seeking the Lord for understanding and guidance in the writing of this manuscript. I shared this dream with the third lady, who was a very friendly person. It is interesting that she was very cool to me afterwards. I don't blame her. Who would believe that the Lord would be telling a deaf person with a severe speech impediment to go to graduate school to prepare for evangelistic work?

Vision – Two priests with Ph.D.'s caps and gowns walking into my yard.

On December 26, 1978 I had a vision of two white-haired men, dressed in black priest's suits wearing derby hats, each carrying a Bible, walking with a brisk pace on the road in front of my house. When they turned and walked into my driveway, they suddenly had Ph.D.'s caps and gowns on. I had knowledge that these two men were the Lord's two witnesses and that they had all wisdom, knowledge, understanding and discernment. Six years later, I asked two people to pray with me for understanding.

> These two men were angels of the Lord coming as Doctors of the Church to bestow the gift of knowledge, and understanding upon you. The angels in priest's suits indicated that the gift of knowledge and understanding related to spiritual matters. The Ph.D.'s garment is symbolic of the highest level of knowledge and understanding.

The second prayer partner received and spoke the following words to me.

> I love you Mike so I will instruct you with wisdom, instruction and love. Continue steadfastly with the work that the Lord has given you the opportunity to present. Pray with these two men for forgiveness of sins of the

people. The prayers and fasting with which you have honored Me, are about to unfold with their reward.

Strong thoughts kept coming to me to write on the Book of Revelation.

The Lord had been prompting me, for several years, to write on the Book of Revelation. I finally began in May of 1980. After I had written 8 to 10 pages, the Lord showed me a vision of what I had written and said, "This will not do." The Lord not only prompted me to write, but also guided me as, I wrote.

The Lord did not allow me to have a spiritual director. He kept me isolated from theologians. One priest told me I was out of my field. The Lord allowed me to share my work with only a few people. He spoke to me through dreams and visions, and guided me through several prayer partners throughout the writing of this manuscript.

The Lord provided me with a prayer partner.

While attending a retreat, I asked someone, whom I had met and spoken to only a few times, to pray with me for a discomfort in my neck. While praying, he started speaking the following message to me. I had not said anything to him about my book.

> Give the first part of the morning to Me. Give the other part of the time to your family. Rest in Me, I have much to teach you. I want you to enjoy the fruits of your labor, as you bring the knowledge of My glory to the people of this planet. At this moment, I have already begun to put into motion the people who will publish and distribute your book to all the people of this planet, so that they may know of My glory.

A week later, the word "Releemer" was spoken and spelled to me as I was coming out of my sleep at 5 A.M. As I prayed for understanding, I had a vision of myself standing on a sidewalk. The Lord, dressed in a white robe, was on the sidewalk. He was bending over, picking up loose bricks and building a brick wall on both sides of the walkway. As the Lord moved forward to pick up more bricks, I would back up. The brick walls were approximately two feet wide and three feet high. The brick walls and walkway led to what looked like a two storey tall building with two large columns about 75 yards away. This building was the Jewish temple. After praying for three days receiving no understanding, I called the friend, who spoke the above prophecy. As we began to pray, he spoke the following words to me.

> Son of man, you will be a witness, as the Apostles of old were witnesses to My Son, Jesus. I have given you wisdom, knowledge, understanding and discernment about the restoration of My people. I will allow you to see this restoration of My people, because I love you. Each brick is symbolic of a person being restored to My bulwark that I am building, for the protection of My Church. This is the Lord God Yahweh Who speaks. I am your Father Who has redeemed you by the blood of My Son, Jesus, Who has brought you to an awareness of My nature through the Person of the Spirit. I am pleased with your prayer time. Be patient, as you continue your work, for through it, many people will come to know the glory of My name. Be conscious of My Word. Research My name, for in it you will find the meaning of life.

"Releemer" is a spiritual term, which refers to a type of communication men receive from Christ. Christ presents His view, objective, direction and guidance, with the help of the Holy Spirit, to many people who believe in His name. This means of communication bridges the gap between God and man in the exchange of ideas.

While in prayer, a prayer partner received the following words.

> My son, walk with Me. Bring Me your burdens, for I am the way, the truth and the life. I am calling you to come to know Me as the Apostles of old. I would have you to

know the nature of My being and the character of My nature. Rest in Me, My son, for it is within Me that I will reveal the mysteries of life to you. You ask to know the meaning and the purpose of life. At this moment, My Spirit wants to reveal Himself to you. Come to Me in order that I may reveal those things you need to know about Me to complete the work that I am doing through you. Be strong; be committed; be humble; be My servant. Allow Me to mold your character to that of one of My chosen. The Apostles of old allowed themselves to be surrounded in My love. Do the same, for I want you to be one of My own. At this moment, all that is of concern to you is in My control. I love you. Be patient; for My work is not yet complete. Your book is in the hands of those whom I would have to come to know My nature. Pray for them daily. Pray for their souls daily in order that My words will fall on fertile soil. For many are called, but few are chosen. The Lord God Yahweh speaks.

Do not have fear.

Fear not, for I have all things under My command. You are the first of many brothers. You are to have no fear, for I am your Father, and all things are under My authority. There is no situation that I would allow, which would disturb the peace that I would have for you. For in the name of My Son, Jesus, all good things will abound to you. Rest in His name (Jesus) and in the light of My name, Yahweh. You are precious to Me, My son, because of your work and love for Me. You need to have no fear, for all things will turn to My good. Continue with your writings, your study and your prayer. Make them one, just as I am one with the Son and the Spirit. Unite yourself to Me in prayer and fasting. Your faith is the faith of Abraham. Your blessings will be the same. Remember that My Son

Jesus, died and rose and ascended to Me. You too will die, and rise and ascend to Me. Be patient with all those people who seem to be annoyances for Jesus has died for them as well. I love them as I love you. Your work (book) will one day be complete. I love you. Continue on unfalteringly with your prayer, studies and writings. I will make your face as that of Moses. I love you.

Nature of God

After I had finished my book on Revelation, I had knowledge that I was supposed to write another chapter on the nature of God. I was puzzled, as this did not seem to fit in with Revelation. I asked a prayer partner to pray with me. The following words were spoken to me.

My son, when you begin to write about My nature, I would have you to pray in the Holy Spirit. Begin at the beginning with what I have given you so far in regard to My nature. I say to begin at the beginning of the Holy Word. It is in the first few chapters of My Word that you will come to an understanding of My triune nature. Seek out what it is about My Holy Spirit that is revealed in the early writings of the book of Genesis, for it is in the beginning, I was. It is in the writings of the prophets that the presence of My Son is first revealed. Carry this particular part of your work on through the New Testament. Flow with the wind of the Holy Spirit. Allow the flow and movement to be the movement of the Holy Spirit. Allow Him to come upon you to engulf you, to refresh you and to use you, to bring about what My love is. I would have the movement of your writings be that of a symphony by starting slowly, moving toward a crescendo, all the time allowing the beauty of My nature to be revealed. Move slowly, but exactly, for this is an important part of My overall work that you are presenting in your writing. I love you for your diligence. I have many blessings in store for you. For he who reads My Word and believes, shall have everlasting life.

Vision of a moon-like trumpet

While in prayer early in the morning of January 19, 1984, somehow in a vision I was walking on the grounds of the U.S. Capitol with some of the national monuments in the background. As I walked on the sidewalk through the park, I saw a soft white moon-like light in the sky, in the form of a long trumpet. The sky was purple.

The Lord had previously revealed to me that purple was a call for repentance. In the Old Testament, the trumpet was an instrument used to give certain signals or calls to the people. Because the moon-like trumpet was in a purple sky, in the presence of the U.S. Capitol, I felt the Lord wanted to sound a trumpet call to the people of this nation to repent for their sins and for the sins of their leaders and their nation. The Lord is asking the people to repent and to turn from their sins and their wicked ways, and to pray for a spiritual revival, so that this nation may be restored as one nation under God. As I continued to seek the Lord about the meaning of this vision, the following words were spoken to me:

> The pen is mightier than the sword and
>
> My sword is the sharpest pen known to mankind.
>
> Take up My pen, which is My Word and
>
> write about the need for national repentance.
>
> Do this now in order that
>
> you will be ready to publish it, at the appropriate time.
>
> All that is important for you to know at this time is that
>
> I would have you to write about the need for repentance in your nation.
>
> Trust in Me, for the message of repentance in your land must come forth.

Allow the Lord to help.

Be still, My son. Allow Me to assist you in your work. You will have the final discernment on the book. Others will proofread, some will try to change. Not all have purity at heart. This is why I chose you for this work. My Word will stand regardless of any effort to change it. Yours is the final decision as to what will come to print. Be patient with those whom I have given to help in assembling your material. Pray for them in order that their discernment will be the same as Mine. Have confidence that your work will be completed as I desire. For my desire is for us to be one.

The Lord calls the book, His book.

My son, be at peace about My book, for I have it in the hands of those I would have to receive great blessings from it. Even though the progress seems minute to you, the blessing has been great for those who have handled it, for a day is as a thousand years and a thousand years are as a day. Do not despair, My son, for many great healings must first take place, in order for your work to be finished. Continue to persevere for My name's sake. Dedicate all your actions, in regard to this book, to Me. All things are in My control. Be patient, persevere and have hope that this work will be complete.

The Lord's book is near completion.

I have given you the means by which I can give My people the solutions to their problems. My book is near completion. Keep in mind My attitude about prayer. Vigilance, persistence and self-denial are the necessary ingredients for successful and victorious encounters against the Adversary. My scripture is the embodiment of

457

all truth. Write as I have instructed you in the past with an open mind, a contrite heart and diligence for the truth. My Word will speak for itself. Concern yourself with only the truth. Trust Me, for I am with you always.

I asked the Lord if I was to write about faith and praying in tongues.

My words at this moment are on their way to you. My thoughts in regard to prayer of faith, you already know. Be direct, descriptive and scriptural. Brevity is important. Directness of trust is imperative. Begin with the description about the Spirit. Begin with a description of the power of praying in the Spirit. All else flows, as the river of life flows in the eternal city in paradise. Ask the saints to pray for you, because the resistance of the Adversary is strong. Call on your patron saint to stand with you and ask for divine guidance. I am pleased with your cooperation and collaboration with My Holy Spirit. Pray as you write, and My thoughts will come forth for you.

Do not be deceived into thinking that this information came from yourself.

You are a storehouse of information. You have had My truths deposited within you because they are part of the nature of My Spirit that has dwelled within you since baptism. These truths are not yours, they are Mine. Be sensitive to the prompting of the Spirit as to who is to receive them. For those who receive them will receive My blessings. The origin of these truths is always Me, your Father. Never be deceived into believing that they came from yourself or another. Test them always, before dispensing them. This way, there will be no error as to the source, from which they came. I would have you, at this time, to bring My truths to a larger number of people. Use these means that I have given you to take advantage of the opportunities that present themselves. For it is important that My Word go forth, for the time of the end draws near.

The Lord speaks on faith.

My son, your faith is as strong as Abraham, Isaac and Jacob. It is, because of your faith that you are able to un-derstand the mysteries of My nature. It is because of your faith in Me, Yahweh your God, that you are able to ask for and receive the desires of your heart. This faith of yours is a gift from Me, Yahweh your God. Cherish and protect it, for it is your children's children's legacy. The enemy tries to weaken your faith by deception and untruths about the mysteries of My plan of salvation and redemption. Remain committed, faithful and strong in your search of scriptural truths, which are contained in the book that I have commissioned you to transcribe. The importance of My truths must be the foremost endeavor of this work (book). In time, you will come to know the totality of My glory. For now be patient, and accept it in the same faith of your forefathers - Abraham, Isaac, Jacobs and Moses. I will draw to you, those people that are needed as helpers for you to finish this work. Be patient, work with dili-gence, and know that I am in control of this project. I love you. Continue with your prayers, as you have in the past. Your reward will be great, when this book is complete. It is Yahweh Who speaks.

The Lord is pleased. (These words were spoken on different days.)

I am pleased with your commitment to search for the deep knowledge hidden in the scripture.

I am pleased with your witness and testimony, your

faithfulness and fidelity to My Word. I am pleased that you yield yourself to the prompting of My Spirit. I love you very much. I have many great gifts for you. Do not look for these gifts to come from the world, for these are not the rewards I have for you. Look for these gifts to arrive through the vehicle of My written Word. I will be giving you a deeper knowledge, wisdom and understanding of My nature. Be open to receive, for I want you to know and experience the totalness of My love for you.

Writing of the manuscript is completed.

My son, your faithfulness in your endeavor to write My revealed knowledge of the Book of Revelation in a clear 20th Century manner is to be commended. The work is now to be entrusted to those in whom you have confidence. Listen to their criticisms, advice and discernment. The part you play, in bringing this manuscript forth, is now complete. I will be in charge of the discernment process, just as I was in charge of the writing. The positive feedback will strengthen your faith. The apparent negative feedback will purify your work effort. Do not allow anyone to hinder or stop this manuscript from being published. The words that you have written for Me are words for this hour. I do want them to come forth at this time. These are My words. I will let no man keep them from being read by others. Be conscious of the enemy, so that he will not distract from the truth that is contained in this manuscript. Pray for those, who will be reading this manuscript in order that they may be guided by the Holy Spirit, just as you were guided by the Holy Spirit in writing it. Your part is complete. It is now time for others to play their part, for it is the Lord God Yahweh Who speaks.

Rest for now.

Rest and be peaceful at this time. In the creation of the universe, there was a day left to rest. You have labored generously with the project that I have given you. You are in the seventh day, the beginning of a new week. Rest for now. The work that I am doing within you is one of developing a peaceful and harmonious spirit. Do your everyday chores of the world. At the same time, allow yourself the opportunity to rest in Me. Your load is light, at this time, in order that you may be more attentive to Me and My will for you. Be cautious of the spirit of hastiness, for I am a God of order, patience, power and might. Your role in the war with the enemy of darkness, death and destruction is one of greatness. I choose, at this time, for you to relax and be peaceful, so that you will be able to discern the part that I would have for you to play. Come quietly before Me each day. Seek ye My face, in order to know My will for you, at this time.

I had a vision of two blue eyes looking at me. Blue is symbolic of holiness, but for some reason, I knew these eyes were evil.

Do not be deceived by those who would appear in the eyes of men to be holy. For not all holiness is of God. The Pharisees appeared to be holy, however, they were as dead inside as Pharaoh of Ancient Egypt. Be cautious in trusting yourself to those who appear to be holy. Trust the Spirit of God that seems to be present in them. Not all of the men that came to Me were of God, My Father. There were those, who wanted to use me (Judas Iscariot) for themselves and for the benefit of others. Know this My son, I have given you all wisdom and knowledge to discern the intentions of those, who would come in the appearance as holy men. I am in charge. Trust in Me, for this is the Lord God Yahweh, Who speaks.

Dream – I was at the top of a large round cube, approximately 18 feet off the ground. I knew it was time to get down.

> I have placed you in a position at the top of the bulwark, in order that you may see the work that is being done in the restoration of My Church, of which you are a part. I am allowing you to see both sides of the wall. I would like for you at this time to allow Me to help you down, in order that you can become part of the restoration, by helping the laborers, who are already at work. For now, I have a new work for you, which I will reveal to you in My time. Be at peace, and know that I am with you and that My Holy Spirit is guiding you. Trust in Me to show you your new place and work.

Dream and prophesy:

I had knowledge that a priest had read my manuscript. This priest walked into a room with about twenty people and said, "Who has Mike's book?" Someone stood up with the book. The priest walked over and took the book, saying something about Revelation. Another person stood up and said, "Revelation makes me not want to be a Catholic. Revelations turns me away from the Catholic Church." The priest said, "This book will bring them to me."

> My son, be not alarmed of those, who would be turned away from the Catholic Church because of the Book of Revelation. This book was written by My evangelist, John. It is My desire that this book be read by all men. My Holy Spirit has been its discerner, and many people will be drawn to Me through it. Trust Me, knowing that My Father has approved this.

Tell the people about the Lord.

> I have raised you up, in order for you to do My work of

telling people, who I am, what I am like, where I am, why I am, because at this time the work of My Church and My Magisterium and My written Words are under attack by the world, self, and Satan himself. The gift of written communication skills comes to you for the purpose of bringing My divine character and nature to others, who do not know of Me. It is also an alternative to those things of the world and the devil that will deceive people from knowing Me as the Lord God Almighty. I am with you at all times. The questions that you have about Me will always be answered, for I have you in the world to be a disseminator of information about Me and My kingdom. This is the Lord God Yahweh Who speaks. (Our desire is to know, love and serve Him and to be happy with Him forever on earth and in heaven.)

While I was praying for those reading my manuscript, the Lord said:

Walk a straight line, Mike. This line exemplifies the Holy Spirit. This Spirit is Who wrote your book. Do not yield to any spirit other than Mine. Your book shall be carried to all nations, so that they may hear. Do not modify or change it in any way. Critics, in whom you have a great deal of respect, will try to change your book. But they were not of the anointing of the Spirit, when your pen was in action. So listen to no one, except those with whom you pray for learning of my truths.

Dream - The Lord revealed that I was involved in a checker game as I was making the moves that involved getting the manuscript written, read and published. The Lord said I was too deeply involved in the game to back out; however, there had been a setback, and I was going to have to make the right moves to get the book published. We prayed and asked the Lord about the setback. The Lord revealed that it had to do with the phrase I had written in the dedication of the book. I dedicated the

463

book to the Father, the Son and the Holy Spirit, under Whose guidance this book was written. Someone felt I was being presumptuous that this manuscript was written under the guidance of the Father, the Son and the Holy Spirit. I knew the manuscript was written under their guidance but since I did not want to be accused of being presumptuous, I decided to remove that part. My prayer partner said the Lord had revealed to him that I had spent considerable amount of time in prayer, as I wrote this book and that this book was truly written under the guidance of the Father, the Son and the Holy Spirit. The Lord said:

> Do not remove the phrase "under Whose guidance this book was written." These words are Holy Fire, which will carry your book throughout this nation and many others, not only in your generation but in generations to come. The adversary is immensely strong, but with just these words the enemy has no power. Give the glory to God.

A picture of a friend who said, "The Lord is well pleased with the book."

I spoke back immediately and said, "Thank you, Jesus."

The Lord said people will come into His Body 1011 ways. Then there was a vision in which I was serving as a Eucharistic minister, holding a golden chalice filled with a powdered form of the Body of Christ. Using a silver spoon, I was spoon-feeding the Body of Christ to the people as they came to the altar. As we began to pray, the Lord spoke.

> My message is for all people, which includes both male and female of all races and creeds. My message comes to them for the washing of their soul and body to regenerate new life. Once new life is formed, it is unsoiled, pure as white linen, with the days of old unable to stain the white garments that bathe and clothe their new life. Sin is no longer a deadly sting to claim its victim. Thousands upon

thousands of people will accept My name in the near future. They will come into My kingdom like you and Mike. Bring My message to them with vigor and steadfast prayer. Have faith in Me so that I may come to them through you and Mike. My message will be heard by millions of people through a book that will be under the authorship of Michael D. Miesch Jr. Stand by Mike when he publishes this book, and believe that it will come forth to My sheep in this generation and generations to come. This book will be a tool to serve as a guideline for millions of people, who will come to Me to accept My glory.

Vision - I was talking with a priest outside a new church building. The priest, wearing a black cassock with a white surplice, walked into the church through a door near the altar. I followed the priest and stood behind him on the altar to his right, facing the people. The church was round and beautifully constructed with a high dome. The seats were filled with people. There was a long procession of priests getting ready to march into the church. Though I was very comfortable standing on the altar behind the priest, the priest was very nervous and uncomfortable with me standing behind him. He kept turning around looking at me, but he did not say anything.

When the Lord walked the streets of His hometown, many people of that so-familiar site refused to have faith in Jesus as a healer of divine origin. God's very own Son was able to do nothing miraculous amongst the people because of their own unbelief. Jesus delivered a message to His people, but the message was not received. Faith is the ultimate receptacle that must be a part of the people before the power of the Almighty Holy Spirit can be made manifest to bring forth a healing. The process is two fold: the people must provide the faith and God will provide the power. The priest within Christ's Church is representative of many of the high priests that were in command of religious order in Jesus' day. If the priest's own faith is as little as the faith of the people of Nazareth, there is little hope of him receiving the power of the Almighty Holy Spirit. Many priests all over the world are with little faith in Jesus Christ. Whatever comments or remarks they may make, about Mike's book, must not be taken to heart, if their words are not guided by the Spirit. They must have receptacles of faith to be responsive to what the Holy Spirit saith. The book will make many of the priests nervous, because it strikes fear into them regarding their own convictions. However, it will bless them in the final moments of their ministries, when they realize the truth of the message is that of the Holy Spirit.

Vision - a priest sitting behind a desk with his feet propped upon the desk reading my manuscript. Then, there was a picture of a man to my right looking at me.

The Lord is going to send some people to talk to you about the manuscripts. One of the people will speak with half-truths. The Lord wants you to listen to what they have to say, but to come before Him, before making any changes or decisions.

Vision – a building was being constructed.

This building was solidly reinforced with different width boards (6,8,10 and 12 inch boards) nailed at an angle, not only on the sides but also on the roof. This building was strongly reinforced to be able to weather a fierce storm.

The Lord said this building was His Church. He said my son (Michael III) and I were carpenters that were helping to rebuild, restore and renew His Church just as St. Francis of Assisi did. The Church is going to have to be reinforced this strong to weather the storm that is coming.

466

The Church is the body. The body is the people. The people are going to have to be strong in their faith to weather the storm that is coming.

While praying for my book, I had a vision of a long and narrow yellow and green ribbon-like flag, flying from a pole.

Yellow symbolizes the presence or the light of the Lord. Green symbolizes new life.

> The door of life shall be opened by your book, to reveal the glory of the Lord upon His people. Thus they will be raised to the height, to which I have called them.

Praying for my book

While praying for my book, I had a vision of a farmer wearing a black, wide brim, flat top hat, white shirt and beige pants like those worn in 1800's. The farmer had his hands on a plow that was being pulled by an ox, breaking the ground for planting. The sun was shining on the farmer's face, but not on anything else.

> As the farmer tills the ground for planting seeds, so am I preparing America and the world for a harvest, unparalleled to this time.

While praying for my book, I had knowledge that there was something within me, blocking the publication of this book.

> I refer to the book as my book. The Lord said this is not my book but His book, that He only used me as an instrument to write the book. I must turn loose of the book and give it to Him, so that he can do with it what He wants.

Vision of a white-hot dove that looks like metal, when it is super heated: This dove, which resembled the emblem of the Holy Spirit, was descending downward head first.

> I have given you My words and have set them in your heart. It is on fire from My Holy Spirit. I shall interpret what it means to each person, as My Spirit speaks to their hearts. You have done all that I have asked of you. You shall have your just reward. Do not turn to change anything. You have given it to Me. Do not try to take it back. Blessing and curse comes from the tongue. So it is with My words. It will divide and join. Many will come to sit at your feet. Be prepared in all areas of your life. I am taking you on a new path, a path of different colors. They shall be joined to Me through you. Turn back to what I have taught you. Be ready to use it. Much joy is coming. Rejoice, for I am near and hear your voice day and night. You have taken a place in My heart. I rejoice in your personal praise and the open love that you show Me. I love you, My son. Know that I love you.

Vision – I had shown a priest something I had written. Later, the archbishop dropped in. As the archbishop was leaving, the priest walked up to him and asked if he had time to look at this paper. To my surprise, he glanced at it, and then he sat down to read it. I had written something about the Holy Spirit. The archbishop looked something up in the Catholic dictionary and said, "That is right" and continued to read. Then he read something about a giraffe. Again, he looked it up in the Catholic dictionary and said, "That is right".

> The Archbishop is symbolic of the higher authorities of the Church. The giraffe meant that this work, at first glance, appears to be too simple and uncomplicated to be valid by the typical, wise learned theologians of the Church. This work appears to be ridiculous. The Archbishop was saying that this was a valid work of the Holy Spirit.

Dream – I had knowledge that I was to be on TV. I asked a friend if he thought my book was from the Lord? He said, "No decision has been made, but they would know tonight." I had knowledge that I was to be interviewed by a lady with premature white hair who had the gift of discernment. Then my friend asked me a question, "What if it is not from the Lord?" I responded by saying, "If it is not of the Lord, I will get rid of the book."

> The "night of decision" mentioned in the dream, does not indicate "tonight", rather "a time" of prayer and discernment about your book, which will be seriously considered. The lady, with white hair, is a spirit of truth who will be interviewing not only you, but those, who will be discerning your book. The question, "What if the book is not of God?" is made to you by God, not your friend. Your answer is the right answer. The "television" you will be on is the deep scrutiny you will be under because of your book.

Dream – Someone said to me, "I understand the Lord has been speaking to you about Abraham Lincoln". I said, "Yes!" Then another person said, "I understand the Lord has been speaking to you about Abraham Lincoln." I said, "Yes!"

> The Proclamation of Emancipation was for all slaves in bondage against their will, and they were set free by the direction of Abraham Lincoln. Such will be the emancipation of all believers and unbelievers alike as they will be guided by the light of God through this book.

Dream – I had written a manuscript or something in which the code to what I had written had been lost. I do not know to whom I was talking, but I told him to interpret it the way it read.

> The Lord has the code. Those reviewing the manuscript are to interpret the document "just the way it reads". This is meant only for reviewers.

Someone with whom I have prayed with on a few occasions, who asked to read the manuscript, said this hit him right between the eyes, as he really had intentions of editing the manuscript.

Vision of a white bearded man, standing close to me, looking sideways to the ground: My prayer partner received the following words.

> This man was Moses. He was standing beside you explaining what is going to happen to the earth. He said you had written of it and will understand. I asked, "Why Mike?" Moses responded, "He will be part of what was, what is, and what is to come!"

Vision of several pieces of white paper blowing with the wind in a pasture or meadow: Each sheet of paper was like a blinding light.

> Something you have written has been rejected by those who should read it. This writing will be found to be of God and will reflect God's will.

Praying before the Blessed Sacrament after Mass:

> I want you to show My people My mercy throughout your book that I gave you. When there is a tragedy or calamity, show My mercy to My people, My children. Show how I love them. I will give you the words to write. My words will be understood by children as well. They will be simple and they will be Mine. I want My children to know why I am doing this for them. I do not want them to have fear. I would have them to be joyous and happy that I would do this for them. My words will be full of peace and love.

Words received

What you have written will endure the test of time.

Vision of an abstract picture - I was in a classroom talking to a teacher. The teacher's face and upper portions of the chest and arms suddenly became as an abstract picture. I saw several different views of the picture. One view had a purple outline of the face. Then the power of God came upon me and the abstract picture became a living person in front of me looking at me.

> The Lord revealed that the full understanding and meaning of an abstract picture is only known to the artist. This is the same with the Book of Revelation. The Book of Revelation is like an abstract picture in which only the Lord knows the full meaning of all the symbols and things written therein. These meanings become clear to those to whom the Lord chooses to reveal them. I could see several different views in an abstract form, but when the power of God came upon me, I could see this person who was a teacher very clearly. I asked my prayer partner to pray with me for understanding as to who this person was. My prayer partner laughed after praying. The Lord revealed that this person was one of several angels that are around me at all times ministering to me.

Dream – a book of perilous verses

I was holding a book that I had seen in a previous dream. I placed the book on a table saying that my book was finished (not referring to the book on the table). There were two young men close by. They were trying to get a glance at the cover of the book that was placed on the table. When a priest picked up the book, I asked him, if it was his book. He said, "Yes". Later, after I woke up and was praying my regular prayers, I had a vision of the priest in the dream. He asked me, "What is your favorite verse?" I replied, "To know, love and serve the Lord, thy God, with thy whole heart, whole mind, and whole soul", which is the first commandment. I had forgotten about the dream, which I remembered after the vision.

> This book is a writing of perilous verses. (My prayer part-ner did not know what perilous meant. Perilous means dangerous or hazardous.) This priest will write a book against your book. He will use your book against you. He will slander your name, misinterpret the scriptures and will almost certainly come to the point of abusing the Holy Scriptures. Scriptures are the sword. Remember the first commandment, have it in your mind and heart at all times for your protection, and the enemy will not penetrate your spiritual realm. Your flesh will be very weak and battered, but your spirit will be unharmed. Do not mind those that believe in what that priest says. They shall also falter in their walk in the Lord. Just remember the words you spoke after the priest asked you what your favorite verse was. People who blindly abuse the Holy Scripture will be smitten by the sword. My people suffer for the lack of knowledge.

The Lord speaks

> My son, do not concern yourself about anyone who would take issue with your work. Your work is unlike any other work undertaken on the Book of Revelation. The book in the dream is not yours because it belongs to someone else. The person to whom it belongs has his own opinion, which is different than yours. Others have already writ-ten and will write on the subject matter that is the same as yours. Yet, their work will not be the same as yours. You need not worry or concern yourself about someone taking issue with your work or discrediting your work or slandering your name, because you have been obedient to My will, which is to know, love and serve Me with your whole heart, soul and mind. The priest represents

the mainline Christian denominations and not a specific priest.

The Lord says:

Be cautious and move with diligence. Gather your materials and make preparation to contact prospective publishers. In time, I will make known to you the responsible agent for the publication, printing and distribution of your work. Gather facts about those, who you believe will be prospective candidates for publication. Move with confidence, knowing that you have a work of God to be brought forth. Anyone who leads you into believing that he is doing you a favor in publishing the work should be eliminated. Those that present themselves as a serving-agent of God's work on this earth are to be considered. Any others, who endeavor to dazzle you with their operation, need not be considered. Only consider the best who are exemplified as Christ-like character. Don't rush, for all things will come to pass in My time. Patience, diligence, discernment, observation and scrutiny are the watch-words for now.

The book

The book will print. It will reprint. It will sell many, but only to those who choose to know.

The sun-clothed woman and the Blessed Mother

I made the statement that the Sun-clothed woman is not the Blessed Mother; yet, there are prophecies, supposedly from the Blessed Mother, saying that she is the Sun-clothed Woman. While I was praying asking the Lord for an understanding, I had a picture of a head of an alligator with its mouth wide open with many teeth. A few days later, while praying, I had a vision of the Blessed Mother. I asked three of my prayer

473

partners to come together and pray with me for an understanding. I asked the Lord if I was to change the statement about the Blessed Mother not being the Sun-clothed Woman. We received the following message and words of knowledge:

> We, who are of many tribes, come together to worship and adore My Father and the Holy Spirit. My message is the same, yet, I speak in a way that those who are searching will understand. I have twelve tribes, not all are understanding in the same way. I speak loudly and intellectually to one, and I give dreams to another. Just as at the Tower of Babel, My people have been confounded. Yet, I am speaking and they are each hearing Me differently. Does this mean what I have spoken or made known to you is wrong? "Nay!" I say, "Nay!" What you have been given is for those of the tribe I have directed you to. Because they challenge, charge, argue, assail, laugh, distort, curse or lie about my revelation to you is no consequence to you. I give this to you that those, who will see or hear it, will be touched, blessed and a part of my whole message which has been imparted to them. My other messengers are speaking the same message and it is disseminated to them in a way that they will understand. Stand firm, speak boldly, do not concern yourself with the message I have given others to speak. They are reaching those that I am sending to them and reaching others that they themselves are reaching out to. My messengers will cross paths and will sometimes be misunderstood. Do not separate yourself from them. Know that I will use those who are willing and even some that are not. Go to those that I have sent you to and be at peace for I am Peace and Love.

Head of an alligator with its mouth wide open with many teeth

The Lord said, "Do you believe what you have written wholeheartedly with all that is within you?" I replied,

"Yes!" Then He replied, "The alligator with its mouth wide open will be the people trying to tear at you and bring you down. " I am a God of covenant. I dwell within My covenant. Apart from it, there are grave consequences. Stay within its protection and there will be blessings and fruits. Apart from it, there is death.

Another prayer partner received the following words of knowledge:

The Lord is the author of your work. You do not need to apologize for what He has given you to understand and how He has instructed you to write. He has a covenant with you in the writing of this book. It is His task to open the understanding of each one, who has access to it.

Vision of the Blessed Mother

Be comforted my son. You do not need to be concerned about tomorrow, for it will take care of itself. Be of good cheer for my Son loves you.

Vision in which three different colored solutions were being injected into the tree. The color of the three solutions was red, blue and yellow.

This tree is the "Tree of Life". Red is the blood of man, which is the manifestation of the Spirit of Life. Blue is the Living Water, which is the Spirit of Life. Yellow is the Light of His Word, which never changes. These colors symbolized the chemistry of our existence. Trust My Word. Let the light shine, as in My Word to show that the blood of man, the once fallen race, shall be saved for all eternity. This is what My Son has done for mankind, to set man free. Thereby, I say unto you, do the same for others, just as He has done for you. Let no man persuade you against the truth, which is My Word, which shall never change. The goodness of your heart is all that will remain from your present physical existence. Stand steadfast in My Word, which will keep your heart in My good will. These three things are the Spirit of existence. The fourth thing is knowledge of the disorder of nature which could not harmonize with the goodness of the tree of knowledge. Because of redeemed man, God had to cut out that portion of the tree, which was the nature of sin through Jesus Christ, Who was the atonement for that portion of the tree, which was man's disobedience to God's Word.

Dream – I had knowledge that I had asked Jesus for permission to ascend upward to be enlightened so I could finish the Book of Revelation. I spoke to Jesus, Who was standing at my right and said, "Thank you Jesus."

Study My heart. Study My soul. Let My mind be in yours. Know Me. Study how I forgive. Study how My revenge will prevail over Satan. Know My love. Know My will. Many have forgotten that have tasted My love and My presence. They have forgotten about My wrath that is to come. All they want is to feel good. They have gone back to pagan ways. They have chosen to be lied to - to feel O.K. I want you to be ready to tell them and so shall those, who will follow you. I love you My son. You are Mine!

Dream - I came upon a man in the street, carrying a package, wrapped in a roll of newspapers. This roll was tightly bound with string. This man and I were in a struggle over this package. I managed to pull out a small package rolled very tightly in newspaper, the size of a hot dog bun. I spoke to the man and said, "I have it." I had knowledge that package contained meat. This man dressed in a brim hat and a coat that covered his hips said to me, "Eat it". I refused to eat it, as I did not know what it was. As I began to unroll the tightly wrapped newspaper off the package, I got a glimpse of a white blinding light, then it looked like white gold. I asked a prayer partner to pray with me for discernment. Is this from the Lord?

Prophecy-

My son, you have fought and struggled to know and understand My Word and Me. I am happy to tell you of the great blessing that has been made ready for you. In the box was My hidden Word. You have brought it to the light. Your work has been tested by fire for the truth. It has produced pure white gold. It is ready to be shared with the world. My Words are that of brilliant gold. My Words are in you and through you about to speak to My people. Your heart is so full that many will reject you as they did Moses. Many will open their hearts to your words of Me. Speak slowly and gently. Let your words be kind and building. Many will be spring lambs. Very few will be able to consume the greatness I have taught you. Let My Words flow from My heart to your heart. Let your lips bring joy, acceptance, and forgiveness. Some you now know will scatter. Know this now and do not be shaken when it happens. I will be with you. Take care of your physical person. Much will be demanded of you.

I asked my prayer partner to pray with me about my book.

Be prepared for disappointment. Have faith that My Word will not come back void. For My Word is like a mighty hammer, driven into the spirit and flesh. Be humble of heart and obedient unto My authority and you shall be blessed. Submit to My perfect will. Send it (the book) to the publishers that have been mentioned. If not those, I will close or open the doors. Trust in Me, for I will choose the one that will publish the book. Be prepared to be tested.

I gave a copy of my book to a friend to read. At that time, she received understanding that she was to speak a word from the Lord to me at another time. Later she received this message.

The Lord says that it is time to publish the books!
Don't get hung up on ecclesiastical looks.
The opinions and statements of man are
only snares and traps to hinder, what I've told you to do before hand.
Go forth and cast down your nets.
The fish are waiting and you will have pockets to let.

It is time for the nation to hear
what I've spoken privately in your ear.
It is time for My people to read about the spiritual truths
that you have paid the price to receive.
Now listen! Don't hold back
for I have gone before you and slain the devilish pack.

My son, you have stayed before Me,
loving Me, delighting yourself in My presence
for surely I will give you the desires of your heart.
You have cried out to Me to open the door.
Now I have unlocked (previously closed opportunities).
Much more, than you have asked, is in store.

Your life is a testimony to be shared
for those beloved saints that have physically been impaired.
For know that you are one chosen to overcome
Even now you have victory and are proof that
battles have been fought and won by the Son.

Your anointed praise and intercession
is a sweet smelling fragrance to Me.
Because of your dying to self, so many have been set free.
Many walk in health and deliverance today,
because I've called you to pray.

478

The days ahead will be busy and time-consuming.
Be aware there are still snares.
Again, doors will swing wide open that have been closed
to speak to the family's unhearing ears.
For you this will be a good spiritual year.

Press on My son, move forward,
for it is time for others to know those
revelations and knowledge to you I did show.
Don't wait! Don't hesitate!

The lull, the pause is over.
Now I'm releasing you to move forward.
I will fill you with My anointing, My love and My power
To enlighten mankind this last hour.

      Selah

A few years ago, I asked the Lord if I was to make any changes in my book. The Lord said:

> No, do not make any changes, you will in time. What you have written will go out on power lines throughout this nation and the world.

While in prayer, the Lord said:

> This book may cause controversy; controversy is not always bad, controversy can do a lot of good.

Dream – Someone spoke to me very excitedly about me teaching Revelation. In a second dream this person said there was a division in the ocean. In a third dream, he said there was a great division in the ocean.

> Michael, the time is now. Go and prepare your notes. Set

into place - markers. Arrange your cards. Prepare your highlights. Make your notes clear. Arrange each step so that my weak will understand. Choose no one to serve you. I will send My own to be by your side. They in turn will go out into the hinterlands. As time passes many will separate themselves through My churches. Many have been misled and wander to know the truth. When the false comes more will separate themselves looking for peace. Go, prepare, write, rewrite. Do not be discouraged. You will be taken away when no more can be done. I have made a place for you and yours.

As I was waking up I heard these words:

"My son, you have been given a trumpet to raise the dead from the dead."

While praying very early in the morning, I had five or six visions of a blinding light.

The Lord said, "I am coming soon. It is time to get your books published.

My beloved holy one of Mine. Prepare to travel. Not as you have done before, for I call you away. I have much for you to do. You must be prepared to travel light. Be prepared to go when My angel beckons. All is cared for. You have much to do for Me. Do not be afraid. Learn now to give up what you do not need for those things you will need. I am your arm chair and comforter. I will bring you to My place for you to rest and work. My eyes are looking into your eyes to see My will.

Embraced by the Lord Jesus Christ

I was sitting in a chair at home with my eyes closed saying my prayers. Someone grabbed both of my upper arms giving me a gentle shake. When I opened my eyes, there was no one in the room. I had assumed this was an angel as I have been touched many times by angels to get my attention. I asked my prayer partner to pray with me for an understanding.

> Jesus said, "It is Me! It is Me! It is Me! It is good that you are here. I will comfort you here."

A month later

I had laid a book down to close and rest my eyes. Suddenly my hands were on the upper arms of a person. I started squeezing and feeling the muscles with my hands. I knew immediately this was Jesus. I started telling him how much I love Him over and over. I pulled His head over my shoulder and to hug Him. I did not dare open my eyes as I knew He would disappear the minute I open my eyes. This lasted for less than a minute.

I received understanding that Jesus was extremely pleased that I wrote and am publishing the two books that He asked me to write. He expressed His appreciation by allowing me to physically touch and embrace Him.

The Lord said, "You have My strength. I have you in the palm of My hands. I will never leave you nor forsake you.

References

1.   *New American Standard Bible*, Foundation Press Publications, Box 277, La Habra, California 90631, 1960.

2.   *New International Version of the Holy Bible*, The Zondervan Corporation, Grand Rapids, Michigan 49506, 1978.

3.   *Saint Joseph Edition of the New American Bible*, Catholic Book Publishing Co., New York, 1970.

3A.   *Saint Joseph Edition of the New American Bible*, (Revised New Testament - 1986 and revised Psalms - 1991) Catholic Book Publishing Co., New York, 1970.

4.   Gordon Lindsay, *Satan's Rebellion and Fall, Satan, Fallen Angels and Demons Series*, Vol. I, Christ For The Nations, Dallas, Texas 75224

5.   The Amplified Bible, Zondervan Publishing House, Grand Rapids, Michigan, 1965.

6.   Pope Benedict XVI, The Role of Andrew – Magnificat, PO Box 822, Yonkers, NY 10702, Vol. 11, No. 9, November 2009)

7.   Hematidrosis, http://en.wikipedia.org/wiki/Hematidrosis

8.   John L. McKenzie, *Dictionary of the Bible*, The MacMillian Company, New York, New York, 1965.

9.   *The Mystery of the Shroud*, National Geographic, Vol. 157, No. 6, page 730 - 753, National Geographic Society, 17th and M Sts. N.W., Washington D.C. 20036, June 1980.

10.   Mary Jo Anderson, *Relic authenticates Shroud of Turin* - Exhaustive tests show scared cloth much older than carbon 14 date

– Wednesday October 4,2000 (http://www.worldnetdaily.com/ bluesky exnews/20001004 xex scientists r.shtml) (joycelang@ prodigy.net)

11. Richard Rooney, SJ *Let's Pray the Rosary*, Liguori Publications, One Liguori Drive, Liguori, Missouri 632057-9999

12. Message via Louise Tomkiel, October 15, 1998 (njkoti@nji.com) October 18, 1998 (Remnant@RCC.org)

13. *The Pieta Prayer Booklet*, Published by MLOR Corporation, 1186 Burlington Drive, Hickory Corners, Michigan 49060, 1996.

14. Luisa Piccarretta's *The lamp of Grace. All the pains that Jesus suffered in His Passion were triple.* Volume 6. September 26, 1904, The Luisa Piccarreta Center for Divine Will, P.O. Box 340, Caryville, TN 37714

15. Maria Jesus reveals details of His Crucifixion http://www.thewarningsecondcoming.com/jesus-reveals-details-of-his-crucifixion/ Thursday, March 29, 201213.

16. The Living Bible, Tyndale House Publishers, Wheaton, Illinois, 1971

17. *Good News For Modern Man, The New Testament in Today's English Version*, Second Edition, American Bible Society, New York, 1966.

18. *The Jerusalem Bible*, Doubleday and Company, Inc., Garden City, New York, 1966.

19. Knox, *Old Testament*, Sneed & Ward, Inc. New York, 1950.

20. *The Holy Bible, The Douay Version of the Old Testament* - Catholic Book Publishing Company, New York, 1954.

20A. *The Holy Bible, The Douay Version of the Old Testament*, Catholic Book Publishing Company, New York, 1962.

21. W. Hautenville Rambout A. B., *Extracts from the writings of St. Irenaeus, Exhibiting the Doctrines of the Second Century*, James Charles & Son, 61, Middle Abbey - St. Dublin 1870.

22. Joachim Jeremias, *Infant Baptism in the First Four Centuries*, (Translated by David Cairns), The Westiminister Press, Philadelphia; SCM Press LTD, Great Britain,1962.

23. Burkhard Neunheuser, O.S.B., *Baptism and Confirmation*, Translated by John Jay Hughes), Herder and Herder, New York, 232 Madison Avenue, New York 16, New York, 1964, page 71.

24. A. George S.M., et. al. *Baptism in the New Testament* (Translated by David Askew), Geoffrey Chapman, London 1964, page 129.

25. t. Cyprian Letters, *The Fathers of the Church*, Vol. 51, The Catholic University of America Press, Washington D.C. 20017, page 216 -219.

26. The New Catholic Encyclopedia, *Baptism*, Vol. 11, McGraw-Hill Book Co., New York, 1967.

27. *The New World Dictionary-Concordance to the New American Bible*, World Publishing, Times Mirror, New York, 1970.

28. Cruden's Complete Concordance, Zondervan Publishing House, Grand Rapid, Michigan 49506, 1970

29. Michael D. Miesch Jr., *Lifting the Veil of Revelation.*

30. Information on Jesuit Fathers off the internet

31. *The Bible - Revised Standard Version*, American Bible Society, New York

32. Cardinal Timothy Manning's prayer - internet

33. Virgin Mary: When I waited with the apostles in the Cenacle for the descent of the Holy Spirit it took ten days of preparation. Wednesday, August 22, 2012, http://www.thewarningsecondcoming.com/virgin-mary-when-i-waited-with-the apostles-in... 8/28/2012

34. Saint Augustine, Bishop of Hippo, 354 – 430 A.D., www.quotedb.com/quotes/215

35. *The Holy Bible, Authorized King James Version*, The World Publishing Company, Cleveland and New York.

36. Nihil Obstat: P.L. Biermann, Imprimatur: George Cardinal Mundelein

37. *Angel of the Judgment - a life of Ferrer Vincent* by S.M.C., Ave Maria Press, Notre Dame, Indiana.

38. T.S. McDermott, O.P., *The Lives of the Dominican Saints*, published by The Dominican Fathers of the Province of St. Joseph, U.S.A. 1940.

39. Derek Prince, *Shaping History Through Prayer and Fasting*, Fleming H. Revell Company, Old Tappan, New Jersey in association with Derek Prince Publications, 1973.

40. *1984 Religion in America*, The Gallup Report, Report No. 222, March 1984, The Princeton Religious Center, Inc., Princeton, New Jersey 08540.

41. John Leary, *Prepare for the Great Tribulation and the Era of Peace, Vol.54*, March 5, 2009, Queenship Publishing Company, P.O. Box 220, Goleta, CA 93116

42. Magnificant Vol. 14, No.6 August 2012, pg 66, PO Box 822, Yonkers, NY 10702,

43. Bishop Robert J. Hermann, "Judgment is coming", St. Louis Review, Archdiocese of St Louis October 17, 2008

44. Bill Gothard, *Institute in Basic Youth Conflicts*, Box One, Oak Brook, Illinois 60621.

45. Adolphe Tanquerey, *The Spiritual Life - A Treatise on Ascetial and Mystical* Theology, translated by Herman Branderis - 1930, Society of St. John The Evangelist, publishers Desclee & Co. Tournai, Belgium.

46. James Robison, *Attack on the Family*, Life's Answer Series, Tyndale House Publishers, Inc., Wheaton, Illinois 1982.

47. Paul Kurtz And Edwin H. Wilson, *Humanist Manifesto II*, Humanist Magazine, Vol. 33, No. 5, American Humanist Association, 923 Kansington, Buffalo, New York 14215, September/October 1973.

48.   United States Defense Committee 1986 Candidate, Questionarie, United States Defense Committee, 3238 Wynford Drive, Fairfax, Virginia 22031.

49.   Gordon Lindsay, *God's Plan of the Ages as Revealed in Bible Chronology*, Christ For The Nations, Dallas, Texas 75224, 1971.

50.   *Community of God's Delight Prayer Watch*, Dallas, TX - Adapted from the Alleluia Community of Augusta, GA

51.   Louise Tomkiel – Public Communication - Message to Louise Tomkiel, Joyce Lang e-mail, Friday, March 10, 2000.

52.   Downs Matthews, *The Monarchs of Mexico*, The Dallas Morning News, Page 8, Section G, Sunday, March 19,1995, Dallas, Texas.

53.   Charles and Frances Hunter, *Angels on Assignment* as told by Roland Buck, Hunter Books, 201 McClellan, Kingwood, Texas 77339, 1979.

54.   Approval and recommendation M. Cardinal Pahiarca, Lisbon, Portugal, March 4, 1936

55.   Carl E. Schmoger, C.SS.R., *The Life of Anne Catherine Emmerich Vol. 2*, Tan Books and Publishers, Inc, P.O. Box 424, Rockford, Illinois 61105 1976

56.   Dr. Kenneth McAll, *"Healing the Haunted"*, Queenship Publishing Company, P.O. Box 220, Goleta, CA 93116

57.   John Leary, *Prepare for the Great Tribulation and the Era of Peace, Vol. I*, Queenship Publishing Co., P.O. Box 42028, Santa Barbara, CA 93140

58.   John Leary, *Prepare for the Great Tribulation and the Era of Peace, Vol. II*, Queenship Publishing Co., P.O. Box 42028, Santa Barbara, Ca. 93140

59.   John Leary, *Prepare for the Great Tribulation and the Era of Peace, Vol. III*, Queenship Publishing Co., P.O. Box 42028, Santa Barbara, Ca. 93140

60.   John Leary, *Prepare for the Great Tribulation and the Era of Peace, Vol. V*, Queenship Publishing Co., P.O. Box 42028, Santa

Barbara, Ca. 93140

61. *The Father speaks to His children,* Pater" Publications, C.P. 135, Via Verrotti 1 – 67100 L'Aquila - Italy

62. John Leary, *Prepare for the Great Tribulation and the Era of Peace,* Vol. 51, Queenship Publishing Co., P.O. Box 42028, Santa Barbara, Ca. 93140

63. Spiritual Communion, Sister Benigna Consolata, a nun of the Visitation, Como, Italy. Internet

64. Fr. Alessio Parente, *Send me your Guardian Angel* Edizioni Padre Pio da Pietrelcina, Piazzale S. Maria delle Grazie, 71013 San Giovanni Rotondo (RG) – Italy First Edition 1993, Fifth Edition 2006

65. Message from St. Michael the Archangel via Littlest of Servant, e-mail August 1, 2009

66. Tiny fossils called oldest ever found, The Dallas Morning News, Dallas, TX, Monday August 22, 2011

67. Dr. Lennart Moller, The Exodus Case – New Discoveries of Historical Exodus, 3rd Extended edition, January 1, 2008. Publisher- Casscom Media/Scandansvia, Virginia, IL.

68. Gordon Lindsay, Creation, Volume 1, Christ For The Nations, Dallas, TX 1980

69. Dakes Annotated Reference Bible, Dake Bible Sales, Inc., PO Box 173, Lawrenceville, Georgia 30245, 1961

70. Mammoth find: Preserved Ice Age giant found with flowing blood in Siberia, estimated to have lived between 10,000 and 15,000 years ago. Internet, Published May, 29, 2013.

71. Fazale Rana and Hugh Ross, *Who was Adam,* NAV Press, P.O. Box 35001, Colorado Springs, CO 80935 2005

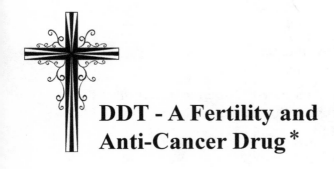

DDT - A Fertility and Anti-Cancer Drug*

Michael D. Miesch Jr., Ph.D.

Paul Muller received the Nobel Prize in 1948 for the discovery of the DDT. It had saved the lives of our troops from malaria, typhus and other insect-borne diseases during World War II. DDT was found to be a fertility and anti-cancer drug. Contrary to popular opinion, the teachings of Rachel Carson and the so-called environmentalists, scientific data do not support their accusations against DDT. DDT is a miracle drug that continues to be used today in many parts of the world where mosquitoes are a problem. This article was written so that the truth will be made known.

FERTILITY STUDIES

Dr. Alice Ottoboni conducted fertility studies with rats and dogs at the California Department of Public Health Labs in Berkeley. Female rats receiving 20 parts per million of DDT in their diet had a longer reproductive life than the control rats that received no DDT. Female rats, which were fed DDT, reproduced for an average of 14.5 months in contrast to 8.9 months for the control. Eight of the DDT-fed rats reproduced 17 months which is twice as long as the average for the control.

*Received words from the Lord in middle of night to write papers on Chlordane and DDT. I have not been able to get these papers published. They will be published here.

Table 1. Average number of months rats reproduced.

DDT- fed Rats	14.5 Months
Rats not fed DDT (Control)	8.9 Months

The DDT-fed rats produced far more offspring than the control. (Effect of DDT on the Reproductive Life-Span in Female Rat, Toxicology and Applied Pharmacology 22:497-502, 1972)

Beagle dogs were fed up to 10 milligrams of DDT per kilogram of body weight per day through three generations with no harmful effects. The female dogs, which were fed DDT, had their first estrus cycle two to three months earlier than the control. A total of 650 offspring were produced. (Archives Environ. Contam. Toxicology 6:83-101, 1977)

Every year, the Audubon Bird Society has a bird count and records the total number of different species of birds seen. This is recorded scientific data. The following Audubon's data was compiled by Philip H. Marvin. It is interesting that the bird population exploded after 1952 coinciding with the use of DDT.

Table 2. Average annual number of birds of all species counted; average annual number of people participating, and average number of birds counted per person.

Years	Birds	Observers	Birds per observer
1949-52	8,606,251	5,160	1,667
1954-57	23,146,380	6,603	3,505
1958-61	34,253,194	8,511	4,024
1962	44,630,257	9,981	4,471

Table 3. Average number of Robins counted annually.

Years	Birds
1949-52	41,214
1953-56	86,386
1957-60	367,733
1961-62	928.905

Contrary to the opinion of Rachel Carson, the Robin population exploded during the time of DDT.

Table 4. Average number of Cardinals, Mourning Doves and Flickers counted annually.

Years	Cardinal	Mourning Dove	Flicker
1949-52	19,576	13,131	4,278
1953-56	31,375	32,752	5,980
1957-60	43,191	59,886	7,500
1961-62	61,942	66,860	9,216

Table 5. Average number of Mockingbirds and Eastern Meadow Larks counted annually.

Years	Mockingbird	Eastern Meadow Lark
1949-52	4,430	11,170
1954-56*	9,802	22,373
1957-60	14,027	32,715
1961-62	15,176	36,809

* 1953 not included

Table 6. Average number of House Sparrows, Crows, Red-wing Blackbirds and Starlings counted annually.

Years	House Sparrow	Crow	Red-wing Blackbird	Starling
1949-52	134,878	122,259	2,858,267	717,477
1953-56	239,073	216,316	6,650,760	1,561,710
1957-60	314,397	289,197	16,025,571	5,799,820
1961-62	400,055	233,524	11,812,060	8,119,410

The annual Audubon bird count shows that the bird population exploded after and during the time of heavy pesticide use. The Congressional Record of Senator Everett Dirksen on October 22, 1965 reported that the Audubon bird count in 1961 was 19 times higher than in 1940.

In 1965, the Fish and Wildlife Service asked Congress to appropriate money to help control the birds in the Arkansas-Mississippi rice-growing region, an area of the greatest pesticide use in the nation. (Senator Everett Dirksen, Congressional Records, Friday, October 27, 1965)

DDT AND THE ROBIN

Ms. Carson said the Robins were on the verge of extinction because they fed on earthworms living under apple trees that had been sprayed with DDT. Experiments were set up to determine the effect of feeding earthworms raised in soil with high concentrations of DDT to Robins. The Robins that were fed nothing but these earthworms for 30 days showed no ill effects. (Farm Chemicals, March 1967, page 68) The Audubon bird count showed that the Robins increased over 1,000% from 1940 to 1961. Roger Troy Peterson, one of America's leading ornithologists and author of Field Guide To Birds, stated in 1962 that the Robin was the most numerous bird in North America. (Chemistry, April 1970, page 37)

There were certainly some isolated cases where misapplication of DDT killed some birds. Misapplication of any chemical can be dangerous, taking an overdose of aspirin for example. Pesticides applied according to the label do not pose any threat to wildlife.

DDT AND BIRD EGGS

Ms. Carson stated that quails, when fed high concentrations of DDT, had only a few eggs hatched. Those few eggs amounted to 75.3% in contrast to 83.9% for the control. In the same experiment above, Ms. Carson neglected to mention that 50 ppm of DDT increased reproductivity in pheasants and Mallard ducks. Bengalese finches when fed DDT had an increase in thickness of the eggshell.

Ms. Carson said DDT caused pheasant sickness, killing the pheasants. In a scientific experiment conducted in 1955, pheasants were fed a phenomenal 15,000 ppm DDT in their diet with no symptoms of illness, - none of the pheasants died. (Chemistry, April 1970, page 37)

In 1966, Fish and Wildlife researchers fed elevated levels of DDT to captive eagles for 112 days. They found no ill effects to either birds or eggs. (Stickel, "Bald Eagle Pesticide Relationships," Transcript of the 31st North American Wildlife Conference, 1966, pp. 199-200) It is a shame that the Fish and Wildlife people knew the truth about DDT and continuously allowed false reports to be circulated.

DDT when fed to some birds at exceedingly high concentrations can affect the hatchability of the eggs but so do half of all chemicals selected at random when fed at high dosage. These same chemicals at appropriate dosage do not affect the hatchability of an egg. (GAC 904-430, Geigy Agricultural Chemicals, 3/72)

HUNTERS AND TRAPPERS
AFFECTED THE EAGLE POPULATION

The Audubon Bird count shows that there were 20% more Bald Eagles in 1961 than 1940. Just because DDT is found in the bodies of birds does not mean DDT killed the birds. A government survey of 118 eagles found dead in 1962 revealed that 91% of the eagles died as a result of physical violence: 77% were shot, 7% were caught in traps, 7% died from other violent causes such as power lines, 9% died from natural causes. ("The True Facts about Pesticides and the Environment", Farm Chemicals, March 1967, page 68)

In 1989 it was reported that Fish and Wildlife agents in Alaska found 50 to 70 eagles that loggers shot out of trees "just for grins."

Another situation is Eagle no. 51, which was taken from a nest in Alaska on July 23, 1988, carried to Indiana, raised and released on September 1. It was spotted in Kentucky on December 29th and January 4th and likely spent the last two months of its life in or near North Texas, a popular eagle wintering area. Eagle no. 51 was found shot to death on the Trinity River near Eagle Mountain Lake in Wise County on March 12, 1989. (Dallas Times Herald, April 23, 1989).

84 ILLEGAL POLE TRAPS FOUND IN NORTH CENTRAL AND NORTHEAST TEXAS

Raisers of gamecocks commonly used steel traps, mounted on the top of poles to ward off predators. These traps kill or maim perching birds such as eagles, hawks or owls. (Dallas Times Herald, April 23, 1989)

PEREGRINE FALCON ALSO KNOWN AS THE DUCK HAWK

DDT was blamed for the decline of the Peregrine falcon. In Wisconsin, where the falcons had decreased in number they had 0.9 ppm of DDT in their bodies. In Canada, where the falcons flourished with no reproduction problems, they had 37 times more DDT in their bodies. (Chemistry, April 1970, page 37)

GROWTH OF WILDLIFE AT TOXIC SITE CHALLENGES U.S. POLICY

Wildlife is thriving at a highly polluted Rocky Mountain Army Arsenal area that once made nerve gases and chlorinated pesticides. Bill Thomas, a former base commander, called this spot the most polluted square mile on earth. Yet, there are 30 eagles and 130 ferruginous hawks living at this site, more than any other site in North America. There are also 240 mule deer, 120 white tail deer and numerous owls. These birds of prey feed on the large number of prairie dogs and other small animals that live in the contaminated soil. The pesticides that were reported to cause birds to lay thin eggshells elsewhere have not affected the birds here. (The Dallas Morning News, April 20, 1989)

DDT FED TO CONVICT VOLUNTEERS FOR TWO YEARS WITH NO ILL EFFECTS

Dr. Wayland J. Hayes of the U.S. Public Health Service testified before the Ribicoff Congressional hearing on pesticides. He had done extensive studies on the effect of DDT on human beings. For two years, from 1956 to 1958, Dr. Hayes fed convict volunteers daily up to 200 times the normal amount of DDT that would be found in an average diet of food and vegetables treated with DDT. Dr. Hayes found that the convicts achieved the maximum storage of DDT in approximately one year and stored no more DDT in their bodies despite a continuous intake of DDT. After two years of daily intake of DDT, the convict volunteers suffered no ill effects and were just as healthy as the convict volunteers who received no DDT in their diet. Dr. Hayes told the Congressional committee that his experiment showed that men could consume DDT daily at a level 200 times greater than the amount consumed in most people's daily diet with no ill effect. Eight of the 24 volunteers claim that their appetite improved after taking DDT. (Congressional Records, October 27, 1965; Evidence of Safety of Long-Term, High, Oral Doses of DDT for Man, Arch Environ Health Vol 22: 119-135, 1971)

Dr. Alice Ottoboni reported that in controlled studies human volunteers taking 35 milligrams of DDT per kg of body weight for 4 to 5 years showed no adverse effects, acute or chronic. (The Dose Makes The Poison, Vincente Books, Berkeley, Ca., pg. 106)

Mr. and Mrs. Robert Loibl, pest control operator from California took 10 milligrams pills of DDT per day to prove that DDT was not harmful. Mr. Loibl said that he feels better and his appetite has picked up, while his wife's dandruff has disappeared and her teeth and gums are healthier. (Weed, Trees and Turfs, I have a copy of the article but no date)

DDT was widely used on man, animals, vegetables and agricultural crops for 30 years before it was banned.

DDT INHIBITED TUMOR FORMATION IN ANIMALS AND CURED MICE WITH MALIGNANT TUMORS

A U.S. Public Health Service Study at John Hopkins University found that DDT inhibited tumor formation in animals and cured mice that were deliberately inoculated with malignant tumors.

Professor J. Gordon Edwards of San Jose State College reported that DDT and its analogs are medicinally effective in the direct treatment of adrenal cancer, infant jaundice and barbiturate poisoning of man. (Dallas Time Herald, February 9, 1971)

NO CASES OF CANCER AMONG WORKER IN DDT PLANT

Dr. Edward Laws and associates of the U.S. Public Health Service made detailed studies of 35 workers who had worked at the Montrose DDT plant from 9 to 19 years. These workers had absorbed from 4 to 8 milligrams (not micrograms) of DDT per day. No cancer had occurred. Over 1,000 workers had worked at this plant during its 23 years of operation with no case of cancer reported. (Archives of Environmental Health 15:766-775, 1967) The Journal of the American Medical Association 212:105, (1970) noted that careful research on pesticide handlers with high levels of DDT in their body fat showed "no interference with their health."

The Wall Street Journal, on April 21, 1993, reported that breast cancer was linked to DDT. A year later, another study with three times the number of participants found there was no link between DDT and breast cancer. ("Pesticide Residue and Breast Cancer?" Journal of the National Cancer Institute, Vol. 86, No. 8, pp 572-3, 589-599 April 20, 1994)

WHY WAS DDT BANNED?

At the conclusion of the 1972 DDT hearing, the EPA examiner, after reviewing over 9,000 pages of scientific documents and the testimonies of prominent scientists, ruled in favor of DDT. His final statement was:

> DDT is not a carcinogenic hazard to man. DDT is not a mutagenic or teratogenic hazard to man...The evidence in this proceeding supports the conclusion that there is a present need for the essential uses of DDT.

Unfortunately, William Ruckelshaus, the EPA administrator, overruled his chief examiner without even reviewing the evidence, and for political reasons, DDT was banned. (PCT, 1985)

The U.S. Department of Agriculture, being stunned at the banning of DDT, requested the EPA sources of information which might justify this action. Mr. Ruckelshaus, defying the Freedom of Information Act, refused to reveal any such sources. After Mr. Ruckelshaus left the EPA, he continued to wage his unjust war on pesticides by his active support of the Environmental Defense Fund (EDF). He sent out thousands of letters (via EDF mailings) urging Americans to donate money to the EDF. The Washington Monthly in August 1973 reported that Attorney Ruckelahaus stated, "At the EPA, I often had to make them think I wanted something else in order to get what I wanted accomplished." (PCT, February 1976) William Ruckelshaus was also the EPA administrator in 1988 when Chlordane was banned.

DDT did not kill the birds or thin their eggshells or hinder their reproduction. Scientific data show that DDT is a fertility drug causing the bird population to explode. The eagle and falcon populations were not affected by DDT or pesticides but by hunters and trappers. DDT does not cause cancer but prevented, inhibited and cured cancer in animals. DDT is a miracle drug that saved millions and millions of lives from Malaria, Typhus, Yellow Fever and many other insect-borne diseases. It protected our food and crops for almost 30 years before it was banned. Could DDT be used as a cure for cancer in humans?

Rachel Carson and William Ruckelshaus did a grave injustice, creating a pesticide phobia among the American people. Ms. Carson made up stories and told outright lies about DDT and other pesticides. For Mr. Ruckelshaus to overrule the recommendations of his chief examiner and the top scientists of the world, to ban DDT without a just reason or cause and to imply that DDT was dangerous or guilty was morally wrong. It has been 52 years since Ms. Carson first published her book in 1962, and the American people still believe the outright lies she told. Will the people ever know the truth about DDT? Will justice ever be known, believed and served? Will DDT ever be restored to its rightful place of honor that it so richly deserves?

SUMMARY

Rachel Carson in her book <u>Silent Spring</u>, intentionally wrote many untruths about pesticides, especially DDT.

Statements of Ms Carson	Scientific Facts
1. Pesticides especially DDT virtually wiped out the Brown Thrasher, Meadow Larks, Grackles, Robins and Pheasants.	The Audubon bird counts showed that the bird population exploded with the use of DDT. The Robin population increased more than 1000%.
2. DDT caused the birds to be sterile.	DDT is a fertility drug.
3. DDT caused bird's egg shells to be thin and break.	DDT increased the thickness of eggshells of Bengalese finches.
4. DDT destroyed the eagles ability to reproduce, causing their population to decline alarmingly	Scientists found that DDT did not affect the eagles or their ability to reproduce. Audubon bird counts showed that the eagle population increased 20%. Hunter and trappers greatly affected the eagle population.

Statements of Ms Carson	Scientific Facts
5. DDT is carcinogenic	Public Health studies at John Hopkins University showed that DDT prevented and cured animals of cancer. It is incredible that there was not one case of cancer among over 1,000 employees of the Montrose DDT plant after 23 years of operation.
6. DDT accumulated in the fat, poisoning man.	Studies on convict volunteers, taking DDT daily for 2 years showed no ill effects. DDT, after reaching 15 ppm was eliminated from the body. Studies of workers at the DDT plants showed that high levels of DDT did not interfere with their health.
7. DDT killed the small animals that were sprayed in the fields	DDT is a fertility drug, increasing the animal's reproductive life and number of offspring.

CHLORDANE**

Michael D. Miesch Jr. Ph.D.

Chlordane was discovered in 1943. For almost 30 years chlordane was one of the leading insecticides used for the control of insects on vegetables. It was widely used in homes, schools, restaurants, cafeterias, hospitals, and lawns to control cockroaches, ants, fleas, and many other insects.

Chlordane was one of the best insecticides ever used to control termites. It protected homes for 40 years. Studies by Dr. Roger Gold of Texas A&M on current pesticides being used for termite control, showed that there is essentially no pesticide left in the soil after four and five years. (Center for Urban & Structural Entomology, Dept. of Entomology, Texas A&M University, College Station, Tx.)

CHLORDANE RESIDUE WAS NOT FOUND IN FOOD OR MAN

In 1962, the Department of Agriculture of the State of California analyzed approximately 12,000 samples of food including vegetables, fruits, meat and dairy products for pesticide residue. Chlordane was not detected. When chlordane is consumed, they found that over 80 percent of the chlordane is metabolized to relatively non-toxic derivatives which are eliminated from the body through urine. Chlordane residue was found to be essentially non-existent in or on food consumed by man or in man. An exception was the production workers at the chlordane plant, which will be discussed below. In almost 500 analyses of human tissue, chlordane and heptachlor epoxide were never detected, though DDT, lindane and dieldrin were found. Chlordane residue has not resulted in any hazard to man. ("A Monograph on Chlordane - Toxicological and Pharmacological Properties", University of Illinois, 1965)

MEDICAL STUDIES OF WORKERS AT CHLORDANE PLANT

Dr. Sidney Shindell, M.D., Chairman of the Department of Preventive Medicine at the Medical College of Wisconsin has conducted three different studies on the health and mortality of 800 employees and former employees of the Velsicol chlordane plant. These workers had worked three months or more at the chlordane plant during the period from January 1946 to June 1985. Many of the employees had worked over 30 years with chlordane. Mortality from cancer of all types was at or slightly below the expected level for comparable U.S. non-production and production workers. Though the production workers had high level of chlordane in their blood, they had a lower incidence of cancer than the general U.S. population. (Journal of Occupation Medicine, 28:7, July 1986)

MEDICAL STUDIES OF PEST CONTROL OPERATORS

Dr. Brian MacMahon, Professor and Chairman of the Department of Epidemiology, Harvard School of Public Health, reviewed the mortality data of over 16,000 pesticides applicators employed between 1967 and September 1981. Studies on pest control operators have shown no evidence of chlordane causing any discernible health problems. (Velsicol Chemical Corporation, Statement to Massachusetts Pesticide Control Board, May 31, 1983)

Dr. Shindell reported that chlordane has been used in 30 million homes since its introduction in the late 1940s. This means that approximately 100 million people or 40 percent of the U.S. population have lived in homes treated with chlordane. If chlordane were a public health hazard, it certainly would have been reflected in our overall mortality and morbidity data. Even in the Air Force housing studies that dealt with detectable amounts of chlordane in the air, there was no report of any adverse health effects. (Statements of Sidney Shindell, M.D., on the Health Effects of Exposure to Chlordane - Velsicol Chemical Corporation)

**Received words from the Lord in middle of night to write papers on Chlordane and DDT. I have not been able to get these papers published. They will be published here.

CHLORDANE WAS ACCUSED
OF BEING CARCINOGENIC

Chlordane was accused of causing hepatic tumors in mice. It has not been found to cause tumors in any other animal. Liver cancer is rare in man with the exception of those who are alcoholic or who have had hepatitis. Cancer in these cases is due to the destruction of the liver by alcohol or hepatitis. (Science, July 31, 1987, Vol. 237, No. 4814, page 473)

Dr. Gary M. Williams, M.D., a pathologist, toxicologist and nationally known cancer research specialist, is the Associate Director of the Naylor Dana Institute of the American Health Foundation. Dr. Williams, who has published over 150 papers on chemicals that cause cancer, testified before the EPA that chlordane was carcinogenic. His testimony was based on another person's data. He has since retracted his statement. After running extensive tests on his own, he now believes that chlordane itself, is not a carcinogen nor is it hazardous to humans. ("Statement on Carcinogenicity of Chlordane", American Health Foundation, Naylor Dana Institute for Disease Prevention, Valhalla, N.Y. 10595 presented May 21, 1984, White Plains Hearing)

TUMOR-SENSITIVE MICE

Special strains of tumor-sensitive rats and mice are used to try to determine if a chemical is carcinogenic. Since chlordane was originally accused of being carcinogenic in mice, this discussion will be limited to tumor-sensitive mice. A certain percentage of these mice, naturally, develop tumors during their lifetime. The procedure for determining whether a chemical or a substance is carcinogenic is to mix the test substance into the diet of the test animal and feed it to the animals daily throughout their life at the highest dosages the animal can tolerate without dying prematurely. Studies are also conducted by adding the test substance to drinking water, through inhalation, injection, skin painting or some other manner. If the treated mice developed more tumors than the control (untreated mice), the test substance is considered to be carcinogenic even if the animal dies at an old age.

FALLACY OF TEST WITH TUMOR-SUSCEPTIBLE MICE

Raymond Everett in review of studies on laboratory mice, compiled a lists of non-chemical, physical and environmental factors that greatly influence the number of tumors mice developed. He showed that tumor-susceptible mice are very sensitive to the type of housing, temperature, type of bedding, altitude, caging practice, diet, germ-free environment, fluorescent lighting, etc. Any kind of physical, environmental stress will cause these mice to develop tumors. These mice are very sensitive to any type of stress. This is probably due to the fact that these mice are born blind. Not being able to see and know what is happening can bring on stress.

LOW STRESS HOUSING VERSUS CONVENTIONAL HOUSING

After 13 months, mice reared in conventional quarters had seven times more mammary tumors than mice reared in low stress, quiet quarters.

Type of Housing	Percent of Mice with Tumor
Low stress quarters	10%
Conventional quarters	68%

TEMPERATURE - After 77 weeks, mice reared at low temperature had eight times more mammary tumors than those reared at 80 degree F.

Temperature	Percent of Mice with Tumors
80 degree F	10%
Fluctuate between 41 and 55 degree F	78%

BEDDING - A strain of C3H-A mice reared in the U.S. had almost 100 percent spontaneous tumor rate. When these mice were moved to Australia, the tumor rate dropped to 29 percent while the second generation was further reduced to 10 percent. It was found that Eastern Red Cedar shavings in the U.S. was responsible for the high mammary tumor rate.

ALTITUDE - Mice reared at high altitude had significantly less spontaneous leukemia than those held at sea level. However, mice held at high altitude had a higher incidence of spontaneous urethane induced tumors.

High Altitude	Sea Level
Less spontaneous leukemia	More spontaneous leukemia
More urethane-induced tumors	Less urethane induced tumors

GERM-FREE ENVIRONMENT - After 48 weeks, the mice in a germ-free environment had developed only half the number of liver tumors as those reared in conventional quarters.

Type of Environment	Percent of Mice with Liver Tumors
Germ-free environment	39%
Conventional quarters	82%

CAGING PRACTICE - greatly affects the number of tumors a mouse developed.

Mice Grouped Together in Cages	Single Mouse per Cage
28% fewer tumors	28% more tumors
46% fewer hepatic tumors	46% more hepatic tumors
27% fewer lymphoreticular tumors More lung tumors	27% more lymphoreticular tumors Less lung tumors

DIET - Type of diet greatly affected the number of tumors a mouse developed.

Restricted Diet	Non-restricted Diet
85% Less Hepatic Tumors in Males	85% More Hepatic Tumors in Males
14% Less Pituitary Tumors in Females	14% More Pituitary Tumors in Females

Overfeeding greatly increases the spontaneous tumor rate in mice. ("Factors Affecting Spontaneous Tumor Incidence Rates in Mice": A Literature Review, Haskell Laboratory for Toxicology and Industrial Medicine, E.I. DuPont de Nemours Co., Newark Delaware, CRC Reviews in Toxicology, Vol. 3, Issue 3.)

FLUORESCENT LIGHTING - Mice born, weaned and paired under three different types of fluorescent lighting for 19 months induced the following percent tumors in female mice.

Type of Lighting	Percent Mammary Tumors
Daylight-stimulating	97%
Cool-white	97%
Pink	100%

("The Effect of Different Types of Fluorescent Lighting on Reproduction and Tumor Development in C3H Mouse", National Institute of Environmental Health Science, P.O. Box 12233, Research Triangle Park, North Carolina 27709)

The above data show that a number of factors including any type of stress will induce tumors in mice. Mustard and horse-radish are considered to be carcinogenic. ("Does Nature Know Best?" - Natural Carcinogens in American Food, A Report by American Council on Science and Health, 47 Maple Street, Summit NJ 07901) Mice fed mustard or horse-radish in their diet developed more tumors than mice which received no mustard or horse-radish in their diet. Does mustard or horse-radish cause the tumors or is it stress induce by its strong or objectionable taste? Or is it due to the stress of having to eat it at every meal throughout its life? If the tumors are due to stress induce by an objectionable taste or an upset stomach, can we really say that mustard and horse-radish are carcinogenic? How can we have a control group of mice, if the control do not received the same strong or bitter taste to bring on stress? How can we eliminate the stress factor in the treated mice or put the stress factor in the control mice? To prove that mustard or horse-radish is carcinogenic, we must eliminate stress due to its strong or objectionable taste. If stress causes tumors, how can we determine if the tumors are due to stress or to the mustard or horse-radish?

NATURAL PROPERTIES OF A CHEMICAL CAN INDUCE STRESS

Was the increase in tumors in mice due to the chemical or was it stress due to the natural properties of the chemical such as being too salty, too bitter, too sour, too sweet, too hot (hot peppers), too greasy, too oily or some other unpleasant, objectionable taste? Or was it stress due to indigestion, upset stomach, diarrhea, stomach cramps, muscular spasms or any other numerous, uncomfortable side-effects? Or was it stress caused by overwhelming these animals with the highest dosage of chemical their bodies can tolerate without dying prematurely? Stress or discomfort of any kind will cause these tumor-sensitive mice to develop tumors. Non-chemical environmental factors and variables can be factored out through a control group of mice by having both the treated and control mice in an identical environmental condition. However, there is no way to factor out stress due to bitter, objectionable taste, upset stomach, diarrhea, pain or any other type of body discomfort caused by the chemical unless the control mice experience the same type of stress. If the tumors are caused by stress or discomfort from the chemical instead of the chemical, itself, then these chemicals are not carcinogenic and we are drawing a false conclusion.

What about the different lights? These mice were confined to an area within 18 inches of the light. I do not know how bright these lights were or how much heat was put out, but for some reason or another, these mice were apparently under stress. Rodents are usually nocturnal animals.

If I had to eat mustard or horse radish at every meal or sleep under a bright light for the rest of my life, I can assure you I would be under a tremendous amount of stress. I cannot sleep with a light in my face. Stress is known to cause serious sickness.

Can an excess of any chemical be given to these mice everyday throughout their lives without bringing on discomfort and stress? If not, then these mice are not reliable for determining whether a chemical is carcinogenic.

MICE ARE BORN BLIND

The tumor-susceptible mice are not normal as they are born blind. *If I was blind and had problems finding food, water and could not see or understand what was going on or being forced to eat unpleasant food, I would be under a lot of stress too.* These mice have too many outside factors that cause tumors. When slamming a door can induce these stress-sensitive mice to develop tumors, they should not be used for carcinogenity tests. Healthy mice are not susceptible to tumors. Most scientists question the reliability of using these blind, stress-sensitive mice to determine if a chemical is carcinogenic.

CARCINOGENS OCCUR
NATURALLY IN HUMAN BLOOD

Formaldehyde averages about 3,000 parts per billion in human blood as a result of normal metabolism. The chlorinating of tap water results in chloroform, which is carcinogenic. ("Carcinogens: We Must Ignore the Trivia," PCT, October 1986) Dioxin, the potent carcinogen in Agent Orange, occurs naturally in the blood of the human population up to 20 parts per trillion. (Associated Press, "Agent Orange Report: Few Vietnam Vets Have High Levels of Dioxin in Their Blood." Dallas Times Herald, July 25. 1987, Page A3) Dr. Williams stated that certain hormones produced in our bodies are cancer causing at high level. ("Statement on Carcinogenicity of Chlordane" presented to White Plain Hearing , May 21, 1984)

All the food we eat contains naturally occurring carcinogenic chemicals. How can we eat food with so many carcinogenic chemicals and still be healthy? The answer is simple - toxicity is dose related. Dr. Alice Ottoman, a scientific advisor for the American Council on Science and Health, and the author of <u>The Dose Makes the Poison</u> summarized the dose-effect concept well:

We survive because we do not take in 100 cups of coffee at one time or 100 pounds of potatoes, or 10 pounds of spinach, or a fifth of liquor. Our bodies can handle small amounts of (natural chemicals). We metabolize them or excrete them unchanged without doing any damage. All living organisms since the beginning of time have had to deal with exposure to numerous noxious substances. No animals on earth could survive a day - if it were not capable of handling small amount of a wide variety of foreign chemicals. It is only when we overwhelm the natural defense mechanisms of our bodies by taking too much at one time, or too much too often, that we get into trouble.

("The Toxicity of Natural Chemicals", PCT, November 1987)

Dr. Gary M. Williams, who original testified before the EPA that chlordane was carcinogenic, has since retracted that statement. There is no scientific evidence that chlordane is carcinogenic.

Dr. Shindell said he would rather put his trust in the data of 800 employees of the chlordane plant and 16,000 pest control operators covering 40 years of working with chlordane than in 50 (blind, stress-sensitive) laboratory mice.

WHY WAS CHLORDANE BANNED?

Mr. William Ruckelshaus was asked again to head the EPA during the Reagon's Administration. Fifteen years after he banned DDT, Mr. Ruckelshaus, for personal and political reasons, banned chlordane. Miss Rachel Carson and Mr. Ruckelshaus have done a grave injustice to the American people. They are responsible for the banning of DDT, chlordane, and many other insecticides, creating an unjust fear of pesticides, bringing forth laws and regulations that greatly hinder the development of new pesticides, and continued registration and use of old pesticides that are essential for the protection our food, livestock, crops, homes and our lives.

Chlordane was used to protect our food for almost 30 years. It has protected our homes from termites for 40 years with no known health problem to the American people. It does not cause cancer, nor has it been detrimental to the wildlife or the environment. Chlordane was used during the same period of times as DDT when the bird population exploded.

Judgmental decisions on chemicals that are vital for the protection of our homes, food, crops, livestock, property and our lives, need to be made with prudent, reliable, scientific facts and not through fear, untruths, bias or pressure of the environmental political groups. Chlordane, DDT, heptachlor, and other pesticides have been unjustly banned.

Chlordane is a safe, non-restricted insecticide that was widely used by the general public for 40 years.

Michael D. Miesch Jr.
B.S. – Texas A&M 1955
M.S. – Purdue 1959
Ph.D. – Oklahoma State 1964

HOPE IS NOT ENOUGH !

We hear a lot about "hope" these days and that has caused me to reflect on my hopes and the efforts I made to achieve my life's objectives. I was born on a cotton farm in Northeast Texas two and one-half months premature. I possessed a severe hearing loss, which ultimately contributed to a severe speech impediment. There were no hospitals in our county and we lacked electricity and running water. My aunt told me that I weighed between two to three pounds at birth with fingers the size of matchsticks. They put me in a shoebox near the open oven door of a wood-burning cook stove, which served as an incubator to keep me warm. It took a year and a half before I was able to walk. Despite this beginning I did not lack intelligence and I started school at five years old in a two-room schoolhouse. My brother, Pete, who had just turned four on September 8th, went to school with me just to get my lesson assignments. He learned the lessons and was promoted along with me. Pete finished high school at the age of 15. Living on a farm, I hoed or chopped weeds out of cotton, corn, and vegetables, plowed the fields, and picked cotton, corn, vegetables and baled hay.

After finishing high school, we hoped to go to college. State employees who worked with the handicapped tried to discourage me from going to college. They said I would never be able to make it. I could hear vowels but not consonants. I did not move my lips or tongue but talked with the back of my throat. Only my immediate family and close friends could understand me. Since I depended on lip reading to understand people I could not read lips and write at the same time. My brother took notes for me through grade and high school. All through college, I depended on other students for notes. If a student did not take good notes, I was in trouble.

My brother and I went to Paris Junior College for two years where I received some speech therapy and then transferred to Texas A&M College. At mid-semester, I had one B, one C, two Ds, and two Fs. They put me on probation and tried to send me home. At the end of the semester, I finished with two Bs, two Cs, one D and one F. The F was due to a 25 on my first physics test. The second semester I made all Bs. A difficult first year but I survived and realized that hope would not carry the day. I had to work twice as hard as others who could hear and speak.

One of my English professors took an interest in me and on his own time, helped me with improving my speech. This is where I learned to relax while speaking.

After receiving my B.S. degree, I was accepted into graduate school. I received Cs in two graduate courses even though my test papers showed that I had an A and a B. My mother wrote the two professors asking what I made on my final exam. One professor did not answer. The other professor said I made 94 but he graded students more on their ability to carry on a discussion in the classroom than on grade points.

I spent the summer in 1955 working for Stroope Pest Control in Waxahachie, Texas checking cotton crops for insect infestation, doing house hold pest control and treating houses for termites. Anita, the wife of Clayton Wright (Purdue -1950), suggested that I go to Purdue University if I was interested in pest control. My mother called Dr. John Osmun in August 1956 and asked if I could get in Purdue. Dr. Osmun told me to come on up. I was told that Dr. Osmun was shocked when he saw that I was deaf with a severe speech impediment. Nevertheless, Dr. Osmun immediately introduced me to J.J. Davis, who had been the head of the entomology department and was famous for his work with pest control operators. Although at the time, I had no idea who J. J. Davis was, this experience stimulated me to pursue my career in the economic phases of entomology.

After finishing my M.S. thesis, everyone on my committee voted against me going for a Ph.D. except Dr. Daniel Shankland, my major professor. Whereas one respected professor told me that my thesis was not acceptable for an M.S. degree, Dr. Shankland reassured me that it was a good thesis. Dr. Leland Chandler agreed to be my major professor for my Ph.D. with the understanding that many on my committee had stated that they would vote against me for a doctorate. Obviously, Dr. Chandler thought I had a good thesis and respected my intelligence and drive or he would not have accepted me as a student for the Ph.D. Truthfully, I do not believe the highly respected professor thought my thesis was bad. More probably he was greatly concerned that a student with a severe hearing loss, speech impediment and one that had difficulty taking notes in the classroom would most likely be a bad reflection on the Entomology Department. He did not want to use my handicap as an excuse but criticized my thesis in an effort to discourage me from going for a Ph.D. Anyone can view my thesis in the Purdue University Library.

I spent the summer of 1959 at Purdue University doing research on my Ph.D. In September Dr. Chandler told me about a fellow from Ohio State with a speech impediment, who had described over 600 new species of leafhoppers. He put his "type insect specimens" up for sale. "Type insect specimens" are used as the museum standard to compare and identify other insect specimens. Dr. Chandler had written him about the type insect specimens and received a very bitter letter from him. Dr. Chandler said this person was upset that he did not get the job he wanted with a university or museum and that he probably wasted his time getting a Ph.D. as he was no longer working as an entomologist. As a consequence of this man's experience, Dr. Chandler recommended that I go out into the field and prove myself before continuing on for the Ph.D. Even Dr. Chandler admitted that my handicap was the reason he asked me to leave.

As an aside I must relate a few brief anecdotes of amusing events during my time at Purdue. In 1958 the Purdue Entomology Department was having a hard time with other departments on the campus taking over their classrooms in Ag Hall. After Christmas break, I brought about fifty scorpions from Texas that I found hibernating all clustered together. The scorpions were placed in a large open cylinder container, which rested on a glass plate. Someone may have picked up the cylinder unaware that there was no bottom. A few of the scorpions got out and scurried into one of the classrooms. The professor and students started screaming and hollering, and climbing on their chairs and desks. When the dust settled and the scorpions were returned to their container the professor asked Dr. Chandler how often these creatures got loose. Dr. Chandler said, "Quite often". The professor and students left giving the entomology department complete control of the classrooms and building.

I have often wondered if Dr. Chandler had purposely released a couple of scorpions under the door of the classroom to frighten the teacher and students. My classmate, Dr. Bill Bowers said this was something Dr. Chandler would do.

Since Dr. Chandler did his B.S. thesis on earthworms. I asked Dr. Chandler what he knew about the two and three-foot long earthworms from Texas. He had never heard of one that long and everyone gave me a hard time because the record for North America was twelve inches. Soon thereafter my mother and dad mailed a few two-foot earthworms from Texas. There was a professor on campus who was an expert on earthworms and Dr. Chandler asked him what he knew about two foot earthworms from Texas. He told Dr. Chandler that the "kid from Texas" must have glued two earthworms together. Dr. Chandler and I walked over to his office with the earthworm. He was stunned. He did not say anything. Soon thereafter a number of live earthworms were mailed to Dr. Chandler including one, which measured 31 inches. Dr. Chandler said it was 29 inches when he received it. This earthworm was placed with the Purdue insect collection. Subsequently, I measured one earthworm at 36 inches. If my mother and dad had not mailed a few two-foot earthworms I believe I would have been kicked out of Purdue before I got my M.S. degree. One professor commented that Texas needed these earthworms to eat up all the bull we shoot in Texas.

The people at Texas Parks and Wildlife were shock to hear about these giant Texas earthworms. An article on these giant earthworms was published in their magazine in November 2008.

Although deeply disappointed in my career trajectory at this time I refused to give up my educational objectives and sought real world field experience. Clayton Wright helped me get a job in Dallas working for two brothers, Dr. Byron Williamson and Dr. Thurmond Williamson, both whom had Ph.D.'s in chemistry. They formulated and sold insecticides for livestock, poultry and pets. Clayton told me to go sweep the floors and do whatever they wanted me to do. The brothers did not have any one to work in the laboratory so they trained me to do laboratory formulation and product development. I spent four years doing research, formulating, developing and testing new products. I was responsible for raising houseflies, cockroaches, dog ticks, taking care of dogs, cats and cattle. We ran oral toxicity tests on white laboratory rats, chronic and dermal toxicity tests on dogs, cats and kittens to support new product registration.

While working in Dallas, I decided to take some more courses in organic chemistry at Southern Methodist University. Dr. Harold Jesky, who was the head of the chemistry department, taught the course. When I went in to register, we were in a small room. Dr. Jesky's booming voice echoed off the ceiling. I had to ask him to repeat three times before I understood what he said. He put his hands on the table and said, "Are you sure you want to take this course?" I said, "Yes!" He would not have anything to do with me the first six week but he wrote everything on the blackboard so I had no problem taking notes. He gave everyone a copy of the questions he had asked on the previous two exams he had given his students in his last two courses. Each exam was an hour and a half. If you knew the answer and wrote as fast as you could write, you could finish the exam. After the first exam, 50% of the students dropped the course. A student next to me was majoring in Chemistry and was taking this course for the third time. He had three "A's, in three other courses in Chemistry. I made an 89 on the first test, which was the second highest grade in the class. The person who made 91 had taken the course before. From that day on Dr. Jesky took an interest in me and tried to get me to major in chemistry. He would stop in the middle of a lecture and say, "Miesch, do you understand?" I took two semesters of Organic Chemistry and felt like a walking textbook, when I finished.

Dr. John Osmun stopped at Love Field in Dallas in 1961. I told Dr. Osmun I would like to go back to Purdue to work on my Ph.D. Dr. Osmun would not give me any encouragement. Dr. Don Schuder told me later that the reason Dr. Osmun did not give me any encouragement was that the one professor who criticized my thesis, was the most influential economic entomologist in the department at Purdue.

I drove to Oklahoma State and talked with Dr. Mike Howell. He told me that they would not hold my handicap against me and for me to get started on my research before starting my residence at Oklahoma State. I had just spent two years working on a Face Fly syrup formulation that was applied to the face of beef cattle to control Face Flies. The company put DDVP into liquid fly syrup to kill the flies. They had to bring all the liquid bait back at the end of the season, as DDVP was not stable in the presence of moisture. I developed a powdered sugar DDVP formulation with a thixotropic ingredient and a stabilizer for the DDVP. It was stable until the farmer added water.

I was trying to come up with a project I could work on the year-round and not just when certain insects were available. I thought about coming up with a roach bait. I bought some dehydrated potatoes and mixed it with powdered sugar using DDVP and the same thixotrophic ingredient and stabilizer that were used for the Face Fly bait. The roaches loved it. I ran tests in roach infested apartments and picked up and counted the dead roaches every morning. At the end of two and/or four weeks I used a pyrethrum flush-out to determine the total number of roaches in each apartment. This enabled me to determine the percent control overnight, the first week and the second week, etc. In one apartment the bait gave 95% control overnight.

I took my bait and data to Oklahoma State and told Dr. Howell that I would like to work on roach bait. "Oh no", he said, "We already have a student working on roach bait." When I showed him my bait and data, he said I was so far ahead that he was going to stop this other person. He wanted me to work on food preferences of roaches. At Dr. Howell's direction, I spent two years working on food preferences for different species of roaches before attending Oklahoma State. I developed a statistical method to test four or nine baits per test. The tests were continued at Oklahoma State especially with liquid baits.

I won a fellowship from National Pest Control Association to attend Oklahoma State and Dr. Howell accepted all the graduate courses at Texas

A&M and the three years at Purdue University. I went to Oklahoma State in September 1963 and earned my Ph.D. eleven months later in August 1964.

The U.S. Forest Service in Maryland wanted me to work for them because of my pesticide formulation experience, but had other candidates ahead of me. I came back to Dallas and visited with my friend, Dr. Ernest Laake who was formerly Director of USDA Man and Animal Research Laboratory in Dallas. Although Dr. Laake had moved the USDA Lab to Kerrville, Texas, he was now working for National Chemsearch at the time of my visit (Now NCH Corporation). Dr. Laake, was responsible for the original work with DDT and toxaphene on the control of insects and ticks on livestock and highly recommended me to National Chemsearch because of my formulation experience. The US Forest Service job offer came the day after I had accepted a position with National Chemsearch. Dr. Laake and I worked together for a year and a half when he retired at the age of 79. Dr. Laake was a graduate of Texas A&M in Entomology – Class of 1913 and lived to be 99. His close association with pesticides did not appear to endanger his longevity.

With more than thirty chemists working in their laboratories National Chemsearch grossed $15 million in 1964. On my retirement in 2000, 36 years later, they grossed over $800 million as a worldwide corporation.

At National Chemsearch I was the head of the pesticide and agronomy section responsible for the formulation and development of insecticides, herbicides, fungicides, rodenticides, fertilizers, growth regulators, wetting agents, etc. I was also in charge of the insectary. We had a colony of houseflies that were originally collected before World War II that had never been exposed to DDT. I kept this colony going by collecting eggs and raising them each week for thirty-six years. The company lost these houseflies within three months after I retired. They asked me to come back each week to maintain the insects which I did for six years after my retirement.

I reported the first case of Baygon resistant houseflies in the nation. They were discovered in a poultry house in Keller, Texas where I was performing some tests. Bayer Corporation did not believe that there were any houseflies resistant to Baygon. Resistant flies were collected and a colony was started in the lab. In a test, the non-resistant flies were dead in a few minutes, while the resistant flies were alive after one hour. Bayer representatives admitted that this was definitely a bona fide case of resistance.

My expertise was in making stable emulsifiable products. Some of my accomplishments include:

- Making the first Delnav formulation that passed the rigid USDA 90 days emulsion stability test that was approved for use in dipping vats in quarantine area to control ticks on cattle.

- Developing a stable emulsifiable Baygon formulation that did not separate or split when added to water.

- I did the original work in developing the Golden Marlin fly bait. DDVP was mixed with powdered sugar and pressed into flakes instead of coating sugar granulars to reduce the repellency of DDVP to houseflies.

- Running toxicity tests with rainbow trout and bluegill sunfish to support dibrom registration for use in trickling filters at sewage treatment plants to control filter flies. A room was constructed with refrigeration to get the temperature down to 45 degree F for the rainbow trout.

- The company sold the roach bait as Roach Strike.

Over the years, I have formulated hundreds of products. Some of the technical pesticides I formulated were DDT, toxaphene, chlordane, lindane, dieldrin, aldrin, heptachlor, DDVP, malathion, dursban, Baygon, Sevin, Lannate, pyrethrum, synthetic pyrethroids, boric acid, rotenone, plus many herbicides and fungicides, etc.

The struggle I went through has been a blessing. If it had been otherwise, I would not have had the opportunity to learn the whole field of formulation and product development, which turned out to be my life's work. I made a lot of friends and learned much everywhere I have been. I ended up with a career I really loved with very good bosses and spent forty years doing research, formulation and product development.

Despite the difficulties, I have kept in touch with all of my professors. Some of the best and happiest years of my life and some of my fondest memories were on the campus of Purdue University where I developed many close friends. The first year at Purdue I lived with a family in Lafayette with whom I have maintained contact through the years. I worked at the Zeta Tau Alpha sorority house next to the campus, washing pots and pans for my meals. Mabel Walker was the cook for the sorority house. My wife and I later spent the night at her house several times when we visited Purdue. Dr. Don and Mary Schuder spent a couple nights in our home during their visit in Irving, Texas. Dr. Leland Chlandler's family also spent a couple nights in our home. Dr. and Mrs. Schuder, and Dr. John Osmun have visited my laboratory and the plant manufacturing facilities where I worked. Dick Wright and I were lab partners in Dr. John Osmun's 515 pesticide formulation course where I did my first pesticide formulation. Clearly, this first experience with pesticide formulation was an important beginning of what became my life's work. Dr. Ralph Killough was a good friend who loaned me his class notes. Dr. Bill Bowers and I continue to keep in touch through e-mail.

One weekend, Mr. Arnold Mallis, the author of the "Handbook of Pest Control", honored us with a surprise visit. Mr. Mallis had an interest in the identification and study of ants. After a brief visit, we looked for ants in our yard and found some tiny black ants, which he put into a small vial and took with him.

I have a beautiful, lovely wife, a family of three married sons and now grandchildren. I retired in 2000, but still collect insects. I have 14 cases of insects on three walls in the house. My wife, Ann, taught science and was chosen as the Texas State Teacher of the Year in statewide competition in 1986.

Michael D. Miesch lll is a Senior Program Manager for Avaya. He is married to Jean Marie who is an accountant for St. Gabriel's Catholic Church. They have one son who was conceived after 16 years of trying to have a family. They reside in McKinney, Texas

Mark David Miesch is the Director of Project Management for a Design-Build-Developer in Houston. He is married to Tracy Lynn, who is self –employed in Sales and Marketing. They have three children, Margaret Ann, Meredith Estelle, and Donovan Andrew Miesch. They live in Magnolia, Texas which is northwest of Houston.

Paul Martin Miesch is a writer. He is married to Christy, who is a pharmacist. They have one son Nicholas Asher who was born on April 27, 2014. They live in Austin, Texas.

I am an Eagle Scout with 76 merit badges, a Vigil member of the Order of the Arrow, and have earned Scouting Wood Badge and Beads. I was awarded the Silver Eagle for the Explorer Scouts, which was supposedly equivalent to the Eagle Badge for the Boy Scouts. The Silver Eagle is no longer offered by the Boy Scouts of America. I have also studied Indian dancing and made numerous performances. The Greater Dallas Pest Control Association presented me a plaque as an honorary member of their association. In 2010 Paris Junior College inducted me into their Academic Hall of Honor for Science with a very beautiful plaque and my picture on the wall. This is a brief story of my life.

I am thankful and grateful for the education and experience I received at Paris Junior College, Texas A&M, Purdue, SMU and Oklahoma State Universities. Each of these fine academic institutions possessed great professors and teachers. I learned a great deal and made many friends that I cherish to this day. I am very thankful to my brother, Pete, for helping me through grade and high school, the students who willingly loaned me their notes and the professors who helped me reach my great desire in college education. My brother, Pete, was awarded a B.S. in petroleum engineering and later went on to receive his Ph.D. in petroleum engineering at Texas A&M. Two of my sons are graduates of Texas A&M University and the other son is a graduate of the University of Texas at Austin.

The professors at Texas A&M giving me C's in graduate school and Purdue sending me home was a blessing in disguise. Otherwise, I would have missed the opportunity to learn chemistry, research, formulation and product development which became my life work and to meet the beautiful and lovely lady who became my wife. It was also helpful that I was able to do two years research on my dissertation at the company before entering Oklahoma State which enabled me to get my Ph.D. in eleven months. I am truly thankful for my family, friends, and for all the blessings I have received. I had a very rewarding career and all of my dreams and desires have been fulfilled.

From this brief safari through my life's adventures I believe you will understand that my hopes were carried forward on a river of perspiration and that hope is not enough.

CPSIA information can be obtained
at www.ICGtesting.com
Printed in the USA
FFHW02n2349181018
48826024-53011FF

9 781478 757573